Supranational Cooperation
and Integration

Roland Eisen (ed.)

Supranational Cooperation and Integration

Goods and Services vs. Information

PETER LANG
Frankfurt am Main · Berlin · Bern · Bruxelles · New York · Oxford · Wien

Die Deutsche Bibliothek - CIP-Einheitsaufnahme

Supranational cooperation and integration : goods and services vs. information / Roland Eisen (ed.). - Frankfurt am Main ; Berlin ; Bern ; Bruxelles ; New York ; Oxford ; Wien : Lang, 2002
ISBN 3-631-37927-7

ISBN 3-631-37927-7
US-ISBN 0-8204-5395-1

www.peterlang.de

Table of Contents

PREFACE AND INTRODUCTION

The fourth Arnoldshain Seminar on
"Supranational Cooperation and Integration:
Goods and Services vs. Information"
September 4-6, 2000

The articles published in this volume were presented and discussed at the Arnoldshain IV seminar in Arnoldshain in September 2000. This seminar is to continue the series of Arnoldshain Seminars which developed to a forum for discussion between the Universidade de São Paulo (USP, Brazil), the Universidad Nacional de Córdoba (UNC, Argentina), and the Johann Wolfgang Goethe-Universität Frankfurt a.M. (JWG, Germany).

Supranational cooperations, free trade zones, and economic and currency unions are of increasing political and scientific interest. However, not only questions about welfare gains and optimal currency policies are the focus of interest. Also questions about explicit and implicit financial equalization between member countries, structural, industrial and infrastructure policies had to be addressed.

The European Union and the South American Mercosur have to introduce reforms during the next years because both unions want to increase the number of member countries. This is the main reason why it is important to strike the balance of results, of the structural changes and of the welfare increases. Furthermore, the globalization and the expanding information and communications technologies will force future changes. The structural changes caused and the repercussions on the process of union enlargement for the old and the new union members have to be analyzed.

The following provides an overview of the contents of each article based on abstracts written by the authors themselves. Financial crises seem to be inevitably connected to the advantages of global and liberalized financial markets. For this reason alone, it is an interesting issue to discuss how financial crises propagate in economic unions, if one considers the different financial systems. Roughly speaking, two typical financial systems can be distinguished: a system guided by the capital markets or a system guided by banks ("house banks"). Both systems have different effects on management policy, corporate governance, and certainly different mechanisms of stabilization. These factors seem to be of great importance for internal financial crises (banking crises etc.), but also for the spread of financial crises. It might be relevant for this spreading effect that the Mercosur consists of two big countries (Argentina and Brazil) and two small countries (Uruguay and Paraguay). Can we learn in this context from Asian countries? The first two papers of **the first section** deal with these problems. Marta Podzun de Buraschi and Aldo A. Arnaudo (UNC) analyze the financial effects of two financial crises (devaluations in Mexico and Brazil) on the member countries of Mercosur, given the increased linkages brought about by the common market. The authors, firstly, look at the degree of uniformity in the reactions of the four countries where some institutional arrangements differ greatly. Second, they focus on the reactions of a small country as a consequence of a large country's monetary shock.

Malcolm Dunn (JWG) examines different explanations of the Asian financial crisis, and questions the explanatory power of the standard arguments. Instead of exchange rate systems, moral hazard and inefficient banking, he sees the reason in the world financial system as a source of credit bubbles and monetary instability.

Amaury Gremaud and Marcio Bobik Braga (USP) analyze the experiences in exchange rate policies of several Latin American countries, in particular Argentina and Brazil. They ask whether fixed or flexible exchange rates or even the substitution of local currency with US-dollars or a monetary union are the best way to overcome the restrictions imposed by the external account and the consequential negative effects.

In his paper, Dante Mendes Aldrighi (USP) casts some doubts on the reasoning that predicts the convergence towards the Anglo-American model of corporate governance. He argues convincingly for factors hindering this way: the importance of human capital in the "new economy", social values, redistribution of "property rights" among stakeholders.

Another interesting aspect, sometimes also connected with globalization, is privatisation of state-owned enterprises (SOEs). Roberto Macedo (USP) discusses the various characteristics of the Brazilian privatization program undertaken in the 1990s. He concludes that this program – on the one hand – contributed to softening both the fiscal and external constraints. However, the objective of reducing the public debt was not achieved. On the other hand, the program was restricted to big business, and the better off could reap the benefits, while the poor did not have access to the assets and will in the end share in the payment of the increased public debt and the larger interest bill.

In **the second part**, the authors look at the consequences of cooperation and integration on the "old" industries. Alejandro D. Jacobo (UNC) analyses the macroeconomic behavior of Argentina, Bolivia, Brazil, Chile, Paraguay and Uruguay during the last 25 years. Here, he distinguishes between two major questions: First, given Mercosur, do economic fluctuations show a more similar pattern? Second, what are the effects of demand and supply shocks on these economies?

In the next paper, Hebe G. Morales de Marega and Eugenio M. Cerutti (UNC) look at the trade flows between Argentina and Brazil and their openness towards the EU and NAFTA. She tries not only to identify the possible changes in the direction of the countries' exports and imports, but also the inter-industry and intra-industry nature of the trade flows.

Graciela Juarez de Perona's (UNC) paper is devoted to the analyses of the linkages between indication of competitiveness (such as market share, growth, productivity, technological innovation) and external trade performance of firms during the economic integration process.

María Luisa Recalde, María Cecilia Ganame (UNC) and Michaela Kuhl (JWG) look in their paper on a central political problem of the EU as well as of the Mercosur. Besides the competitive distortions of the subventions and other trade restrictions of agricultural policy, environmental issues increasingly play an important role. This is relevant not only for the "old" member countries but also for the new candidates: the process of integration leads to shifts of trade flows and of the spatial allocation, thus to changes in the residuals and use of natural resources. Consequently, the positive and negative effects on the environment and the social welfare must be accounted for. Again, the question is posed whether Mercosur can learn from the experience of the EU.

The third part contains three papers dealing with the fundamental changes of the communications and information technology as "global" technologies which affect the international capital mobility, the cost advantages of alternative locations, and the international outsourcing of certain activities. The most discussed consequences relate to employment chances of differently educated people. Direct effects on the destruction and creation of employment and indirect effects on the re-employment are certainly decisive and intensify the structural transformation of "knowledge societies". Therefore, it is important to make clear the role of regulation for competition in the telecommunications market which is the topic of the first paper by Rinaldo A. Colomé, Á. Enrique Neder and Carlos Ceballos Ferroglio (UNC). Kirsten Lenz and Andreas Oberweis (JWG) analyze the interorganizational work-flows for international business processes: To support those processes, the author proposes so-called XML-nets, a new kind of high-level Petri-nets. These XML-nets can easily be modified and extended to meet the needs of international workflows.

Finally, Ulrich Peter Ritter (JWG) describes the development of internet academic teaching and learning, and asks whether the sceptics or the optimists will be right. Furthermore, he compares the methods and designs used in the internet university with those used in the traditional "face-to-face-universities". As a conclusion, the author outlines a model of the university of the future.

In **the fourth part**, the consequences of globalization and technological shocks on labor markets are taken up. Alberto Díaz Cafferata, Alberto Figueras and José Luis Arrufat (UNC), focus on the impact of changes in trade and the constitution of Mercosur on the spatial allocation of resources in Argentina. The process of regional restructuring which is in progress in the countries of the Southern Cone, is analyzed with respect to its optimality in terms of economic efficiency as well as the economic reasons for this process. Finally, they discuss the general problem of government intervention and the implications for unemployment policies on the federal, provincial or local levels.

Roland Eisen, André Kolodziejak and Dimitrios Gotsis (JWG) focus on regional unemployment in Germany. One of the astonishing facts of economic development in recent years was the high and persistent unemployment – not only in Germany but in nearly all European countries and in the so-called emerging economies in Latin America. Furthermore, the regional spread of unemployment rates within some member countries of the EU is larger than the spread between the national unemployment rates. The authors take this as their starting point. The effects of external shocks, e.g. of the oil price increases, can explain only 50 percent of unemployment changes, the considerable rest stems from other factors, e.g. the changing (female) labor supply and the regional differences in industrial structure.

While the real wage resistance and the regionally unresponsive wage structure may also be of interest in the explanation of unemployment, Mariana de Santis and Héctor R. Gertel (UNC) look at the supply and demand as well as the wages of teachers. The author is particularly interested in teachers' supply, and participation and unemployment rates are estimated.

In the last paper, Maria Cristina Cacciamali (USP) analyzes the informal labor markets in Argentina and Brazil. Although the institutional frameworks adopted by these countries differ, their labor market development during the 90's shows more similarities than differences: High unemployment, high underemployment, illegal contracts and a high degree of informality. The hypotheses proposed to explain the increase in illegal contracts are the loss of fiscal morality and the instability of economic growth.

I have to thank several persons and sponsors who made this seminar and this book possible: Prof. Steinberg, President of the Johann Wolfgang Goethe-University Frankfurt a.M., Prof. Kelm of the "Stiftung zur Förderung der internationalen wissenschaftlichen Beziehungen der Johann Wofgang Goethe-Universität", Dr. Franceso Papadia, Director General Operations of the European Central Bank, and Dr. Jürgen Stark, Vice-President of the Deutsche Bundesbank, as well as the German Academic Exchange Service (DAAD). I also thank all the participants for their collaboration and the lively discussions; and I thank Ulrich Peter Ritter for helping organize a wonderful day in Kronberg. Last but not least, I thank Dimitrios Gotsis who has done most of the work of the local organization committee and the publishing of this book.

Frankfurt a.M., April 2001 Roland Eisen

Financial Services and Crises

UNEQUAL TRANSMISSION OF FINANCIAL CRISES IN MERCOSUR

Marta Podzun de Buraschi and Aldo A. Arnaudo (*)

1. Introduction

During the nineties, Latin America faced two important financial shocks, both consequences of devaluation of exchange rates. First it was Mexico in December 1994 and second came Brazil in January 1999. These shocks brought about financial crises in most Latin American countries. Balance-of-payments crises and financial crises are difficult to separate and in many cases may have the same causes; however, they can be isolated and treated as different.[1] A financial crisis is defined as "a situation in which a significant group of financial institutions have liabilities exceeding the market value of their assets, leading to runs and other portfolio shifts, collapsing of some financial firms, and government intervention" (Sundarajan and Baliño, 1999).

This paper aims at comparing the effects that those crises had in the financial sectors of the member countries of MERCOSUR, i.e. Argentina, Brazil, Paraguay and Uruguay, given the increased linkages supposedly brought about by the common market.[2] First, the analysis focuses on whether any degree of uniformity in the reactions could be observed; second, it centres on the reactions that a small economy may confront as a consequence that a larger one is affected by a monetary shock. An analysis and comparison of the behavior of several financial indicators is therefore carried out for the four countries.

However, it is important to point out that some institutional arrangements were completely different in the four countries, i.e., the exchange rate regime and the degree of dollarization of the financial sector. Brazil followed in the past an adjustable exchange rate accompanied with high interest rates and some official indexation of financial assets; in 1993, it introduced an exchange system with an adjustable peg and fluctuating bands, until the country underwent a large devaluation at the beginning of 1999. Argentina had, except for 1990 and part of

(*) Facultad de Ciencias Económicas, Universidad Nacional de Córdoba, Argentina; mpodzun@eco.uncor.edu ; aaa@eco.uncor.edu

[1] Recently, Kaminsky and Reinhard (1999) have analysed both kinds of crises and the simultaneity of their appearance. According their Table 1, banking crises alone were less than a half in the last three decades.

[2] For Argentina and Brazil, the financial sector is taken as the commercial banking sector, whereas for Paraguay and Uruguay it may include other financial intermediaries besides banks. Anyway, the figures represent adequately the financial sector.

the following year, a fixed exchange rate regime. Paraguay had an adjustable peg system, and Uruguay had a managed exchange rate regime, mostly operating as a floating rate one. As a consequence, the price level and nominal interest rates in each country are supposed to show a corresponding behavior.

Furthermore, the second issue is a particular instance of contagion, whereby the economy of a country is affected by the disturbances occurring in another country or group of countries (Calvo and Reinhart, 1996). The financial sectors of Paraguay and Uruguay were believed to be somehow linked to those of the other two larger economies of Argentina and Brazil. The disturbances to be considered here, whatever their origin (internal or external), are only those affecting the financial sector, disregarding the effects on the real sector of the economy.

Finally, the paper is organized as follows: the next section presents a brief account of the effects of a common area; Section 3 discusses linkages in the real sectors of the member countries of MERCOSUR, followed by Section 4 on financial connections. Section 5 presents the financial indicators chosen for the analysis and the methodology used. Next comes Section 6 with the description of the indicators' behavior during the two crises, followed by a brief summary in Section 7.

2. A Brief Note on Trade Theory

Frenkel and Rose (1998) have observed that the economic purpose of a common market is to enhance welfare among member states, and it is usually accomplished by the following formula: increasing trade between the countries concerned and/or harmonizing their macroeconomic policies. Not necessarily should the first method be interpreted as a means to obtain the second, although in general an increase in trade brings about heightened needs for macroeconomic coordination. However, macroeconomic homogeneity or convergence only fosters welfare under certain conditions, i.e. the real exchange rates of the member countries remain stable or unchanged.[3]

Take the simple example of two economies with strong commercial connections. When both face a boom (or a slump) they will try to eliminate any upward (downward) pressure on the economy by implementing similar or convergent policies; for instance, by a revaluation (devaluation) of the exchange rate or by a restrictive (expansionary) monetary policy. However, if one is in a boom while the other is in slump, opposite policies will alter the relative prices between the two countries and trade will be hampered. The change in relative prices becomes evident, for example, when one country has a fixed exchange

[3] Obviously they assume bilateral real aggregate rates; later eventually individual prices for traded goods would be equalised by the allocation and payment of resources in each country.

regime and stable prices, and the other a managed peg which does not take into consideration domestic prices, as it has been the case of Argentina and Brazil, respectively.

For the moment, however, MERCOSUR has taken the road of increasing trade. For this purpose, member countries have removed import and export taxes between themselves, eliminated non-tariff barriers (Asunción Treaty, 1991), and agreed an external common tariff (Ouro Preto Accord, 1994). This approach has been the general rule, since there are numerous exceptions or the rules are only applicable to specific sectors. Uniform macroeconomic policies were only mentioned in the discussions, but left for the future.

3. The Performance of the Real Sector

The macroeconomic performance of MERCOSUR's member countries was relatively heterogeneous during the 1990s. In terms of gross domestic product, annual growth figures were asymmetric, as shown in Chart 1a (in the appendix). Taking a longer period (1970-1994), a similar tendency has been documented for MERCOSUR countries (Arnaudo and Jacobo, 1997) and for Latin American countries (Loayza et. al., 1999). Similarly, Carrera (1998) has revealed an analogous pattern for Argentina and Brazil during different time spans. However, the figures also hint at some, though weak, relationship between the economies of Paraguay and Brazil, on one hand, and those of Uruguay and Argentina, on the other.

Total trade of MERCOSUR countries increased for the most part of the 1990s. This was mainly due to the important effects of the trade liberalization policies followed by member countries. However, trade figures showed only some of the fluctuations seen in GDP. Chart 1b presents how the erratic behavior observed in GDP was only partially reproduced by trade figures, which in general were much higher than GDP growth rates.

Likewise, since the start of the common market in the early 1990s, the share of intra-MERCOSUR trade in total trade for each member country increased consistently (See Chart 2a). In fact, every country experienced an expansion in trade with other members in addition to the general trend in trade mentioned before. Argentina and Brazil were the countries that benefited the most from this situation, relative to the smaller Paraguay and Uruguay.

That tendency is in part confirmed by trade figures between the smaller economies of Paraguay and Uruguay on one side, and those of Argentina and Brazil, on the other (See Chart 2b). Although the two smaller countries have stronger connections with Brazil (something anticipated given the size of its economy, relative to that of Argentina), the Uruguayan economy appears more akin to the Argentine (Chart 2b). Further, only a rather weak connection is implied between the economies of Brazil and Paraguay, and those of Argentina and Paraguay. Therefore, such expansion in trade is seen as the only source of potential heightened linkages among the financial sectors of the member countries. As a matter of fact, it is difficult to expect much financial uniformity given that the economic performance of MERCOSUR countries depended on many other factors, i.e. geography, society, etc., widely different among them.

4. Financial Linkages within MERCOSUR

There are mainly three factors that could bring about linkages between the financial sectors of the two countries. They are: a. connections of their real sectors through trade, or perhaps through macroeconomic coordination; b. connections of their financial sectors per se; and c. contagion effects due to shocks experienced by either one of the countries involved or a third country.

When an economic disturbance affects the trade sector of a country, with further effects on the current trade balance with a smaller one, there also may be some repercussions in the financial sector of the latter. The general condition for this to happen is that the proportion of exports and imports of the smaller country to/from the larger one be substantially high. This has not been the case of MERCOSUR members because the volume of trade of Paraguay and Uruguay with Argentina and Brazil has been shown to be relatively small. Nor has the increase in trade, although substantial as the common area moved forward, changed that view. Further, given that the coordination of macroeconomic policies has been negligible within MERCOSUR, increased linkages in the financial sectors are not to be expected on these grounds.

On the other hand, unless established arrangements exist, the most common linkages between countries' financial systems per se come from the behavior of economic agents. Credibility, for example, plays a key role in the way investors (mainly international) regard the financial systems, usually investing in those countries whose domestic policies are the most credible. Therefore, the direction of financial flows to a country or group of countries or from one country to another will depend on investors' attitudes toward those countries and whether they perceive them as similar or can differentiate them. Furthermore, given that these views usually change with time, it would be possible to see changes in the direction of the flows as time passes.

Finally, and connected to the previous point, contagion is observed when a financial shock endured by a large country is transmitted to a smaller one in the same direction. In those cases, the repercussions in the smaller country may even be more severe than in the country undergoing the initial crisis.

5. Financial Indicators and Methodology

The following key variables have been selected to evaluate the financial disturbances endured by the member countries of MERCOSUR during the 1990s: international reserves, monetary base, type and composition of deposits, credit to the public, and interest rates.

However, it should be kept in mind that deposits and credit to the public are affected by the dollarization of the economy, experienced to different degrees by all countries with the only exception of Brazil. Further, the definition of monetary base in a dollarized economy must be adapted. Traditionally the domestic concept has been attached to the monetary multiplier, giving a measure of the other monetary aggregates, including bank loans to the private sector. If deposits and credits are in two currencies, and bank reserves may additionally be indistinguishable held in one or the other, the concept loses a great deal of meaning. Nevertheless, the monetary base used here refers to the unambiguous traditional domestic way.

Additionally, in the case of deposits, a distinction is to be made on whether they function as currency or asset substitute since the behavior of the public is different for each class. Demand deposits, belonging to the category of money (in the restricted sense), are used for current transactions and have a low possibility to be substituted for foreign currency. On the contrary, savings and time deposits are easily transformed into foreign currency and used for asset accumulation (Baliño et al, 1999, Section II; Guidotti and Rodríguez, 1992).

The methodology for the analysis would be to compare the evolution of the indicators selected independently. Nevertheless, this gives rise to different answers in regard to the duration of the disturbances, depending on the indicator or indicators selected. There are three possible ways to sort out the problem: first, to take an average of all the indicators; second, to select just one in particular; or third, to take discretionary units of time and compare the values of the indicators. The last solution is embraced in this paper after looking at the behavior of the variables. Therefore, the six months before and the six months after the financial crisis are considered to be the fall and recovery experienced by the variables.[4]

Complementarily, the time required for domestic savings and time deposits to recover, i.e. the time elapsed until the decline stops, is considered because it best represents the voluntary behavior of the public. A similar pattern does not occur with the credit to the private sector since it is less responsible to the disturbance.

---

[4] Since both perturbances turned to happen in December and taking into account the strong seasonal component of this month, the account starts in November.

6. Performance of the Financial Sector During the Crises

Shock I: Tequila, December 1994

a. Argentina - Brazil

Let us first compare the situation in the two largest economies, those of Argentina and Brazil. In the first six months after the shock both countries faced an important fall in international reserves of around one fifth. While Argentina was not able to overcome the decline during the second semester of 1995 the tendency was reversed in Brazil and the reserves reached a level higher than that before the crisis. In other terms, the initial impact of the financial shock was transitory in Brazil and substantial in Argentina. A similar pattern is found in the monetary base measured in real terms: in Argentina, it decreased vis-à-vis the international reserves given that due to the Convertibility Law, international reserves are the main component of the monetary base. Further, during the following semester, the monetary base kept falling, although more gradually. In Brazil, the fall in the monetary base was not as big because it had an important component of domestic credit; moreover, in the subsequent semester, the effects of the disturbance have practically disappeared. (See table 1 in the appendix)

The behavior of demand deposits was relatively similar. In Argentina, they fell in a limited proportion, approximately 5% in the first six months and even less in the following semester. This may be a consequence of that demand deposits attained a lower long-term equilibrium. In Brazil, the fall in deposits was initially greater (almost one quarter), but later they got back to pre-crisis level.

On the other hand, the behavior of savings and time deposits was just the opposite. In Argentina the decrease in this kind of deposits in the first six months was substantial; deposits denominated in pesos fell one third, whereas those denominated in dollars fell 15.4%. In Brazil, given that financial intermediaries were not allowed to take deposits in foreign currency, an increase in saving and time deposits took place; or at least partially, a conversion of demand deposits into interest bearing instruments.

As a consequence of the fall in these deposits, there was a disequilibrium in the Argentine financial market, which brought a substantial increase in interest rates of both peso and dollar denominated deposits. During the subsequent six-month period, deposit rates dropped, but without reaching previous levels.

On the credit side, financial intermediaries did not react immediately to the fall in deposits, as one could have expected. This was due to the downward rigidity of the demand curve for loans, because borrowers were reluctant to cancel abruptly their loans since they usually have long run informal agreements with their lenders. Besides, given the apparent deterioration of the economic conditions, the reluctance or inability to pay their debts was even bigger.

This phenomenon explains the comparatively larger fall in deposits to the private sector than that of loans in Argentina, which is confirmed by the figures in table 1. In the first six months, the diminished supply of funds to the financial system brought a significant increase in interest rates on loans, which was larger on loans denominated in pesos than on those in dollars. After this initial rise, interest rates on loans decreased but did not reach those low levels prior to the crisis. In the case of Brazil, however, domestic interest rates on both deposits and loans remained quite stable during the whole period.

Summarizing, the Tequila had tremendous consequences on the Argentine financial system whereas it did not significantly affect the Brazilian economy. Despite the shock's extensive repercussion in Argentina, its duration was relatively brief. Deposits started to recover approximately after five months; furthermore, six months later, the credibility of a wise monetary policy made it possible for savings and time deposits reach pre-crisis levels, though some were converted into foreign currency.

b. Paraguay

The financial sector of Paraguay appears to have escaped the Tequila crisis. A glance at the figures in Table 1 confirms this fact; none of the variables analysed were affected. However, it is also true that the financial system underwent several troubles a few months before the crisis began, and therefore, new disturbances might have overlapped existing ones. On the other hand, the financial system of Brazil, whose economy was pre-eminent for Paraguay, was lightly affected.[5]

By the end of 1988, Paraguay began a process of financial liberalization; this started with the exchange rate being subjected to a kind of administered crawl, deposits in foreign currency being permitted, the release of credit restrictions to banks and the imposition of liquidity coefficients. In this new environment of freedom and credibility, a number of new financial institutions, banks and the like were established, making possible the acceptance of deposits and the granting of loans in foreign currency.

As long as it ran large budget superavits, the Government provided an important source of funds to the financial system. However, when the budget came to balance or even to deficit, those funds in the form of deposits were withdrawn, thus shrinking the system's credit capacity.

---

[5] The main problems in Paraguay began in mid-1995 when the Tequila shock had been almost overcome in Argentina. One may wonder whether this disturbance did not influence directly, but without doubt indirectly aggravated the situation in the future.

The magnitude of loans may give a distorted view of the health of the financial system because the portfolio of many banks and other financial institutions suffered a permanent deterioration as debtors began to default on interest charges and amortization re-payments. Obviously, this phenomenon also happened in Argentina, and was perhaps widespread in all MERCOSUR countries; however, the case of Paraguay was remarkable.

Unfortunately, the degree of default in Paraguay can not be compared to that of other countries because a risk based classification of loans was unavailable for a period before the analysis. Likewise, the criteria to measure the risk of loans was not available, nor the conditions for a change in category. Besides, Basle's risk based framework, which became popular later in Latin America, would give risk measures greater than those reported by Government officials. In any event, the figures register an increase in risking in 1994 and 1995.

This deterioration in the solvency of the financial system was clear in the years following the Government's closure or nationalization of many banks, representing approximately 4.7% of total loans in 1994 and 13.3% in 1997 (International Monetary Fund, 1999).[6]

c. Uruguay

International reserves and the monetary base increased in Uruguay during the first six-months after the Tequila; however, the figures in table 1 show that while the former practically stabilized in the following semester, the latter decreased a little further. Compared to the case of Argentina, this phenomenon appears to be exactly the opposite, giving the impression that the financial system in Uruguay was less affected by the crisis. In fact it was; a similar conclusion can also be reached for demand deposits.

The difference is even more remarkable in the case of savings and time deposits denominated in domestic or foreign currencies. In Argentina, for instance, these deposits decreased in the first period after the crisis, whereas they increased in Uruguay; during the following six months, they increased –almost to previous levels- in Argentina, while the increase was much smaller in Uruguay. The presumption is that a portion of those deposits were Argentine funds that flew to Uruguay because of the more credible economic conditions. The geographic proximity of the two countries and the connection between their financial intermediaries could make the flow relatively smooth.

Moreover, this hypothesis is reinforced because of three additional facts. First, the significant flexibility of financial flows, in the sense that they can easily change locations or countries. This occurred in Argentina during the first

[6] As said, these figures do not follow the Basle rules for loan classification.

months of 1995, when the reduction of deposits accompanied a parallel increase in Uruguay, which could not be explained by domestic factors. Obviously, in nominal terms the percentage increase of deposits in Uruguay is not the same as that in Argentina, however, they are in opposite directions. Second, when the deposits reversed their tendency in Argentina and began to increase, their increase in Uruguay was at a lower rate.

Third, interest rates responded in line with the change in deposits. They increased a lot in Argentina, almost double the previous level, and later decreased to approximately the same portion; in Uruguay, however, interest rate on deposits had minor changes, which is at odds with the increase in deposits.

In the case of loans to the private sector, a similar tendency was found. Not only did they increase in the period next to the disturbance, but also during following months at a rate commensurate to that of savings and time deposits. It is possible that in a small scale financial intermediaries took a conservative attitude of increasing liquidity (not interest investments) when faced with financial flows that did not deem permanent. Interest rates on loans, either in domestic or foreign currency, remained almost invariable.

Shock II: Brazil, January 1999

a. Brazil – Argentina

In contrast to the first financial shock that affected mainly Argentina, the consequences of the second financial crisis, which hit its peak with the devaluation of the real, was confined to Brazil itself. Two special characteristics distinguish the Brazilian crisis from the Tequila. First, it was preceded by a general deterioration of investor's confidence in the emerging markets of Southeast Asia and Russia. Second, it took a longer time to hit the Brazilian economy; even though a similar loss of credibility abruptly led to the Tequila in Mexico and Argentina.

Given that it would be impossible to make a full comparison of the two shocks because there has not elapsed enough time to appreciate the phenomenon and its consequences, an analysis of the initial impact of the crises will be carried out (see table 2 in the appendix).

In Brazil, the loss of international reserves was extensive, on top of that observed during the final months of 1998. However, the monetary base did not decrease due to the sterilization carried out by the monetary authorities. Argentina, on the other hand, did not experience a decrease in international reserves, which in fact increased a little, nor in the monetary base.

The level of demand deposits in Brazil also dropped substantially, while that of savings and time deposits remained roughly the same. Loans to the private sector plummeted during this initial period, but these figures might be biased given that they are measured in real terms and there was a sharp increase in nominal prices.

The Argentine case is special because the shock brought about higher interest rates for both deposits and loans, rather than modifications in the level of credit. Although the loan capacity of the financial sector increased as a consequence of a higher level of demand, savings and time deposits, no effective change in private credit occurred. This may be a consequence of a decreased demand for credit as the cost of borrowing went up and probably because the conditions established by the financial sector had changed. Additionally, the increase in interest rates was due to an external deterioration on the credibility of the country's policies. Nevertheless, the overall liquidity of the banking sector increased.[7]

b. Paraguay and Uruguay

Paraguay and Uruguay did not follow the financial patterns of the other two countries; on the contrary, they stuck to the particular forces that governed their economies. These forces do not show a uniform character, but the deteriorated credibility - in general, similar to that experienced by other emerging markets - had a rather neutral influence. Interest rates remained relatively stable, even six months after the shock.

In Paraguay, while international reserves decreased, the monetary base went up; also, the level of demand deposits increased, and that of savings and time deposits fell. In the case of Uruguay, the reverse took place. The effect on the level of loans to the private sector is difficult to assess, apart from the change in denomination observed in Paraguay.

7. Summary

The two financial shocks affecting Latin America during the 1990s had different effects on the financial systems of MERCOSUR countries. This was mainly due to the particular characteristics of each economy. The supposed increased linkages associated to the trade agreements under the common market did not materialize, nor was the lack of homogeneity among the countries affected. The bilateral relationships between the two largest economies (Brazil's and Argentina's) and the two smaller ones (Paraguay's and Uruguay's, respectively) hardly affected the already existing financial connections, being the case of Argentina and Uruguay the clearest.

[7] The liquidity restrictions imposed by the monetary authorities do not prevent the banks from compensating less credit by investing their reserves in the United States.

References

Arnaudo, A. and A. Jacobo. (1997): Macroeconomic Homogeneity within Mercosur: An Overview. Estudios Económicos, January-June

Arnaudo, A. and M. Podzun. (1999): Two Policies to Face Financial Crises: The Cases of Mexico and Argentina during the Tequila. Twelfth World Congress of the International Economic Association, Buenos Aires, August 23-27.

Baliño, T. et al. (1999): Monetary Policy in Dollarized Economies (Washington: International Monetary Fund)

Calvo, G and C. Reinhart. (1996): Capital Flows in Latin America: Is there Evidence of Contagion Effects?, mimeo

Carrera, J. et al. (1998): Análisis Integral de las Fluctuaciones Macroeconómicas en Argentina y Brasil. Documento Técnico CACES No.1

Frenkel, J. and A. Rose. (1998): The Endogeinity of the Optimal Currency Areas Criteria. Economic Journal, July

Guidotti, P. And C. Rodríguez (1992): Dollarization in Latin America: Gresham's Law in Reverse. Staff Papers, December

Kaminsky, G. and C. Reinhart (1999): The Twin Crises: The Causes of Banking and Balance-of-Payments Problems. American Economic Review, June

International Monetary Fund (1999): Paraguay: Recent Economic Developments

Loayza, N. et al. (1999): Sectorial Macroeconomic Interdependencies: Evidence for Latin America, East Asia and Europe. FMI.WP/99/11

Sundarajan, V. and T. Baliño (1991): Issues in Recent Banking Crises, in V. Sundarajan and T. Baliño (eds.). Banking Crises: Cases and Issues (Washington: International Monetary Fund, 1991)

APPENDIX

Table 1: Key Financial Variables 6-month Changes,

May 1995-November 1994, November 1995-May 1995, in percentages

Variable	Argentina	Brazil	Paraguay	Uruguay
International Reserves (dollars)	-18.5 / 11.6	-24.9 / 42.5	20.6 / -6.7	12.2 / 0.2
Monetary Base (1995 prices)	-16.7 / -13.9	-9.8 / 8.0	24.2 / -9.2	26.0 / -3.1
Demand Deposits (1995 prices)	-5.6 / -2.3	-25.3 / 21.4	10.8 / -0.9	6.6 / -2.5
Savings and Time Deposits.				
Domestic Currency (1995 prices)	-36.5 / 11.0	10.4 / 2.9	6.7 / 7.2	18.5 / 9.6
Foreign Currency (dollars)	-15.4 / 18.3		-1.1 / 2.5	19.7 / 3.9
Loans to the Private Sector				
Domestic Currency (1995 prices)	-7.3 / 3.1	20.3 / -0.7	2.6 / 9.9	6.2 / 5.2
Foreign Currency (dollars)	3.2 / 1.8		-7.5 / 11.3	13.3 / 5.9
Nominal Interest Rates *				
Deposits, Domestic Currency	8.4 / 15.7 / 8.8	65.7 / 61.6 /40.4	15.3 / 16.3 / 9.4	38.6 / 37.6 /36.1
Foreign Currency	5.8 / 9.8 / 7.1		7.4 / 6.7 / 5.8	4.1 / 4.8 / 4.1
Loans, Domestic Currency	9.8 / 22.0 / 12.1		34.7 / 34.7 /34.1	97.2 /101.6/95.0
Foreign Currency	8.2 / 17.6 / 10.8		14.0 / 13.5 /14.0	12.5 / 14.3 /13.7
Time (months) elapsed for a change in direction Domestic Savings and Time Deposits	5	8	3	3

*Annual rates (%). November 1994, May 1996, November 1995, respectively

Table 2: Key Financial Variables 6-month Changes, May 1999-November 1998, in percentages

Variable	Argentina	Brazil	Paraguay	Uruguay
International Reserves (dollars)	1.4	-23.8	-10.1	10.7
Monetary Base (1995 prices)	0.9	5.0**	8.5	-6.5
Demand Deposits (1995 prices)	3.5	-10.2**	-0.2	-5.1
Savings and Time Deposits				
Domestic Currency (1995 prices)	3.3	1.1**	15.2	7.2
Foreign Currency (dollars)	5.3		3.5	4.0
Loans to the Private Sector				
Domestic Currency (1995 prices)	1.0	-36.9**	-3.3	1.1
Foreign Currency (dollars)	-0.1		4.5	2.2
Nominal Interest Rates * for Depos.				
Domestic Currency	6.1 / 7.8	24.3 / 32.0	19.7 / 20.4	14.3 / 14.2
Foreign Currency	5.6 / 6.5		5.7 / 5.5	4.8 / 4.8
For Loans				
Domestic Currency	8.3 / 11.6	...	32.8 / 31.7	51.2 / 53.8
Foreign Currency	7.5 / 9.8		12.0 / 12.5	13.1 / 12.5

* Annual rates (%). November 1998, May 1999, respectively

** April 1999

... n.a.

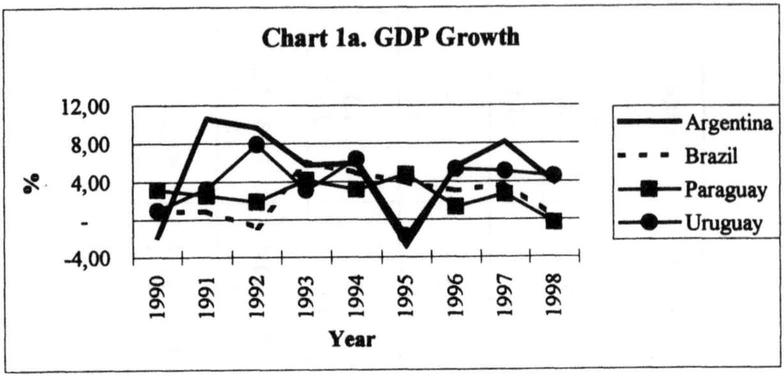
Chart 1a. GDP Growth
12,00
8,00
4,00
-
-4,00
%
1990
1991
1992
1993
1994
1995
1996
1997
1998
Year
Argentina
Brazil
Paraguay
Uruguay

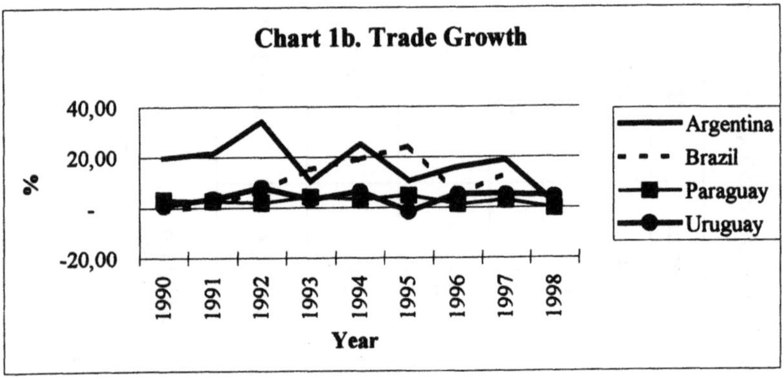
Chart 1b. Trade Growth
40,00
20,00
-
-20,00
%
1990
1991
1992
1993
1994
1995
1996
1997
1998
Year
Argentina
Brazil
Paraguay
Uruguay

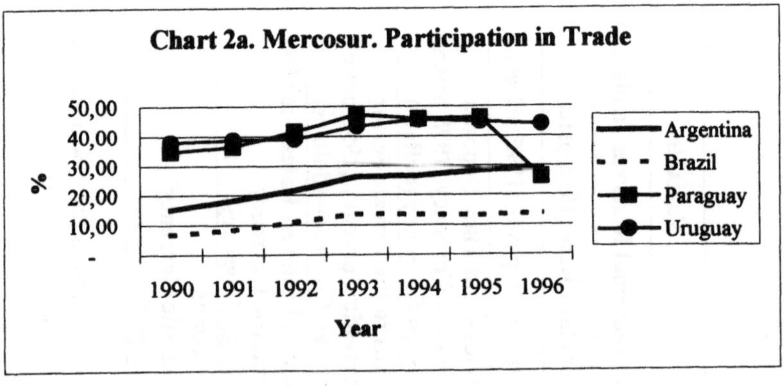
Chart 2a. Mercosur. Participation in Trade
50,00
40,00
30,00
20,00
10,00
-
%
1990 1991 1992 1993 1994 1995 1996
Year
Argentina
Brazil
Paraguay
Uruguay

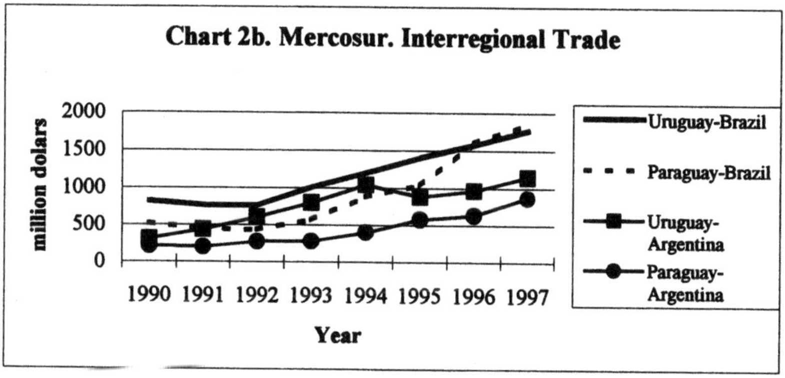
Chart 2b. Mercosur. Interregional Trade
million dolars
2000
1500
1000
500
0
1990 1991 1992 1993 1994 1995 1996 1997
Year
Uruguay-Brazil
Paraguay-Brazil
Uruguay-Argentina
Paraguay-Argentina

THE ASIAN FINANCIAL CRISIS – CAUSES AND CONSEQUENCES: A CRITICAL COMMENT ON THE CURRENT DEBATE

Malcolm H. Dunn

1. Introduction

Prior to the so-called Asian crisis, many economic journalists regarded the vigorous economic growth of the emerging economies of Southeast and East Asia as exemplary. The successful linking of the Southeast Asian currencies' exchange rates to the US dollar testified to their stability. Many cities in Southeast Asia experienced a construction boom, share prices on the Southeast Asian stock exchanges rose considerably year after year and billions in foreign capital poured into the region. Observers were virtually unanimous in the belief that the reason for this success was the 'right' economic policy, based on the free movement of capital, a market-led economy and international trade, while at the same time keeping a tight rein on public debt. Relatively low inflation rates, moreover, seemed to confirm that the expansion of business activities in the region was not built on sand but rather the result of real economic growth.

Once the crisis had erupted and as it progressed in East Asia, the experts all of a sudden knew better; many of the economic successes of the Southeast Asian countries were now considered mere illusion that no one should have been taken in by. The fact that growth rates were so high should have been enough to give cause for scepticism; the construction boom had been a sign of purely speculative capital spending projects, and the enormous imports of capital had of course only been made possible 'artificially' with the aid of high long-term interest rates. Furthermore, they pointed out, the countries of Southeast and East Asia had omitted to ensure supervision of private banks. As a consequence of these institutional deficiencies, many loans had been channelled into extremely unreliable and risky business sectors. In short, the economic policy of these countries had been a complete failure and the IMF should be called upon to support reform efforts in the emerging economies of Southeast Asia by imposing strict credit conditions.

What is striking in the current interpretation of the crisis is that virtually all of the phenomena that were regarded as indicators of success prior to the crisis then came to be identified, after its onset, as the causes of it. Running through all the declarations like a scarlet thread is the firm conviction that it was all down to policy failure – primarily that of economic policy – in the countries concerned, but also failure on the part of the IMF and the World Bank which, by granting credit all too readily, contributed to the moral hazard in the private banks. "Financial crises" – so the tenor of the argument goes – "are not inevitable. When they nevertheless happen, it is because economic policy, both national and international, has failed".

Is the financial crisis in Asia really the result of misguided political decisions, such as the decision to link the Southeast Asian currencies to the dollar or negligence regarding banking supervision? In the course of this presentation, these interpretations of the Asian crisis will be subjected to critical appraisal. Contrary to the usual explanations, this presentation will demonstrate that the fundamental reason for the Asian crisis lies in the nature of money as credit. For the same reason it is also basically impossible to prevent financial crises without doing away with the very function of financial markets. This does not mean that we must dispense with financial markets altogether, but rather that financial market operations need to be regulated. The presentation concludes with some reflections on the consequences of the financial crisis in Asia.

2. Did fixed exchange rates cause the Asian crisis?

In order to gain the confidence of the international capital markets, many of the emerging economies of Southeast Asia had tied their currencies firmly to the US dollar. As a result, the Southeast Asian currencies mirrored the depreciation of the dollar against the Japanese yen in the first half of the 90s, and then the appreciation of the dollar against the yen in the second half of the 90s.[1] The overvaluation of the Southeast Asian currencies that went hand in hand with being linked to the dollar is considered by many authors to be one of the prime causes of the financial crisis. According to the critics, the disadvantages of being tied to the dollar are confirmed by three of its effects.

First, linking the currency to the dollar encouraged the inflow of short-term capital from abroad, as currency-related risks seemed low. Under a flexible exchange rate regime, the inflow of foreign capital would soon have led to appreciation of the Southeast Asian currencies; this in turn would have made foreign direct investment less profitable, the inflow of capital would have taken on less dramatic proportions and over-investment in unprofitable sectors could have been avoided.

1 "In the process, they recorded an appreciation of their real (trade-weighted) effective exchange rates relative to trend (where trend is captured by the 1987-97 average). By that measure, at the end of June 1997, the Thai baht stood about 7 percent above its long-term average; the corresponding figures for the Indonesian rupiah, the Malaysian ringgit, and the Philippine peso were 4, 9, and 12 percent, respectively." (Goldstein 1998, 15.)

Second, tying the currencies to the dollar undermined the price competitiveness of Southeast Asian export products. Since the appreciation of the US dollar relative to the Japanese yen and the European currencies was followed by the Southeast Asian currencies, this meant higher export prices to other countries. At the same time, the price competitiveness of other suppliers (e.g. China and Vietnam) improved, to the disadvantage of the emerging economies of Southeast Asia. Under a flexible exchange rate regime, therefore, the sharp slump in exports could have been prevented.[2]

Third, being tied to the dollar placed the Southeast Asian countries under pressure to sacrifice their foreign currency reserves to defend US dollar parity as soon as the financial markets began to speculate against their currencies. Abandonment of their currency reserves precipitated a loss of confidence in their solvency and forced a drastic devaluation of the Southeast Asian currencies. Under a flexible exchange rate regime, in contrast, the need for support buying operations would not have arisen.

The arguments that are advanced regarding why the currencies should not have been tied to the dollar are directed in principle against any fixed exchange rate regime, irrespective of the currency used as the anchor: fixed exchange rates and exchange rate target zones are always fraught with problems because they restrict the informative and guiding function of the price mechanism and thereby increase the risk of misallocations. It should not be inferred from this, however, that a system of freely floating exchange rates is generally superior to a fixed-rate system.

First of all, it is also possible to restrict short-term capital inflows under a fixed exchange rate regime by regulating movements of capital. This begs the question whether the liberalized capital account of many developing and emerging economies since the 70s might in fact have been a more significant causal factor in Asia's financial crisis than the pegging of their currencies to the dollar.[3] Consider Taiwan and China, which remained largely unaffected by the Southeast Asian financial crisis because they prevented the inflow of short-term capital. Consider also the Federal Republic of Germany, where capital market deregulation did not begin until quite late on (in the mid-sixties).

What about the effects of the dollar peg on the trade balance? There is no question that the appreciation of the Southeast Asian currencies as a result of be-

---

2 "In Thailand, merchandise exports were practically flat (0.5 percent increase) in 1996, after rising by 23 percent in 1995. In South Korea, merchandise exports grew by less than 4 percent in 1996 – a big change from the 30-percent-plus growth rate of a year earlier. In Malaysia, Indonesia, and the Philippines an export slowdown was likewise in evidence, albeit on a more moderate scale." (Goldstein 1998, 16.)

3 See Stiglitz 1999.

ing linked to the dollar had a detrimental effect on the competitiveness of Southeast Asian export goods, even though the effect was mitigated by the fact that import prices factored in dollars, such as that of oil, could be kept stable.

Early devaluation of, say, the Thai baht, would have brought down export prices of Thai goods and raised import prices. Whether this would in fact have brought about a sustainable improvement in the balance of payments depends in the short term on export supply and import demand elasticities, and in the long term on the knock-on effects of higher import prices; if the impact of higher import prices on domestic price levels is too strong, then the costs of producing the commodities for export also rise. In the worst-case scenario the inflationary effect then over-compensates for the exchange rate effect, resulting in higher export prices. The more inelastic the response of import demand to price increases, the more pronounced this effect is.

It is therefore by no means certain that early devaluation on the part of the Southeast Asian countries would have brought about a sustainable improvement in the balance of trade. Moreover, it must be borne in mind that the sharp decline in export growth cannot be attributed solely to the overvaluation of the Southeast Asian currencies. At least two other factors have to be taken into consideration, first the general decline in the global economy in the mid-nineties, and second the increased supply-side competition from Chinese products.

In 1996 growth in world trade fell to 5.6 per cent from 9 per cent in the previous year. Hale (1997) points especially to the importance here of the electronics industry and in particular of semiconductors, prices of which fell by around 80% in 1996. This sharp decline had a profound effect on the emerging economies of Southeast Asia as exporters.[4] From the mid-nineties, overproduction could also be seen in industries such as chip manufacture, vehicle production, steel and petrochemicals. These developments were entirely independent of the exchange rate-related fall in price competitiveness of Southeast Asian export goods. One other factor affecting Southeast Asian exports, if to a lesser extent, was that foreign direct investment going to China was rising and China was making its presence felt increasingly as an exporter. Thurow (1998), indeed, considers this to have been the most important factor behind the trade deficit in many ASEAN countries.[5]

---

[4] According to Hale (1997), 57 per cent of Singapore's exports, and 49, 40 and 17 per cent of the exports of Malaysia, the Philippines and Thailand are electronic goods. In particular, semiconductors account for a large share of exports from Asian economies to the United States. (See Fernald/Edison/Loungani (1998)).

[5] In contrast, Fernald/Edison/Loungani (1998) come to the conclusion that the increase of Chinese exports did not contribute very much to the outbreak of the Asian financial crisis.

Lastly, the significance of the dollar peg as a possible cause of the financial crisis in Asia is put into perspective also by the fact that under a floating exchange rate regime, the currencies of Southeast Asia would have appreciated much earlier on due to the influx of foreign capital. The growth in exports from Southeast Asian countries to Japan in the first half of the 90s would most probably have been more modest if the ASEAN currencies had not depreciated against the yen as a result of being tied to the dollar. Thus if one wants to compare the effect of a free exchange rate regime and that of a fixed exchange rate on the dynamics of the trade balance, it should be borne in mind that Southeast Asia's export growth in the early 90s did in fact benefit from being pegged to the dollar.

Under a floating exchange rate regime, Southeast Asia's exports would not have grown to such an extent in the first half of the 90s or slumped so dramatically in the second half of the 90s as under a fixed exchange rate regime. There is therefore good reason to believe that the success or failure of an economy as a supplier of products that are saleable on the world market depends less on the exchange rate regime than is commonly supposed. The Meltzer report, for example, comes to the same conclusion.[6] Although a flexible exchange rate relieves central banks of the need to deploy their currency reserves to defend the exchange rate, it also exposes private foreign investors to the risk of having to cover themselves *individually* against exchange rate fluctuations. A fixed exchange rate places central issue banks under pressure to defend the exchange rate and steer a more restrictive course as regards monetary policy, but it can also, for this very reason, enhance a country's attractiveness as a location for international capital.

3. Moral hazard

During the 1990s, the emerging economies of Southeast Asia experienced a significant expansion of bank and non-bank loans to the private sector that were used to a large extent for the purchase of equities and real estate. This led to asset price inflation and a further expansion of credit, extended on the basis of the increased collateral represented by the assets whose value had risen. At some point, however, this self-perpetuating process of lending expansion came to an end. The

---

6 "A critical point is often overlooked. The long-run position of an economy does not depend on the choice of the exchange rate system. Exchange systems determine how a country adjusts to external events or domestic policies. ... Two important lessons of experience under many different exchange-rate regimes are: First, countries that follow stabilizing monetary, fiscal (and other) policies can successfully maintain either a fixed or a fluctuating exchange rate. Second, countries that adopt policies that are excessively expansive or contractive have difficulty maintaining a fixed exchange rate or avoiding appreciation or depreciation of a fluctuating rate. Stabilizing policies are more important than the choice of exchange-rate regime." (I.F.I.A.C.-Report 1999, Chapter 3, 36.)

circular process was reversed. Asset price deflation led to loss of collateral for secured loans, to which financial intermediaries responded by reducing their lending volume, which in turn triggered a further decline in asset prices.[7]

What was it that caused things to go so badly wrong? Many authors regard the inflated volume of credit as a consequence of an inefficiently operating banking sector. Three arguments are used to support this view:

First, the very low equity ratios in private banks encouraged moral hazard since in the event of collapse the banks had little (i.e. only their equity capital) to lose. Borrowing from outside sources, meanwhile, promised high returns in the event of a successful outcome.[8] In addition, credit was often extended to bank directors, bank managers and businesses connected to them ('connected lending'), which led to a higher concentration of credit risk.[9]

Second, the risk of a sudden outflow of capital was increased by the fact that most foreign borrowing was short-term in order to keep borrowing costs down and avoid currency-related risks. Contrary to one of the important rules of financing, short-term loans were used to finance long-term investments.[10]

Third, the closely interwoven nature of relationships between the private banks and the government reinforced the assumption of private bankers that in the event of an emergency they could count on government assistance. Due to the fact that the government had an interest in ensuring that banks lent generously, banking supervision was grossly neglected.[11] Consequently, many authors believe that part of the solution lies in improving banking supervision, increasing the share capitalization of banks, closing down ailing banks and – last but not least – privatizing state-owned banks.

---

7 See Menkhoff 2000, 6 and Sarno and Taylor 1999, 1.

8 "The major problem underlying financial relations is the incentive for borrowers to follow overly risky policies, because in the case of success they would reap most of the advantage; but in the case of failure, the burden is substantially shared by the lender. Unfortunately, the behavior of the borrower – the agent – cannot be completely observed by the lender – the principal. From this originates the moral hazard problem." (Menkhoff 1999a, 3.)

9 See Goldstein 1998, 12ff.: "There was too much 'connected lending' (lending to bank directors, managers, and their related business) with all the attendant dangers of concentration of credit risk and lack of arms-length credit decisions ('crony capitalism'). ... Based on past behavior, there was a strong expectation that, should banks get into trouble, depositors and creditors would get bailed out, and bank supervisors lacked the mandate to counter strong political pressures for regulatory forbearance. On top of all this, the quality of public disclosure and transparency was poor."

10 See Goldstein 1998, 9.

11 See Krugman (1998) "The problem began with financial intermediaries – institutions whose liabilities were perceived as having an implicit government guarantee, but were essentially unregulated and therefore subject to severe moral hazard problems."

In retrospect, the massive influx of short-term foreign capital into the emerging economies of Southeast Asia seems like a bad investment of gigantic proportions. The risks involved in many investments were underestimated or were not covered adequately by risk premia. The question raised by the *moral hazard* hypothesis is how does one explain this systematic misjudgement of investments by both domestic and foreign lenders? Is it really the case, as Krugman (1998) suggests, that "the Asian crisis ... was mainly about bad banking..."? There are several factors that cast doubt on this explanation of the financial crisis.

First, inadequate share capitalization of the domestic private banks does not necessarily mean that their lending practices will inevitably be lax. One could also argue that the reverse is true; the fact that even small losses pose a danger to the bank could motivate the bank's management to be more cautious. A moral hazard problem can only occur if the bank's shareholders are themselves involved in the bank's business operations, not when the bank's management runs the risk of losing its job. It is even less appropriate to infer that if the bank's equity position is excessively thin then the credits extended by private banks must have been rated as highly risky by the banks themselves. If it is true that before the financial crisis the emerging economies of Southeast Asia were considered by the biggest and most highly renowned international financial institutions to be an exceedingly lucrative area for investment – characterized by a high degree of political stability, restrictive financial and monetary policy, with low government debt, high growth rates and stable currencies – then why, of all the banks, should the private domestic banks arrive at a completely contrary risk assessment?

It is far more reasonable to assume that investments that had previously received financing were also basically regarded by the private domestic banks as perfectly justifiable. Even the fact that domestic funding needs were met through foreign borrowing does not in itself signify bad banking. What kind of private bank would meet its capital requirements at home if that entailed a high burden of interest, when it could avail itself of much more favourable refinancing terms in the international financial markets?[12] It is only the failure, in retrospect, of many investments financed through external borrowing that lends any plausibility to the argument of excessive external debt.

Second, Moral hazard can also result from relationship banking. The emphasis here is on the word 'can', however, because the type of relationship banking that is typical in many Southeast Asian countries is not in itself inefficient. This gives us another qualifier to the moral hazard argument. As Menkhoff 1999a, 5 emphasizes, the nature of relationship banking is based on the idiosyncratic character of its business relationships. "Relationship banking is, typically,

[12] Cf. Montiel and Reinhart (1997).

banking within a wider family or a group of otherwise related persons (such as friends, colleagues, religious groups or other social networks."

The economic rationale of this type of business relationship resides in the fact that the lender has a personal impression of the borrower. Long-standing personal relationships and the fact that people belong to the same social group mean that the danger of opportunistic behaviour is significantly reduced. The problem of lack of legal security that arises in many developing and emerging economies, and the attendant question of contract enforcement, is offset by the potential damage it could do to the borrower's reputation. Because of this, *Menkhoff* sees the real problem not in 'moral hazard' and 'bad banking', but rather in the overly rapid liberalization of the capital market, which presented operators in Southeast Asia with new problems relating to information and supervision that the banking system was institutionally not yet able to cope with.

The *third* qualifier to the moral hazard argument relates to the supposedly negative role of the government in guaranteeing private banks' liabilities and, in doing so, encouraging them to engage in risky lending activities.[13] The argument that excessively lax banking supervision in the emerging economies of Southeast Asia was responsible for the risky lending behaviour of private domestic banks ignores the fact that renowned foreign banks were also involved to a significant extent in this lending. "One could almost say that they could hardly place enough capital in these countries ... These institutions, however, were regulated according to current (western, M.D.) standards" which, according to Menkhoff 2000, 15, produces the argumentum e contrario that "there is little reason to suppose that international regulatory standards alone could help to prevent banking crises like the one in Asia."

4. Financial crisis, money and the nature of credit

Theoretical explanations of the crisis in Asia that fall back on the exchange rate regime, moral hazard behaviour of privately-owned commercial banks and the government's failure as regards banking supervision assume international capital flows without taking the trouble to seek an explanation for them. The question of "how did banks and their customers in these countries obtain the external financing that helped to support such lending decisions?" (Goldstein 1998, 13) is often barely touched upon. Instead, their analysis concentrates on identifying mechanisms and institutional deficiencies that might have induced the private

13 Krugman (1998, 4) describes this mechanism as follows: "It is a familiar point that such intermediaries then have an incentive not merely to undertake excessively risky investments, but to pursue investments with low expected returns as long as they have 'fat right tails' – that is, the owner of a guaranteed intermediary likes investments that could yield high returns if he gets lucky, even if there is also a strong possibility of heavy losses."

market participants and governments to take the wrong course of action. The only ones to make 'mistakes', however, are those who are in a position to recognize the really worthwhile investment opportunities, together with the risks entailed, in advance. The indicators that were interpreted *ex post* as sure signs of an impending financial crisis – high interest rates, short maturities, large capital inflows, rising real estate prices, etc. – were interpreted *ex ante* as a sign that exceptionally high rates of return on investments were to be expected – at least from the perspective of those who believed that they had to get involved in the upswing of the emerging markets before their competitors did.

In order to find an explanation for the Asian crisis one must first identify the origins of the massive inflows of capital that were a crucial contributor to Southeast Asia's economic upswing, and the reasons behind them. Here we come to the growth of the financial markets, which in the past twenty years have expanded far more rapidly than global production. The share of corporate investments that are financed via the financial markets is declining. This means that financing from internal resources, i.e. from company profits and depreciation, has risen considerably in the last two decades.[14] With this development financial markets have undergone a fundamental change in character.

Whereas in the past financial markets served primarily to finance enterprise investment projects by means of raising bank loans or issuing shares and promissory notes, today financial investments predominate. As *Tobin* noted in 1987, the way in which the securities industry operates nowadays has very little to do with the financing of real investments. Much the same may be said of currency trading. In the period from 1979 to 1998 currency trading increased twelve-fold, to 1.5 trillion dollars *per working day*. This means that it takes only five days of currency trading to process the equivalent of the total world trade in goods and services *for the whole of 1998* (6.5 trillion dollars). Even taking into account hedging transactions it is clear that the scale of currency trading has very little to do with movements of real goods and services. This leads us on to the subject of the derivatives market, the fastest-growing segment of the international financial markets.

Derivatives originally served as a means of safeguarding income from trade in commodities that are subject to fluctuations in price and are time-consuming to produce. Often it was agricultural products or raw materials that were involved. The protection of prices works as follows: buyer and seller pledge to buy/sell a certain amount of a product at a certain price – set out in a contractual agreement

---

14 The share of the retained earnings (depreciation excluded) as inflow of financial resources in enterprises has increased during the period 1975-95 from 50 to 66.2 per cent. Banking credits amount to one-fifth, and stock financing 7.6 per cent of total funds. Raising loans plays a minor role as a source of finance. Cf. Huffschmid 1999, 19.

– on a designated date. This symmetrical transaction provides both parties with a secure basis for calculation. The introduction of commodity futures exchanges, such as the Chicago Mercantile Exchange (CME) in 1872, considerably facilitated these hedging agreements, since the buyers and sellers no longer had to enter into contact with one another directly. Nowadays, meanwhile, the vast majority of derivatives business involves financial products, such as currency, interest rates and stock index futures.

Trade in derivatives, then, rather than serving to safeguard prices, is used to speculate on movements in prices and as a result it has become increasingly like a form of betting.[15] Speculation does not start with derivatives trading, however; it starts with the simple commodity bill, where a payment is replaced by a promise to pay which functions as a means of payment until such a time as the bill is redeemed. *All* loans are speculative inasmuch as they are extended on the basis of an *expected* future profit out of which the interest will be serviced and the repayments financed. Each loan adds to the mass of promises to pay, which in turn forms the basis for new loans. Securities and other assets are bought on credit terms in the expectation that their price will rise. If their price then indeed rises, then this provides the basis for new credit, and the new credit is in turn invested in new assets. In this way we end up with a continual inflation of lending, and with it monetary claims, that becomes increasingly disconnected from the dynamics of the real economy and its true earning power.

The Asian crisis is a prime example of this process of expanding demands for payment without a corresponding increase in the ability to pay, increasing monetary exploitation rights and real surplus production. Every loan places the borrower under an obligation to generate profits from which the interest on the loan can be serviced and the credit debt repaid. The crisis in the financial markets exposes the general disparity that exists between accumulated monetary claims and wealth actually accumulated and thereby reveals the true nature of credit business:

Credit itself brings no return; it participates in the returns of others! The interest earned by banks is the price that has to be paid for *other* market participants (enterprises) to be able to expand their business activities without having to wait for the return on capital they themselves have employed. In this respect credit is the anticipation of profits expected in the future. If these profits fail to materialize and a situation arises where many borrowers are no longer servicing their loans, then credit contraction will follow. Instead of once again accepting promises to pay and thereby extending the debts, lenders now demand actual payment. The consequences of this are not only to be seen in the Asian crisis.

---

15 An expression of this development is the high turnover rate of derivates. For example, a short-term interest rates futures contract changes hands on average eight times.

There ensues a general flight to liquidity, with the result that there is a contraction not only in the extent of credit business, in the value of national credit, but in economic activity as a whole. At the same time a massive outflow of foreign capital occurs, and not only from the emerging markets of Asia. This is because doubts as to whether the capital invested short-term has genuinely increased in the less developed countries are not confined to the region but become generalized. Other countries are then swept along in rapid succession by waves of speculation (Russia 1998/ Brazil 1998/99) that plunge their financial systems too into serious crisis.

Not least the way in which the financial crises spread – often referred to using the medical term contagion – provides further indication that the underlying reason for the Asian crisis is not to be found in Asia itself than the Asian Miracle can be adequately explained by the exceptionally favourable growth conditions in Asia. For the Asian crisis underscores a further point: When speculative attacks against economies and their currencies is enough to bring about the collapse of economic life as a whole, this tells us something about the *nature of wealth* in those economies.

The financial strength of these countries thus turns out to be not so much the result of a flourishing domestic economy as the result of speculation on the part of foreign investors regarding the future economic growth of the countries. It had simply become increasingly difficult for international players with surplus money to find lucrative investment opportunities in their usual favourite investment locations, especially as the public authorities there were in the process of reducing indebtedness on a massive scale. A way out was found in the shape of the emerging markets, which for their part appeared attractive with high interest rates, low inflation, minimal current account deficits and exchange rates that were tied to the dollar. In other words, it was because the huge influx of foreign capital had turned the countries of Southeast Asia into 'emerging markets' that they were particularly hard hit when the foreign capital withdrew. Any economic policy that aims to prevent financial crises of global proportions must therefore give priority to reforming the way financial markets operate rather than devising remedial programmes for the crisis countries.

5. Some lessons from the Asian financial crisis

The possibility of financial crisis is inherent to the financial market system, because financial market growth of necessity becomes disconnected from the *dynamics* of the real economy. On the other hand, the efficiency of the free market system is in fact based on the 'decoupling' of the monetary economy from the real economy; financial markets foster economic growth by providing advance finance enabling business activities to expand and they fulfil a vital guiding role. They ensure, ideally at least, that capital is invested where it will bring the greatest increase in welfare and, in addition, they also have a disciplinary effect in that they reward 'good' and penalize 'bad' economic policy (cf. Jochimson 1997).

The aim of the reform debate underway at present, therefore, is not to abolish financial markets but to limit the scale of financial crises and the risks associated with them. Before these goals can be achieved, however, there are some fundamental and difficult decisions to be made. If the aim is to stabilize the financial system while at the same time maintaining a high degree of national sovereignty with regard to monetary and economic policy, then this implies restriction of the free capital market; if, on the other hand, one dispenses with financial market regulation and gives precedence to the free movement of capital, this will entail relinquishing monetary and fiscal policy autonomy to a substantial extent. In other words, it is not possible to achieve financial market stabilization while at the same time retaining both an autonomous (national) monetary policy *and* free movement of capital. In view of this, we can divide the reform proposals into those that place greater emphasis on allowing leeway for national economic policy and accept that this will mean limiting the free movement of capital and – the reverse – those that give priority to the free movement of capital and accept that this will mean limiting national autonomy in terms of monetary and economic policy. Let us take a closer look at the different strategies.

(1) Regulation of international capital transactions

Since the 70s, many emerging economies have liberalized their capital markets. This means that restrictions on foreign investments and restraints on currency exchange were eliminated, and bans prohibiting ownership of domestic assets by foreigners were lifted. The theory behind this policy of 'deregulation' is based on the view that liberalizing movements of capital increases the efficiency of capital markets. The financial crises of the 80s and 90s have nevertheless raised doubts as to whether it was sensible to liberalize the capital markets so rapidly, particularly since free capital markets can only function properly if the appropriate financial sector institutions (e.g. banking supervision, adequate equity capitalization of private banks) have been put in place. For this reason, a significant number of authors consider premature liberalization of the capital markets to have been one of the major reasons for the high level of volatility of short-term capital movements.

Capital market regulation serves first and foremost to lessen the risks of highly volatile capital and price fluctuations. A fundamental distinction needs to be made between two different methods for restricting movements of capital. One method consists in imposing a tax on currency transactions (cf. *Tobin* 1978). Taxation of currency transactions increases transaction costs and reduces incentives to speculate on or against a currency.[16] The other instrument consists of controls on the movement of capital, which might for example take the form of non-interest-bearing minimum reserves for foreign currency denominated borrowing, or quantitative restrictions on inflows and outflows of capital. The stabilizing effect of both approaches derives from the fact that they enable exchange rates to remain fairly stable while keeping a significant degree of autonomy as regards monetary policy in the hands of national governments. These advantages are offset, however, by certain disadvantages; if the cost of financial transactions, for example in the derivatives market, increases too much, then this jeopardizes the risk hedging function of currency transactions. If on the other hand the tax levied on currency transactions is set at too low a level relative to the exchange rate expectations of the market participants, then the Tobin tax has no impact at all.

Controls on the movement of capital are also problematic: capital export restrictions can curb inflows of capital and therefore also economic growth if foreign investors begin to fear that they might not be able to repatriate the profits from their direct investments. In addition, there is a danger – common to all government regulatory mechanisms – of efficiency-reducing rent-seeking behaviour on the part of some market participants who exploit their good relations with the political decision-makers and engage in patronage activities in order to ensure that exceptions are made in their favour within the regulatory provisions. These problems notwithstanding, the experiences of China, Taiwan, Malaysia and Chile show that restricting short-term capital movements can be a useful instrument for reducing the damaging impact of contagion in the event of financial crisis.

(2) International co-ordination of monetary and fiscal policy

Calls for international co-ordination of monetary and economic policy are also based, as are those for regulation of international capital transactions, on the proposition that liberalizing capital markets increases the volatility of financial flows and thereby increases the likelihood of financial crises that have a negative impact on the real economy. However, advocates of this strategy emphasize that regulation must be *international*. The reason for this, it is argued, is the global nature of financial market crises, which cannot be tackled adequately by provisions for capital market regulation ordained at the national level.[17] Eatwell and

---

16 Short-term investments are particularly affected because, as a rule, these bring a lower return than long-term investment projects, whereas the same level of tax burden is spread over a shorter period.

17 Cf. *Eatwell/Taylor* (1999, 282): "Since international financial liberalization results in a major increase in risk to both the national and the international real economy, an effective policy toward capital markets must be international in character."

Taylor (1999) point in this direction with their suggestion for setting up a 'World Financial Authority' (WFA), whose task would be "to develop a framework for international financial regulation (...) and to ensure, via the powers ceded to it, that those rules are implemented." (p. 284). In addition, this organization should also become a forum for international financial co-operation. Once national monetary and finance policies were brought into line with each other within the regulatory framework of the WFA, the signatory countries would then be bound mutually to support each other's stabilization policies.

The advantage of an international financial institution vested with appropriate powers as opposed to capital market regulation ordained on a purely national level resides firstly in the fact that unilateral regulatory provisions can actually reinforce contagion by encouraging speculative movements of international capital to countries where no such regulation of capital markets is in place. In addition, national regulatory measures pertaining to movements of capital are *reactive* in the sense that they have no impact whatsoever on the real cause of international financial crises, i.e., on the essentially unjustified inflation of international lending. In contrast, measures that combat the over-expansion of international credit volume arising as a consequence of essentially unjustified expansionary monetary and fiscal policy will indeed tackle the roots of the problem. There is, however, an important down-side to this advantage: a precondition for establishing a World Financial Authority is willingness on the part of the member states to co-operate, and this cannot be taken for granted. This is because – first of all – individual countries are affected to different extents by the contagion effect and – second – the member states would be forced to accept a substantial loss of sovereignty as regards economic policy which, due to the first reason, they are not willing to do.[18]

The strategies discussed in this presentation – i.e. regulating international capital transactions, imposing a tax on currency transactions, engaging in international co-ordination, perhaps even setting up a world financial authority vested with appropriate powers – are all based on recognition of the fact that the reasons why international financial crises occur and the mechanisms by which they spread have less to do with economic policy misjudgements on part of the developing and emerging economies than with the nature and composition of international financial markets. At the samc time, it also becomes clear that the implementation

---

[18] Eatwell and Taylor (1999, 284) consider the World Trade Organization to be a good example "that it is possible to establish an international executive authority with enforcement powers." The history of the WTO negotiations and conferences demonstrates, however, that the 'authority' of international organizations diminishes if the economic and political interests of the major trading nations, i.e. those with bargaining power, are affected. No wonder, then, "that there is no appetite today (especially in Washington) for the creation of a new international bureaucracy."(284/5)

of these policy recommendations is fraught with considerable difficulties and carries with it substantial risks that are ultimately due to the information problems confronting political decision-makers. Finally, it should be borne in mind that volatility in international financial markets and exchange rates is not necessarily an indication of the failure of capital markets.

First it is inherent in the nature of the price mechanism that actual prices deviate temporarily from equilibrium prices and only come to approximate them in the longer term. We therefore need to verify whether the price deviations recede from or oscillate around their constant mean values. *Second*, prices also fulfil their informative function when they are volatile, indeed especially then. It is precisely when they are volatile that they reflect the uncertainty of the market participants, whose expectations are subject to erratic fluctuations. *Third*, market participants are not entirely defenceless in the face of volatile prices. They are able to hedge against risks related to price fluctuations, and indeed frequently do so. Hedging transactions increase the costs of economic transactions and may reduce incentives to engage in speculation. For this reason it is important to gauge accurately whether and to what extent highly volatile prices and capital movements bring about changes in behaviour that will reduce volatility in the medium and longer term.

Even if the market failure theory were correct, regulating movements of capital is not always the best course of action. Demands for regulation appear to be justified only in cases where the costs and the risks associated with the free movement of capital are higher than the cost of government intervention and measures to regulate capital transactions, since these too involve uncertainties and risks. It seems, finally, that the question raised by Eatwell and Taylor as to whether it is possible "to secure the benefits of a flexible financial system, ... whilst at the same time ensuring that [...] the [...] world economy [is] protected from the systemic risks which financial liberalization brings in its wake?" (1999, 282), will have to remain unanswered for the time being – in spite of the flood of specialist literature on the subject of financial crises – or at least as long as the economic costs of government regulation remain unknown, as do the risks that indisputably arise when capital markets are highly liberalized.

References

Eatwell, John and Lance *Taylor* (1999), Towards an Effective Regulation of International Capital Markets, International Politics and Society, 3/1999, 279-286.

Fernald, John, Hali *Edison*, and Prakash *Lounganie* (1998), Was China the First Domino? Assessing Links Between China and the Rest of Emerging Asia. Washington: Board of Governors of the Federal Reserve System (March).

Goldstein, Morris (1998), The Asian Financial Crisis: Causes, Cures, and System Implications, Institute for International Economics Washington, D.C.

Hale, David (1997), The East Asian Financial Crisis and the World Economy. Testimony before the House Banking Committee, Washington (13 Nov).

Huffschmid, Jörg (1999), Politische Ökonomie der Finanzmärkte. Hamburg.

International Financial Institution Advisory Commission (1999) (Meltzer-Report), Washington, D.C.

Jochimsen, Reimut (1997), Eher Schiedsrichter als Störenfried: Internationale Finanzmärkte und nationale Wirtschaftspolitik, International Politics and Society, 4/1997, 399-411.

Krugman, Paul (1998), What happened to Asia? From: Paul Krugman's home page.

Menkhoff, Lukas (1999a), Relationship Banking and Thailand's Crisis: The Difficult Transformation from Personal Relations to Market Relations. Working Paper, Aachen.

Menkhoff, Lukas (1999b), Bad Banking in Thailand? An Empirical Analysis of Macro Indicators. Working Paper, Aachen

Menkhoff, Lukas (2000), Die Rolle der Finanzmärkte in der Asienkrise. In: Renate Schubert (Ed.) Ursachen und Therapien regionaler Entwicklungskrisen - Das Beispiel der Asienkrise. Schriften des Vereins für Socialpolitik, N.f. Duncker & Humblot, forthcoming.

Montiel, Peter, and Carmen *Reinhart* (1997), The Dynamics of Capital Movements to Emerging Economies during the 1990s. Williams College and the University of Maryland. Photocopy.

Sarno, Lucio, and Mark P. *Taylor* (1999), Moral Hazard, Asset Price Bubbles, Capitals Flows, and the East Asian Crisis: The First Tests. Working Paper University of Oxford.

Stiglitz, Joseph E. (1999), Reforming the Global Architecture: Lessons from Recent Crisis, Journal of Finance, Vol. 54, 1508-1521.

Thurow, Lester (1998), Asia: The Collapse and the Cure. New York Review of Books (5th Feb.).

Tobin, James (1978), A Proposal for International Monetary Reform, Eastern Economic Journal, Vol. 4, 153-159.

Tobin, James (1987), On the Efficiency of the Financial System. In: J. Tobin, Policies for Prosperity. Essays in a Keynesian Mode. Cambridge, 282-296.

EXPERIENCES IN EXCHANGE RATE POLICIES IN LATIN AMERICA IN THE 90s: HISTORY AND PERSPECTIVES

Amaury Patrick Gremaud, Márcio Bobik Braga*

1. Introduction

Throughout the 90s several exchange rate experiences were observed in various Latin American countries, the last of which occurred in Ecuador, whose economy has been undergoing a dollarization process since January 2000. These experiences have brought at least two issues to the forefront of discussions on policies of stabilization and growth in the region: the use of so-called "exchange rate anchors" as the best form of overcoming instability in Latin American countries; and the possibility of using dollarization of the economy as a means of resolving the restrictions imposed by the performance of external accounts. These restrictions are manifested through elevated interest rates and exchange rate instabilities, factors that contribute to low economic growth. Recently, there has been more discussion on the creation of a monetary union, especially among the countries of Mercosur, as a form of overcoming some of the exchange rate problems of these countries and of strengthening the economic union among them. The objective of the present article is to synthesize the main characteristics and implications of the different forms of exchange rate treatment that have been adopted in Latin America, as a means of defeating the current scenario of economic instability faced by its countries.

2. Exchange Rate Regimes: the various options

Exchange rate regime is understood as the set of rules and institutions that regulate the functioning of the exchange rate market. In general, there are two major groups of exchange rate regimes that differ as to the formation of price (that is, exchange rate) in the exchange rate market: that of fixed rates and that of flexible rates. Indeed, there is a great variety of policy options. Associated to models of fixed exchange rate, there can be:

i) an exchange rate rule that involves the government's determination to intervene in the market so as to maintain the exchange rate stable for an indefinite time period;

* Professors of the Economics Department at FEA/USP, Ribeirão Preto campus and of PROLAM – Graduate Program in Integration of Latin America.

ii) a *currency board*, which institutionalizes that rule and formally associates the monetary policy to the exchange rate regime; and
iii) a policy of exchange rate fixation but with systematic adjustments, which can be made using previously defined rules or in a discretionary manner (crawling peg).

Within a flexible exchange rate regime it is further possible to have:

iv) a market totally free of government interventions; and
v) a partially managed market – using so-called dirty floating – in which the government interferes in this market when the exchange rate levels start to compromise certain goals of economic policy.

There are also some intermediary schemes possible, such as:

vi) a system of symmetrical bands, in which within certain limits the rates behaves as a free market; and
vii) asymmetrical bands, where there is only one limit, either the maximum or the minimum.

Finally there are the options of simply giving up having an exchange rate policy of one's own. In a way this option represents a deepening of the consequences of a fixed exchange rate regime. In this case we have:

viii) the adoption of another currency as the local currency (dollarization of the economy, for example); and
ix) monetary union with other countries, promoting a joint monetary and exchange rate administration.

In general, in the system of floating exchange rates there is freedom in the exchange rate market. In this case, the government intervenes only as supplier and demander of exchange rate values according to its needs, just as the private sector does. Thus, the alterations in the supply and demand of exchange rate values have an effect on the exchange rate, which should value or devalue as a result of these alterations. A system that has been frequently used as of the mid-70s is dirty floating. This system differs from the previous in that it is subject to unanticipated interventions from the government with the objective of diminishing the volatility associated to a free exchange rate market. Hence, if the market is stable, it works as a floating market. On the other hand, if the market behavior is unstable or if the exchange rate level is hampering economic performance, intervention is aimed at stabilizing or directing the rate to a desirable level.

In the case of the regime of fixed exchange rates, as the very name suggests, the exchange rate of the country is constant. What is adjusted in the exchange rate market is only the quantity demanded and supplied at that value. Indeed, in this regime, the government intervenes in order to balance the supply and demand of exchange rate values at the level of the established exchange rate. Thus, the oscillations in the supply and demand of exchange rate values do not have repercussions on the exchange rate, but only on the volume of international reserves of the country, with implications on the supply of money.

At the end of the 70s, with the emergence of the European Monetary System, another exchange rate regime, denominated "band system", gained strength. This system possesses the following logic: limits are defined for the exchange rate and, within these limits, the system functions like the floating exchange rate. Thus, a central rate is established along with a variation interval, for example, more or less x%. When pressure for devaluation of the national currency takes the system to the lower limit, the Central Bank intervenes by selling foreign currency and buying national currency. Conversely, when the market is pressured towards an exchange rate valuation, the Central Bank acts in the opposite direction. In many cases the Central Banks intervene in the markets before the limits are reached, avoiding possible speculative attacks. These are so-called intra-marginal interventions. The difficulties associated to this regime are: defining the central rate (difficulty similar to defining the exchange rate in a regime of fixed exchange rate) and defining the breadth of the margins.

The economic implications on the adoption of this or that exchange rate regime, particularly on the performance of the balance of payments and on the capacity of the economic authority to execute monetary and fiscal policies are well known in the literature. Nevertheless, from the recent exchange rate experiences in Latin America, it is possible to explore other important questions surrounding the exchange rate options in a context of macroeconomic instability, particularly with respect to chronic inflationary processes and intertemporal inconsistency in the external accounts. Thus emerges the concept of “exchange rate anchoring”. On the other hand, utilizing the exchange rate as a key variable in policies of macroeconomic adjustment depends on the capacity of the economic authority to maintain credibility for its intention to control this variable. Following we shall examine these points.

3. "Exchange rate anchoring" and credibility

After the end of the international monetary system in the early 70s - a system that prevailed post-World War II and was based on a regime of relatively fixed exchange rate -, there was vast instability in the international exchange rate markets and many oscillations in the exchange rate regimes. In general, many of the developed countries adopted floating exchange rate regimes, with less government intervention. As for developing countries, especially in Latin America, the exchange rate was utilized as an instrument of economic policy, with strong government influence in the exchange rate market. Oftentimes the exchange rate (or its devaluation) was utilized for the purpose of resolving balance of payments problems, promoting competitiveness gains in the economy and avoiding that the adjustments in external accounts occur in an overly recessive manner.

At the end of the 70s and especially throughout the 80s, the fixation of the exchange rate in several developing countries began to be part of a broader set of measures aimed at ending inflation. The transition from a situation of chronic inflation to price stability required, at least at first, some type of nominal anchor, that is, setting the value of one or more economic variables, with the objective of curbing the advance of the other nominal variables. This is because, in these processes, prices, salaries and exchange rate begin to rise in an autonomous fashion: prices rise because salaries rose; and salaries rise because prices rose; and so on. In this process, it is not enough to suppress the basic causes of inflation - generally monetary decontrols given the need to finance elevated fiscal deficits -, the so-called inflationary inertia must also be overcome.

In this set of measures, prices and salaries were the variables chosen as priority nominal anchors in innumerable economic plans adopted in several countries, such as the Astral Plan in Argentina and the Cruzado Plan adopted in Brazil in 1986. These plans, called heterodox because they utilized instruments other than monetary control, had as a basic presupposition the freezing of prices and salaries of the economy, in an attempt to end inflationary inertia. The failure of these plans ended the use of heterodox proposals for battling inflation, bringing about orthodox propositions such as market liberalization, struggle against fiscal deficits, and strict monetary control. However, in this context, the need for an anchor must not be discarded, leaving this role to the exchange rate in the new context of policies, because it brings advantages in the process of market liberalization and/or contributes to greater fiscal and monetary control.

A problem faced by the stabilization plans that utilized some type of anchoring in the exchange rate was the credibility of this measure. The problem of credibility of "exchange rate anchoring" takes two forms. On one hand, there is the traditional doubt in face of fixed exchange rate regimes, which is the capacity of the government to maintain the exchange rate in the short term given the behavior of the balance of payments and the reserves. On the other hand, there is a strong expectation on the part of agents that the government, despite announcing a policy of fixed exchange rate, won't keep its promise. Indeed, while the fixed exchange rate has advantages associated to inflationary control, the devaluation of the exchange rate involves competitiveness gains, at least in the short run. Despite the losses from the inflationary standpoint, the gains in exports and possibly in employment and income in the short term are the motives that would lead the government to break with the anchor. It is interesting to observe that these gains can be even greater (and the losses smaller) if the devaluation is done unexpectedly by the government. Thus, in addition to the relatively deep-rooted tradition of the government to make use of exchange rate policy in order to obtain competitiveness gains, there are strong incentives, perceived by the agents, for the government, in certain circumstances, to renege on the announced policy.[1]

This, at least in part, explains the difficulties of some stabilization plans with "exchange rate anchoring": their lack of credibility induces a non-cooperative behavior on the part of economic agents. Faced with this problem, there were some options for the different countries that chose "exchange rate anchoring" as a stabilizing strategy:

a) persistence in the policy, seeking to obtain this credibility by means of reputation and/or signaling, using correlated policies (such as elevation of interest rates) intensely; that is, the governments enter the war of expectations firmly, maintaining policies even when they are unnecessary, or increasing the use of some instruments beyond what is needed, in order to show the market its determination in the utilization of fixed exchange rate policies;
b) the construction of institutions that lower the capacity of the governments themselves to promote alterations in the exchange rate policy, not so much to convince the agents of the exchange rate stability, but rather to give them greater assurance as to the government's disposition in relation to the policy and the possibility of altering it. Within this context the main example is the institution of the *currency board.*

In general, these strategies have been considered in various experiences with "exchange rate anchoring" in Latin America.

[1] This point is discussed by Agenor, P.R & Montiel, P.J. **Development Macroeconomics**. Princeton: Princeton University Press, 1996.

4. The Regime of a Currency Board[2]

In Argentina, the willingness of the government to maintain the fixed exchange rate regime was reinforced by constitutional determination as to exchange rate parity. That is, it tried to maintain credibility by implementing a *currency board*. In Argentina, this was differentiated from simple "exchange rate anchoring" by the fact that it was implemented by constitutional determination, creating legal and political difficulties for the government in the case of its inclination to alter the regime, thus giving the anchor credibility. Therein the Argentinean case is symptomatic, since the "exchange rate anchor", together with the currency board, is law and it also includes the monetary policy, which is conditioned to the performance of the balance of payments. The issue of currency becomes a function of the volume of reserves of the economy. The national currency becomes backed by the international reserves of the country.

Ultimately, the objective of the currency board is to bring greater discipline to the monetary and fiscal policies in the economies that adopt them. In this regime, the exchange rate is pegged to an internationally accepted standard (generally the dollar), guaranteeing the convertibility between the currencies and the monetary issue linked to the stock of international reserves. In one model of the currency board, the monetary authority loses its discretionary power over the money supply and the government begins to experience strong spending restrictions, since it cannot issue currency to finance deficits. Another interesting aspect associated to the adoption of a credible "exchange rate anchor" is the potential reduction of the interest rates due to the lowering of the risk of exchange rate devaluation. These aspects, together with the determination of an important price of the economy (the exchange rate), end up stabilizing the prices of so-called tradable goods, thus bringing additional gains in the control of inflation. In other words, the causes of inflation and some of its autonomous components are eliminated at the same time. The greater the liberalization of the economy, or promotion thereof, the truer this is.

This exchange rate regime, however, presents some inconveniences. The first to be stressed is the diminution of the instruments of economic policy: monetary policy, which remains conditioned to the behavior of the country's external accounts and, mainly, exchange rate policy. Depending on the institutional structure of the currency board, it is possible to compromise the daily operations of liquidity control and the monetary authorities' capacity to intervene in the face of possible bank crises.

But the great difficulty of this type of regime resides in the assessment of the market, national and international, as to the capacity of the government to

---

[2] On the experiences of Currency Board see Baliño, T. & Enoch, C. "*Currency Board Arrangements: Issues and Experiences*" **IMF Occasional Paper** n. ° 151, August 1997.

guarantee the convertibility of the currency. For this it is necessary to possess foreign currency reserves and/or a reasonable entry flow of foreign currency. This flow, in turn, depends on the amount of trust that foreign investors place in the country. In a world of uncertainty and of great speculative movements, that flow is far from being stable. On the other hand, if the country begins to present successive deficits in the balance of current transactions, with no perspective of reversing that deficit in future (a scenario of intertemporal inconsistency), the market can assume that the parity chosen is not one of equilibrium, anticipating the exchange rate devaluation by means of a strong flight of exchange rate values.

This possibility is reinforced if we take into account two aspects. First, all the stabilization processes based on "exchange rate anchors" have heated up the economy immediately following the plan, which puts negative pressure on the trade balance. Add to this a tendency of real valuation of the exchange rate due to a residual inflation that is generally higher than international inflation, reinforcing the deterioration of the trade balance. In the short run, equilibrium is obtained by means of capital accounts. This normally has a very positive tendency due to the improvement of the risk conditions of the economy and to the maintenance of high interest, combined, normally, with financial liberalization. In the case of the 90s, this process is further reinforced by a favorable situation of liquidity in the international market of capitals.

The flow of capitals is, therefore, more than enough to resolve the problem of the trade balance. However, new problems arise. On one hand, the logic of the monetary policy would lead to a rise in the supply of currency in the country, which could compromise the goals of inflationary control. This possibility however tends not to occur because the authorities generally activate sterilization operations.[3]. These operations, in turn, can signify the deterioration of the government's fiscal conditions due to the elevation of the public debt. On the other hand, there is the temporal problem relative to the entry of external capital. These flows are, as we have seen, extremely volatile, and in the long run demand the generation of a greater capacity to attract resources in order to deal with the resulting services.

All these elements – deterioration of the trade balance, of the public accounts, and uncertainties in relation to the stability of the balance of capitals and future conditions to service the debt – recast the problem of risk and expectations in the scenario of "exchange rate anchoring". Hence, in order to maintain the credibility of the regime, economic policy begins to have clear

[3] Sterilization operations are the placement of public bonds on the market in an effort to remove some of the currency from circulation.

recessive contours[4], at the same time as it reinforces the need to make structural adjustments in this economy. These adjustments aim to obtain competitiveness gains and reinforce the possibility of generating future surpluses.[5]

5. The options to an "exchange rate anchor"

Obviously the likely recessive situation resulting from the adoption of a currency board regime is one of difficult policy sustenance. Therefore some alternatives need to be considered. The most evident is the abandonment of the anchor, devaluing the exchange rate and thus relieving the recessive pressures. The presupposition for this measure is solving the problem that justified the anchor in the first place: inflation. Thus, despite running the risk of a return to the inflationary process, it is assumed that the years of anchoring were enough to overcome that problem. This is a question that takes on a greater complexity when the country frequently adopts the anchor – the dollar – as unit of account. In this situation, which seems to be that of Argentina, the inflationary effects of devaluation should not be underestimated.

The passage to a floating exchange rate system, however, does not seem to be simple; and the risks of exchange rate crisis and flight of capital are not negligible. On the other hand, one must consider the patrimonial question. In the case of Argentina, an extremely high indebtedness in foreign currency is observed; that is, the liability of its economy is practically entirely dollarized. Exchange rate devaluation could signify a loss of great dimensions to the Argentinean economy, which would place at risk the entire private sector and the public sector as well. These losses could lead the country into a strong recessive phase.

Thus, the option for devaluation involves, besides the possibility of a return to the inflationary process and the risk of exchange rate decontrol, problems resulting from the patrimonial losses that must be imposed on a part of society. It is interesting to note that these losses must, somehow, be negotiated, since the devaluation involves legal changes that go through the Argentinean legislative branch. In a way devaluation was the Brazilian option. However, Brazil started out from another situation, since its strategy was a little different from Argentina's. Brazil initiated a stabilization policy – the Real Plan – with an asymmetric band system (with an upper limit only) and switched to a symmetric band system, albeit with controlled devaluations of this band.

Another option for the Argentinean case is complete dollarization of its economy, which is what Ecuador adopted. The advantage is the elimination of

[4] The main sign of this policy is the elevation of interest rates, which also sustains the flow of capitals.

[5] The major dilemma is to what point is it possible to obtain such gains without a significant volume of national investments, since these are constrained by the interest rate.

any exchange rate uncertainty, making possible a rapid convergence of the interest rate to close to international levels. This would further allow better financing conditions of a possible resumption of economic growth, in addition to continuing to guarantee the stabilization of the inflationary process. However some costs can also be observed. Let's examine the Brazilian case and the option of dollarization in closer detail.

5.1 From the system of asymmetrical bands to dirty floating

Brazil's stabilization strategy was different from Argentina's, despite their both utilizing "exchange rate anchors". Whereas Argentina, faced with the question of credibility previously raised, made use of the legalization of a currency board, Brazil embarked on a war of expectations, seeking gains in reputation and signaling a strong willingness to stick to the "exchange rate anchor". Its anchoring, however, was done on a band system, initially asymmetrical.

As to the issue of reputation, it is important to stress the persistence of the Brazilian government in not using the exchange rate to obtain competitiveness gains even in moments of greater political and economic pressure. This created a cooperative attitude on the part of agents, in the face of the government's firm determination to go forward with the anchoring. This point is reinforced with innumerable signals sent by the government to the market; and one of these signals was the formidable rise in interest rates, which, while on one hand served to compensate the risk of international investors and attract a greater flow of capitals to the country, on the other imposed not unsubstantial internal political costs.

The band system can be considered a "lighter" form of "exchange rate anchoring". In the Brazilian case, the fixation of the exchange rate below an established maximum ceiling was permitted by means of an asymmetric band. In a situation of heavy entry of exchange rate values, the exchange rate tends to value. This exchange rate valuation (possible in the Brazilian case, but not in the Argentinean) reinforces the positive impacts of the anchoring, which becomes an "exchange rate super-anchor", since its impact was to cheapen tradable products, an effect reinforced by the economic opening.

On the other hand, there was an elevation of imports and disincentive to exports, thus contributing to a deterioration of the trade balance. Successive deficits in the trade balance end up creating problems in the external accounts, elevating the dependence of the country in relation to the international flow of capitals, in addition to increasing the risk of loss of exchange rate control on the part of the economic authority. The major problem of this model consisted in the need to maintain high internal interest rates, which reduces investments and, consequently, compromises the growth of the country, in addition to raising the level of internal nonpayment. The situation is particularly grave when there is strong instability in the movement of international capitals. This instability demands ever-higher interest rates, which can cause the country to undergo a strong recessive process. In the Brazilian case, the difficulties faced on the occasion of the Mexican, Asian, and Russian crises are notorious. These crises led Brazil to raise internal interest rates to extremely high levels, thus generating a strong recessive scenario.

This scenario was partially assuaged with the establishment, as of the Mexican crisis, of a now symmetrical band system (with floor and ceiling)[6], which was utilized by the government to manage a light process of nominal devaluation of the exchange rate, without signifying, however, a break with the anchoring system.[7] Even with this slight controlled devaluation, the anchoring problems, notably the recession and the difficulties in the balance of payments, continued and led to a break with the "exchange rate anchor" policy.

At the beginning of 1999, Brazil saw a change from the exchange rate band regime (symmetrical with light devaluation since 1995) to a dirty floating system. The passage was not smooth, with an overshooting occurring in the exchange rate, but there were few inflationary consequences[8]. This passage, however, was not undertaken before a process of protection of the private sector with liability in dollars could occur in order to avoid great losses caused by devaluation for those sectors.[9] These two problems however do not seem to be so easily confronted by Argentina due to the greater utilization of the dollar as unit of account in that country, and due to the existence of a large volume of commitment of the liabilities of the Argentinean economy with the dollar.

Since then the exchange rate in Brazil has floated; but this oscillation suffers governmental influence. In theory these interventions aim mainly at the inflationary control that began to be exercised by means of a policy of *inflation targeting*.

---

[6] At first, the floor is more important since it avoids the continuity of the exchange rate valorization, however, the ceiling later becomes the important reference, when the market pressure is for devaluation.

[7] On various occasions the government's capacity (and willingness) to maintain that anchor was tested. It was maintained, with the justification that breaking with it could lead to a return of the inflationary process.

[8] Despite the fall of interest rates and the recuperation of the Balance of Payments occurring slowly.

[9] This protection was given by the public sector (operations in the futures market and the internal issue of public bonds with an exchange clause), with the government itself the most harmed by devaluation. See Gremaud, A and Toneto Jr, R "*Politica cambial, velhos problemas, velhos dilemas*" **Revista Praga** n.° 9, 2000.

5.2 The extreme case: dollarization

The most radical regime of "exchange rate anchoring" is dollarization, the latest example of which can be credited to Ecuador. After facing a severe exchange rate and bank crisis, in addition to a recession of 7% of the GDP and high inflationary rates (the highest of the continent at present), the country opted for a process of replacing the Sucre, the local currency, with the dollar. Though this process is still recent, the previously pinpointed problems can be expected to occur. The fact is that the exchange rate issue in Ecuador has reinforced the position that the so-called "exchange rate anchors" are the best form of overcoming the problems resulting from exchange rate instability and are an alternative for the difficulties that the "exchange rate anchors" also face, as is the case of Argentina.

In this regime the local currency is replaced by the dollar, where the monetary authority is totally conditioned to the performance of the international accounts of the country and to the volume of ingress of external currency. The objectives are the same as those of the currency board: greater monetary and fiscal discipline. The major difference is that maintenance of the exchange rate stability is no longer necessary, which is a positive factor from the standpoint of international investors, who would have no reason to fear unanticipated exchange rate devaluations. Thus, a fiscal discipline is imposed from the exterior that cannot be obtained by internal determination, while at the same time exchange rate instability disappears. The main issue associated to dollarization, however, is its almost total irreversibility, which causes its advantages and disadvantages to be more potent.[10]

A great advantage of the measure has to do with the lessening of the costs of international financing associated to the risk of exchange rate devaluation. Among the greatest disadvantages is the loss of financial gains from the issue of money (*seigniorage*) that would result from dollarization. For a country that possesses a pure currency board, where the monetary base is totally backed by the reserves, the loss is equal to the amount of gains from international financial investments of these reserves. In the Argentinean case, these gains rise to over U$ 700 million per year.[11]

Another problem of dollarization is the loss of sovereignty in monetary policy, which remains subordinate to the decisions made in the USA. This would involve, for example, the loss of capacity of the local government to succor the financial system in the case of major bank runs. If it is true that the practice of furnishing daily liquidity would not be totally lost with dollarization

---

[10] Berg, A. and Borensztein, E. "*The pros and cons of full dollarization*" **IMF Working Paper** WP/00/50, 2000.

[11] See Berg, ª and Borensztein E. Op. cit.

as long as adequate institutions were created and endowed with net resources in dollars, the role of a lender would ultimately be very difficult to play given the need for a high volume of net resources in the hand of the institution responsible. On the other hand, dollarization can provide a stronger financial sector that is less dependent on this type of succor. In this case however the tendency also involves a strong denationalization of the financial system of the country.

The great dilemma in this regime has to do with the cyclical evolution of the dollarized country in face of the USA and the impact that a crisis provokes in each of these economies. The more disparate the economies are the greater the problems are. As the economies do not behave with a single pattern and receive different impacts from an alteration in the international conjuncture, the steps taken in the USA, as to monetary policy, may be the opposite of that recommended for the dollarized country at that same conjuncture. However, that country no longer can avail itself of instruments to face that conjuncture and relies on policies over which it has no control and which are most likely unfavorable to it. The positive expectation, however, refers to the greater approximation with the American government. That approximation leads the dollarized country to take advantage of being under a healthy monetary regime, making it possible to increase confidence in the private sector and, consequently, in investments. The trend is also towards a convergence, especially, of the monetary variables, such as inflation. The end of monetary and exchange rate differences can also diminish the transaction costs involved in trade between the two countries, intensifying said trade.

Another problem related to dollarization refers to its impact on the structure of assets and indebtedness of the country in the passage from one regime to the other. When the differential between the internal and external interest rates is great, it is common for enterprises to seek loans in the international financial system. These loans are corrected by the external interest plus exchange rate variation. The problem is that in the moments prior to dollarization, corrective devaluations generally take place. These devaluations end up raising, in dollars, the value of the debt, making payments unfeasible and elevating the level of nonpayment of the country.

One last aspect in relation to dollarization, especially its adoption by Argentina, is the impacts on Mercosur. To be precise there are no great changes between dollarization and the present situation of a currency board in terms of Mercosur and its present stage[12]. The problem however is that dollarization is difficult to revert, so that the strengthening of Mercosur which will potentially require a monetary integration, could be compromised, unless this strengthening occurs at a broader regional level, involving all of America.

---

[12] See Berg and Borensztein (2000) Op. cit.

6. Conclusion: Would the "guarani" be a way out[13]?

The formation of a monetary union is, without doubt, an option to be considered for the Latin American countries, particularly those that make up Mercosur[14]. We can pinpoint at least three important benefits resulting from this option. First, if the union is effective, it can contribute to the reduction of the internal political pressures in the management of economic policies. This is because, given the degree of integration, there would be high costs in imposing policies not coordinated with the rest of the bloc. Second, if there is an agreement among the members, it is possible to draw up changes in the management of economic policy as a result of shocks that affect the blocs. Insomuch as it is likely that these shocks would be more symmetrical among the countries of Mercosur than between those countries and the USA, for example, therein lies an advantage for this strategy over dollarization. Finally, there would be no loss with *seigniorage* among the countries of the monetary union.

The doubt, however, is to know whether there is a possibility of effectively acquiring the credibility noted above, thus avoiding the problems that prevail in the present exchange rate strategies of the countries. This doubt is even stronger the more we observe that none of the Mercosur countries has a tradition of maintaining a healthy monetary policy. Furthermore, the differences of size and structure of the countries may cause their positions as to behavior of the exchange rate and monetary policy to differ over time. On the other hand, no country is large enough within Mercosur to absorb without major problems the possible impacts of measures unfavorable to that country, but favorable to the other members. These elements place in doubt the possibility of managing a coordinated policy.

Nevertheless, it is important to emphasize that monetary unification can be a possible way out of the exchange rate difficulties of countries like Brazil or Argentina, but not the only one and not necessarily the best one. Moreover, the present stage of economic integration still requires some degree of oscillation in the exchange rate among these countries, due to their differences in size and structures, despite being lower than the recent variations[15]. The exchange rate stability resulting from a monetary unification is only required if the intention is

[13] The " guarani" is the name suggested for the single currency in the arena of Mercosur

[14] See Eichengreen, B. "*Does Mercosul need a single currency?*" **NBER Working Paper** n.° 6821. Cambridge: NBER, December 1998.

[15] The argument that the devaluations, like Brazil's at the beginning of 1999, get in the way of the growth of intra-bloc trade is not untrue. However the main explanation for this is the intensification of the defense of protectionist interests. The income effects seem to be more important than the price effects if we take into consideration the aggregate behavior of the trade balance. Hence the current impasses of Mercosur reflect the fact that two main partners of the bloc are in recession simultaneously.

a strengthening of the economic integration among the countries that make up Mercosur; and this seems to be the greatest difficulty at present. At any rate, the effective intention of the countries to construct a monetary union is a necessary condition for the construction of credibility in the process; and that credibility can generate gains in the harmonization of macroeconomic policies, particularly in terms of exchange rate policies, and in the power of governments in the face of pressures from interest groups.

References

Agenor, P.R & Montiel, P.J. **Development Macroeconomics**. Princeton: Princeton University Press, 1996.

Baliño, T. & Enoch, C. "*Currency Board Arrangements: Issues and Experiences*" **IMF Occasional Paper** n. ° 151, August 1997.

Berg, A. and Borensztein, E. "*The pros and cons of full dollarization*" **IMF Working Paper** WP/00/50, 2000.

Eichengreen, B. "*Does Mercosul need a single currency?*" **NBER Working Paper** n.° 6821. Cambridge: NBER, December 1998.

Gremaud, A and Toneto Jr, R "*Política cambial, velhos problemas, velhos dilemas*" **Revista Praga** n.° 9, 2000.

IS GLOBALISATION SAPPING THE STAKEHOLDER MODEL? AN ASSESSMENT OF THE GERMAN CASE

Dante Mendes Aldrighi*

1. Introduction

Since the 1980s, the financial scene has been rapidly and hugely modified around the world. The relentless harsh competition among financial institutions – strictly associated with the broad and acute deregulation of their activities – has promoted the continuous integration of financial markets, both within and across national frontiers. Moreover, the increasingly ubiquitous recognition that the public pay-as-you-go pension system could not meet the rising liability resulting from the provision for ageing population has led many governments to strive for offloading this burden on to individuals and companies. Indeed, in a great number of countries, funded pension schemes have expanded at a fast pace, fostering, in turn, capital markets and non-bank financial intermediaries supplying this type of contractual savings. Simultaneously, individual and institutional investors have been increasingly aware of, as well as sensitive to, the returns from the broad range of alternative investment instruments – made available by the deregulation of financial markets together with the reduction in transaction costs resulting from the spread of information technology. Completing this picture, the preparation for and the actual launch of the European single monetary currency have been another leading force affecting financial markets and institutions – chiefly, but far from solely, those located in Europe.

Transformations have also been outstanding in the product markets. Competition has become increasingly ruthless as a result of deregulation, globalisation, and pressures on companies arisen from financial markets. This process triggered a surge of corporate restructuring world-wide, still in course, embracing cross-border as well as domestic mergers and acquisitions (hostile takeovers included), disposal of non-core businesses, and strategic alliances.

Some commentators have predicted that greater international integration in the product and financial markets is bound to force patterns of corporate governance to converge towards those prevailing in the United States – which rely essentially on legal and market mechanisms and aim primarily at maximising the shareholder value. This claim is grounded on the belief that the most efficient form of governance (as any other input or technology) will inevitably emerge

* Department of Economics, University of São Paulo. E-mail address: aldrighi@usp.br.

from severe global competition. At the heart of this reasoning, there lie two assumptions. One is the superior efficiency of the Anglo-Saxon system of corporate governance. The other is that the corporate governance pattern is ultimately determined by economic forces, which will ineluctably eradicate whatever historical and political "hurdle" opposes their course.[1] Accordingly, governance arrangements whereby corporate non-owner constituents have voice and power are condemned to be replaced by the "shareholder model".

This paper casts doubt on such account. Firstly, the decisive assumption underlying this argument cannot be taken for granted. There are circumstances, which now tend to grow in importance, where the so-called "stakeholder model" turns out to be efficient. Hence, there is room for challenging the view that the search for efficiency stemming from globalisation is increasingly and irreversibly undermining that model. Furthermore, reasons other than the quest for efficiency may contribute to shape the particular design of corporate governance prevailing in an economy. Moves to better arrangements may be thwarted due to non-economic forces (such as politics, laws, and social values). Path-dependence renders complex the evolution of patterns of corporate governance, inasmuch as the mechanisms regulating the distribution of authority and power among firms' constituents are strongly influenced by the underlying Political Economy.

The article is structured as follows. The first section probes the widespread view that the shareholder model is inherently superior to other methods of corporate governance. Beginning with the conceptual discussion of corporate governance, Section I attempts to demonstrate that, as regards efficiency, a more comprehensive concept, embracing also non-owner stakeholders, is needed. The corollary is that the "stakeholder model" is not necessarily inefficient even if profit maximising is the pursued goal. Section II turns to some factors that, irrespective of efficiency considerations, may render corporate governance path-dependent and sharply subject to Political Economy constraints. It is claimed that even in the event that globalisation pressurises some leading economies to adopt market-led governance patterns, politics may operate as a powerful countervailing force hampering this move, since deep-rooted interest groups will fight off endeavours to reform existent arrangements if changes deprive them of power. The ensuing section, focused on Germany, tries to collect some concrete evidence to underpin the theoretical logic put forward previously. Notwithstanding the mountainous changes occurring in the German corporate governance landscape, it is argued that political and structural barriers coupled with efficiency reasons hinder a big chunk of German companies from moving, at least before long, to Anglo-American governance patterns. The article ends summing up the findings of the former sections.

[1] For an in-depth review of this perspective, see Coffee (1999).

2. Corporate Governance and Efficiency

Much has been discussed about the effects on corporate governance engendered by ever increasingly competition brought about by globalisation. A frequent claim is that legal rules and practices shaping corporate governance in developed countries will ineluctably converge to the most efficient arrangement, supposed to be that pursuing the maximisation of the shareholder value.

To evaluate this proposition, it is convenient to begin with the analysis of the meaning of corporate governance, specifying the reasons for which it emerges and its possible goals. In a world wherein contracts are complete and enforceable and information is perfect,[2] corporate governance is needless. Every party involved with the functioning of the firm has her duties and rewards determined *ex ante*, and their *ex post* enforcement is fully ensured. The need for corporate governance springs from both the incompleteness of contracts and their costly and/or imperfect enforcement in the real world. Contingencies not dealt with contractually imply residual rights of control, whose allocation has strong influence on incentives and power among firms' constituencies. Neither their efforts nor the distribution of the firm's surplus among them can be determined contractually in a precise way.

It is noteworthy that there still remain some variations on the way corporate governance is defined. In their excellent survey, Shleifer and Vishny (1997, p. 737) put forward that "*corporate governance deals with the ways in which suppliers of finance to corporations assure themselves of getting a return on their investment. How do the suppliers of finance get managers to return some of the profits to them? How do they make sure that managers do not steal the capital they supply or invest it in bad projects? How do suppliers of finance control managers?*". Zingales (1998, p. 498), in turn, defines corporate governance as "*the complex set of constraints that shape the ex post bargaining over the quasi-rents generated by a firm*", whilst Bebchuk & Roe (1998, p. 4) understand the term as "*how authority is distributed among owners, the board of directors, senior managers, and employees*".

Focused on the scope for management's opportunistic behaviour at the expense of their principal – the outside investors – as well as on the need for protecting the latter, Shleifer's and Vishny's demarcation of corporate governance is more restricted. This definition somewhat reflects the prevailing arrangement of corporate governance in the United States, the usually dubbed *shareholder model*.[3]

---

[2] Incomplete contracts mean that it is impossible or at least too costly to determine in advance what should be done in all feasible contingencies in the uncertain future.

[3] As Roe (1998a, p. 345) notes: "*American work on comparative corporate governance has focused on the triangular relationships among the shareholders, the board of directors, and*

On the other hand, Zingales' together with Bebchuk's & Roe's definitions seem to be more comprehensive, inasmuch as they also attach importance to the existence and power of other non-owner stakeholders. This approach appears to be especially appropriate to the *stakeholder model*, supposed to characterise the predominant arrangement of corporate control in some continental European countries, notably Germany. The decision-making in that model takes into account other interests besides those of shareholders – such as the interests of employees, creditors, suppliers, customers, and the local community. Thus, firms' policies and strategies reflect "*a political compromise*", which is generally mediated by the board of directors.

The rationale lying behind the stakeholder model is that the quest for efficiency in a firm hinges at least partly on firm-specific investments made by non-owner constituencies.[4] It is likely they will invest in these assets on condition they are granted enough protection (by a contract or a practice) against "*early termination or opportunistic renegotiation of the terms of the production relationship*" – the so-called *hold-up problem* (Milgrom & Roberts, 1992, p. 31).[5] This form of post-contractual opportunism derives from the combination of imperfect contracting and the specificity of assets. So far as uncertainties over their share in the surplus are significant, outside investors and corporate non-owner stakeholders will have weak incentives to make sunk, firm-specific investments needed to enhance the value of the firm.[6]

In light of this, corporate governance should also concern the influence of the rules constraining the interactions of stakeholders who somehow contribute to increase the value of the firm on the ex post surplus division and, consequently, on their incentives to make efforts or irrevocable specific investments.[7] Therefore, arrangements of corporate governance should distribute the residual rights of control so that constituencies who enhance the value of the firm would be empowered to actively participate, or at least have their interests represented, in the *ex post* bargaining over the surplus they created. That could grant the incentives for every stakeholder to make the correspondent firm-specific

---

senior management. Other basic elements of commerce – suppliers, customers, and employers – have been viewed as outside the core institutions of governance".

[4] Specific investment is that investment that would lose value outside its specific use.

[5] According to these authors (p. 599 and 136), the hold-up problem emerges when "*one who makes a relationship-specific investment is vulnerable to a threat by other parties to terminate that relationship. This threat then permits these parties to obtain better terms than were initially agreed.*"

[6] See Blair (1995) and Zingales (1998). In contrast with the usual view that those undertaking firm-specific investments should be protected against managerial expropriation by means of "explicit property rights", Rajan and Zingales (1998a, 423-24) understand that "*insecurity may encourage rather than discourage specific investment by stakeholders*".

[7] These rules may be formal or informal, mandated by law or by firm-statutes.

investment, allowing the maximisation of the value of the firm and the productive efficiency. Neglecting non-owner stakeholders' interests would amount to sub-optimal level of firm-specific investments.

As the risks of a significant fraction of the investments needed to make firms work efficiently are not borne exclusively by shareholders, Blair & Stout (1999) argue that corporate governance should aim primarily at maximising "*the joint welfare of all the firm's stakeholders – including shareholders, managers, employees, and possibly other groups such as creditors or local community – who contribute firm-specific resources to corporate production*". Needless to say that achieving this objective is no easy task.[8] According to them, this is the reason for the existence of the board of directors. Its rationale lies in "*the team production problem*", which stems from the impossibility of devising contracts to distribute the output created by the different stakeholders' joint firm-specific investments. This problem is legally coped with by stakeholders jointly relinquishing, for their own benefits, "*control over those resources to a board of directors*", who should represent the team's interests and arbitrate the distribution of rewards among constituents. Notwithstanding higher agency costs, boards' intervention, ensured by corporate laws, in the bargaining over the surplus created by the stakeholders may succeed in providing incentives for specialised investments in the firm.

Besides fostering investments in firm-specific assets (especially in human capital), arrangements of corporate governance wherein shareholders' property rights have no overwhelming primacy over other stakeholders' interests may reduce costs of transaction, co-ordination, and dispute resolution, building on "*greater trust, loyalty and commitment among the various parties*" (OECD, 1996, p. 119, 148). Moreover, pressures to maximise profits over the short-term in such approach are expected to be less demanding, attenuating the bias for myopic strategies. In brief, shoring up long-term implicit contracts among stakeholders would facilitate co-ordination in addition to circumventing hurdles associated with incomplete contracts and difficult and costly enforcement of contracts.

[8] Blair (1995) argues that "ownership-like incentives" should be delivered to "*those who control critical, specialized inputs and to align the interests of these critical stakeholders with the interests of outside, passive shareholders*". For her, the ideal arrangement consists in an ownership structure wherein each stakeholder's share reflects the contribution of his/her accrued firm-specific investments. Employees, in particular, "*would be paid a fixed wage for the opportunity cost of their general human capital and then in equity for their specific skills*" (OECD, 1996, p. 148-9).

Evidently, this model is not devoid of drawbacks. Co-ordination of interests that hardly ever are immediately harmonious, and sometimes not at all,[9] requires complex, time-consuming negotiations. Past commitments and consensus-building impose severe constraints, implying that responses to external shocks (such as sudden changes in markets and technology) may be sluggish. The clumsy question of how far companies should be accountable to their different stakeholders, left by companies' multiple foci, makes the stakeholder approach inherently contentious, not least when companies' financial links together with their marketing and production strategies become increasingly global.

Although this model may appear to be unfit to cope with rapid changes in markets and technologies, it may enable firms, as indicated above, to deal efficiently with several types of market failures, reaping benefits largely exceeding its underlying costs. Mayer (1997) reckons that the stakeholder model is particularly good for activities whose technological and managerial best practices are more stable, allowing consequently their slower and smoother changes to be timely met by companies' stakeholders engaged in long-term implicit contracts.

But it is worth noting that the spread and increasing importance of young and innovative firms with high-growth potential characterising the "New Economy" seem to call for a type of governance whose characteristic features are rather similar to those identified with the stakeholder model. As Rajan & Zingales (1998b, p. 3) point out, "*recent changes in the nature of the organisations, the extent and requirements of markets, and the availability of financing have made specialised human capital much more important, and also much more mobile. But human capital is inalienable, and power over it has to be obtained through mechanisms other than ownership. As the importance of human capital has grown, power has moved away from the top and is much more widely dispersed through the firm*".[10] As a consequence of the changing corporate landscape, the concept of the firm should be revised and the goal of corporate governance no longer should be circumscribed to that advanced by the agency theory – that is, to prevent outside investors from being expropriated by managers or controlling shareholders. Firms primarily need to retain their employees, whose evasion may lead to the disintegration of the firm itself. This is so because: 1) of the outstanding importance of human capital as a source of value for firms and 2) human capital cannot be "appropriated" by a third party (since it is embodied in the employees). Rajan & Zingales (1998b, p. 19-20) claim that employees' firm-

---

[9] For example, the choice among projects involving different combinations of return/risk is likely to set apart debt-holders, who are primarily concerned with bankruptcy risks, and shareholders, willing to support high-expected-return/high-risk investments.

[10] Even for traditional enterprises, tangible assets are responsible for a minor fraction of their value (Blair & Roe, 1999).

specific specialisation may be an important means of cementing the company's integrity, since links of complementary dependence make both firm's and employee's rewards larger if they operate jointly rather than apart.[11]

3. Corporate Governance, Path Dependence, and Politics

On top of efficiency, other factors appear to obstruct the way to convergence. Management decisions are not taken in a void. The relative power of the different groups of stakeholders (such as management, employees, shareholders and creditors) is strongly embedded in deep-rooted social values as well as in the political environment, both of which cannot be promptly expunged. Changes in the rules of corporate governance imply redistribution of rights among stakeholders and, consequently, they will be pushed through so long as political constraints allow. Otherwise politics may overwhelm economic rationale.

Overall these inertial forces pervading corporate governance arrangements arise from path dependence. From this standpoint, Bebchuk & Roe (1998) provide a thorough theoretical analysis of corporate governance and ownership. They claim that path dependence may impede corporate law rules as well as corporate structures in the advanced economies from converging.[12] They try to show that rules across developed countries may remain different owing either to high transformation costs (since they affect which set of rules is efficient) or to the opposing political action of vested interest groups. Recognising the influence of corporate rules on corporate structures, they stress notwithstanding that even if rules converged (against their own conviction) differences in corporate structures may persist among advanced countries. The reason is that either the locally efficient structure often is path dependent (due to sunk adaptive costs and network externalities) or changes enhancing firm's efficiency may be barred by stakeholders benefiting from the extant structure.

As for how path dependence affects corporate rules, Bebchuk & Roe (1998, p. 2, 13-15) explain that "*a country's initial pattern of corporate structures will create interest groups and determine the power of groups to influence which corporate law rules persist and which ones change. If a pattern of ownership creates a group with positional advantage inside the firm, that group will often have the motivation and the means to preserve rules that favour itself. Consequently, the rules that a country will have down the road will depend on the type of corporate structures and corporate rules that it began*

[11] It sounds rather ironic that the apparently demise of the stakeholder model has coincided with the stark decline in the relative importance of physical and financial capital vis-à-vis human capital.

[12] For them, corporate structure is basically associated with the degree of corporate ownership concentration and the firm's distribution of authority.

with". By the same token, globalisation can coexist with rules supporting inefficient corporate governance, since the same interest group which managed to pass these corporate rules may use again its political sway to obtain subsidies from the state. In the case of convergence of rules, corporate stakeholders "*with positional advantages will often refuse to initiate the transactions* (needed to move to more efficient structures), *or block them if someone else initiates them. Thus rules could converge without structures converging*".

In order to assess the adherence of Bebchuk's and Roe's thesis to reality, it is worthwhile to regard how corporate governance has lately evolved in Germany, endeavouring to highlight the influence of politics and path dependence on it.

4. Recent Evolution in the German framework of corporate governance

Several peculiarities shape the German arrangement of corporate control, a great portion of which derived essentially from regulation. The most important are: the Supervisory Board; the highly concentrated structure of corporate ownership – mostly held by controlling investors; the proxy voting rights exerted primarily by banks; and the web of cross-shareholdings amongst the largest companies, wherein the four big banks and a couple of insurers stand at critical positions. The combination of these characteristics is the backbone of the stakeholder approach on which the German system of corporate governance rests.

4.1 The Supervisory Board

Limited companies are obligated to set up a supervisory board (SB) as an internal mechanism of governance. Its chief mandatory duty resides both in appointing the members of the management boards (MBs) and in controlling their decisions. The Co-determination Act (*Mitbestimmungsgesetz*), enacted in 1951, established that every joint-stock corporation,[13] regardless of the number of its employees, had one-third of its SB members elected by employees. In 1976, this law was redefined, matching the number of shareholder and employee representatives for public limited companies (*Aktiengesellschaft*, AGs) gathering more than 2,000 employees. The chairmanship of the SB is, however, a prerogative of the shareholder representatives. The importance of this post derives from the chairman's entitlement to cast the tie-breaking vote in the case of stalemates in the SB's decision making. By law, SB's members must be accountable to the interests of the firm as a whole – rather than just to the

[13] There are two types of limited liability companies in Germany: public company (*Aktiengesellschaft*, AG, literally "joint-stock corporation") and private limited company (*Gesellschaft mit beschränkter Haftung*, GmbH, literally "limited liability company").

interests of the groups they represent. The Act also sets the SB size, which varies from twelve to twenty members, according to the company's number of employees.

4.2 Regulation and Large Voting Block-Holders

In comparison with their U.S. counterparts, German financial institutions are subject to a less stringent regulation concerning ownership and control of non-financial enterprises. Commercial banks encounter no major hindrance to hold equity stakes in other enterprises, except for "some generous prudential rules".[14] Moreover, non-financial enterprises are not legally curbed from owning equity stakes in each other nor antitrust legislation used to be severe – now an issue under the EU's control. As a general rule, every shareholder whose control on a listed company crosses 5%, 10%, 25%, 50% or 75% of its votes should notify the financial authorities (the threshold was 25% until 1994). Legal rules preventing insider trading were adopted only in July 1994 (being effective from 1995), mainly as a result of the imposition of bringing German securities trading supervision rules in line with the European standards.

Bearing in mind this tolerant legal background, small wonder that, in sharp contrast to the United States, the ownership and voting structure of German large non-financial corporations is distinguished by: (i) the high concentration and great incidence of majority-owned listed enterprises; (ii) a deep bank involvement, both through equity stake or via proxy voting rights; (iii) and a widespread web of cross-shareholdings.

(i) Concentrated shareholdings, types of shareholders, and controlling blocks

Large German listed enterprises typically show a relatively high degree of ownership concentration, often implying that the separation of control from ownership is not widely disseminated. Families and non-financial enterprises account for the lion's share of the large ultimate shareholders. Privatisation has contracted the fraction of shareholdings the German government owns whereas foreigners have considerably built up theirs since the end of the eighties (DB, April 1998, p. 57). Even though the slice of the total equity shares of listed companies held by institutional investors in Germany has augmented at a fast pace in the last few years, it still lies far behind that held by their American and British counterparts (DB, January 1997).

---

[14] As a proportion of their own capital, they are allowed to hold shares of any unrelated company up to 15%. But their total shareholdings in other companies cannot exceed 60% (Prowse, 1994; OECD, 1995; OECD, 1996).

It is remarkably high the frequency of German listed enterprises with at least one single shareholder holding a controlling equity stake. More than 80% of the total number of German listed companies have at least one shareholder owning a stake of at least 25% of the company's total capital.[15] Most of listed companies are controlled by only one single shareholder, albeit for the relatively small number of listed companies lacking a majority-control multiple blocks are frequent.

(ii) Banks' governance role

However high from an international viewpoint, banks' stake in non-bank equity is not overwhelming – around 10%. Notwithstanding, banks' own shareholdings clearly understate the actual power they are enabled to exert over management. That is so because, along with the significant leverage over firms coming from their role as lenders, banks are entitled to exercise by proxy the voting rights belonging to shareholders for whom they provide services of both safe administration and custody of shares. Voting proxy rights coupled with their own equity voting rights confer on banks a significant proportion of the total votes at shareholders' meetings, paving the way to ensure their representation on the company's SB. Nonetheless, as a condition to exercise voting rights by proxy at shareholders' meetings, banks are legally compelled, since 1965, to inform depositors their intention of vote as well as to request instructions from depositors about how they should vote on each item of the agenda to be dealt with at every meeting.

It has been argued (Allen & Gale, 1995; Löhnert, 1995) that German banks perform a crucial role in the governance of large companies. Managing to obtain a seat on the SB by means of their control of proxy voting rights,[16] banks would be empowered to appoint, monitor and dismiss the management of a public company, acting as "delegated exercisers of equity's control rights". However, this thesis has been lately contested. Edwards & Fischer (1994), for example, state that "*the argument that German banks perform a corporate control function is, therefore, one which lacks both a solid theoretical foundation and convincing empirical support*".

However disputable the monitoring role of banks, their sway over companies, thanks mainly to the control of proxy votes, is above doubt. In this respect, it is noteworthy the very high proportion of the attending votes at the

[15] See Becht & Böhmer (1998); Jenkinson & Mayer (1992); and Jenkinson & Ljungqvist (1999).

[16] At the end of 1992, banks had control over nearly 84% of all voting rights on the annual meetings of the 24 largest German firms without a single majority owner – 13% from own shares, 10% from associated investment funds, and 61% from proxy votes (OECD, 1995).

shareholders' general meetings of the German DAX companies cast by banks – in particular, by the "big 3" banks (see Becht & Böhmer, 1998).

(iii) Companies' equity stakes and cross-shareholdings

German large corporations, notably banks and insurance companies, usually have a significant portfolio of equity stakes in other companies. In 1995, Deutsche Bank, Allianz Holding, HypoVereinsbank, Dresdner Bank, and Commerzbank owned direct stakes in, respectively, 23, 19, 15, 11, and 8 AGs. Direct stakes, however, by and large underestimate voting power inasmuch as this may be leveraged through some legal devices, the most important of which are banks' proxy voting rights (Becht & Böhmer, 1997).

In addition, some large corporations have long engaged in an extensive and intricate web of cross-shareholdings and/or cross-voting-power. At the hub of the web lie Allianz, Munich Re, Deutsche Bank, Dresdner Bank, and Bayerische Vereinsbank. Allianz Holding is the largest ultimate voting blockholder in Deutsche Bank (5%), Dresdner Bank (22%), Munich Re (25%), HypoVereinsbank (17%), BASF (12%), Bayer (5%), and Veba (11%) whereas the largest voting blockholders in Allianz are Munich Re (26%), Bayerische Vereinsbank (15% plus 1500 votes), Deutsche Bank (10% plus 1500 votes), and Dresdner Bank (10%). Munich Re's voting rights, in turn, are in the hands of Allianz (25%), Bayerische Vereinsbank (9.9%), Deutsche Bank (9.9), and Dresdner Bank (9.9%). Allianz AG and Munich Re, besides their 25% mutual cross-shareholdings and outstanding importance among German listed companies' blockholders, also concentrate voting power owing to their shareholdings in the big banks and in regional banks.[17] For example, the Bayerische Hypotheken-und Vereinsbank's largest voting block-holders are Viag (10.83%), Allianz (9.2%), and Munich Re (5.4%). Controlling jointly a majority of voting rights in each other, German large banks and insurance companies manage to evade outside control.

The combination involving mandatory employee representation on SBs and cross-shareholdings is decisive to understand the predominance of the stakeholder approach of corporate control in Germany.[18] Edwards & Fischer

---

[17] Merrill Lynch estimated that "*Allianz's combined shareholdings in DAX 30 companies was worth a total 128 billion euro last month. Together with fellow Bavarian insurer Munich Re, it is said to control nearly a quarter of the index*" (Financial Times, March 7th 2000).

[18] According to Schneider-Lanné (1992, p. 11), in addition to enforcing the efficient use of the company's assets, "*corporate control also has to ensure that the interests of the other stakeholders, such as the company's employees, clients, buyers, suppliers, and the community at large are looked after*". She adds (p. 15-16) that "*the objectives of German companies, however, do not stop at maximisation of the return on investment. Their philosophy is based on 'the concept of the interest of the company as a whole', a key concept of German*

(1994) and OECD (1995) highlight the benefits stemming from cross-shareholdings among companies and representation on each other's SBs, notably the contribution to efficiency improvement due to economies on transaction costs. These studies argue that shoring up long-term implicit contracts among companies would facilitate co-ordination and circumvent hurdles associated with incomplete contracts and difficult and costly enforcement of contracts.[19]

4.3 Some Alleged Deficiencies of the German Corporate Governance System

Over the last decade, the German model has been blamed for several faults. Main criticisms have revolved around four major issues: 1) the ineffectiveness of SBs in monitoring management; 2) the poor legal protection of investors; 3) companies' unsatisfactory disclosure requirements; 4) and the absence of a market for corporate control, resulting in the neglect of efficiency concerns and shareholders' interests. These claims are briefly reviewed below.

(i) The SBs' poor monitoring role

Some analysts have claimed that SBs are ineffective in monitoring MBs.[20] They argue that SBs are too big; the frequency of their meetings is low; the information flow, fed by MBs, is scanty, biased, and untimely delivered (for example, important documents are available to SB's members just at the meetings); and their members face varied forms of conflicts of interests (members sitting on too many boardrooms). The result, so the argument goes, is feeble control on MBs. Even though much of those issues are still an open question, a fraction of them has been addressed by recent legal changes.

However, if a number of deficiencies actually prevents SBs from performing their fiduciary duty, why have not they been removed yet? For Roe (1998b), improvements in SBs' performance (attainable by, for instance, better release of information, fewer members, and more frequent meetings) are hindered by controlling shareholders who deliberately weaken SBs because they prefer to

---

corporate culture... The creation and maintenance of jobs with attractive working conditions has special priority. There is also a growing sense of responsibility towards the environment. In Germany the enterprise is considered to be embedded in society, and since it profits from society it also has obligations towards it. This commitment is rooted in the German constitution which says that ownership entails obligations".

[19] As for the effects on competition occasioned by these arrangements, Kester (1992) reckons they are immaterial since inter-firm relationships usually take the form of vertical linkages, horizontal competition tending to be preserved.

[20] Roe (1998b) and Coffee (1999) question the efficacy of SBs while Schneider-Lenné (1992) asserts that "*experience has shown that the SB is certainly an effective body of control*".

leave labour ill-informed. He argues that the predominance of block-holdings in the ownership structure of German listed companies stems essentially from the mandated co-determined structure. A widely-held ownership structure would either imply unbound MBs or weak equity representation vis-à-vis labour in the boardroom – both alternatives translating into lower firm value.[21] The concentrated ownership, in turn, debilitates SBs because monitoring can be performed through informal meetings between blockholders' representatives and managers. He advocates that therein lies the crux of German corporate governance, not in SBs' formal meetings. This "public choice hypothesis" could also help to understand why securities and corporate laws (and their enforcement) are so deficient in Germany.

(ii) "Strong block-owners, weak minorities":[22] the legal scope for expropriating minority shareholders

Although the existence of block-shareholders coupled with interwoven shareholdings may provide better monitoring and economies on transactions costs, it also gives management and controlling shareholders vast latitude to expropriate minority shareholders. In the first place minority shareholders in Germany lack satisfactory legal protections. Rules are poor, unclear and, of uncertain and costly enforcement.[23] In the event of transfers of large block-holdings, there is virtually no mandatory public bid requirement. Minorities are seldom offered a buy-out and when such offers are made, prices are set at a significant discount to the price paid to the block-shareholder. If left with too little residual amounts of shares, minority shareholders will encounter liquidity loss while controlling shareholders will enjoy greater discretionary power.

The fertile legal ground for leveraging voting power vis-à-vis share ownership in Germany is an outstanding facet of the comparatively loose legal environment regarding protection for minority investors. Although the concentration of voting power via the detachment of voting rights from ownership may be a legitimate mechanism for creating incentives to monitor without

[21] He argues that "capital" would have incentives to prevent labour representatives from accessing firm's information flow because better information might lead either to conflict increase or internal rent-seeking favouring labour, both of which leading to a reduction in the firm value.

[22] Whereas the gist of corporate governance problem in the United States is greatly grasped by the slogan "*Strong managers, weak owners*", the main agency-problem in continental Europe seems to concentrate on the minorities' exploitation by controlling investors (Jenkinson & Ljungqvist, 1999; Becht & Röell, 1999).

[23] Courts have shown little consistency in ruling litigation, with a bias in favour of controlling shareholder.

harming liquidity,[24] large voting blockholders are granted, however, the incentives and power to reap private benefits at the expense of minorities – especially through circumventing the one-share-one-vote principle.

Among the legally-underpinned devices available in Germany for manipulating voting power, the following are noteworthy.[25] First, the Stock Corporation Act permits the issue of non-voting shares (preferred shares) up to the outstanding volume of ordinary shares. Nonetheless, if the firm issuing this class of share fails to pay the preferred dividend in two subsequent years, the German corporate law determines that preference shares must be converted in ordinary shares. Second, some companies (such as Allianz AG and Munich Re) have issued "registered shares", whose transfers require consent from the MB. Third, until recently, AGs could have in their articles of association provisions stipulating an upper limit to the voting power some single shareholders were enabled to exert, irrespective of the amount of equity s/he held. Conceived mostly as a way to bar unsolicited takeovers, voting caps could be notwithstanding easily evaded – for example, by depositing shares with friendly parties (Becht & Böhmer, 1997, p. 53).[26] Fourth, multiple voting rights, however unusual, were issued by Siemens and a few formerly state-owned enterprises.[27] Fifth, proxy voting rights are the easiest, and thus the mostly used, expedient to consolidate voting power. Last but not least, block-shareholders may engage in cross-shareholdings, voting pacts, pooling contracts and pyramids to expand their voting powers beyond cash-flow rights in a way that is harmful to minority investors.

(iii) The low corporate transparency

German standards concerning companies' disclosure requirements have long been criticised. With respect to the accounting standards in Germany, they are generally blamed for requiring too little information to be released and for

[24] The reason is that, other things being equal, the higher the ownership concentration, the lower the share liquidity (Becht, 1999).

[25] For a thorough empirical analysis of these devices, see Becht & Böhmer (1997).

[26] According to The Economist, voting caps were instituted in the seventies as a means to prevent German companies from the influence of investors enriched by oil revenues, who had bought large chunks of their shares. Nonetheless, a glance at the main German listed companies wherein the Kuwaiti Government has a significant stake (such as Hoechst, Daimler Benz, and Metallgesellschaft) reveals that they did not resort to that device.

[27] Since the *Law on Control and Transparency in the Corporate Sector* (KonTraG, to be discussed in detail below) took effect in May 1998, voting caps and multiple voting rights are forbidden. Voting caps previously existing have to be phased out by May 2000, whereas enterprises that had issued shares with multiple voting rights have to extinguish them by May 2003.

relying more on a realisation principle in the treatment of companies' assets rather than on an accrual principle, as the British accounting rules do. This means that, instead of periodic revaluation of fixed assets, these are recorded at historical prices (less depreciation). Though this legal procedure may be warranted for prudential purposes, since it allows the smoothing of profits over time, the consequent build-up of "hidden reserves" leaves vast leeway for management allocating profits (OECD, 1995). This additional discretionary power in the hands of managers is seen as a serious fault by foreign investors.[28] Opaqueness also prevails regarding companies' liability to employees owing to pension commitments. Firms are not obliged to make provisions for that purpose, which may lead them to be under-funded with respect to future pension obligations.

Notwithstanding improvements brought about by the transposition of the EU Transparency Directive, there remains by and large the traditional view of treating ownership and control issues *as "private, sensitive and not for the eyes of the general public*" (Becht and Böhmer, 1997).

(iv) The rarity of hostile tender offers

Needless to say that a number of requisites should be met so that hostile bids may effectively function as a governance tool: a big chunk of listed companies' voting shares must be available for trading at the stock exchange; potential bidders should have access to company's in-depth and updated information; and laws regarding takeovers along with the infrastructure to enforce them should not give rise to uncertainties about both the extension and observance of the rights of all parties concerned. In the light of all these requirements, it is hardly surprising that unsolicited tender offers are so rare in Germany.[29]

First, and the most important, the concentrated ownership structure makes unlikely the operation of the market for corporate control in Germany. According to the Stock Corporation Act, the SB is entitled to replace the management team

---

[28] Having been just listed on NYSE, Daimler-Benz exhibited, according to German accounting rules, a DM168 million profit for the period over the first half of 1993, whereas, following the GAAP, it yielded a loss of DM949 million (OECD, 1995).

[29] Franks & Mayer (1998) thoroughly analyse the circumstances surrounding the only three cases of hostile tender offers launched in Germany from the end of the Second World War to 1996. Two other hostile bids were attempted thereafter. The first, in 1997, involved Krupp AG (an engineering and steel group) as the raider and Thyssen AG as the target. The attempt failed mainly due to pressure from trade unions and politicians, who managed afterwards to transform it into a friendly merger (Bowley, November 20th 1998). This bid "*was possibly Germany's first ever truly Anglo-US tender offer, being open to all shareholders and offering a 25.5% premium*" (Jenkinson & Ljungqvist, 1999). The second will be discussed ahead.

before the end of the term for which they were originally appointed so long as an "important reason" justifies this measure and, in addition, the request is approved by simple majority of its members. If all employee representatives support the incumbent MB, a raider may reach a simple majority of the SB's total votes providing s/he manages to win over all shareholder representatives, once the SB's chairman, a shareholder representative, has a double vote when deadlocks occur. If any of the incumbent shareholder representatives on SB does not uphold the proposal for dismissing the MB (indeed, the event more probable), the bidder will not be able to carry it out unless s/he replaces part of the SB before the expiration of their appointed term, for which it is necessary a three-quarter majority at a shareholders' meeting. Given the ownership structure prevailing in German listed companies – 82% of which have at least one controlling shareholder whose stake in the company's voting capital exceeds 25% – the condition for a hostile bidder to gain control over the SB is hardly satisfied. This occurs because the shareholder who owns a stake of at least 25% in a listed company is entitled to "*block various decisions at the shareholders' general meeting, and is likely in most cases to give the holder the effective control of the votes at this meeting*" (Edwards & Fischer, 1994). In particular, shareholdings above 25% entitle their owners to block statute changes. This prerogative renders her or his stake worth more than its market price, weakening therefore the incentive to hostile takeover bids.

Second, as public disclosure requirements have usually been flimsy in Germany, those within, or closely linked by long-term business relationship with, the company may appear to have a massive informational advantage over outsiders, reducing incentives to hostile bids. The predominantly insider composition of the board (their members are mostly stakeholders potentially better informed about the company) is likely to make it easier to tackle management inefficiencies by internal channels, since SB members have, at least formally, the duty and the means to monitor executives.

Third, controlling shareholders and managers may avail themselves of the wide range of legally-underpinned devices (such as non-voting shares, restrictions on share transferability, and proxy voting rights) to obstruct hostile takeover bids, though these devices on their own are not enough to impede the deal. Another stumbling-block to hostile takeover bids in Germany are the big stakes in large companies held by states, or by the banks they own (*Landesbanken*). State stakes can, and often do, block hostile or friendly takeover bids that are likely to shed jobs.

Regarding banks' behaviour towards hostile takeovers, the widely accepted view that relationship banking protects companies lacks full support. There are several occurrences wherein "house-banks" upheld predators. As Jenkinson & Ljungqvist (1999) assert, proxy voting rights place banks in a privileged position, enabling them to know about stake-building and, thus, choose the best strategy to undertake – if to be neutral, to defend the target company, or to support the raider.

The difficulties in carrying out a hostile takeover in Germany is paradoxically well illustrated by the recent, successful Vodafone AirTouch's hostile bid for Mannesmann, the biggest ever in history (roughly US$190 billion).[30] Making up the tiny group of large companies with a dispersed-held ownership structure[31] and with more than two-thirds of their voting equity capital held by foreigners, Mannesmann clearly cannot be taken as representative of the majority of German enterprises. Furthermore, resistance against the deal was not so strong because the takeover embraced only Mannesmann's mobile-phone division, wherein unions lack control – not the engineering operations where labour has a great deal of influence (The Economist, February 12th 2000).[32] Though the success of this unsolicited bid is indisputably a breakthrough in the German corporate setting – it emerges indeed as "*Germany's first properly contested takeover*" – it should not be seen, for all the idiosyncrasies surrounding it, as foreshadowing a smooth, fast and inevitable transition to an active market for corporate control.

Summarising this section, it seems that legal investor protection and companies' transparency have been indeed the Achilles' heel of the German system of corporate control. As regards SBs' ability to exert their mandatory duty along with the harmful consequences coming from the fact that hostile takeovers are scarce in Germany, they appear to be controversial claims.

4.4 Recent Changes in German Corporate Governance

Changing economic and financial conditions have induced significant reactions in Germany. The most prominent among them are: the emergence of the Neuer Markt and its startling performance – which must be partly ascribed to fresh governance rules; shifts in companies' strategy; and actions taken by politicians and governmental authorities to face these challenges. The refurbishment of the legal and institutional infrastructure underpinning securities markets and investor rights clearly reveals the Germans' awareness of global institutional competition for attracting companies and investors. Below, each of these responses is commented.

---

[30] Without enough support from shareholders, the Mannesmann's board accepted the bid and the call, imposed by the bidder, for its CEO to resign.

[31] Out of 32 companies composing the DAX index, Mannesmann along with Commerzbank are the only which have "no known blockholders" (Becht & Böhmer, 1998; Edwards & Fischer, 1994). Curiously, Mannesmann' statute establishes a 5% voting cap to any single shareholder.

[32] Being a conglomerate based chiefly on engineering and automotive divisions until 1990, Mannesmann has shifted its core since then to the mobile phone business.

(i) The Neuer Markt and the rise of new governance standards

An important reason accounting for the Neuer Markt's astonishing success so far resides unequivocally in its compliance with what are generally accepted as good corporate governance rules. Investor protection has been the mainspring of its efforts. Its endeavour to eschew the faults believed to plague German stock markets for large, traditional companies has been decisive to its success in attracting venture capitalists, innovative entrepreneurs, as well as individual and institutional investors.

To begin with, the Neuer Markt, however operating as a regulated market (as a new trading segment of the Deutsche Börse Group), is constituted as an entity subject to "private law". Thus, listing requirements are set up by the Deutsche Börse, its "market organiser", which is freer to set rules and procedures "in line with international standards", that is to say, meeting international investors' demands (notably the protection of minority rights) (DBG, 1999).[33] In this regard, Neuer Markt's purported distinctive features may be assembled into three groups: 1) high standards of transparency imposed on firms; 2) mechanisms to foster liquidity; 3) investor protection, especially to avoid unfavourable treatment of small shareholders.

With respect to transparency, firms are required to disclose updated, detailed and comprehensive information about their plans and financial condition. Disclosure rules required in the Neuer Markt are tighter than those binding in the first segment trading. When applying for going public in the Neuer Markt, companies have to submit to the Deutsche Börse an "accurate and complete" issuing prospectus, both in a German and English version, containing "*all factual and legal matters which are necessary for the evaluation of the shares offered*". This is the key requisite for the admission process.[34] The prospectus must include all the relevant financial accounts for the last three years and observe either the International Accounting Standards (IAS) or the American Generally Accepted Accounting Principles (GAAP). Once listed, companies have to publish quarterly and annual reports conforming to the IAS or the US-GAAP and in German and English versions. In addition, they have to inform the issuer's overall shareholdings in the hands of SB's and MB's members.

The rationale of these informational requirements is straightforward: since young, innovative firms are a risky investment, finance will be available on the condition that providers of funds have easy and low-cost access to reliable

[33] The other segments of the German capital markets operate under public law, which makes it difficult to adjust their rules to the rapidly changing financial and corporate environment.

[34] Its overarching contents cover topics from prospectus responsibility to the requirements of in-depth information about issuer's shares, capital, business, financial accounts, MB and SB, and risk factors. On Neuer Markt's prospectus contents, see DBG (1999, § 4.1).

information, which enables them to assess the risk they will face. The adoption of international standards of accounting and the requirement of an English version for the prospectus and for the annual and quarterly reports aim evidently at widening the base of investors, wary of German accounting rules. Entrepreneurs, on the other hand, are willing to exchange transparency for the availability of equity financing and lower risk premium, besides the benefits of risk-sharing and diversification (DBG, 1999).

As regards provision of liquidity, the Deutsche Börse sets two requirements for the admission to the Neuer Markt. One is that companies must guarantee a free float of at least 25%. The other condition is that firms nominate two "designated sponsors" for trading their shares on the Neuer Markt. The sponsors' essential function is to boost liquidity in specific shares by announcing "*either voluntary or on request ... binding bid and offer limits for the equities sponsored*". In other words, they commit themselves to buy at a bid price and sell at an offered price. The greater volume of trading resulting from the intervention of this idiosyncratic financial intermediary helps reducing the risk and cost of liquidity as well as the bid-offer margins.

Last, discrimination against small shareholder is curbed in three ways. First, with a view to matching voting power and cash flow rights, exclusively ordinary shares are admitted to the Neuer Markt (unless statutory provisions force the issuer to issue only shares whose acquisition requires approval). Second, companies should agree to observe the Takeover Code. Third, the existing shareholders (the founding owners and venture capitalists) are obligated to relinquish offers and sale of shares, directly or indirectly, within a period of six months from the date of admission to the Neuer Markt.

(ii) Changes in corporate strategy

Greater international integration of capital markets along with harsh competition in the product-market have incontestably spurred a profound overhaul in companies' strategies. The struggle for funds in the international arena has forced German enterprises and financial institutions to comply with a broad range of expectations and requirements (as a rule carved out conforming with the Anglo-American mould) posed by international providers of capital.[35] This demand has been even tougher for those enterprises planning cross-border mergers and acquisitions, inasmuch as gearing to the American way of doing

[35] In the words of the Ministerial Counsellor of the Federal Ministry of Justice (FMJ, 1998), "*national capital markets are no longer isolated. Our quoted companies raise finance internationally. German stock corporations are in direct competition with other demands for venture capital worldwide. The shareholder structure is becoming more international. The influence of foreign institutional investors and their expectations are growing*".

business will make it easier and cheaper to fund these international deals by means of share swaps.[36] Given the prevalent complaints raised against German putative obfuscated accounting practices and the importance international investors have granted to maximise the so-called "shareholder value", it is expected that companies intending to raise money or make forays abroad align their accounting and managerial patterns to those adopted in the United States.

Globalisation has prompted individual and institutional investors to be increasingly conscious of, as well as highly reactive to, the returns of every investment instruments. This has compelled German enterprises to improve their profitability,[37] reason for which they have restructured their mechanisms of control. Changes in investors' behaviour have also dented the long inertia favouring banks on raising cheap funds from traditional forms of savings – what enabled them to supply low-cost external finance to companies. Sharp competition for funds and businesses has obliged German large banks to be more permeable to the *modus operandi* of global financial markets. Instead of the traditional drift to diversification embracing a broad range of businesses, often relied on cross-subsidisation, German large banks have currently been echoing mantras of shareholder-value maximisation (especially of focus on core activities) in unison with international institutional investors, investment banks, and media specialised in finance.[38] Benefits associated with the potential for enhancing business relationships and with the financial stability this type of diversification may provide may be a disincentive to big banks sell out their long-standing holdings in other companies. Indeed, there is still little hard evidence as yet that they are effectively engaged in disposing of their shareholdings in non-financial

[36] The merger of Daimler-Benz with Chrysler (now Daimler-Chrysler), "*in what was essentially a stock for stock exchange*", was preceded by the listing of the German company on the New York Stock Exchange in 1993 (Coffee, 1999, p. 76). So did Veba in October 1997 with a view to easing U.S. acquisitions. About this, Veba's chairman said "*it was a step into the Anglo-Saxon culture that we consciously wanted to make*" (*Financial Times*, May 11th 1999).

[37] As said by the Ministerial Counsellor of the Federal Ministry of Justice (FMJ, 1998), "*The inflexible structure of shareholdings in Germany is gradually falling away. At the same time, a better stock market culture is developing. It is being fed by the demand side: investment behaviour is changing. A generation of heirs is investing in shares. The return on German share investment is becoming more attractive*".

[38] Deutsche Bank, for example, announced in December 1998 that it was set to spin off its US$24bn industrial stakes into a separate holding, entirely under its control, which would manage these investments as a portfolio whose value should be maximised. It is estimated that the total value of shareholdings German companies hold in other companies "*certainly runs to more than US$106 billion*", of which Allianz owns 40%, 20% are in the hands of Deutsche Bank, 14% with Dresdner Bank, 11% with Hipo Vereinsbank, and 2% with Commerzbank. Munich Re is another large holder of minority stakes in industrial companies. See The Economist (January 8th 2000); OECD (1998); FMJ (1998); and Bowley (December 17th 1998).

enterprises. Nonetheless, a major "outside" hindrance to this scrapping is presumably ready to be jettisoned. Companies are currently subject to a punitive 50-60% capital-gains tax should they opt for the disposal of their stakes in other companies. On December 21st 1999, the finance ministry announced a tax package proposing among other things to exempt sales of share stakes from capital gains tax after January 2001. Without the mountainous tax burden they would have to pay if they realise their hidden reserves (the difference between the market value of the shares and their book value), big banks as well as other large non-bank financial institutions (as Allianz, the mammoth insurer group, and Munich Reinsurance) are left only with strategic concerns when deciding their scope of investments. What is more, if the proposal really turns into law, it may lead to an unwinding of the cross-shareholdings (worth roughly US$252 billion) that cement "insider" relationships and help shelter German firms from hostile takeovers and bankruptcy.

Intense global competition in the product markets combined with increasing pressure coming from the financial markets have, in addition, triggered a wave of restructuring throughout German corporate scene in the last few years. As a consequence, mergers, acquisitions, spin-offs, and divestments have been shifting German companies from diversification to both specialisation and concentration.[39]

[39] The suppression of trade and financial barriers together with the European single market and single-currency zone are some of the leading forces heightening global competition and pressurising companies to be more efficient in Germany. To tackle the challenge posed by these changes, German conglomerates and companies belonging to different sectors have been gripped by restructuring initiatives. Krupp and Thyssen concluded their merger last year. Daimler-Benz and Hoechst pioneered the jettisoning of non-core activities in the mid-nineties – perhaps a first stepping-stone on the path to their subsequent cross-border mergers with, respectively, Chrysler and Rhône-Poulenc. The ex-state-owned conglomerates Viag and Veba announced recently their merger (worth DM 122 billion) and the intent to focus on energy and chemicals, disposing of divisions turning over up DM 50 billion. Indeed, even before the merger, Viag had released its plan to get rid of its logistic and other minor activities with a view to concentrating efforts on power, telecommunication and its other industrial interests, while Veba had manifested its intention to focus on energy markets. In fact, the major German large conglomerates (*Mischkonzerne*) have embarked on selling off non-core businesses. Mannesmann and Preussag, in turn, have moved from their former heavy-industry base into, respectively, new technologies (mobile phone) and package tourism (*The Economist*, July 17th 1998; Bowley, November 20th 1998; Barber, June 1st 1999). According to Heribert Meffert, from the University of Münster, diversified conglomerates accounted for two-thirds of all German enterprises, whilst today they represent only one-quarter.

(iii) The overhaul of the legal and institutional setting

Conscious of the rapid changes under way and zealous both to lift Frankfurt as the European financial centre and to prevent German stock exchanges from losing trading and liquidity to American or other European rivals, German financial authorities and politicians have not spared efforts to actively promote capital markets and reform corporate governance mechanisms in Germany. After the successful flotation of a significant fraction of Deutsche Telekom's shares in 1996 (for many analysts, a turning-point awakening the interest of a multitude of savers in purchasing shares as an instrument of savings), several legal changes have been enacted by the German parliament, with the aim of gearing the legal framework surrounding both capital markets and corporate governance to the changeable financial environment.[40] These moves towards a regulatory level playing field have been partly motivated by the transfer of a great deal of authority from national regulators to EU's agencies and committees together with stronger international integration of financial markets.[41] Also shareholder activism cannot be left out among the prime forces conducting to the revision of German rules of corporate governance.

Among the fairly extensive pieces of legislation focusing on streamlining capital markets and investors' protection that have been sanctioned in the last few years, two laws deserve to be underlined. The first, the *Law to Ease Capital Procurement*, taken effect on April 24th 1998, authorises listed German companies to follow internationally mainstream accounting standards for disclosing their consolidated financial statements. The objective lying behind this law is clearly the removal of the above-mentioned hurdle obstructing German enterprises to obtain finance from global capital markets.

The other, the *Act on Corporate Control and Transparency* (the *KonTraG*), which came into force in April 1998, appears to be the most ambitious attempt to amend the legal arrangement on which German corporate governance affairs rest. Conceived after "*wide-ranging talks with the parties concerned and with academics*" and seeking to fix some of the "shortcomings" pervading the former arrangement, the KonTraG attempted to set governance rules in line with other OECD countries' standards, lest Germany be left behind

---

[40] Discoursing upon the passage of the law on corporate governance reform, the Ministerial Counsellor from the Federal Ministry of Justice depicts clearly the thorough awareness German official authorities have about the changing financial environment scenery. He stated: "*for the legal and political framework, this means that against a background of institutional competition, there is growing pressure for changes and adaptation of our company law, stock market law and accounting law*" (FMJ, 1998).

[41] For example, the Investment Services Directive has prompted competition among regulators since companies in Europe may choose where to list.

in the institutional race for attracting companies and investors. Those who proposed this law refrained from inflating it with "*strict legal directives*", opting instead for "*control to be provided by the existing SBs and the markets*".

Besides tightening public disclosure requirements, the KonTraG improved the dual-tier governance structure, trying to secure that SBs effectively scrutinise management and both SBs and MBs become more accountable to the interests of minority shareholders (FMJ, 1998). Thus, the law laid down a host of regulations defining mandatory duties and affecting the incentives and strength of all stakeholders (SB members, management, banks, block-holders, and minority shareholders). Below the main changes are pinpointed.

As regards information, 1) management are required to release detailed information concerning company's planning to SBs; 2) companies and banks are obligated to inform shareholders about the available options for taking part in ballots; 3) banks have further to inform shareholders whose shares are deposited with them about their own stake in the company as well as whether any of their executives takes a seat on the company's SB; 4) listed companies and banks must disclose all germane links every member of their SBs has with other enterprises.

Among the constraints placed on management and large shareholders with the purpose of curbing them from obtaining private benefits at the expense of minority investors, two are noteworthy: 1) the suppression of both plural voting rights and maximum voting rights; and 2) the prohibition for companies linked by cross-shareholdings from exercising voting rights on each other's general meetings convened for the election of SB members (preventing management, therefore, from "controlling" themselves).

Regarding incentives, shareholders' annual general meetings are set freer to offer stock options as a form of compensation for companies' senior executives, whereas the enforcement of penalties for "*serious neglect of responsibilities*" against members of both the SB and the board of managers has been strengthened.

Another important deregulatory measure lies in the permission for companies to buy back their shares. Enacted with a view to both stimulating the stock market and enhancing companies' flexibility, it also equips managers with an additional defence tool against hostile bids. Together with the obvious appeal of capital gains for investors, share buy-backs allow companies to exploit financial markets' opportunities (the cost differential between debt and equity finance) and to choose what they reckon to be their best capital structure. The removal of the 50% capital-gains tax on selling equity stakes in other companies is due to leave the repurchase of companies' own shares especially attractive.

4.5 Some Remaining Shortcomings

Despite changes in the regulatory setting, small shareholders continue lacking legal protection in the event of takeovers. The takeover code stipulates two specific clauses, in addition to the general rules of conduct directed to prevent market manipulation.[42] One is that investors purchasing 30% (50% before 1997) of the target company's overall equity capital should make a "*reasonable takeover bid*" for the remaining shareholders. The other is that companies should commit themselves to refrain from defensive measures if subject to a public tender offer (Hoffmann-Burchardi, 1999). Notwithstanding, instead of making it legally binding, the government has preferred to rely on self-regulation and leave its enforcement voluntary. Despite code's laxity, companies have been so far reluctant to adhere to it,[43] including some comprising the stock market index (DAX). Given that the decision to observe it is at the discretion of the company's MB, it is unlikely that companies with controlling shareholders adhere to it voluntarily, since this would increase the company's risk of being taken over (Hoffmann-Burchardi, 1999).

Regarding the recommendation for reducing the size of SBs, trade unions' strong opposition has managed to block it to date. Their fear is that therein lies a strategy to dilute labour power on the board (OECD, 1998). As for corporate transparency and disclosure, though improvements were made and are still in progress, there is much to be done, especially with respect to information about companies' holders of voting power.

5. Concluding remarks

Much has been said about the ultimate effects globalisation is bound to engender on corporate governance. Relentless competition in both product and financial markets stemming from greater international integration would inevitably eliminate inefficient arrangements of corporate governance. Inasmuch as one regards maximisation of the shareholder value as amounting to maximising the value of the firm, the inescapable conclusion is that the quest for efficiency will force firms to jettison rules, mechanisms and practices whereby their non-owner stakeholders have voice and influence on firms' decisions, leading firms to adopt the "shareholder model" of control.

---

[42] This code was laid down by the German Stock Exchange Expert Committee of the Federal Ministry of Finance in October 1995.

[43] One year after coming into force, the Takeover Code had a too low adhesion rate – nearly one-third of all listed companies (Jenkinson & Ljunqvist, 1999, p. 21). The major sanction against offenders is the prohibition against companies to go public in the Deutsche Börse.

Throughout this paper, I have tried to demonstrate that there are both theoretical reasons and empirical support to believe that sharp competition can coexist with the stakeholder model. In the first place, one can be sceptical about the prediction that globalisation severely undermines that model on the grounds of its ability to create the appropriate incentives for stakeholders to invest in firm-specific assets which maximise the value of the firm. Moreover, decision-making process considering also the interest of groups other than shareholders may help avert the penchant towards short-term horizons that liquidity risk and pressure for high returns impose. The building of commitment, trust or complementarities among stakeholders may turn out to be an efficient solution to cope with some market failures (such as asymmetrical information, incomplete or unenforceable contracts, and lack of co-ordination). The increasing importance of human capital as a source of value for the firm reinforces the need for arrangements ensuring employees will be granted the appropriate reward during the *ex post* bargaining over the rents created thanks to the contribution of their firm-specific investments. In the light of this, the reach of changes on corporate governance arisen from globalisation is likely to be circumscribed.

Along with efficiency issues, some political forces and deep-seated structures appear to be major roadblocks on the way to convergence. Needless to say, the legal system defining the available set of corporate governance practices enshrines a given allocation of rights among company stakeholders. Changing this system would inevitably entail political struggles. Thus, as Bebchuk & Roe (1998) clearly argue, public choice and politics may explain why rules and structures, however inefficient, persist. Path dependence may constitute a difficult-to-obviate hurdle to "convergence". Extant ownership structure may determine the local optimal rules and structure, fuelling the persistence of divergence.

Examining the German corporate scenery in order to know if it could flesh out this plausible reasoning with empirical stuff, the main finding is that, even though outstanding changes in corporate strategies as well as in legal and accounting rules have undeniably rendered German companies in several respects akin to their American counterparts, there remain some political and legal hurdles obstructing the closing of the huge gulf still separating German and U.S. patterns of governance. One and arguably the most important of these political, path-dependent hindrances to bridge that gap is the *Co-determination Act*. Entitling employee representatives, at least *de jure*, to have voice and power on the SB, this law may be a stumbling block to the quest for shareholder value (hostile takeover bids included). Against the German political background, wherein labour is traditionally a powerful player, divesting it of the right to the co-determined control of management is surely no easy task. Combined with socially embedded values taking companies "*as social institutions, not just as the property of their shareholders*", the Co-determination Act makes the consensus-led stakeholder model somewhat resistant to economic shocks. Unless something especially severe affecting the whole economy saps this model (like an impressive loss of competitiveness coupled with mounting unemployment rates), it is unlikely that its dominance will be disputed.

Another path-dependent reason for which the governance gap still persists is the public limited companies' concentrated ownership structure, wherein single controlling shareholders predominates. Firmly established beneficiaries of that structure, as management and block-holders, are likely to resort to all their power and influence to oppose to changes in rules which shift authority away from them to, for example, minority shareholders – however efficient for the whole economy this change might be. Concentrated ownership also makes it difficult the functioning of the market for corporate control. An additional obstacle lies in the ownership of large equity stakes by Länder or by other governmental institutions in both producing enterprises and banks. Fearful of arousing political opposition, they would hardly ever support hostile raids, inasmuch as such bids are motivated, as a rule, by the goal of promoting job-loss restructuring in the target-firm. Furthermore, the intricate web of cross-holdings casts uncertainties over the outcome of hostile bids, since controlling block-holders may have strategies focused on the group rather than on individual firms. This allied with companies' representatives on each other's SBs tend to favour the stakeholder approach.

Evidently, this structural, path-dependent hurdles may end up being swept away by economic forces. Increasingly harsh competition in product markets – especially within the EU area – as well as in global capital markets is likely to urge (cross-border and domestic) mergers and acquisitions in key industries (financial services included). The run-up to the anticipated market concentration is expected to lead German firms to streamline their asset portfolio. Focus on some few core activities and disposal of peripheral activities, practices highly valued by global investors, may place large German corporations in a better position to undertake acquisitions or mergers – either in cash or through share swaps. The repeal of the tax on capital gains earned from the realisation of hidden reserves, releasing large corporations, especially banks, from the current locking-in effects, should reinforce the incentives to jettison their non-controlling stakes in other enterprises. In this respect, the fact that the four big banks and the two big insurance groups stand at the hubs of the complex web of cross-shareholdings (holding controlling interests in a great number of limited companies) may catalyse and accelerate a startling overhaul of German large corporations' ownership structure. If they opt for relinquishing their stakes in other companies, liquidity in the market for blocks of shares may be strengthened, prompting the market for corporate control. A less concentrated shareholding structure may also be stimulated by the parallel development of venture capital and exit channels (like Neuer Markt).

All the same, if it is true that some large steps have been taken leading German companies to adopt some practices of governance used by their American counterparts, there still remains stark contrasts between them. It is not clear whether convergence is the best route to reach efficiency, and even if it turns out to be, the way is sinuous, long and full of hurdles. Consequently, the completion of this journey cannot be taken for granted. As Bebchuk & Roe (1998, p. 39) accurately summarise the issue:

"*the case for predicting rapid, substantively complete convergence is not strong. Prophets of convergence may well be predicting convergence for quite some time. The direction of convergence or persistence will be the resultant of the two offsetting vectors of competitive globalization (allied with structural imperatives and the pressures toward efficiency) and path dependence (allied with natural local variation). Where the resultant vector will point is, in the end, an empirical question, but the deductive case for rapid, substantively complete convergence has yet to be made out.*"

REFERENCES

ALLEN, Franklin & Douglas GALE. A Welfare Comparison of Intermediaries and Financial Markets in Germany and the United States. *European Economic Review*, 39, 1995.

BARBER, Tony. Capitalism's changing face. *Financial Times*. June 1st 1999.

BEBCHUK, Lucian Arye & Mark J. ROE. A Theory of Path Dependence in Corporate Governance and Ownership. Working paper # 131, Columbia Law School, 1998.

BECHT, Marco & Ailsa RÖELL. Blockholdings in Europe: an international comparison. *European Economic Review* 43, 1999.

BECHT, Marco & Ekkehart BÖHMER. "Ownership and Voting Power in Germany". European Corporate Governance Network, December 1998.

BECHT, Marco & Ekkehart BÖHMER. "Transparency of ownership and control in Germany". European Corporate Governance Network, October 1997.

BECHT, Marco. European corporate governance: trading off liquidity against control. *European Economic Review* 43, 1999.

BLAIR, Margaret & Lynn A. STOUT. A Team Production Theory of Corporate Law. *Virginia Law Review*, 1999.

BLAIR, Margaret & Mark J. ROE (eds.). *Employees and Corporate Governance*. Washington, D.C.: Brookings Institute Press, 1999.

BLAIR, Margaret. *Ownership and Control: Rethinking Corporate Governance for the Twenty-First Century*. Washington, D. C.: Brookings Institution, 1995.

BOWLEY, Graham. Shaking off historic legacy. *Financial Times*, December 17th 1998.

BOWLEY, Graham. Germany's new shop window: corporate change in Germany lies behind the wave of pan-European restructuring. *Financial Times*, November 20th 1998.

COFFEE JR, John C. "The future as history: the prospects for global convergence in corporate governance and its implications". Working paper # 144, Columbia Law School, October 2nd 1999.

DB. Deutsche Bundesbank. Structural changes in the German capital market in the run-up to European monetary union. *Monthly Report*. Frankfurt: Deutsche Bundesbank, April 1998.

DB. Deutsche Bundesbank. Shares as financing and investment instruments. *Monthly Report*. Frankfurt: Deutsche Bundesbank, January 1997.

DBG. Deutsche Börse Group. Neuer Markt rules and regulations: valid from 15/09/1999. Available from http://www.neuer-markt.de, 1999.

EDWARDS, Jeremy & Klaus FISCHER. *Banks, finance and investment in Germany*. Cambridge: Cambridge University Press, 1994.

FINANCIAL TIMES (various issues).

FMJ. FEDERAL MINISTRY OF JUSTICE. "Control and transparency in the business (KonTraG): corporate governance reform in Germany". Bonn. Available from http://www.bmj.bund.de, 1998.

FRANKS, Julian & Colin MAYER. Bank control, takeovers and corporate governance in Germany. *Journal of Banking & Finance* 22, 1998.

HOFFMANN-BURCHARDI, Ulrike. "'Barbarians in chains' – Takeover regulation and minority shareholder wealth". Working paper, The London School of Economics, Financial Markets Group, 1999.

JENKINSON, Tim & Alexander LJUNGQVIST. "The role of hostile stakes in German corporate governance". Unpublished, Oxford University, 1999.

JENKINSON, Tim & Colin MAYER. The assessment: corporate governance and corporate control. *Oxford Review of Economy Policy*, v. 8, n. 3, 1992.

KESTER, W. C. Industrial groups as systems of contractual governance. *Oxford Review of Economy Policy*, v. 8, n. 3, 1992.

LÖHNERT, Bettina. "The structure of the German banking system and its ethical implication". In: Antonio Argandoña (ed.), *The ethical dimension of financial institutions and markets*. Berlin: Spring, 1995.

MAYER, Colin. The City and Corporate Performance: Condemned or Exonerated? *Cambridge Journal of Economics*, 21, 1997.

MILGROM, Paul & John ROBERTS. *Economics, organization & management*. New Jersey: Prentice-Hall, 1992.

OECD. *OECD Economic Surveys, 1994-1995, Germany*. Paris: OECD, 1995.

OECD. *OECD Economic Surveys, 1995-1996, United States*. Paris: OECD, 1996.

OECD. *OECD Economic Surveys, 1997-1998, Germany*. Paris: OECD, 1998.

PROWSE, Stephen. Corporate governance in an international perspective. *BIS Economic Paper*, n. 41, 1994.

RAJAN, Raghuram & Luigi ZINGALES. Power in a theory of the firm. *The Quarterly Journal of Economics*, May 1998a.

RAJAN, Raghuram G. & Luigi ZINGALES. The Governance of the New Enterprise". University of Chicago, 1998b.

ROE, Mark. Comparative corporate governance, in Peter Newman (ed.), *The New Palgrave Dictionary of Economics and the Law*. London: Macmillan Reference Ltd., 1998a.

ROE, Mark. German codetermination and German securities markets. Working paper # 128. Columbia Law School, 1998b.

SCHNEIDER-LENNÉ, Ellen R. Corporate control in Germany. *Oxford Review of Economic Policy*, vol. 8, n. 3, 1992.

SHLEIFER, Andrei & Robert VISHNY. A survey of corporate governance. *Journal of Finance*, vol. LII, No. 2, 1997.

THE ECONOMIST. (various issues).

ZINGALES, Luigi. "Corporate Governance", in Peter Newman, *The New Palgrave Dictionary of Economics and the Law*. London: Macmillan Reference Ltd., 1998.

PRIVATIZATION AND THE DISTRIBUTION OF ASSETS AND INCOME IN BRAZIL[1]

Roberto Macedo

For he that hath, to him shall be given
St. Mark's gospel

I. Introduction

This paper analyses the privatization program undertaken in Brazil in the nineties and focuses on its relation to asset and income distribution. Section II reviews the old and ongoing discussion of the causes of income inequality and shows that it focuses primarily on incremental and minor changes, often ignoring the high inequality itself and the role of the asset distribution in shaping it. Against this background, a huge privatization program has been in progress since the early nineties, the result of which, until 1999, was the transfer to private groups, both Brazilian and foreign, of US$71 billion worth of equity capital in state owned enterprises (SOEs).

The impact of this transfer on asset and income distribution is therefore an important issue, particularly as it was accompanied by trade liberalization, increasing exposure to external financing, a serious fiscal crisis, high interest rates and an overvalued exchange rate. This complex combination has been a source of income gains and losses of various sorts, together with changes in the value and in the property of assets.

It is in this context that we shall focus on asset and income distribution, following the thread of privatization, attracted by the size of the program, and by the fact that it peaked in 1997 and 1998, when fiscal and external imbalances were at their worst in the decade. Section II also sketches an analytical framework for tackling some of the issues involved in the relation between privatization and asset and income distribution.

Section III describes the privatization program and its outcomes. Section IV presents a picture of the fiscal side, involving deficits, debt, interest rates and other ingredients of a problem that privatization was supposed to help, but that was mishandled in such a way as to damage the positive impacts of privatization on the fiscal crisis and harm income distribution as well. The mishandling also

[1] This paper was originally prepared for the Carnegie Endowment for International Peace, where it became a discussion paper (Number 14, July 2000). The complete version can be downloaded at http://www.ceip.org/files/publications/pdf/14macedo.pdf

included the external side as shown in section IV. Section V relates these macroeconomic developments and the privatization process to income and asset distribution in Brazil, and presents other conclusions of the paper.

II. SETTING THE ISSUES AND ANALYTICAL BACKGROUND

Income distribution in Brazil

Studies on income distribution in Brazil are abundant, as it is one of the worst cases of inequality in the world. According to 1998 data from IBGE, the Brazilian Census Bureau, the income share of the poorest 50% was only 14% while the richest 10% took a hefty 46% of the total income.[2] Most of the analyses take a measure of inequality, such as the Gini coefficient, or the income of a particular group in society, and after looking on how it has changed over time, proceed to investigate the causes of the change, leaving aside or taking for granted the reasons, such as the asset distribution, that make up for the very high degree of inequality itself.

For instance, after census figures revealed a worsening of the income distribution in the sixties, an intense debate emerged about the causes. On the one side of the discussion, were those who blamed the wage policies of the military government then in power, particularly the erosion of the purchasing power of the minimum wage. On the other side, were those who, instead, blamed the change on the larger income gains made by educated people in short supply in relation to unskilled workers, as demand for labor expanded rapidly following a period of very high rates of economic growth.[3]

In another and more recent instance, as since the mid-nineties the income of the poorest groups has improved a bit, this time explanations have emphasized the price stabilization achieved by the Real Plan, unveiled in 1994. As the plan has been successful in curbing very high inflation, this improved the fate of the poorest as they had been the major victims of the "inflationary tax" implicit in the very high rates of inflation, which reached as high as 84% a month in March 1990.[4] An increase in the value of the minimum wage, whose major impact is now on the incomes of retired people and pensioners of the

---

[2] PNAD (National Household Survey), 1998, as quoted by Folha de S. Paulo (December 1st, 1999).

[3] For a review of this debate, see Macedo (1977).

[4] As a rule, the poorest groups in Brazil have no access to the mechanisms available to the middle-class and the rich to protect the purchasing power of money holdings, such as indexed checking and savings accounts.

INSS (National Social Security and Welfare System), where it is the floor of the monthly individual benefits, has also been appointed as an important factor.[5]

The objectives of the privatization program and the neglect of asset and income distribution

It was against this background of a very high income inequality that a huge program of privatization of public assets, in the form of equity in SOEs, has been in progress since the early nineties, following earlier but weaker moves in the same direction.

Law 8031, of April 12, 1990, established the legal framework for program.[6] Six objectives were set in its first article: (1) to reestablish the strategic position of the State in the economy, by transferring to the private sector the activities unduly undertaken by the public sector; (2) to contribute to the reduction of the public debt, by helping in the process of adjusting the finances of the public sector; (3) to make room for increased investments in the companies and activities transferred to the private sector; (4) to contribute to the modernization of the country's industrial sector, by improving its competitiveness and by strengthening entrepreneurial skills in the various sectors of the economy; (5) to allow the public administration to concentrate its efforts in the activities in which the presence of the State is fundamental for accomplishing the national priorities; and (6) to contribute to the strengthening of the capital markets, by increasing the supply of securities and by democratizing the capital ownership of the SOEs included in the program.

Thus, from its conception the Brazilian privatization program has shown no explicit concern with income distribution, except in the blurred form of democratizing capital ownership. In any case, the privatization of a SOE will cause an impact on asset and income distribution, and in this respect the program raises many interesting questions, among them the following: (i) who benefited most from the previous public ownership of the SOEs that have been privatized? (ii) which benefits came with privatization? (iii) how was the access to privatization and who bought the SOEs? (iii) was money the only asset received by the government in exchange? (iv) could the government have devised alternative forms of privatization, with different impact on asset and income distribution? (v) how did the government use the money from the program? (vi) what has been the impact on personal asset and income distribution?

---

[5] Inequality was slightly reduced from 1993 to 1998, as the Gini coefficient fell from 0.60 to 0.575.

[6] Law 9491, of September 9, 1997, is the most recent version.

These are complex questions, which will be addressed in the limited scope of this paper. It has no claim of providing a complete and finished picture, as it rather sketches the major facts and issues involved, and provides some paths following which these questions could be further investigated. In any case, by doing this it claims to having dealt with an important and neglected issue that shapes income inequality in Brazil – the asset distribution – and to having brought into the discussion the impact of a major asset redistribution, the undergoing privatization program.

Even within this limited scope, it is important to sketch an analytical background for the issues to be examined. When a SOE is privatized, the buyer gives the government an amount of money or other form of payment, that was either its property or borrowed from some source. Thus, the privatization is an exchange of assets. As the interest of this paper is on income distribution, the question to be examined is whether or not this exchange of assets was neutral in its impact on income inequality.

As the transaction occurred, we can assume that the sale was made at the right price or, in any case, at a price that did not preclude a gain of another nature, and which we see as the major one. This gain is an expected one and will come from the buyer's belief that he will be able to better manage the company, profiting from the previous incompetence of the government managers in obtaining a higher return, or from government policies – such as wage and price policies – that precluded these managers from doing so.

Thus, implicit in the sale there is an expected gain to the buyer, a testable hypothesis, as, barring data difficulties, the efficiency and the profit rate of the privatized firms can be evaluated before and after the sale. Another testable hypothesis is that the rent gainers around the SOEs will lose from privatization, as prices of products, services, suppliers and workers will more closely follow the market rules.

Another issue to be analyzed is how the government spent the money it has received from the sale. Finally, looking at the source of funds for privatization, as in some cases the buyers of the state enterprises have borrowed money from a government bank, we will have to examine if this was done at a rate below the market rate, and to whom this benefit was given.

A major issue: the access to the opportunity to profit from privatization

Among these issues, we have singled out one for additional analysis, as we see it as the major one in shaping the relation of privatization to asset and income distribution. It is the access to the condition of buyer and to the efficiency and profit gains provided to the new owners of the former SOEs, as the rules of privatization have excluded some groups from participating in the process.

In putting the process into practice, among the objectives of Law 8031 the government has emphasized the reduction of the public debt. It also opted for auctioning its shares of the SOEs, in order to get the highest value for them, above a minimum price evaluated by outside consultants. The auctions have attracted big business, both national and foreign. This course of action prevailed over democratization of capital, a component of objective (6), which would have lead to another form of asset exchange and a different impact on income distribution.

Democratization of capital can be made mainly in four ways: management-employee buyouts, mass privatization in the fashion undertaken in some countries of Central and Eastern Europe, large scale flotations as adopted in Great Britain, or, as it could have been done in Brazil, by recognizing unfunded pension liabilities, and other liabilities owed by the government in its social security and welfare area. That is, the government could also use the privatization process to fund liabilities in this area, by transferring its equity capital in the SOEs to those entitled to these liabilities.

The manager-employee buyout, which has been partially and scarcely adopted in Brazil, deserves specific attention because again it opens the opportunity to profit to a particular group only. That is, this group would be one among other buyers who benefited from the opportunity to purchase the firms, and should be analyzed along the same lines.

Mass privatization of the Central and Eastern European style has never received a serious thought in Brazil, as the country does not have the same socialist tradition, nor was it necessary to use the idea to gain political support for the privatization program. Large scale flotations have not yet been adopted in Brazil.[7]

The fourth way to democratize capital deserves close attention as unfunded pension liabilities and other liabilities in the social security and welfare areas are enormous in the Brazilian public sector, including the SOEs.[8] Thus, we have to bring into the discussion the possibility of the recognition of

[7] At the moment, however, it seems that the government is considering this alternative, as the press has repeatedly reported on the idea of "pulverização" , or scattering of property, being discussed in government circles. See, for instance, *Veja* (November 3rd, 1999).

[8] As will be detailed in the next section, the pension liabilities of the SOEs enterprises have had an impact on the privatization process, by reducing the sale price of the privatized companies, as the buyers have assumed the responsibility for their funding. This can be considered a bonus for the workers of these companies, an issue largely ignored in the process. The existence of these unfunded pension liabilities in the SOEs can also be viewed as a result of their lack of adherence to the profit maximization rule, since the private sector has avoided them.

these liabilities, a course of action that was not followed by the government, but that would have led to very different results of the privatization process in terms of asset and income distribution. For later reference, we shall call this proposal the redemption of social security and welfare liabilities.

This idea has been raised by some economists, who have also suggested that the equity received from the government should go into private pension funds to gain from efficient management. It could also have the purpose of starting a new pension system following the capitalization rule, as the present one follows an explosive combination of the pay-as-you-go rule with schemes indigenous to Brazil, the receive-more-than-you-pay and the don't-pay-as-you-go, and is virtually broke.

The idea, however, has never gained wide audience, nor major political initiatives and support. On the side of the present government, only cosmetically social-democrat, its lack of ideological consistency, plus the anxiety of the economic team to get local and foreign money from privatization to help in the fiscal crisis and in the financing of the balance of payments, plus the pressure of big business, have not given any room for the idea to prosper. Notice also that Law 8031 has conflicting objectives in this respect, as democratization of capital in this or another form - for instance, large scale flotations based on a fixed price -, does not maximize the reduction of public debt.

To further clarify what we mean by the fourth above mentioned way to democratize capital ownership, we shall now resort to an imaginary balance sheet of assets and liabilities of the public sector, but containing only the items relevant to the analysis. A balance of this sort is not usual in the traditional analysis of public finances, but it is a key element in this kind of "Chapter 11" situation in which the government releases assets to reduce liabilities. This balance is shown in Table 1.[9]

As the government sells its equities in a SOE to reduce debt, in Table 1 this would mean a reduction in both A-1 and L-1 or L-2, as the government has also accepted as payment a part of its debt in the form of securities such as those of the Agrarian Debt (issued to pay landowners who had their land used in agrarian reform projects), and Siderbrás (the former holding of the government steel companies) Bonds.[10]

The fourth scheme mentioned above would tantamount to use the equity capital in the state enterprises, that is, A-1 to cover L-3-1 to L-3-3. Moreover, to

[9] All tables and figures are in the appendix.

[10] Both are long term securities sold at below par values in the market and which became known in the privatization process as "rotten money". As demand for these securities increased, their owners had a capital gain or a recovery of capital loss. Those who bought these securities to be used in the privatization process at a par value, have had a capital gain. These are changes in property of assets followed by capital gains or losses, therefore also having an impact on asset and income distribution.

the workers of the formal labor market the government also owes a liability of another form, the deposits in the FGTS or Workers' Tenure Guarantee Fund. Brazilian employers are required to deposit in this fund the equivalent of one month's wages per worker per year in an account in his name, and the money can be drafted only if the labor contract is broken, if the money is used to buy a house, or upon retirement. FGTS is thus a funded form of unemployment compensation or social security. In the course of privatization, another idea that from time to time came into discussion, was to allow workers to use their FGTS balances to buy equity capital of the SOEs being sold.[11] It is important to mention that in the revised version of law 8031, that is, Law 9491, of 1997, a provision was made to allow individuals to place of 50% of their balances in the FGTS account into "Privatization Mutual Funds", designed to participate in the National Program of "Desestatization" and in the programs at the state level. These funds, however, have not come into existence thus far.

If democratizing capital ownership and asset and income distribution were the purpose, the group better qualified for it would be the contributors and pensioners of the INSS, the National System of Welfare and Social Security, whose pension liabilities are in L-3-3 in Table 1. They comprise around 20 million workers and 18 million pensioners, who receive pensions having the monthly minimum wage – roughly US$70 in late 1999 – as the floor, and 10 times as much as the ceiling. Rural and informal workers, as well as the handicapped and the aged without other sources of income, are also among the pensioners and therefore the INSS combines social security with welfare or social assistance benefits. This system covers some of the major poorest groups, while those in L-3-1 and L-3-2 are essentially middle-class or even rich people, with favored pension schemes that include 100% of active pay and no ceiling. Pensions in the value of US$1,500 to US$3,000 are not uncommon in this minority group and some are even higher.

Although not explicitly considered in the privatization process, the provision for unfunded liabilities has been made only in the case of the workers of the SOEs, by means of a reduction in the auction price to compensate for the existence of these liabilities. That is, part of A-1 has been used to cover L-3-1. This has been the source of another asset and income distribution impact of the privatization process and in the direction of maintaining or increasing inequality, as this group of workers is among the better off.

To sum up: if democratizing capital ownership, asset and income distribution were the purpose, the groups better qualified to participate in the

[11] The FGTS balances have been used by the government's CEF, a savings and loan bank, to finance public sector projects in areas such as sanitation, on a long term basis. Thus, the FGTS deposits are not an unfunded liability, but the loans are long term and difficult to recover.

privatization, by means of the redemption of social security and welfare liabilities, would be, in this order, L-3-3, L-4, L-3-1 and L-3-2, the last two having roughly the same status.

Still looking for income distribution effects of privatization, as liabilities such as L-1 and L-2 are reduced, the government ceases to pay interest on the amount of the reduction, saving money which, in turn, would reduce the fiscal deficit, if the objectives of the program were to be followed. Moreover, a sizable debt reduction could have reduced the interest rate paid, as the shaky government finances have increased the risk premium paid to buyers of government bonds. The impact on income inequality would be to lessen it, as the interest paid go mainly to the highest income groups. This course of events can be analyzed following the usual framework of analysis of the taxation and expenditure policies. Within the same framework, we can also fit the future increase in tax receipts that will come from the larger profits of the privatized companies, as well as the expenditures that the additional revenue will finance. In this case, the impact will depend on who will benefit from the expenditures.

Table 2 summarizes the assumptions, consequences and hypotheses that have emerged from the analysis in this section. The drawing line between consequences and hypotheses is not a strict one. The former are of a more general nature and come first in the sequence of causation, while the latter are more specific and are more at the end line. In the analysis of the next two sections, the evidence presented will cover only those cases marked with (*).

III. THE PRIVATIZATION PROGRAM, ITS CHARACTERISTICS AND RESULTS

In the process of privatization, the decision was taken by federal and state governments to sell their minority or controlling shares in various companies – some of them had private capital as well – by means of auctions in the stock exchange. In the case of roads, bridges and other public works, the privatization has been in the form of concession of public services, with the selection of the interested parties occurring by means of competitive bidding. Due to the limits set for its scope, this paper will not deal with the case of concession of public services.

In privatizing its companies, the government has advanced by industries, starting with the steel and mining companies, then moving into the electricity, telecommunications and other industries. In the case of electricity, where the state governments have strong participation, major advances have been in the area of distribution. On the production side, a large part of the program remains to be completed. Major state enterprises still exist not only in the area of electricity, but also in the banking and petroleum industries.[12]

The privatization program is composed of three parts. The first is the federal National Program of "Desestatization" (NPD), started by President Collor in 1991. The second is a similar program at the state level. The third is the privatization in the telecommunications industry, thus far the largest one in terms of value, which was initiated by the federal government in 1997, as a program separated from the NPD, but running parallel to it. We shall call it the Telecom program, for later reference. The auctions under this new program resulted in US$ 28.7 billion in only two years (1997 and 1998), while the NPD came to a total of US$28.9 billion in eight years (1991-1998)[13].

Table 3 shows the total proceeds of the privatization program from 1991 to 1999, and also the sum in each of its three parts. The total value, US$88 billion, is impressive and certainly places the Brazilian program among the largest in the world. Two years, 1997 and 1998, have concentrated 74% of the total value of the program thus far. This will have important implications for the analysis, to be undertaken in the next section, of the impact of the program on the fiscal crisis and the external imbalances, as in these two years both were seriously aggravated.

The number of firms privatized from 1991 to 1998 was 115. The whole program has been confronted by the opposition, in particular by the Workers Party. The disputes have ranged from battles in the courts, including last minute petitions against the sales, to attempts to disrupt the scheduled auctions. In some cases, this has led to confrontation with those attending the auction and the police.

Nevertheless, the government has showed competence in overcoming these difficulties and the program first gained speed in the early nineties. Management of the program was a crucial issue and the task was given to BNDES, the National Bank for Economic and Social Development. Its major

[12] Some major state banks, such as those of the states of Minas and Rio de Janeiro, have already been privatized. The largest one, Banespa, formerly owned by the state of São Paulo, has been federalized and its privatization is scheduled for the year 2000. The federal government has a commercial bank, Banco do Brasil, and a savings and loans institution, CEF, which will be at the end line of the process, if ever privatized. The government participation in the petroleum industry includes production, importing and refining and it is dominated by a monopoly (Petrobrás), with a minority participation of private shareholders. It will also be at the end line of the program, in a date not yet established, as even the decision to privatize it remains to be taken. In any case, the monopoly rule has been broken recently and Petrobrás is likely to be exposed to increasing competition in the years to come.

[13] Unless otherwise stated, the BNDES (National Bank for Economic and Social Development) is the source of all data presented in this paper on the privatization program, including the part developed at the state level. The reports and other documents used as references in this paper are listed at the end of it as BNDES (1999a and 1999b).

role is the provision of long term financing to the private and public sectors, such as a petrochemical plant, in the first case, or a subway line, in the second. As a rule, private banks in Brazil do not finance long term projects, because of the risks involved, particularly in the past, when inflation was rampant, and because they get more profits with government securities and short term financing to private clients. The BNDES' bureaucracy is among the best in the public sector and it has acted effectively in organizing the actions, in informing the interested parties, in the court battles, and also in providing assistance to the state governments in their own privatization programs.

The government is clearly running the program at low speed at the moment. Notice, in Table 3, that the results in the first half of 1999 have been minor ones.[14]

In Chart 1 we present additional characteristics of the privatization program, in three panels. The first shows the share of its three components, NPD, Telecom and the privatization by the states; the second shows the share of the various industries; and the third shows the nationality of the buyers. All the shares are measured in terms of the total value of the program from 1991 to 1999. The first two panels put numbers to issues already raised in the previous discussion. The third one reveals that the program has been liberal in terms of foreign participation, as it reached a share (43.5%) not very far from the one taken by Brazilian investors (56.5%). This will have major implications for the discussion on asset and income distribution, as well as on the future pattern of the current account balance, as will be discussed in more detail later in this paper.

In Chart 2, composed of four panels, we present information covering the NPD only. The federal privatization program consists only of the NPD and Telecom components. The first panel on the upper left side shows the share of each industry. The other three panels show data which are crucial for clarifying issues under discussion. Proceeding in a clockwise fashion, the second panel shows how the NPD total of roughly US$20 billion was paid for, a total that does not include the debt owed by the companies and assumed by the buyer. Worth mentioning is the acceptance of the "rotten money", in the form of Agrarian Debt Securities, Privatization Certificates and Siderbrás Bonds. Using the terms adopted in the balance sheet of Table 1, this acceptance meant a gain to the owners and buyers of L-4, thus benefiting high income groups as the poor

[14] One of the reasons for the current stalemate is that the program was supposed to make further advances in the electricity industry, but this is an industry very complicated from the institutional point of view, as it involves producers and distributors in various companies, some of them owned by state governments. Moreover, to further advance, the program would also have to move into industries such as oil and federal banks, where the opposition is fierce, as it includes strongholds such as Petrobrás and Banco do Brasil.

people and even the middle classes are not among the typical holders of securities in Brazil.

With regard to the buyers, the following panel shows that in the NPD the participation of foreign investors has not been as large as in the total program, the reason being that they had took the largest part of the Telecom program. Worth mentioning, for later reference, is that pension funds took 12% of the NPD. However minor, this represents a democratization of capital, handicapped, however, in terms of income distribution, by the fact that these pension funds are largely those of workers of state enterprises themselves, who have been privileged among other groups covered by the government pension schemes. In the last panel, the relevant information is that the public offer and the amount offered to employees have been minor initiatives, particularly as that they have not been undertaken in the case of the Telecom program.

The conclusion with respect to democratization of capital ownership is that the program allowed only minor room for it. When democratization of capital ownership did occur it benefited the middle and higher class workers, such as those at the SOEs themselves who participated in the manager-employee buyouts and those covered by pension plans. Sizable pension funds in Brazil have emerged mainly in the realm of the state enterprises, and it was the funds existing in these companies which took most of the share sold to pension funds.[15]

Even when privatized, these funds and their covered workers benefited from the privatization. Given the presence of unfunded pension liabilities, the value was discounted from the price by which the SOE enterprise was sold, so that in the end they moved from unfunded to funded pension plans. This is a gray side of privatization in Brazil as it is largely unknown to the public in general, and no precise account has yet been given of how much the government lost in the process, for having to cover the funding implicit in the lower privatization price. A recent article on the press mentioned a figure around R$10 billion in the case of the federal state enterprises privatized in the last five years.[16] In one of the interviews we arranged for gathering information for this paper, a fellow economist who works in the electricity industry, called my attention to the case of Eletropaulo, a distributing company in the São Paulo area, privatized in 1998. He said that the unfunded pension liabilities cost the government around R$2 billion. Later on we have had the opportunity to look at data related to the auction of this company. It had an estimated net asset value of

[15] For instance, a major player among pension funds which have participated in the process has been PREVI, the pension fund of Banco do Brasil. It is also the largest pension fund in the country.

[16] Suely Caldas, "Fundos de pensão dão prejuízo bilionário ao País", *O Estado de S.Paulo* (October 11th, 1999). In dollars, this total would be roughly equivalent to US$8 billion, using the average exchange rate in the same period.

R$5.2 billion, but was sold for only R$2 billion. Putting together these two pieces of information, it seems that the unfunded pension liabilities accounted for most of the difference.

This scheme of implicitly funding the pension plans of the privatized companies has another interesting aspect. As the buyer assumes the responsibility for the funding, by reducing the price offered for the company, he has also another opportunity to gain from the acquisition, as he can negotiate new rules for the pension plans with the workers, and these new rules are likely to go in the direction of the contention of benefits, as the new managers are profit maximizers and the workers lose political clout in the privatization. One case mentioned by the same journalist quoted in footnote 14, the one of CSN-Cia. Siderúrgica Nacional, or National Steel Company, is illustrative of the gains obtained in restructuring the pension plan after privatization. In the words of its own president, after privatization the company reduced the unfunded pension liabilities, estimated at R$450 million by the time of the privatization, by shifting 48% of their cost to the workers, in the form of higher contributions and lower benefits. Thus, the privatized company also profited from the government's inability to negotiate a similar arrangement before privatization.

In sum, although the government has not shown a major concern for the issue of democratization of capital ownership in the privatization process, some moves have occurred. These have been in the form of manager-employee buyouts and of pension funds buying part of the equity capital sold in auctions, or implicitly as unfunded liabilities of the pension funds meant lower prices for the enterprises sold. The benefits of this partial democratization of capital did not reach, however, the lower income groups, as the program did not open room for their participation in the process, despite their entitlements to government liabilities.

With respect to the privatization by the states, Chart 3 shows the share of each industry and reveals that in this case electricity has been by far the dominant one.

Turning to the efficiency and profitability gains, an overall evaluation of the performance of the federal SOEs in the period 1981-94 was done by Pinheiro and Giambiagi.[17] Their findings show disappointing results by the SOEs, both in terms of profitability and of dividends received by the Treasury. Taking the whole period, the ratio of profits to net assets was, on average, a negative 2.5%, and the situation became worse at the end of the period, when this rate fell to minus 5.4% between 1988 and 1994. Taking into account only the major groups in mining, electricity, oil and telecommunications, this last ratio was positive, but only 3.5%, after having reached 11% in the 1987-94 years. Moreover, from 1988 to 1994, a period for which data on dividends are

[17] Pinheiro and Giambiagi (1997).

available, their total was only 0.4% of the total capital invested by the federal government in the SOEs.

One of the causes of this disappointing performance was the wage policies of the SOEs. We undertook a comprehensive analysis of wage differentials between private and SOEs in the mid-eighties, using surveys of wage and other characteristics of individual workers, based on forms filled by the firms every year, as required by the Ministry of Labor.[18] In ten industries, we compared the wages of the workers in private and state-owned enterprises. After correcting for differences in education, age, gender and experience, we found sizable differentials in favor of the workers of the SOEs, reaching as high as 80% of the wage differential net of the workers' characteristics. This occurred when the characteristics of the workers were valued according to the criteria of the private sector, as measured by the regression coefficients of the workers′ characteristics in the wage equation of that sector.

Turning to the impact of privatization, a major study was concluded in late 1996. It is the most technically solid and comprehensive produced thus far on this issue. The study, by Pinheiro (1996), analyzes the performance of 50 former SOEs before and after privatization. It uses a methodology that has been adopted by other studies directed at evaluating the change in performance of the firms following privatization.[19] The methodology includes the sign test and the Wilcoxon Signed Rank Test. As the author describes both, "the first measures the proportion of firms that have shown changes in the expected direction, while the second adjusts this measure taking into account the size of the change... In both cases, what is being tested is whether there has been a change in performance by comparing the arithmetic average of the variables before and after privatization".[20] For the large number of firms in his sample, Pinheiro obtained data for periods covering 1 to 4 years before and after privatization and did not take into account the data of the year when the sale became effective, as the change of control occurred within that year.

The study covered eight variables: net sales, net profit, net assets, investment, fixed investment, number of employees, debt and an index of liquidity. From these variables, other six were derived to measure efficiency (sales and profit by employee), the rate of return (profit to sales and to net assets) and the propensity to invest (investment to sales and to assets). Pinheiro separated the companies privatized in the eighties from those sold thereafter, and

[18] Macedo (1985).
[19] Among them, Meggison et al. (1994) as cited by the author.
[20] Pinheiro (1996), p.365.

the number of observations ranged from 29 to 46, depending on the variable (14 to 19 in the first period, and 11 to 27 in the second).[21]

The conclusion was that "in general, the obtained results confirm that privatization brings a significant improvement... of the performance of the firms. Thus, for most of the variables, the null hypothesis of no change in behavior is rejected in favor of the alternative hypotheses that privatization increases the production, the efficiency, the profitability and the propensity to invest, reduces employment and improve the financial indicators of the firms."

The analysis by Pinheiro is full of details and extensive tables of data and results. In addition to the general conclusion, for the purposes of the this paper is important to underscore some specific points. First, the improvements are stronger in the case of change of control than in the cases where only a minority participation was sold, thus confirming that the change in property brings more incentives to managers and workers. Second, the improvements are also stronger for the companies more recently privatized, thus showing that the results are better when combined with other policies, such as liberalization of the economy, positive interest rates and reduced access to Treasury resources. Third, the reduction in employment, particularly for the privatization of the nineties, was sizable– on the average, 48%– and was lower in the case of production workers – 27%–. This confirms the hypothesized practice of overstaffing presented in section II. Finally, some of the improvements occurred when the firms were prepared for privatization, thus showing that when there is political will the management of the SOEs can be improved. The problem was that this political will was not present in the past, nor could it be guaranteed for the future and under other governments.

Thus, from the point of view of bringing more efficiency, profitability and better financial indicators to the privatized firms, the evidence shows that the program has been a success. Of course, an analysis such as the one developed by Pinheiro is needed for the privatization of the late nineties, and continued monitoring of the former SOEs would be important to follow their future developments.

---

[21] Pinheiro's analysis did not address the effects on top executives, but taking into account that 115 SOEs were privatized from 1991 to 1998, and an average of 10 directors per company, this means that 1150 directors ceased to be appointed largely by political criteria, not to mention managers, secretaries and others chosen in the same fashion. Another important area offering room for increased efficiency by the private sector is the management of advertising expenditures. These expenditures in the SOEs have been an important source of political patronage, as in the cases of careless support of cultural events and sports competitions and teams. Moreover, the patronage often goes directly into the political process, such as when an advertising firm that gets a SOE account provides expertise and resources for candidates favored by the government.

Higher profitability could have been achieved alone by higher prices at the expense of the consumer in concentrated markets, without an increase in efficiency in the managerial and technical sense. However, as a rule this has not been the case. Notice that major privatized companies such as Companhia Siderúrgica Nacional , Embraer, Usiminas, Siderúrgica Tubarão and Vale do Rio Doce also operate in international markets where they have no role as price setters. Moreover, the country has been opened to import competition, which was particularly enhanced by an overvalued exchange rate from 1994 to early 1999.

Another important issue is the fact that foreign investors are a major part of the new owners of the privatized companies. This leads to two important consequences. In the case of asset distribution, it means that a larger part of the capital stock of the economy now belongs to foreigners. In the case of income distribution, a group thus far neglected in the Brazilian literature – foreign investors – must receive a greater attention than in the past, as it will get a larger share of income. An alternative procedure would be to limit the discussion to the national income alone.

Table 4 shows that foreign direct investment increased sharply in 1997 and 1998, in large part as the result of the privatization program. As we have seen, it was in these two years that a major component of the program, the telecommunications sector, was pushed ahead, and it was in this program that foreign participation was stronger. The table also shows that the share of foreign direct investment that came to buy existing firms, as in the case of the privatization program, sharply increased in 1997 and 1998. The result of the larger investments has been the sharp growth of the remittances abroad by foreign investors, as profits and dividends, as revealed in the last column of the table.

These remittances are placing under further strain the disequilibrium in the external accounts, as measured by the current account balance, and it is likely that they will increase further in the future as foreign investors follow the above mentioned cycle in which, after a period of capitalization of the companies, comes another where the emphasis is on receiving earnings. Moreover, as a large part of the money has come for investment in the privatized companies that produce non-tradable services, such as energy and telecommunications, the strain on the tradables sector will be stronger.

Moving to the question of financing, a criticism that has been directed at the program refers to the fact that in some cases the buyers of a SOE have received loans from BNDES at favored rates. This has occurred in the case of the electric companies auctioned by state governments and also in the federal area when some groups interested in the Telecom program had access to the BNDES resources. The government has repudiated the allegations that a subsidy is implicit in the lower than market interest rates charged by the bank, as the BNDES is the only domestic source of long term financing, and cannot be compared to external markets offering short-term financing. Moreover, the government argues, the BNDES resources come mainly from marked funds, such as those whose interest costs are below the lending rate for all borrowers, not just participants in the privatization program. Regardless of fitting a strict definition of subsidy, it is clearly a favored scheme. Again, as in the access to the efficiency gains that come with privatization, there is the question of access to the opportunity of profiting from a scheme of this sort, which is not open to everyone, in general, and to the poorest groups, in particular. The conclusion is that these loans at favored rates also make inequality worse.

Although the privatization can be rated a success in terms of gains in efficiency and profits, the same cannot be said, however, of its impact on income distribution, as this opportunity to gain has been limited to Brazilian and foreign capitalists. Even when democratization of capital ownership was found in the process, it has been a minor component and, again, to the benefit of those already relatively well-off. The funding of the pension liabilities of workers linked to the National Social Security and Welfare System and the use of the deposits of the FGTS in forming funds that would participate in the privatization process, alternatives that could have ameliorated asset and income inequality, have not been adopted. Other income and asset gains, such as those in the trade of the "rotten money" used in the process and the loans at favored rates, have also gone to the wealthy. Thus, the privatization process has led to increased asset and income inequality.

In the medium and long term, there is room for some alleviation of this result. This depends on how the government uses the increases in tax collections brought about by privatization to expand social expenditures targeted to the poorest groups.[22] Moreover, there are still some companies to be privatized and they could be used to redeem social security and welfare liabilities in such a way as to reduce asset and income inequality.

We will now turn to examining another objective of the program, the use of revenue from privatization to reduce debt. This could have lowered interest rates, with a favorable impact on income distribution.

IV THE FISCAL CRISIS AND THE EXTERNAL DISEQUILIBRIUM

We will proceed by analyzing the more recent developments, namely, those that occurred since President Cardoso came to power in 1995.

[22] Interestingly enough, the recently elected President of Argentina, Fernando De La Rúa, said immediately after election that he plans to increase taxation of the privatized companies (*Folha de S.Paulo*, October 26th, 1999).

Privatization was to help in the fiscal crisis and in the external imbalance. For various reasons, however, the government lost its direction and the intended positive impact disappeared in the middle of major negative moves. First, it started to play the game of reelection, by pushing in Congress a constitutional amendment to allow it. This move harmed the fiscal adjustment in 1996 and 1997, as the government had to engage in pork barrel politics to approve it. Second, as its prestige was linked to price stabilization, and the government was afraid of the impact of a devaluation on prices, it started to defend the real, which became clearly overvalued immediately after its release. It was initially set equal to US$1.00, but soon came down close to R$0.80 to the dollar.[23] A very high interest rate was the major tool in defending the real.

These developments had the effects of aggravating the fiscal crisis and the external imbalance. In the former, by means of deficits in the so-called primary result, which excludes the payment of interest and therefore reflects more genuinely the fiscal policy of the government, and also in the nominal result, which includes interest on the debt. In the external sector, the overvalued exchange rate led both to a deteriorating trade balance and to the worsening of the current account balance, in this case due to the higher interest payments and to the sharp expansion of foreign travel, among other major items.

Let us now show data that illustrate these points. Table 5, which covers the public sector finances, and Table 6, which shows data on the external accounts, reveal several aspects of the worsening of the macroeconomic scenario, which became particularly serious in 1997 and 1998. Thus, the aggravation coincided with the peak of privatization program.

Table 5 shows that the fiscal side had improved from 1990 until 1994, when there was a large primary surplus and also an operational surplus, the latter concept reflecting the nominal deficit, inclusive of interest paid, but net of the effect of indexation. Notice that the primary surplus practically disappeared in 1995, and this led to a serious reversal of the operational result. The net public debt as share of GDP also came down in the early nineties. From 1995 to 1997, the fiscal result became negative, the operational deficit remained high and was seriously aggravated in 1998 and 1999, because of higher interest on a growing debt. From 1994 to 1999 the net public debt as percentage of GDP increased sharply, from around 30% to close to 50%, with most of the increase occurring in the last two years. The very high values of the debt and interest in the first

[23] Overvaluation became the rule for four and a half additional years. By the time the real was finally devalued, in January 1999, the exchange rate was only R$ 1.20 to the dollar, against an inflation which then reached an accumulated rate around 70% since the real had started at parity level in July 1994.

semester of 1999 occurred because of the devaluation, as part of the debt is in dollars and the devaluation is counted as nominal interest.

Notice, in particular, that the increase in debt from 1997 to 1998, that is, R$77.5 billion, or roughly US$65 billion at the prevailing exchange rate is equivalent to 73% of the total value obtained from the privatization (US$88 billion). Looking also at the growth of the debt before and thereafter, the unfortunate and inescapable conclusion is that the contribution of the whole program to the adjustment of the public sector finances was lost as their conditions were seriously aggravated by higher deficits and debt. To put it simply: the money from privatization went down the drain of the disarray in the public finances.

An argument that could be raised against this conclusion would be that without the privatization the fiscal crisis would be even worse. To this, we can counter argue by saying that the privatization has somehow relieved the hard budget constraint of the government. As the budget constraint became the sum of tax receipts plus debt plus privatization resources, there was more room to expand expenditures, including interest, and the government has shown its adherence to Kornai's concept of soft budget constraints, typical of centralized governments whose budgets are only vaguely, if at all, monitored or controlled by Congress and society. Without privatization, the debt would have increased even more and in the end would have faced restrictions from the financial markets. It does not follow, therefore, that without privatization the fiscal crisis would be even worse.

Our argument can be further explained with the help of Chart 4. It shows the public sector net debt as percentage of GDP, from 1990 to 1999, and the shares of the federal government inclusive of Central Bank, the state and local governments and the state enterprises. Notice, in particular, the reduction in the share of the state enterprises following the adjustments of the SOEs for privatization and the program itself, and the increase of the total debt and the growth of the shares of the federal and state and local governments. In the chart, the reduction of the black part of columns opens room for the increase of the gray parts. Without privatization, including restructuring of the SOEs, and assuming a constant share of GDP for the debt owed by them, total debt would have reached not 49.5 % but 66.5% of GDP at the end of the period, plus the reduction in the government debt achieved by the program. This is unthinkable given the conditions of the financial markets. Thus privatization really relaxed the hard budget constraint of the government, or made it softer by reducing the SOEs' debt, as otherwise the other part of the total debt owed by the government could not have increased as it did.

Turning to the external imbalance, which is related to the fiscal disequilibrium as the high interest rates to defend the real compounded in the fiscal deficit and debt, Table 6 also reveals a dramatic worsening of the picture from 1994 to 1998. This is the case for all variables except international reserves, which increased between 1994 and 1996 and decreased thereafter. With the 1999 devaluation, the disequilibrium was reduced, except in the case of interest payments. In the table, the 1999 figures cover the first semester only. The higher interest payments in this semester reflect the higher debt and the reduction in interest receipts due to the loss of reserves.

The use of the interest rate to defend the real is clear from Chart 5, which covers the period September 1997 to September 1999. As international reserves began to fall at the end of 1997 due to the "speculative attack" that followed the crisis in the countries of Southeast Asia, the government raised the basic interest rate from around 20% to about 45%, as shown in the bottom part of the chart. The result was a recovery of reserves which came to renewed pressure in the third quarter of 1998, this time due to the crisis in Russia. The government tried again to reduce the loss of reserves by increasing the interest rate, this time without success. Devaluation became inevitable, but the interest rate increased anyway to contain the overshooting of the exchange rate, which reached R$2.14 in February. The increase in reserves in April 1999 reflects the effect of the IMF rescue package.

It is also interesting to look at what was left from the increased exposure of Brazil to financial globalization in the period 1994 to 1999, as shown by Chart 6, which covers the flow of foreign resources in the period. As expected, foreign direct investment came to stay, with repatriation representing less than 10% of the total inflow. Short run money, in the form of financial investments, came only to profit from the high interest rates and only roughly 10% of the total inflows remained at the end of the period. External debt increased by R$84 billion and together with foreign direct investment actually financed the external disequili-brium. Privatization brought foreign direct investment as expected, but as in the case of fiscal crisis its contribution was overshadowed by the misguided macroeconomic policies of the period.

In the same fashion as the effect of privatization in softening the hard fiscal budget constraint, the foreign direct investment that followed privatization also relieved the external constraint, as it allowed the financing of higher current account deficits. Although this is usually considered a positive consequence, it can also be viewed as negative, in the sense that it also postponed adjustment in the form of devaluation. Interestingly enough, the devaluation in early 1999 came after the wave of the Telecom privatization program in 1998, in which the presence of foreign direct investments was stronger. These investments were seen by the market as a sign that the government could hold on to the overvalued real. Thus, if the privatization program had proceeded with full force, a likely outcome is that overvaluation could have been further extended; as the program came to a halt, privatization came sooner.

V THE IMPACT ON ASSET AND INCOME DISTRIBUTION AND OTHER CONCLUSIONS

Most of the consequences and hypotheses listed in the analytical framework of Table 2 and marked with an (*) have been confirmed by the Brazilian privatization program, as presented in this paper. An exception occurred in the case of the last hypothesis listed in the table, namely, that the program would reduce debt, opening room for lower interest rates and having a positive impact on income distribution. This has not occurred because the program has been developed in a context of macroeconomic policies that have aggravated fiscal crisis and external disequilibrium. Worse yet, by providing additional resources for the government, the program has contributed to softening the hard fiscal budget constraint and to delaying the adjustment of the external sector as it brought inflows of foreign resources that helped in defending the real.

However complex this combination of privatization, fiscal crisis and external imbalance might be, the conclusion with regard to income distribution is straightforward. The poorest people did not have access to the immediate gains from privatization, did not see their pension and welfare liabilities covered in the process, and have not gained from the high interest rates that came in the wave of the fiscal crisis cum overvaluation. The government has shown no firm commitment to democratizing capital ownership, an objective initially set for the privatization program but that was never forcefully pursued.

The unraveling of this complex combination of events go well beyond this. At the start of this paper, we were primarily concerned with the impact of the changes in asset and income distribution that follow a privatization process. However, privatization has been carried out in a context of aggravated fiscal crisis and external disequilibrium, which has left as a major consequence a sharp increase in the public debt, thus more than nullifying the intended positive impact of the privatization on the fiscal side. As a consequence, public assets have been sacrificed in the privatization process, but in the end the liabilities of the society in general have sharply increased. Returning to our "Chapter 11" metaphor, the situation can be compared to a firm that sells assets to cover liabilities, but in the end is worse off because the liabilities have enlarged instead of diminishing. These increased liabilities, with the interest that accrue to them, constitute an enormous, very serious and lasting problem

As the budget is now showing again a primary surplus, taxes are now being used to pay at least a part of the interest bill. Moreover, as tax receipts have increased and indirect taxes respond for the largest share of taxes in Brazil, the poorest will bear a relatively high share of the burden. In any case, the largest part of the increased liabilities, plus interest, on income distribution, will not be felt immediately, as the government debt and interest simply piles up. Thus, except for part of the interest bill, the burden of the enlarged debt is not distributed and will be left for generations to come.

In any case, we can speculate about who will more likely suffer the burden in the future. If the larger debt is to be serviced by taxes and if the regressive tax system is maintained, the poorest will bear a disproportionate share. In the short run, the effects of the larger liabilities, even of the interest bill actually paid, might not appear or will come up only marginally in the income distribution statistics of the Census Bureau. Foreign capitalists do not fill the Brazilian census questionnaires and domestic owners of government debt might hide or understate the increase in their interest income, given that compounded interest on their government securities is not disposable income. Moreover, as part of the gains accrue to banks and companies, the profits might not be distributed, therefore not revealing themselves as personal income. Many people also confuse composed interest with indexation, as in the past it was difficult to separate one thing from another. Thus, asset and income distribution is being aggravated, but it will not necessarily be revealed by the collected income data and the inequality indices based on them.

In contrast with the poorest groups, some middle class groups and rich Brazilians, together with foreigners, have reaped most of the gains that have emerged from the opportunities open by the privatization, and have also gained from the disarray in public finances and in the external sector that led to advantages to the owners of financial capital. However minor, some alleviation of these distortions can be made if the resources raised by the government, by taxing the increased profits of the privatized companies, are used in government social expenditures targeted to the poorest groups. These groups will also benefit by the increased efficiency of the former SOEs, if this leads to lower prices and increased investment. As most of them operate in concentrated markets, their efficiency and their prices should be closely monitored, together with their ability to promote investment thus contributing to the growth of the economy. In the end, with privatization Brazil is seeking a new engine of growth, the work of which will be crucial to generate employment and income for the poorest groups. Moreover, since there are still some firms to privatize, the government will have another opportunity to use these assets to democratize capital ownership and to improve asset and income distribution.

The need of resources dictated by the fiscal crisis and by the external imbalance has been appointed by government officers as the main reason for neglecting the objective of democratization of capital, in general, and asset and income redistribution, in particular. Other excuses have also been presented, such as the fact that the redemption of social security and welfare liabilities would have required time consuming and politically difficult changes in legislation, even in the Constitution.

Changes would have included a new social security system parallel to INSS, in the form of private pension funds covering formal-sector workers and public servants, the transfer of liabilities from one system to another, the end to the existing guarantee of fixed benefits, and a reform of the legislation of capital markets, in the areas of corporate governance, in general, and rights of minority shareholders, in particular. Another difficulty would have been to calculate the balances owed individually to those entitled to the social security and welfare liabilities. This would have required the action of other ministries not linked to the privatization program, such as the Ministry of Welfare and Social Security, as well as a coordination among the various branches of the government that has not yet taken place. These difficulties are impressive, but the major reason for not undertaking a different course of action was because a genuine concern with the idea of democratizing capital ownership has not existed either at the bottom or at the top of the government hierarchy. The privatization program has also been full of other obstacles, but they have been surpassed because was, at least until 1998, strongly committed to the idea. Only now, that most of the SOEs, including major "jewels" have gone, is the idea of democratizing capital ownership resurfacing again in some areas of the government, in the weaker form of large scale flotations.

One cannot underestimate the major difficulties that would lie ahead if another course of action were to be taken, as suggested by this paper. They could be a combination of the problems involved in the large scale flotations of the British type and in the mass privatization undertaken in transition economies, with those typical of the Brazilian institutions and of the expectations of the country's common citizens. Many Brazilians are not familiar with the institutions of modern capitalism, such as shareholding, pension funds and capital markets, and have shown an enormous resistance in moving from state guaranteed fixed benefits to variable ones, either in social security and welfare or financial markets, which have been indexed because of high inflation.

Both the pensions of the INSS and the FGTS deposits have been accordingly indexed, the latter plus interest. Would the citizens be willing to move into the riskier realm of share or fund holdings, voluntarily buying shares in large-scale flotations? Would they politically accept the exchange of the liabilities that the INSS and the FGTS owe to them for shareholding or fund participation? Would efficient management of the former SOEs be guaranteed? How to avoid having the control of these enterprises fall into the hands of the groups referred to by Nellis (1999) as the "resourceful, agile and well-connected", as was typical of the privatization in many transition economies?

In spite of all these difficulties, we insist the alternative route suggested in this paper, or others along the same line, should have been tried and must be given a chance what remains to be privatized in Brazil. This would be tantamount to creating a new model, to compete with the one developed thus far, in a dispute stimulating to both, and healthy for the economy, as it would bring to the scene the discussion of neglected issues such as democratizing capital ownership, reform of capital markets, and popularization of pension funds, which we see crucial for changing the asset distribution which is at the root of the high income inequality.

This alternative course is full of difficulties, but if bold measures are not undertaken now, no relevant changes will be made, and for times ahead we will continue to discuss marginal changes in the Gini coefficient. Governments are judged not only for what they accomplish, but also for what they attempt, as this allows them at least a face-saving alternative. At this moment, the government has no alternative to offer, not even one to save its blushed face.

REFERENCES

BNDES (Banco Nacional de Desenvolvimento Econômico e Social), Secretaria Geral de Apoio à Desestatização, *Privatizações no Brasil – 1991/99*. Rio de Janeiro: BNDES, 1999a.

_______, *Sistema de Informações*. Rio de Janeiro: BNDES, 1999b.

MACEDO, Roberto B.M., "A Critical Review of the Relation Between the Post-1964 Wage Policy and the Worsening of the Brazilian Income Distribution in the Sixties", *Explorations in Economic Research* (No.1, 1977).

MACEDO, Roberto B.M., *Os Salários nas Empresas Estatais*. São Paulo: Nobel, 1985.

MEGGISON, W.L., R.C. Nash and M. van Randenborgh, "The financial and operating performance of newly privatized firms: an international empirical analysis". *Journal of Finance* 49(2), 1994: 403-452.

NELLIS, John, "Time to Rethink Privatization in Transition Economies". *International Finance Corporation, Discussion Paper* 38 (1999)

PINHEIRO, Armando Castelar, "Impactos microeconômicos da Privatização no Brasil", *Pesquisa e Planejamento Econômico* 26(3) (Dec.1996): 357-98.

PINHEIRO, Armando Castelar, and Fabio Giambiagi, "Lucratividade, dividendos e investimentos das empresas estatais: uma contribuição para o debate sobre privatização no Brasil". *Revista Brasileira de Economia* 51 (January-March, 1997).

Table 1 : Relevant Items of an Imaginary Balance Sheet of the Brazilian Public Sector

Assets	Liabilities
A-1 Equity in State Enterprises	L-1 Short Term Debt (Treasury Bonds)
A-2 Loans from the FGTS (Workers' Tenure Guarantee Fund)	L-2 Long Term Debt (such as Agrarian Debt Securities and Siderbrás Bonds)
	L-3 Unfunded Pension Liabilities L-3-1 Workers of SOEs L-3-2 Public Servants L-3-3 INSS – National Social Welfare and Security System
	L-4 Deposits in the FGTS

Table 2: Privatization, Assets and Income Distribution - Assumptions, Consequences and Testable Hypotheses

Assumptions	Consequences	Testable hypotheses
SOEs are profit maximizers.	SOEs have suffered from technical and pricing inefficiencies (*). Access to privatization represents opportunity to profit from the correction of such inefficiencies(*).	Productivity and profit will increase after privatization(*). Overstaffing will be corrected(*). Wage and price(*) policies of privatized firms will more closely follow market rules. Groups used to rents from the state enterprises will lose(*) Privatized companies will pay more taxes after privatization. Check how the government will spend the money, for the impact on income distribution.
	State enterprises will accumulate unfunded pension liabilities (*).	Minimum price set by evaluation will compensate for them(*). In relation to other groups entitled to the unfunded liabilities, workers of privatized firms will gain, maintaining or worsening income inequality(*).

Table 2 (continued)

Assumptions	Consequences	Testable hypotheses
Strategic concerns, political reasons and scale of capital led the government into public services and concentrated sectors. Pressure from fiscal crisis and from external disequilibrium have been dominant in setting the rules and the timing of privatization.	No concern for democratization of capital, except in a few cases of manager-employee buyout(*).	Access to privatization and its gains becomes limited to some groups(*). Scale and expertise required will attract big business and foreign investors; income gained will flow to foreigners and the wealthy(*). Domestic inequality will be worsened (*).
	To push privatization, money was lent to buyers(*).	Check if this was done at favored rates and who benefited from them(*).
	The use of "rotten money" was also allowed to pay for privatization(*).	Owners and buyers(*) of the securities have benefited from the rule. Income inequality will worsen.
	Privatization will be followed by regulatory practices managed by government agencies.	Check for biases in regulatory practices, such as favorable prices, and groups who benefited from them.
	Revenue from privatization is to be used to reduce debt, opening room for lower interest rates(*)	Owners of financial capital will be paid less; income inequality will be lessened(*)

Table 3: Brazilian Privatization Program – 1991/1999 By Components – US$ million (*)

Year	NPD	Telecom	States	Sum
1991	1,988	-	-	1,988
1992	3,383	-	-	3,383
1993	4,188	-	-	4,188
1994	2,315	-	-	2,315
1995	1,628	-	-	1,628
1996	4,749	-	1,770	6,519
1997	7,824	4,734	15,116	27,674
1998	2,737	23,948	10,857	37,542
1999(**)	49	421	2,603	3,073
TOTAL	**28,861**	**29,103**	**30,346**	**88,310**

(*) Includes transferred debt.

(**) Until July

Table 4: Foreign Investments in Brazil
Total, for the Acquisition of Existing Firms, and Remittances Abroad 1993-97

Year	Total US$ billion (A)	For Acquisition of Existing Firms US$ billion (B)	[(B)/(A)]%	Remittances Abroad US$ billion
1994	2.1	0.008	0.38	2.5
1995	5.5	1.5	27.3	2.6
1996	10.5	3.1	29.5	2.4
1997	18.7	10.4	55.5	5.6
1998	28.7	21.3	74.1	7.2

Source: SOBEET (Brazilian Society for the Study of Transnational Companies), Central Bank and *Conjuntura Econômica*, as published by *Folha de S.Paulo* (October 3rd, 1999)

Table 5: Public Sector(PS) Results, Interest Paid and Debt - 1991-1998

Year	Primary Result as % of GDP	Operational Result as % of GDP	Interest on Debt in R$ billion	Interest on Debt as % of GDP	Net Public Debt in R$ billion	Net Public Debt as % of GDP
1991	2.8	-1.4	(...)	(...)	(...)	37.9
1992	2.3	-2.2	(...)	(...)	(...)	37.2
1993	2.7	0.3	(...)	(...)	(...)	33.0
1994	5.3	1.4	(...)	(...)	(...)	29.2
1995	0.4	-4.9	(...)	(...)	(...)	30.5
1996	-0.1	-3.8	46.4	5.8	269.2	33.3
1997	-1.0	-4.3	45.6	5.1	308.4	34.5
1998	0.0	-7.5	73.1	8.1	385.9	42.4
1999(*)	3.2	-9.4	89.8	18.4	495.3	49.5

Source: Secretary of National Treasury, Minister of Finance.

(*) Until June. (...) Data not relevant to the arguments developed in the paper and whose inclusion would require correction for inflation of the figures in R$, not important from 1996 to 1998.

Table 6: External Accounts - 1990-1999 - US$ million

Year	Trade Balance	Current Account Balance	Net External Debt	Internat'l Reserves	Net Interest Payments
1990	10,753	-3,782	86,753	9,973	-9,748
1991	10,579	-1,407	83,590	9,406	-8,621
1992	15,308	6,144	87,081	23,754	-7,253
1993	12,938	-592	82,059	32,211	-8,280
1994	10,440	-1,689	80,862	38,806	-6,338
1995	-3,158	-17,972	77,473	51,840	-8,158
1996	-5,554	-24,347	83,982	60,110	-9,840
1997	-8,357	-33,054	115,587	52,173	-10,391
1998	-6,484	-34,981	166,096	44,556	-11,947
1999(*)	-524	-13,830	(...)	42,156	-8,644

(*) Until July.

Source: Central Bank.

Chart 1:

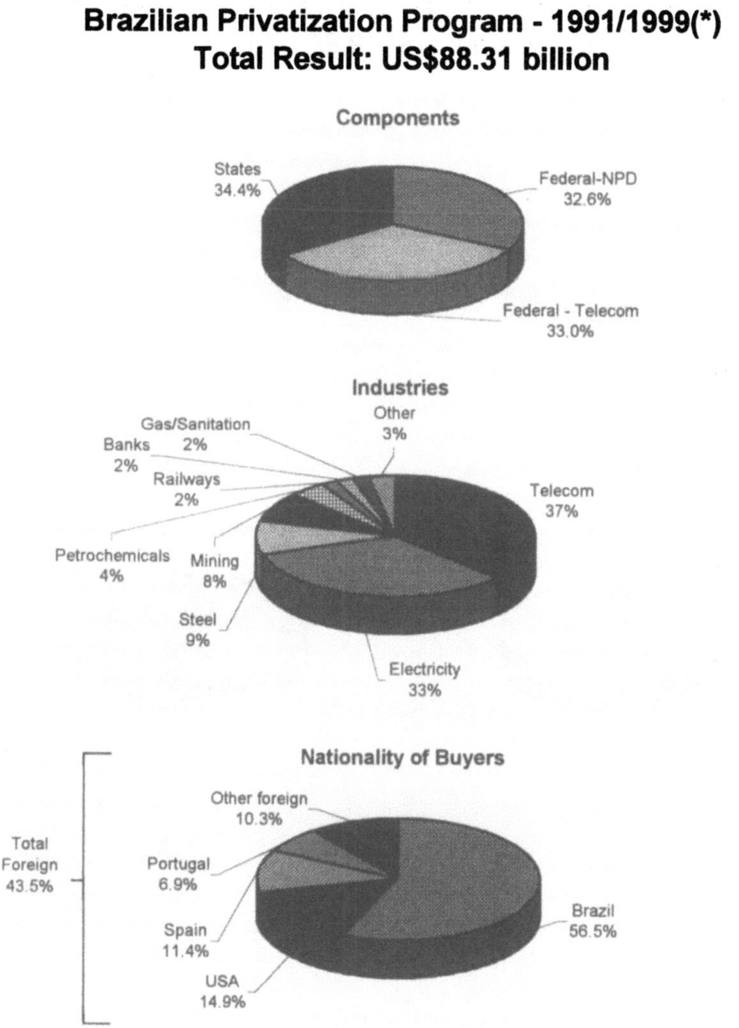
Brazilian Privatization Program - 1991/1999(*)
Total Result: US$88.31 billion
Components
States
34.4%
Federal-NPD
32.6%
Federal - Telecom
33.0%
Industries
Gas/Sanitation
2%
Other
3%
Banks
2%
Railways
2%
Telecom
37%
Petrochemicals
4%
Mining
8%
Steel
9%
Electricity
33%
Nationality of Buyers
Other foreign
10.3%
Total
Foreign
43.5%
Portugal
6.9%
Spain
11.4%
USA
14.9%
Brazil
56.5%

Chart 2:

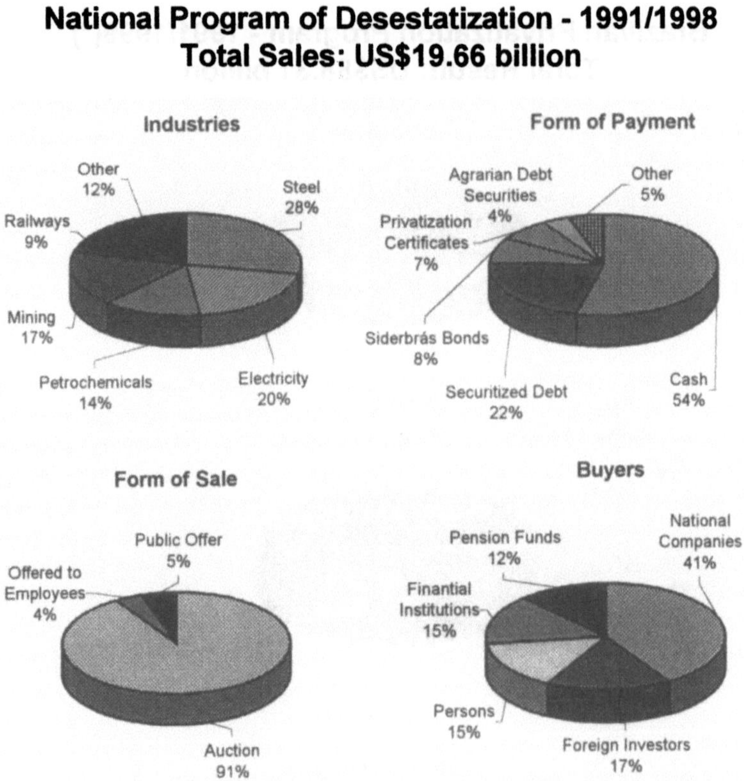
National Program of Desestatization - 1991/1998
Total Sales: US$19.66 billion
Industries
Other 12%
Steel 28%
Railways 9%
Mining 17%
Petrochemicals 14%
Electricity 20%
Form of Payment
Agrarian Debt Securities 4%
Other 5%
Privatization Certificates 7%
Siderbrás Bonds 8%
Securitized Debt 22%
Cash 54%
Form of Sale
Public Offer 5%
Offered to Employees 4%
Auction 91%
Buyers
Pension Funds 12%
National Companies 41%
Finantial Institutions 15%
Persons 15%
Foreign Investors 17%

Chart 3:

Privatization by the States - 1996/99
Total Sales in Auctions: US$28.605 billion

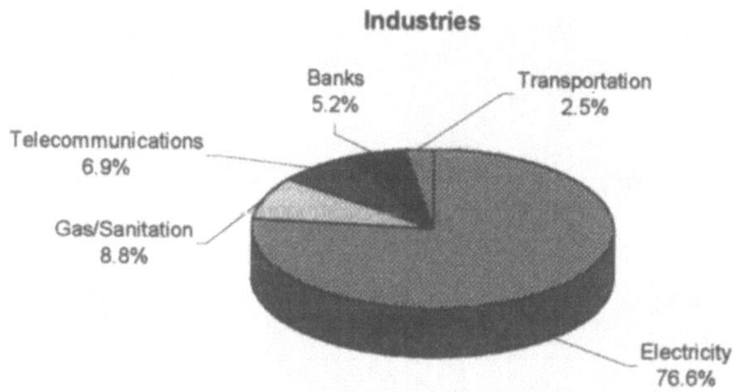

Chart 4:

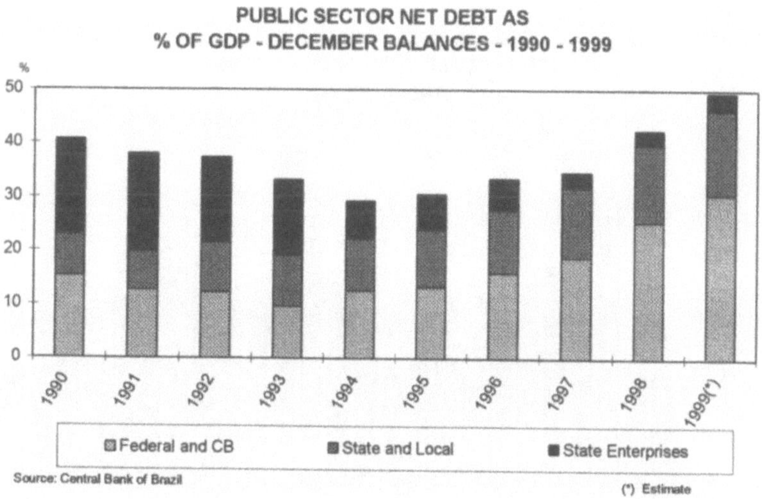

Chart 5:

International Reserves (*) - 1997 - 1999
US$ million

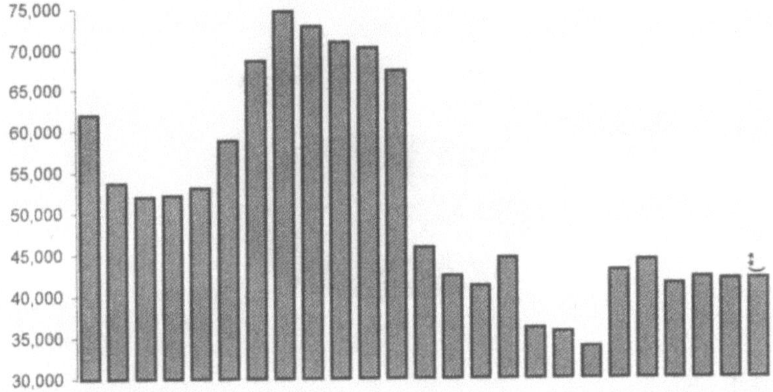

(*)International liquidity concept
(**) Estimate

Interest rate (*) - % per annum
1997 - 1999

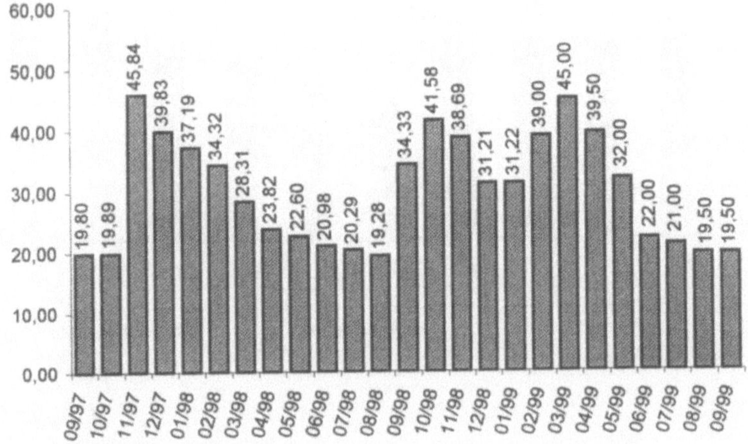

Source: Central Bank of Brazil
(*) SELIC rate per annum at the beginning of each month based on daily rate and 252 days.

Chart 6:

Flow of Foreign Resources - 1994/1999 (until July)
US$ million

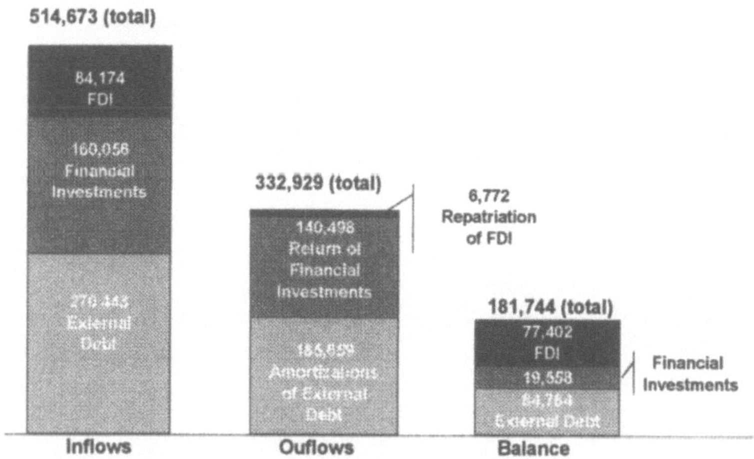

Source: Banco Bilbao Vizcaya, Working Paper by Octávio de Barros, Folha de S.Paulo (8-22-99)

Cooperation and Integration in Goods Markets

SOME EMPIRICAL EVIDENCE ON THE MACROECONOMIC BEHAVIOR OF MERCOSUR COUNTRIES

Alejandro D. Jacobo[1 2]

I. Introduction

The process of creating a European Union has triggered a substantial amount of research, both theoretical and empirical, to better understand the preconditions of this development for Europe. Some of these studies have adopted the idea that the existence of similar business fluctuations is a necessary condition for the harmonization of economic policies and institutions (Christodoulakis *et. al.*, 1995; Fiorito and Kollintzas, 1994). In fact, the synchronism in the cycles facilitates common policies among countries involved in an integration process. In this case, where coincidences exist, policies to cope with the cycle can be effectively designed since the phases are going to be similar across countries. In spite of the fact that this is of extraordinary relevance for the region, there is not any study about Latin American economies by which one could determine the existence of such a uniform behavior.

It is true that there is an enormous literature trying to document some evidence about cyclical fluctuations after Kydland and Prescott's (1990) reports of the U.S. business cycle facts, but this reactivation (with a different methodology) of the research agenda of Burns and Mitchell in the 40s at the NBER generated worldwide country-specific works with the same structure as that of Kydland and Prescott's. Although there are some studies about individual economies, Latin American countries were left aside from this line of research mainly for lack of stability and lack of data (Fullerton and Araki, 1996; Mena, 1995).[3] Notwithstanding one should recognize the existence of other studies, their authors are interested in using some "econometric pyrotechnics" rather than in determining the existence of a "rhythmical beat" among the economies.[4] In other words, because of the problems mentioned above, and a lack of emphasis in the comparison of business cycle facts among countries, Latin America is still behind in its evaluation of the preconditions of the integration process.

---

[1] The author would like to thank Roberto Macedo for helpful remarks on a previous version of this paper.

[2] Instituto de Economía y Finanzas, Facultad de Ciencias Económicas, Universidad Nacional de Córdoba.

[3] For a recent study about Chile see Belaisch and Soto (1998).

[4] The study of Carrera et al. (1999) seems to be aligned with those interested in the use of different econometric methodologies.

A related literature investigates the extent to which the countries appear to be symmetric or asymmetric with respect to the nature of shocks underlying their economies. The argument is that if the shocks that are impinging upon a particular economy and the rest of the countries do so differently (asymmetrically), then the monetary and fiscal policies cannot be carried out efficiently. The curiosity in such behavior arises because the integration process tends to its *momentum* when a monetary union takes place. If this is the case, in response to country-specific shocks the governments will no longer have the option of adopting a monetary policy which differs from that of the union as a whole, and the weight attached to these arguments depends on the incidence of the shocks.

There are some studies for Europe that focus on these "shocking aspects of monetary unification" (Bayoumi and Eichengreen, 1992b). Although with an explicit recognition that the monetary union is at all times a political decision (Eichengreen, 1993), these studies want to show the existence of an economic argument that supports the currency area. About this argument, the starting point of the literature is the work of Mundell (1961). In his framework, the incidence of disturbances across regions is a critical determinant of the design of a currency area, and countries would find it optimal whenever the nominal exchange rate is not necessary to adjust the real one at every time that these economies face asymmetric shocks. Again, and not surprisingly, Latin American countries have been ignored. In fact, while numerous empirical studies have been developed for the case of the European Union, only marginal attention has been given to the case of MERCOSUR (Southern Common Market).

The paragraphs above constitute merely an outline to intuitively discover the goals of this paper. About its first aim, the reader could infer the implicit interest to find the degree of homogeneity of Latin American economies, and hence the feasibility of policy harmonization. The countries to be examined are those related with the integration phenomenon that in the Southern Cone is named MERCOSUR (Argentina, Brazil, Paraguay and Uruguay). Currently, MERCOSUR has further extended its scope by entering free trade agreements with Bolivia and Chile, and that is why these two additional countries have joined to the study. The period selected for the analysis is the last quarter of the century (1970-1997), and the characterization of the GDP fluctuations in the past will be use only to predict the likely outcome of the integration process.

The second aim is related with the mechanisms underlying the business fluctuations with special reference to the size and correlation of shocks. While this featuring helps to describe the economies, it also helps to discover whether the economic argument for an optimum currency area exists.

With both aims, the remainder of the paper is organized as follows. Section two is devoted to some generalities about cyclical fluctuations and shocks; together with the methodologies employed to remove the trend from the data and to discover the shocks. Section three presents the results. The concluding comments are in Section four.

II. Fluctuations and Shocks

II.1 Fluctuations

Although the characterization of GDP fluctuations is an interesting and motivating feature, their discovery is not less attractive. In fact, cyclical fluctuations are not such if the trend is not properly defined. For this reason, the first step is to separate the fluctuations from the GDP growth trend, something that is a common practice in macroeconomics.

The usual exercise for this purpose is to consider that the economic aggregates wave around a long run uniform trend line (Burns and Mitchell, 1946). This point of view is supported by the hypothesis that the growth rate of real variables is explained by exogenous factors such as population or technological changes. The notion that the secular component does not fluctuate much over short periods of time, but it does slowly and smoothly with respect to the cyclical component, has led to the practice of "detrending" the series using time as an explanatory variable.

However, the evidence has suggested that the secular movement change over time, and most of the theory has rejected the hypothesis that these rates of growth are constant. Therefore, it is assumed that transitory changes modify the rate. Once this assumption is accepted, the economic literature admits the existence of a stochastic trend as a variable in modeling macroeconomic fluctuations (Beveridge and Nelson, 1981; Nelson and Plosser, 1982).

These recent theories arose mainly after the re-definition of the cycle made by Lucas (1977) who thinks that business fluctuations are deviations of aggregate output from trend (without an explicit explanation of what trend to use).[5] His incomplete definition gives the chance to use the trend considered more appropriate for the economies under analysis.

Lucas' point of view of the cycle is in clear contrast with that of Mitchell's. In fact, while Mitchell represents business cycles as sequences of expansions and contractions, particularly emphasizing turning points, Lucas does not think in terms of sequences of the cycles as inevitable waves of economic activity, and he does not consider necessary to distinguish the different phases of the cycle either. While it is true that with Lucas the detailed description about the phases is also abandoned, it is also true that with him the interest in the cycles is recovered.

[5] His definition was completed by Kydland and Prescott (1990) who provided an explicit procedure for calculating the time series trend that successfully mimics the smooth curves most business cycle researchers would draw through the plots of the data.

The studies of business cycle flourished from the 1920s through 1940s; but in the 1950s and 1960s, with the development of the structural system of equations approach that Koopmans advocated, business cycles ceased to be an active area of economic research. Now, once again, the study of business cycles, in the form of recurrent fluctuations, is alive, and instrumental in bringing cycles back into the mainstream of economic research is the important paper of Lucas (1977) (see Kydland and Prescott (1990) for a quick reference).

In short, what matters here is that if the rate of technological change were constant, then the natural logarithm of real GDP would be a linear function of time. Since the rate of technological changes varies (both over time and across countries), detrending using a linear function of time could be inappropriate. Formally, the key question is to perceive which is the trend of GDP series, and for this one can distinguish two kinds of process.[6]

The first one is the process through which the series could be modeled by a deterministic trend plus a stochastic process with zero mean. This is known as a "trend stationary" process.

This first procedure is associated with the traditional point of view of business cycle through the equation $y_t = a + bt + e_t$ in which y_t is formed by a stationary fluctuation (e_t) around the time trend ($a + bt$). Since y_t is not stationary due to the presence of t, stationarity is easily achieved by removing the trend, that is, using time as an explanatory variable. In this context a stationary fluctuation appears after the trend is removed.

The second process is related to one in which the first (or higher) difference of the series is a stationarity and an invertible autoregressive moving average (ARMA) process.

This procedure appears when the series is $y_t = a + y_{t-1} + e_t$, *id est*, the series could be modeled using its past values, a drift (a) and a stationary disturbance (e_t). This is known as a random procedure with a drift, and the first difference of the series ($y_t - y_{t-1}$) is a stationary process ($a + e_t$). The fact that stationarity is achieved through differencing justifies labeling it as a "difference stationary". This model represents the unit root hypothesis.

The test of unit root is useful to distinguish which of the two processes best explains the non-stationarity behavior of the series, contributing to answer if the non-stationarity arises from a deterministic or a stochastic trend. From the macroeconomic point of view, it suggests whether a shock influences the growth of the economy in a transitory way or in a permanent one. Although the Augmented-Dickey Fuller test is a formal one to identify if the variable should be considered in levels or in differences (each unit root needs a difference for an ARMA model to fit

[6] In other words, it is necessary to discompose the GDP series into a stationary (trend) and stationary (cyclical) components, because certain characteristics of the data are valid only if the series are stationary.

the data), sometimes it tends to overdifference the series (Enders, 1995; p. 251). For this reason, Box and Jenkings methodology is preferred here.

The first step in this methodology is to choose *d*, the number of times the series should be differenced to make it "approximately" stationary.[7] A plot of the series over time gives a clue as to the nature of the series. If the series appears to grow exponentially, one should take the logarithm and then plot it against the time. If a linear trend is apparent, one should difference the series (or its logarithm) once and plot the differenced series. If this also exhibits a trend, a second differencing might be required.[8] A second way to identify whether differencing is required is to calculate the Autocorrelation Function (ACF) and plot the correlogram. If this plot declines slowly, then differencing is suggested. Then, plot the correlogram of the first difference. If this plot also declines slowly, a second difference is indicated.

With a visual examination of the Autocorrelation and the Partial Autocorrelation Functions (PACF) one can perceive the order of the moving average and the autoregresive processes (see Ramanathan (1992) and Larrain (1981) for further details).[9] The parameter estimates are something intricate. Since there are programs that not only compute ACF and PACF, but also do the estimation, it is not necessary to give further contents. When the procedure is finished the residuals are white noise, or "approximately" white noise.

II.2 Shocks

A rich description could be made distinguishing fluctuations as consequences of different shocks. This analysis is useful since it improves the characterization of the economies. By the way, the analysis is also related to the possibility of an optimum currency area (as stated in Section one). The renewable interest for this concept is the result of the dynamism of the integration phenomena (with special reference to Europe), together with monetary integration as an element of such phenomena.

Although it should be recognized that the political impulse and the economic relations have improved during the last years, a monetary union in MERCOSUR is not in a short distance. In fact, a common currency means an extraordinary sacrifice of monetary autonomy, which turns to be useful against some specific shocks. In a monetary union, the governments will not be able to use a different monetary policy giving up the chance to modify nominal prices. Since monetary policy is useful for adjustments, some problems may arise, and the relevance of these problems depends on the incidence of the shocks.

---

[7] Analysis of time series is not a perfect science. Something may force the researchers to terminate their analysis even if there is still fairly regular residual element.

[8] Economic time series rarely require differencing more than twice (Ramanathan, 1992; p. 497).

[9] Also Nelson (1973) and Vandaele (1983) could be helpful in understanding the processes.

The cost and benefits of a monetary union are estimated in most of the cases on the symmetry or asymmetry of the shocks.[10] Using a shocking perspective, Bayoumi and Eichengreen (1992b) concluded in their study between Germany and other European countries that the European Union is divided in a core and a periphery. In the core the shocks are highly correlated, but this does not happen in the periphery.[11] Besides, the size of the shocks is similar among the core countries, but it is not alike in the rest of Europe. Bayoumi and Einchegreen compare their results with those of a consolidated monetary union as represented by the United States, stating that the correlation in eight regions of the United States is similar to that of the central region of Europe, but is higher than the one of the periphery.

The shocks are going to be obtained using the procedure described by Blanchard and Quah (1989). The purpose of these authors was to reconsider the decomposition of GDP made by Beveridge and Nelson (1981) in its permanent and transitory components. It is with this aim that they developed a model in which supply and demand shocks may influence the GDP: the demand shocks having a transitory effect on output, the supply shocks a permanent one on it.

Consider a system in which the true model can be represented by an infinite moving average representation of a vector of variables X_t and an equal number of shocks E_t:

$$X_t = A_0 E_t + A_1 E_{t-1} + A_2 E_{t-2} + A_3 E_{t-3} + \ldots \tag{3.1}$$

where the matrixes A_i represent the impulse responses functions of the shocks to the element of X. Specifically, let X_t be made up of changes in output and in the monetary aggregate:

$$\begin{bmatrix} \Delta y_t \\ \Delta(m-p)_t \end{bmatrix} = \sum_{i=0}^{\infty} L^i \begin{bmatrix} a_{11i} & a_{12i} \\ a_{21i} & a_{22i} \end{bmatrix} \begin{bmatrix} \varepsilon_{dt} \\ \varepsilon_{st} \end{bmatrix} \tag{3.2}$$

where y_t is the logarithm of output, m is the logarithm of the monetary aggregate, p is the logarithm of the price level, L is the lag operator, a_{11i} is the a_{11} element in A_i, and ε_{dt} and ε_{st} are, respectively, the demand (monetary) and supply shocks.

As stated before, supply shocks have permanent effects on the level of output while demand ones have only temporary effects. Since output is written in a difference form, this implies that the cumulative effects of demand shocks on the change in output must be zero. This implies the restriction:

[10] For a fresh list of the costs and benefits of a monetary union see Fondo Monetario Internacional (1997), p. 14-16.

[11] Although the authors correctly use the term "periphery", it sounds pejoratively. Hereinafter, this expression will mean, strictly, the area beyond the limits of some common characteristics, but without a pejorative connotation.

$$\sum_{i=0}^{\infty} a_{11i} = 0 \tag{3.3}$$

The model defined by equations (3.2) and (3.3) can be estimated using a vector autoregression. Each element of X_t can be regressed on lagged values of all elements of X. Using B to represent these estimated coefficients, the equation becomes:

$$\begin{aligned} X_t &= B_1 X_{t-1} + B_2 X_{t-2} + \dots + B_n X_{t-n} + e_t \\ X_t &= (I - B(L))^{-1} e_t \\ X_t &= (I + B(L) + B(L)^2 + \dots) e_t \\ X_t &= e_t + D_1 e_{t-1} + D_2 e_{t-2} + D_3 e_{t-3} + \dots \end{aligned} \tag{3.4}$$

where e_t represents the residuals from the equation in the vector autoregression. In this case, e_t is comprised of the residuals of a regression of lagged values of y_t and m-p on current values of each in turn; these residuals are labeled e_{yt} and e_{pt}.

To convert equation (3.4) into the model defined by equation (3.2), the residuals from the VAR must be transformed into demand and supply shocks. Writing $e_t = C\varepsilon_t$, it is clear that in the two-by-two case considered four restrictions are required to define the four elements of the matrix C.[12] Two of these restrictions are simple normalization, which define the variance of the shocks. A third restriction arises from the fact that demand and supply shocks are orthogonal. The final restriction that allows C to be uniquely defined is that monetary shocks have only temporary effects.[13] In terms of VAR this implies:

[12] In applied work the nature of the identified shocks has differed. Some studies identify only one generic shock to aggregate demand (e.g. Blanchard and Quah, 1989), whereas others identify multiple shocks to aggregate demand (e.g. Shapiro and Watson, 1988; Galí, 1992). Likewise, some of these studies identify only a single supply shock (e.g. Blanchard and Quah, 1989; Galí, 1992), whereas others identify several supply shocks (e.g. Shapiro and Watson, 1988; Fackler and McMillin, 1998). However, one should be cautious in identifying shocks. King *et al.* (1991), for example, identify three shocks one of which is a real interest shock, but it is not clear how to classify this shock because it could be interpreted either as an aggregate demand or supply shock, or as a mixture of the two. In summary, the shocks are identified by imposing a number of restrictions, and in spite of the fact that in applied work the nature of the identified shocks has differed, they could be labeled either as demand or supply ones.

[13] This restriction excludes the possibility that aggregate demand shocks permanently affect the level of output. The assumption allows the data to choose a description closer to the Keynesian view in which fluctuations are predominantly transitory, or to fit a description closer to the real business cycle view in which they are largely the result of permanent shocks.

$$\sum_{i=0}^{\infty}\begin{bmatrix} d_{11i} & d_{12i} \\ d_{21i} & d_{22i} \end{bmatrix}\begin{bmatrix} c_{11} & c_{12} \\ c_{21} & c_{22} \end{bmatrix}=\begin{bmatrix} 0 & \cdot \\ \cdot & \cdot \end{bmatrix}$$

In summary, the disturbances are in general not directly observable, but these can be inferred from the joint behavior of two series. This joint behavior is characterized by a vector autoregression, and the underlying shocks are identified by imposing some restrictions, one of which is the long-run neutrality of nominal shocks.

III. Results

The data to obtain the cyclical fluctuations are from *Anuarios Estadísticos de America Latina y El Caribe* for they provide consistent information for the period 1970-1997. The information was computed in constant prices. Although this procedure is no difficult to follow, it may show some distortions in very long periods of time as a consequence of changes in the statistical procedures.

It is difficult to obtain overlapping time series of national accounts under different base periods in Latin American countries. It is typical that, once the base period is changed, the old time series (based on the previous base period) are discontinued and the new time series are not extended backward for a significant number of years (Mena, 1995).[14] This makes unclear if the observed differences in the output growth rate across base periods effectively reflects changes in the structure of the economy (input-output matrix) or merely shows the peculiarities of statistical procedures. Anyway, this "second best methodology" related with the simple "chain" of the series is adopted.[15]

As to money, the construction of the series of the relevant monetary aggregate generated an additional problem since Argentina, Bolivia and Brazil were very unstable economies and had changed their monetary units several times.[16] To overcome the difficulties that may arise from this situation, it was necessary to consult the International Financial Statistics provided by the International Monetary Fund. The series constructed were checked with the information provided by *Estudios Económicos de América Latina*. These early-based *Estudios* bring a short description of the performance of the economies that helps to find inconsistencies with the data and to avoid the introduction of distortion in the series.

---

[14] Argentina, Chile and Uruguay are the only Latin American countries that do not present these difficulties in obtaining such national account statistics (Mena, 1995; p. 89).

[15] Macroeconometric testing in Latin American countries requires a country-specific detailed knowledge of the economic policy evolution throughout the period investigated. Such information needs to be incorporated into both the specification and estimation procedures. These "pressing restrictions" suggest the adoption of a second best methodology.

[16] This is due to the episodes of hyperinflation.

The general procedure was to use the last volume of *Anuarios Estadísticos de América Latina*, and then to construct the series from the present to the past. It is done in this way on the assumption that the last data was properly elaborated. The same procedure was employed for the monetary aggregate series.

III.1 GDP Fluctuations and their Characteristics

The adoption of a deterministic trend implies that the growth rate of the GDP was a constant one. Table 1 (in the appendix) summarizes the results for the period 1970-1997 under this assumption. The growth rate for the economies were different among the countries selected. It was necessary to include a dummy variable for the eighties, which turned to be relevant for the cases of Argentina, Bolivia, Chile and Uruguay. The growth rate of Paraguay was 5.1% while the one of Brazil was 3.8%. The growth rate for the rest of the countries (dummy included) was 4.9% for Chile, 2.9% for Bolivia, 2.4% for Uruguay, and 2.2% for Argentina.

Despite the satisfactory results obtained, the procedure could be useful only for some economies since it is probably not true that all of them followed a constant growth rate.

The autocorrelation and partial autocorrelation functions suggested that the series of GDP be differentiated in the cases of Brazil, Chile and Paraguay. The correlograms insinuated the use of a first autoregressive process for all the economies.[17] The residuals are shown in Graph 1 (see Appendix), and they are approximately white noise. The Graph also presents the residuals from a deterministic trend.

The coincidences in expansions and recessions have been checked with the description of the economies provided by *Estudios Económicos de América Latina*, and a high number of coincidences have been found. Although there is no way to do this procedure directly due to methodological matters (related to fluctuations along a trend line or to the previous year), one could construct a table in which expansions and contractions are listed and then compare them with those given by *Estudios*.[18]

Once the fluctuations are obtained, the next step is to characterize them. Christodolulakis *et al.* (1995) suggest their duration, intensity and persistence as the most relevant characteristics; while their simultaneity and temporal correlation are also useful to perceive the joint behavior of the countries.[19]

III.1.a Duration, Volatility and Persistence

Table 2 presents the duration (in years) of the cyclical fluctuations given the alternatives selected. Argentina and Paraguay have shorter expansions; while

[17] This is probably due to the use of annual data.
[18] A similar practice is employed in Arnaudo and Jacobo (1998).
[19] See Arnaudo and Jacobo (1997).

Bolivia, Uruguay and Chile have longer ones. Brazil is somewhere in between. In the cases of contractions, they are similar in all the cases with the exception of Brazil.

Since the estimated residuals show a great variability, it is useful to evaluate their volatility. The volatility of the fluctuations is measured through the standard deviation of the cyclical component. Table 2 shows that volatility is small for the cases of Bolivia, Brazil, Chile and Paraguay when a stochastic trend is selected; while there is no significant differences in the cases of Argentina and Uruguay. This situation seems to confirm the trend selected for the economies.[20]

The persistence is measured through the autocorrelation coefficient. The results indicate that the persistence in the economies is not relevant, although one should recognize some persistence in the cases of Argentina, Paraguay and Uruguay.

III.1.b Simultaneity

The analysis of expansions and contractions showed a number of coincidences that should be recorded. The question is, in this case, which is the expected number of coincidences. If the fluctuations were happening simultaneously, the number of years should be equal to that of the years analyzed, whereas if the fluctuations were in opposite directions, the number should be zero; thus, it is reasonable to think that half the number of periods corresponds to a random situation.

Since due to statistical procedures it was necessary to sacrifice one year in some cases, the number of periods in which the economies experimented coincidences was related to the years analyzed, and then the number was expressed in percent. This method does not invalidate what is stated above. In fact, a number near 50% suggests a random case.

Table 3 gives some information about simultaneity in these geographically linked countries. The coincidences are high between Argentina and Brazil (71%). Something similar is observed between Brazil and Paraguay (71%), and between Uruguay and Bolivia (73%). Chile and Bolivia also have an interesting number of coincidences (69%), and the same occurs in the cases of Chile and Uruguay (65%).

In summary, the countries do not have a very different behavior and demonstrate a high number of coincidences in their expansions and recessions; with the exception of Chile and Brazil (where the coincidences seem not to occur).

[20] It is judicious to remember that the time series trend should mimic the smooth curves most cycle researchers would draw trough the plots of the data.

III.1.c Temporal Correlation

Up to now the analysis focuses only on the number of years during which conditions were similar, disregarding the relative size of such fluctuations. This difficulty could be overcome by looking at the temporal correlation of economic fluctuations. The data included in Table 4 give the temporal characteristics of the fluctuations in each country, as well as their correlation with other economies. These figures, in general, confirm the basic measure mentioned before. Although one should recognize the existence of some correlation among the economies, its value is small.

The cyclical fluctuations of Brazil are simultaneously correlated with the fluctuations of the rest of the countries. In fact, the relationship is a positive one with Argentina (0.28), Bolivia (0.25), Paraguay (0.53) and Uruguay (0.21); while the correlation with Chile is negative (-0.20).

Paraguay's cyclical fluctuations are positively related to those of Argentina (0.21), Bolivia (0.49), and Chile (0.30). The business fluctuations of Uruguay are negative correlated with those of Chile (-0.20).

It is also possible to observe what happens when a current fluctuation in one country is compared with the fluctuation in the rest of the countries lagged one period. Although the selected indicator (cross-correlation) gives the chance to see if the fluctuation of one country leads the other country's cycle, the lack of significance of the indicator is an excuse for not giving conclusions in this sense.

While all the economies were contemporaneously correlated with the fluctuation of Brazil, there is no business fluctuation correlated with Brazil's lagged one. This means that even if the economies are influenced by the situation of this country they can recover themselves after a period (a year in this case). Nevertheless, some economies save information about their own experience (Argentina, Paraguay and Uruguay).

Just for explanatory purposes, one could assert that there are some economies in the region that due to the size of their GDP could seldom be affected by the rest. In fact, while Argentina, Brazil or Chile may influence each other, rarely could the situation of Bolivia, Paraguay or Uruguay influence on them.

The cyclical fluctuations of Bolivia seem to be correlated with those of Chile lagged one period (0.32), and with those of Brazil lagged two years (0.21). In the case of Paraguay, its fluctuations are related to the expansions and recessions of Argentina lagged one period (0.23), and to those of Brazil (0.22) and Chile (-0.37) lagged two years. Uruguay's cyclical fluctuations are related to those of Argentina lagged one year (-0.24), and to the ones of Chile lagged two (0.39).

Argentina's business fluctuations are weakly correlated with those of Brazil lagged two periods (0.25), which means that Brazil's influence on that country probably occurred two periods after. There is no other significant correlation among what could be called the "big economies".

Bolivia's fluctuations are influenced by Paraguay's lagged ones (0.23), while the opposite is not true. Uruguay's cyclical fluctuations are correlated with those of Paraguay' lagged one period (-0.24).

III.2 Monetary Shocks

The VAR was estimated using the Akaike Information Criteria giving some priority to the use of the correlograms of the residuals since they avoid the employment of an unnecessary number of lags. While in most of the cases the estimation and simulation results (by way of "illustration") show the impulse response functions and forecast error variance, they are not going to be exhibited here.[21] The shocks are shown in Graph 2 (see Appendix).[22] In this case, the characteristics of the shocks are concentrated in their correlation and size.

III.2.a Correlation

Table 5 presents the correlation for demand shocks. Argentina and Uruguay are weakly correlated (0.42), and something similar occurs with Argentina and Brazil (0.22). If now Brazil is the referential country, its demand shocks are weakly correlated with those of Bolivia and Paraguay (-0.36 and -0.43 respectively).[23]

For the supply shocks, the figures in Table 6 show that the weak correlation observed in demand shocks between Argentina, Brazil and Uruguay is not preserved. Nevertheless, it is possible to find a weak one between Argentina and Paraguay (0.22), Brazil and Bolivia (0.21) and Brazil and Paraguay (0.49).

The immediate conclusion is that while Argentina, Brazil and Uruguay have their demand shocks correlated (although this correlation is a weak one), the supply shocks show a different situation, and make Brazil look close to Paraguay and Bolivia.

---

[21] The impulse response functions and forecast error variance are usually computed from vector autoregressive models in order to investigate the interrelationship within the system. However, the authors usually provide no measures of estimation uncertainty. In contrast to common practice in econometric works where t-ratios or standard errors are usually reported, measures for estimation uncertainty are often not supplied. One reason for this "silence" on the estimation precision may be the fact that the relevant asymptotic distributions are not sufficiently easily accessible to applied researchers.

[22] The precision in the estimation results is usually not spread before the view of the reader. In this sense, applied researchers seem to extend their silence.

[23] The description only includes the most relevant correlations. In doing so, it considers Argentina and Brazil as referential countries due to their GDP size.

III.2.b Size

The employed methodology makes it possible to observe the size of demand and supply shocks. The wider the supply shocks, the bigger the usefulness of the monetary policy. In other words, there will be extraordinary difficulties to fix the exchange rates if supply shocks do not have the same size in all the economies.

In the case of demand disturbances, their interpretation is rather different. In fact, Bayoumi and Eichengreen (1992b) suggest that the different size of the demand shocks through the different regions of the United States are such due to the higher specialization of each region. In other words, if the region is diversified in its production the demand shocks should be small. But in the cases of the economies under analysis, the size of monetary shocks seems to be more related with stabilization plans. Since these plans were exchange rate based ones, the size of demand shocks tends to confirm the importance of exchange rates as a mechanism of adjustment.

The size of demand and supply shocks was computed using the estimated residual correlation matrix from the VAR, but not using the variance- covariance one. In fact, the normal procedure implies an identity variance- covariance matrix due to the assumption of variance equal to unity and orthogonality of the shocks. The transformation suggested only changes the scale factor.[24]

Table 7 shows the standard deviation of the shocks. The standard deviation of Argentina's supply shock is 0.055 (5.7%). The size of the supply shocks in Brazil is 0.063 (6.3%), and in Uruguay 0.069 (6.9%). In the case of demand shocks, those of Argentina, Brazil and Bolivia were the biggest ones.

In summary, supply and demand shocks are different among the economies. Besides, they seem to be bigger than those of European countries. In fact, while in the European core countries (Germany, France, Belgium, and Denmark) the size of supply shocks is between 1-2%, this is not the case here.[25] Moreover, the size of the supply shocks is bigger than those of the European periphery (United Kingdom, Italy, Spain, Portugal and Greece) where the size is between 2-4%. The demand shocks are also different suggesting that monetary policy should be different.

IV. Concluding Comments

An interesting exercise was to assume that the group of countries under analysis did not have a strong economic linkage. This was, of course, the period previous to the integration, and it could be identified as "the initial situation", opposite to the time when the integration process is taking place. This kind of

---

[24] See the modification of the VAR decomposition discussed in footnote 10 of Bayoumi and Eichengreen (1992a;p. 6).

[25] Notice that some methodological differences may exist. For further details about Europe and the United States, see Bayoumi and Eichengreen (1992b).

partition may be applied to the countries now joining MERCOSUR where the *Tratado de Asunción* (1991) should be taken as the boundary between the two periods, marking the performance of the economy in the past and its likely behavior in the future. However, the results of the integration took time to emerge, and their first evidence may have occurred in the middle 1990s. Therefore, it seems more appropriate to take this latter time as a dividing point, and thus, the usefulness of considering the analysis up to 1997.

To determine the feasibility of policy harmonization before the countries had started the integration process (that is what was called the initial situation), the analysis focused on the behavior of the economies which is well summarized in the GDP fluctuations.

The macroeconomic fluctuations of Argentina, Bolivia, Brazil, Chile, Paraguay and Uruguay were variable and not time uniform during the last quarter of the century. As a consequence, the possibility of homogeneous policies in the future is difficult to predict.

Although there is a high discretion in separating the fluctuations from the GDP growth trend, the growth rate of these economies was different. The duration of expansions and recessions were variable, and the persistence was small.

While the simultaneity of expansions and recessions showed a great number of coincidences, with the exception of Brazil and Chile, the size of their association is small. Nevertheless, Brazil is positively correlated with all the economies (with the exception of that of Chile). Paraguay is also positively correlated with all. Argentina is not correlated with Bolivia, nor is it with Chile. When lagged fluctuations are analyzed, there is no relation with Brazil's past ones.

As a result, the arhythmical beating among these countries reveals that the case for policy harmonization is weak. Similar policies could work in expansions and contractions, but their strength should be different: very high in one country, very small in the other. This is probably why the alignment of economic policies up to the moment is mainly due to the abandonment of inflationary finance.

When analyzing the underlying mechanism to the cyclical fluctuations, Argentina, Brazil and Uruguay have their nominal shocks (weakly) correlated, while the supply ones make Brazil closer to Paraguay and Bolivia. The supply shocks of Chile are also weak, but negatively correlated with those of Argentina and Brazil.

In spite of the fact that there are three countries (Argentina, Brazil and Uruguay) that have their supply shocks similar in size, these are not correlated. The supply shocks that show some correlation are only those of Bolivia and Paraguay, but the size of these shocks is different.

For the demand shocks, Argentina, Brazil and Uruguay have correlated ones, but their size is not equal. This simply means that their monetary policy is distant.

A well understood rule is that if the shocks are different the institutional agreement and the policies that may be accorded tend to exacerbate fluctuations since the governments should relinquish their tools for stabilizing their economies. Following this rule, the shocks underlying these economies were different. As a consequence, there is no economic reason for a monetary union.

Nevertheless, and just to finish the paper with a small degree of optimism, one could inquire oneself as Wyplosz did (1997): "Would the United States have passed the currency area test a century ago? And had it failed, all things considered, was it a mistake for the country to adopt a single currency?"

References

Agénor, Pierre-Richard, C. John McDermott and Eswar Prasad (1998): "Macroeconomic Fluctutations in Developing Countries. Some Stylized Facts", EDI *Working Papers*.

Arnaudo, Aldo A. and Alejandro D. Jacobo (1998): "Policy Harmonization in MERCOSUR", *Economia Aplicada*, **2** (4): 757-766.

Arnaudo, Aldo A. and Alejandro D. Jacobo (1997): "Macroeconomic Homogeneity within MERCOSUR: An Overview", *Estudios Económicos*, **12** (1): 37-51.

Bayoumi, Tamim and Barry Eichengreen (1992a): "Is There a Conflict Between EC Enlargement and European Monetary Unification?, NBER Working Paper Series, *Working Paper* No. 3950.

Bayoumi, Tamim and Barry Eichengreen (1992b): "Shocking Aspects of European Monetary Unification", NBER Working Paper Series, *Working Paper* No. 3949.

Belaisch, Agnès and Claudio Soto (1998): "Empirical Regularities of the Chilean Business Cycle", *Banco Central de Chile*, draft.

Beveridge, S. and Charles Nelson (1981): "A New Approach to Descomposition of Economics Time Series into Permanent and Transitory Components with Particular Attention to Measurement of the 'Business Cycle'", *Journal of Monetary Economics*, **7** (2): 151-174.

Blanchard, Oliver J. and Danny Quah (1989): "The Dynamic Effects of Aggregate Demand and Supply Disturbances", *American Economic Review*, **79** (4): 655-673.

Burns, Arthur F. and Wesley C. Mitchell (1946): *Measuring Business Cycles*, National Bureau of Economic Research.

Carrera, Jorge, Mariano Féliz and Demián Panigo (1999): "Una medición de los canales de transmisión de las fluctuaciones económicas. El caso de Argentina y los Estados Unidos", 34 Annual Meeting, Asociación Argentina de Economía Política, draft.

Christodoulakis, Nicos, Sophia P. Dimelis and Tryphon Kollintzas (1995): "Comparisons of Business Cycles in the EC: Idiosyncrasies and Regularities", *Economica*, **62** (245): 1-27.

Eichengreen, Barry (1993): "European Monetary Unification", *Journal of Economic Literature*, **31** (3): 1321-1357.

Enders, Walter (1995): *Applied Econometric Times Series*, John Wiley & Sons Inc., New York.

Fackler, James S. and W. Douglas McMillin (1998): "Historical Descomposition of Aggregate Demand and Supply Shocks in a Small Macro Model", *Southern Economic Journal*, **64**(3): 648-664.

Fiorito, Riccardo and Tryphon Kollintzas (1994): "Stylized Facts of Business Cycles in the G7 from a Real Business Cycle Perspective", *European Economic Review*, 38 (2): 235-269.

Fondo Monetario Internacional (1997): "Zonas monetarias óptimas: un desafío de políticas", *Boletín*, **26** (1): 14-16.

Fullerton, Thomas M. (Jr.) y Eiichi Araki (1996): "New Directions in Latin American Macroeconometrics", *Economic and Business Review*, **38** (12): 49-73.

Funke, Michael (1997a): "How Important are Demand and Supply Shocks in explaining German Business Cycles?: New Evidence on an Old Debate", *Economic Modelling*, **14** (1): 11-37.

Funke, Michael (1997b): "The Nature of Shocks in Europe and in Germany", *Economica*, **64** (255): 461-469

Galí, Jordi (1992): "How Well Does the IS-LM Model Fit Postwar U.S. Data?", *Quarterly Journal of Economics*, **107** (2): 709-738.

International Monetary Fund: *International Financial Statistics*, various issues.

Karras, Georgios (1993): "Sources of U.S. Macroeconomic Fluctuations: 1973-1989"; *Journal of Macroeconomics*, **15** (1): 47-68.

King, Robert G., Charles I. Plosser, James S. Stock and Mark Watson (1991): "Stochastic Trends and Economic Fluctuations", *American Economic Review*, **81** (4): 819-840.

Kydland, Finn E. and Edward C. Prescott (1990): "Business Cycles: Real Facts and Monetary Myth", Federal Bank of Minneapolis *Quarterly Review*, Spring.

Larrain, Felipe (1981): "El uso de las series de tiempo con fines predictivos", *Trabajo Docente Nro. 33*, Instituto de Economía, Pontificia Universidad Católica de Chile.

Lucas, R. (Jr.) (1977): "Understanding Business Cycles", en K. Brunner y A. Meltzer (Ed.), *Stabilization of Domestic and International Economy, Carnegie-Rochester Conferences Series on Public Policy*, Vol. 5, North-Holland.

Martirena-Mantel, Ana M. (1997): "Reflexiones sobre Uniones Monetarias: pensando el MERCOSUR desde el Caso Europeo", Academia Nacional de Ciencias Económicas.

Mena, Hugo (1995): "Pushing the Sisyphean Boulder? Macroeconometric Testing in Latin American Countries", *Review of Income and Wealth*, **10** (1): 81-99.

Mundell, Robert (1961): "A Theory of Optimum Currency Areas", *American Economic Review*, **51** (4): 657-665.

Naciones Unidas- Comisión Económica para América Latina y El Caribe: *Anuario Estadístico de América Latina y El Caribe*, various issues.

Naciones Unidas- Comisión Económica para América Latina y El Caribe: *Estudio Económico de América Latina*, various issues.

Nelson, Charles and Charles Plosser (1982): "Trends and Random Walks in Macroeconomic Time Series", *Journal of Monetary Economics*, **10** (2): 139-162.

Nelson Charles (1973): Applied Times Series Analysis for Managerial Forecasting, Holden- Day Inc.

Ramanathan, Ramu (1992): Introductory Econometric with Applications, Harcourt Brace Jovanovich Inc.

Shapiro, Matthew D. and Mark W. Watson (1988): "Sources of Business Cycle Fluctuations", NBER *Macroeconomic Annual*: 112-148.

Sterne, Gabriel and Tamim Bayoumi (1995): "Temporary Cycles or Volatile Trends? Economic Fluctuations in 21 OECD Economies", *The Manchester School*, **63** (1): 23-51.

Vandaele, Walter (1983): *Applied Times and Box-Jenkins Models*, Academic Press, New York.

Wyplosz, Charles (1997): "EMU: Why and How it Might Happen", *Journal of Economic Perspectives*, **11** (4): 3-22.

APPENDIX

Tables

Table 1: Growth Rate for Selected Latin American Countries

Countries	Growth Rate[a);b)] without a Dummy	Growth Rate[a);b)] with a Dummy	r^2
Argentina	1.3 (7.84)		0.71
		2.2 (8.30)	0.82
Bolivia	1.7 (8.05)		0.72
		2.9 (9.36)	0.85
Brazil	3.8 (12.47)		0.86
		4.2 (6.95)	0.57
Chile	3.7 (12.36)		0.85
		4.9 (5.27)	0.89
Paraguay	5.1 (19.05)		0.93
		5.1 (9.56)	0.93
Uruguay	1.4 (6.85)		0.65
		2.4 (6.99)	0.76

Note: (a) in %; (b) t-statistic in parenthesis

Table 2: Characteristics of GDP Fluctuations

Type	Country					
	Argentina	Bolivia	Brazil	Chile	Paraguay	Uruguay
Duration[(a)]						
Expansions	2.6	6.2	4.0	4.7	2.3	5.0
Contracions	1.6	2.0	3.3	2,0	2.2	2.3
Volatility[(b)]						
D	5.3	6.2	9.4	9.5	10.3	7.2
S	4.8	2.6	6.2	6.2	3.8	8.1
Persistence[(c)]						
D (t-1)	0.46					0.29
S (t-1)		-0.10	0.01	0.02	0.36	
D (t-2)	0.10					-0.12
S (t-2)		0.05	0.45	0.05	-0.07	

Notes: (a) in years; (b) following a deterministic (D) or a stochastic (S) trend;
(c) autocorrelation coefficient

Table 3: Simultaneity of Cyclical Fluctuations

Countries	Argentina	Bolivia	Brazil	Chile	Paraguay	Uruguay
Argentina	.	65	71	65	54	67
Bolivia		.	58	69	65	73
Brazil			.	50	71	65
Chile				.	58	65
Paraguay					.	62
Uruguay						.

Note: Number of coincidences over the number of years analyzed (in %).

Table 4: Temporal Correlations of Cyclical Fluctuations

Countries		Argentina				Bolivia				Brazil				Chile				Paraguay				Uruguay			
	Lags	0	-1	-2	-3	0	-1	-2	-3	0	-1	-2	-3	0	-1	-2	-3	0	-1	-2	-3	0	-1	-2	-3
Argentina	0	1.00	0.46	0.08	-0.1	-0.0	-0.2	-0.0	0.08	0.28	0.01	0.25	-0.0	-0.1	-0.2	-0.3	0.13	0.21	-0.2	-0.2	-0.01	0.08	0.23	0.17	0.00
	-1		1.00	0.46	0.07	0.12	-0.0	-0.2	0.0	0.14	0.32	0.01	0.25	0.09	-0.1	-0.3	-0.3	0.23	0.24	-0.3	-0.23	-0.2	0.07	0.22	0.15
	-2			1.00	0.49	-0.0	0.10	-0.0	0.2	0.19	0.17	0.35	0.01	-0.0	0.09	-0.1	-0.3	-0.0	0.25	0.23	-0.3	-0.2	-0.25	0.06	0.21
	-3				1.00	-0.3	-0.0	0.10	0.0	0.11	0.23	0.13	0.32	-0.0	-0.0	0.04	-0.1	-0.0	0.04	0.26	0.27	-0.2	-0.29	-0.29	0.00
Bolivia	0					1.00	-0.1	0.03	0.34	0.25	0.13	0.21	-0.0	0.02	0.32	-0.4	0.05	0.49	0.23	0.02	-0.23	0.05	-0.06	0.34	-0.02
	-1						1.00	-0.1	0.04	0.34	0.23	0.10	0.17	-0.0	0.02	0.31	-0.4	0.14	0.50	0.23	0.02	0.00	0.05	-0.06	0.33
	-2							1.00	-0.1	-0.1	0.34	0.25	0.13	0.02	0.00	0.02	0.31	0.04	0.15	0.50	0.23	-0.0	0.00	0.05	0.06
	-3								1.00	0.22	-0.1	0.25	0.24	-0.0	0.04	0.02	0.02	0.17	0.06	0.14	0.51	0.02	-0.02	0.00	0.03
Brazil	0									1.00	-0.1	0.43	-0.1	-0.2	0.07	-0.1	-0.2	0.53	0.12	0.09	-0.13	0.21	0.11	0.12	0.21
	-1										1.00	-0.0	0.52	0.03	-0.2	0.07	-0.1	0.00	0.53	0.12	0.09	0.02	0.21	0.11	0.12
	-2											1.00	0.01	-0.3	0.07	-0.2	0.07	0.22	0.01	0.53	0.12	0.10	0.03	0.21	0.11
	-3												1.00	-0.0	-0.3	0.03	-0.2	0.16	0.22	0.00	0.54	-0.2	0.10	0.02	0.2
Chile	0													1.00	0.00	-0.0	0.09	0.30	0.35	-0.2	-0.09	-0.2	-0.08	-0.54	-0.28
	-1														1.00	0.03	-0.0	0.09	0.32	0.35	-0.28	0.10	-0.30	-0.08	-0.56
	-2															1.00	0.01	-0.3	0.12	0.32	0.36	0.39	0.08	-0.31	-0.11
	-3																1.00	-0.1	-0.3	0.12	0.32	0.31	0.40	0.08	-0.32
Paraguay	0																	1.00	0.23	-0.1	-0.12	-0.0	-0.03	-0.15	-0.11
	-1																		1.00	0.25	-0.14	-0.2	-0.04	-0.02	-0.12
	-2																			1.00	0.25	0.02	-0.25	-0.05	-0.03
	-3																				1.00	0.15	0.03	-0.25	-0.04
Uruguay	0																					1.00	0.36	-0.04	-0.31
	-1																						1.00	0.37	-0.10
	-2																							1.00	0.36
	-3																								1.00

Table 5: Correlations of Demand Shocks

Countries	Argentina	Bolivia	Brazil	Chile	Paraguay	Uruguay
Argentina	1.00	-0.28	0.22	0.08	0.01	0.42
Bolivia		1.00	-0.36	0.01	0.11	-0.04
Brazil			1.00	-0.02	-0.43	-0.10
Chile				1.00	0.23	-0.27
Paraguay					1.00	-0.14
Uruguay						1.00

Table 6: Correlations of Supply Shocks

Countries	Argentina	Bolivia	Brazil	Chile	Paraguay	Uruguay
Argentina	1.00	-0.16	0.06	-0.31	0.22	0.03
Bolivia		1.00	0.21	0.30	0.31	-0.05
Brazil			1.00	-0.42	0.49	0.15
Chile				1.00	-0.05	-0.59
Paraguay					1.00	-0.08
Uruguay						1.00

Table 7: Standard Deviation of Shocks

Country	Demand Schock	Supply Shock
Argentina	1.872	0.057
Bolivia	2.561	0.024
Brazil	3.172	0.063
Chile	0.774	0.050
Paraguay	0.118	0.037
Uruguay	0.146	0.069

Note: The variables are measured in logarithms, so that 0.057 is 5.7 %.

Graph 1: GDP Fluctuations

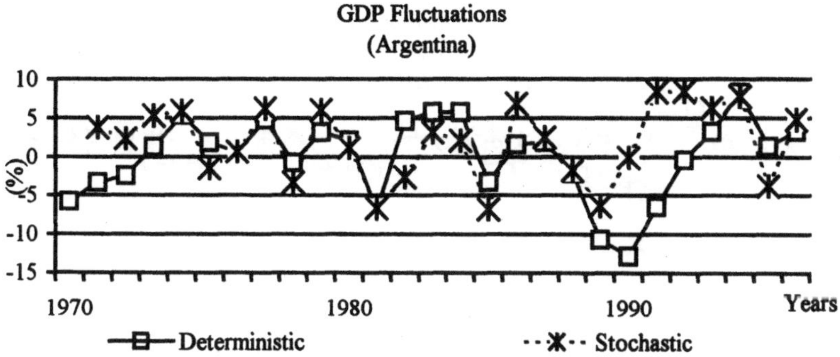

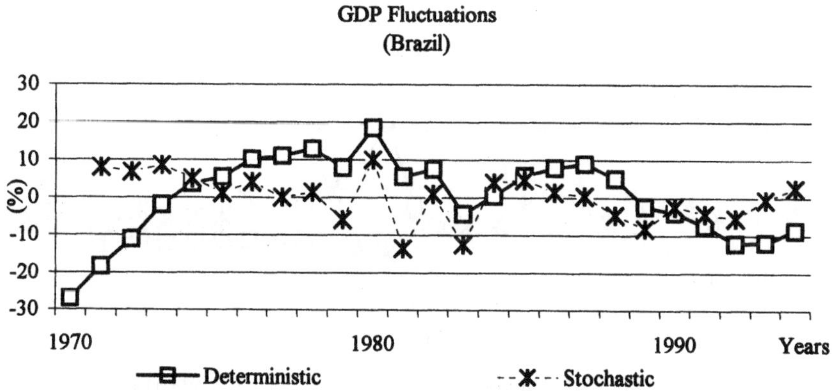

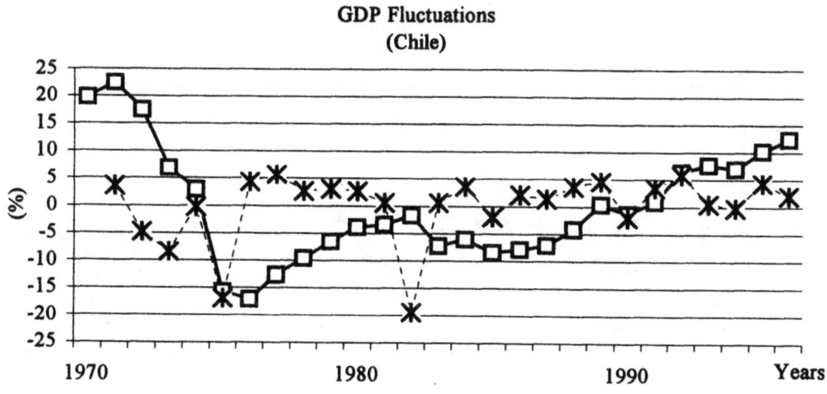

GDP Fluctuations
(Uruguay)

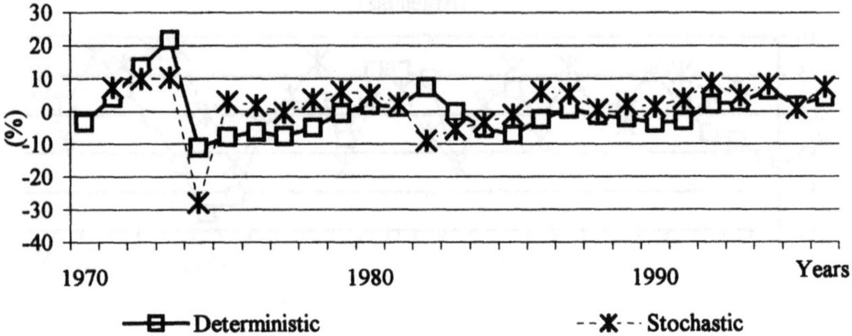

GDP Fluctuations
(Bolivia)

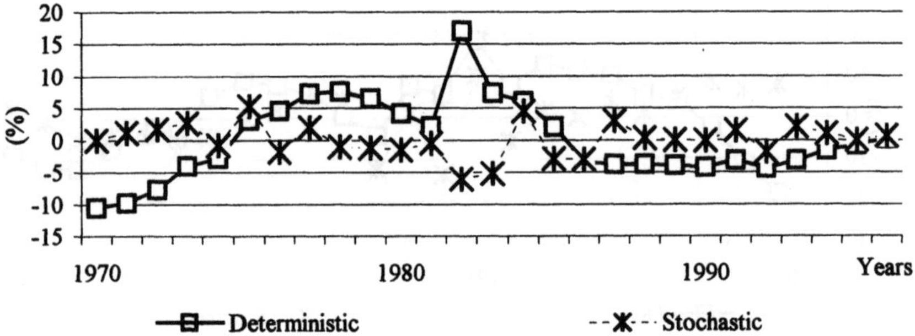

GDP Fluctuations
(Paraguay)

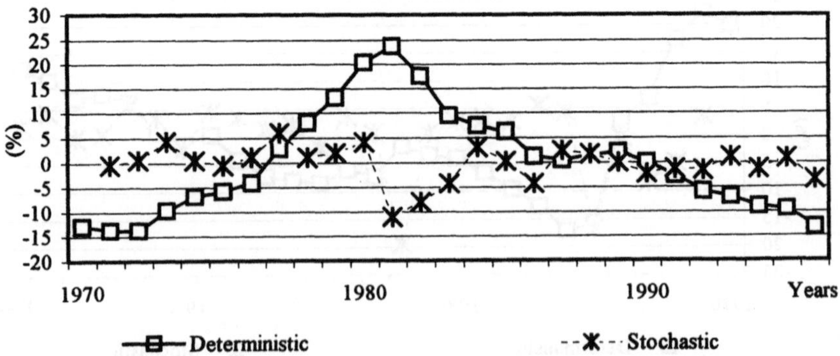

Graph 2: Demand and Supply Shocks

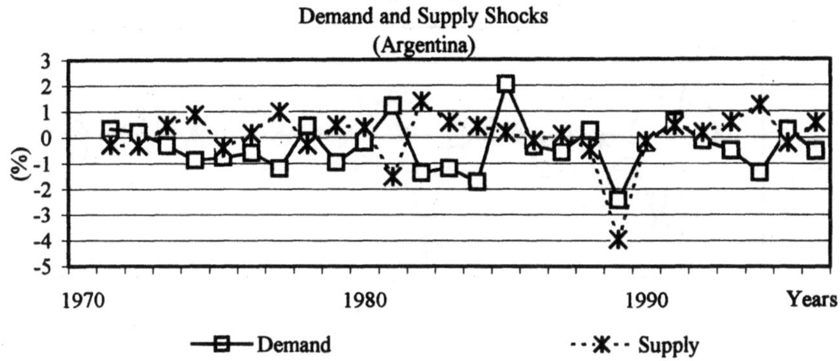

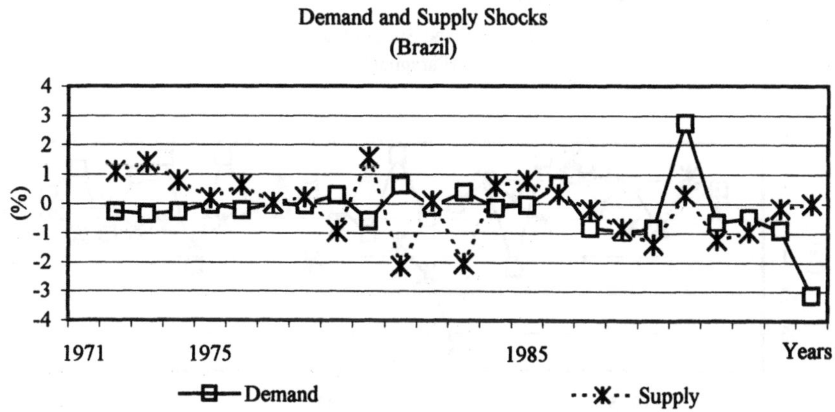

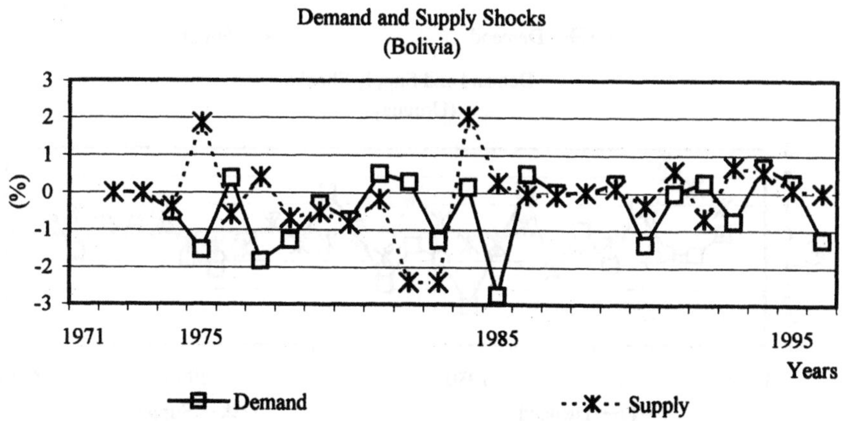

Demand and Supply Shocks
(Chile)

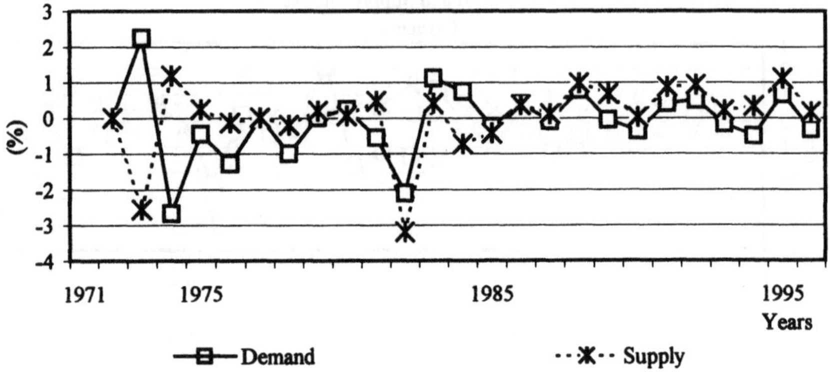

Demand and Supply Shocks
(Paraguay)

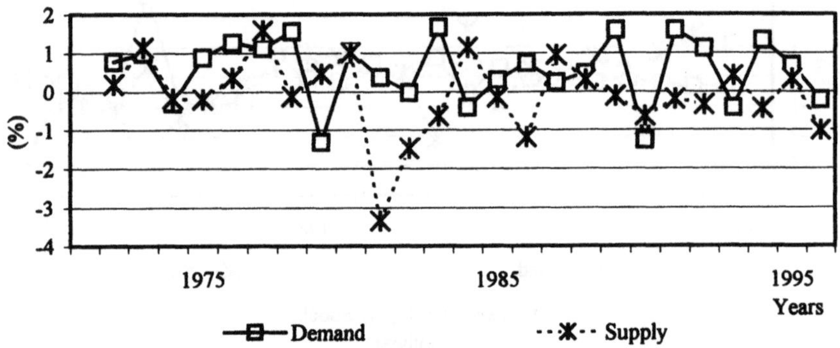

Demand and Supply Shocks
(Uruguay)

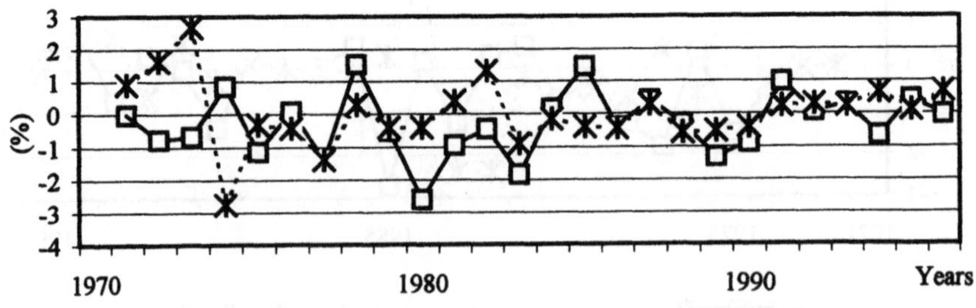

INTRA-INDUSTRY TRADE BETWEEN MERCOSUR, THE EUROPEAN UNION (EU) AND THE NORTH AMERICAN FREE TRADE AGREEMENT (NAFTA)

By Hebe G. Morales de Marega and Eugenio M. Cerutti

I Introduction

In the last years of the twentieth century, four South American countries (Argentina, Brazil, Uruguay and Paraguay) started the long process of building a common market, called MERCOSUR. However, this regional integration agreement was not the only factor that had effects on the commercial relationships of the partner countries, because Argentina and Brazil implemented a unilateral commercial opening during the regional integration process.

In this direction, this paper wants to evaluate the trade flow evolution between Argentina and Brazil, the two most important countries in MERCOSUR, in the 1986-1996 period, and also the changes in the commercial relationship of both countries with the members of the two biggest occidental integration agreements, the European Union (EU) and the NAFTA. The analysis of the commercial flows will be directed to identify not only the possible changes in the direction of the countries' export and imports, but also the inter-industry and intra-industry nature of the trade.

The last aspects are really relevant because we can observe the sectors where comparative advantages of each country have prevailed and the trade has taken inter-industry nature as the traditional Heckscher – Ohlin model predict, or the sectors where an intra-industry trade relationship is more significant[1]. Both kinds of trade have different consequences and will play an important role in the relationship of the MERCOSUR countries, and in a future MERCOSUR association with NAFTA or EU.

In order to achieve the objectives announced above, firstly, we will summarize the trade flow evolution between Argentina and Brazil, and the trade of both these countries with the NAFTA and EU. Secondly, we will summarize the potential gain and different explanations of the intra-industry trade. Also in this section, we will describe the different measurements used to reflect the intra-industrial trade. Thirdly, we will analyze the empirical evidence of the presence

[1] We should also mention that some of the theories that explain the presence of intra-industry trade do not necessarily have to step aside from the conceptual background of the H-O classic model. This topic will be dealt with within item III in this paper.

of intra-industry trade between Argentina and Brazil and the integration agreements mentioned above. Finally, we will write the conclusion that can be derived from this analysis.

II Trade Flow Evolution

Before starting a brief analysis of the trade flow evolution between 1986 and 1996; it is important to mention that The Economic Integration and Cooperation Program between Argentina and Brazil was established in 1986 precisely. This free trade and cooperation agreement between both countries is the most important precedent for MERCOSUR integration which took place in 1991 signing the Asunción Treaty together with Paraguay and Uruguay.

However, we should also consider the fact that the trade flow evolution between Argentina and Brazil was influenced not only by the tariff preferences granted by both countries all along the period being analyzed in this paper but also by the unilateral process of commercial opening to other countries that both countries implemented parallel to the economic integration process. Argentina, after the two hyperinflation crises in 1989, went deeper into the unilateral, non-restrictive, and not negotiated process of commercial opening which had been occurring at different levels since 1976. For Brazil, instead, the commercial opening period started in 1988 and was strengthen in 1990 by eliminating a list of 1300 item that had been previously banned for imports.

In chart 1 (in the appendix), we can see the evolution of Argentine Exports classified with one digit in the Standard Industrial Trade Classification (SITC)[2]. The total Argentine exports change from U$S 6.8 bn in 1986 to 23.8 bn in 1996, which means an increase of 13% annual average. In chart 1, it can also be seen that there is no substantial change in the composition of Argentine exports, but there is a sharp decrease in Section 0 (Food Products), a greater participation in Section 3 (Fuels and Lubricants) and-to a lesser extent than for the previous case-a greater participation in exports of products from Section 7 (Machines and Transport Equipment).

It can be seen that Brazil's participation goes up significantly as the destination for Argentine exports, from 10.2 % of the total in 1986 to 27.8 % in 1996. The high percentage of Section 7 being absorbed by Brazil from the total of exports in said Section is particularly noticeable. We can also say that the proportion of exports whose destination is the EU falls from 29.4 % in 1986 to 20% in 1996 and those exports whose destination is NAFTA go up slightly reaching 12.5% in 1996.

---

[2] This classification comprises around 2,100 titles divided into 233 groups (3 digits level) grouped in 63 chapters (2 digits level) which in turn belong to 10 sections.

In chart 2, it can be seen that the evolution of Argentine imports increased from U$S 4.7 bn in 1986 to U$S 23.7 bn in 1996. This figure represents an annual average increase of 18%, or in other words, a five-fold increase from 1986. Alike Argentine exports, the composition of Argentine imports do not show big changes, but imports of manufactured goods grow, especially those comprised in Section 7 - Machines and Transport Equipment (46% of the total in 1996) and in Section 6 - Manufactured Goods classified according to Material (14% of the total in 1996). In imports according to origin there is an increase in products coming from Brazil which now represents 22.4% of Argentine imports, a higher percentage compared to 14% in 1986. This growth in Brazil's participation meant reaching the percentages that the countries belonging to NAFTA and EU have altogether, which are 23% and 29% of the total respectively. However, the participation in Argentine imports regarding the two regional blocks did not show a homogeneous variation at lower levels showing growth in the significance of imports from Section 5 (Chemical Products), Section 6 (Manufactured Goods classified according to Material) and Section 7 (Machines and Transport Equipment) originated in NAFTA and the imports of European origin in Section 3 (Fuels and Lubricants) and Section 4 (Animal and Vegetable oils, wax).

Regarding Brazilian foreign trade and following the pattern used to analyze the evolution of Argentine foreign trade, we can see in Chart 3, that Brazilian exports also had a growing behavior, going from U$S 22.2 bn in 1986 to U$S 46.7 bn in 1996 that means an increase of 7.7% annual average (they are about double in the period being studied). The composition shows a slight increase in the participation of manufactured goods, being the most significant in 1996 -at 1 digit level from the SITC - Section 6 corresponding to Manufactured Goods classified according to Material (24%), Section 0 corresponding to Food Products (23%) and Section 7 corresponding to Machines and Transport Equipment (20%). Argentina -as the destination for these exports- shows an increase in all the concepts analyzed going up from 3% of the total in 1986 to 11% in 1996. In this regard, we can see that the participation of the EU remains the same while the participation of NAFTA falls down (except for Section 2 corresponding to Crude Materials).

The behavior of Brazilian imports is analyzed in Chart 4, where we can see a growth of 13% annual average, going up from U$S 15.7 bn in 1986 to U$S 52.9 bn in 1996. The structure of Brazilian imports shows a fall in Food Products (from 12% in 1986 to 6% of the total in 1996), Raw Materials (from 7% in 1986 to 5% of the total in 1996) and Fuels and Lubricants (from 23% in 1986 to 13% of the total in 1996). But there was also an increase in imports of Manufactured Products, especially those comprised in Manufactured Goods classified according to Material (from 7% in 1986 to 10% in 1996) and Machines and Transport Equipment (from 31% in 1986 to 39% in 1996). The Argentine participation as the origin of Brazilian imports grew from 5% of the total in 1986 to 12.7% in 1996 being the most remarkable the growth in Argentine Food Products (from 20% in 1986 to 44.9% in 1996) and Fuels and Lubricants (from 1.5% in 1986 to 17.9% in 1996) in the total of imports of each title respectively. Products coming from the NAFTA and the EU account for about 26% of the total, showing a slight fall for the period but a moderate increase regarding 1986 respectively. A drop in the significance of Food Products from both these blocks can be noticed at a lower level.

Summarizing, we can see that both Argentina and Brazil realized a significant growth in their exports and imports during the period being analyzed; especially in that referring to bilateral trade between these two countries. Among the most significant products we can mention the increase in the bilateral trade of Machines and Transport Equipment, the growth in Argentine exports of Food Products and Fuels and Lubricants and the growth in Brazilian exports in Manufactured Goods Classified according to Material. However, although Brazil constitutes the most important trading partner for Argentina (first importance destination for Argentine exports and very close to the participation that the other blocks being studied hold altogether respectively), Argentina is below the participation percentages that Brazil has with the NAFTA and the EU (this situation has shown a reverse trend during the past few years).

Regarding the commercial relationship of Argentina and Brazil with the NAFTA and the EU respectively there are no big changes, except for the lower increase of Argentine exports to the EU and the Brazilian exports to the NAFTA which suffered a drop of about 10 points in the percentages of participation of those two blocks in the total exports of each country.

But, as stated in the introduction, this account of the foreign trade evolution of MERCOSUR main partner countries does not say anything about the nature of the kind of commercial relationship held among the different countries (inter-industry or intra-industry trade) and about the different implications that each kind of trade hold on the economic structure of each country. These topics will be focused in the coming sections of the paper.

III Intra-Industry Trade

III.1 Potential Gains due to the presence of Intra-Industrial Trade

The regional integration and free trade processes tend to produce a structural change in the production function of each of the partner countries, and an internal movement for the allocation of production resources. According to the international trade theory, through the Heckscher-Ohlin (HO) traditional model, it can be understood that each country shall produce and export those goods which are intensive in the use of the factor of production relatively abundant in that country.

In this way, the production resources, such as labor, will be reallocated as the outcome of the differences in salaries among the different activities. When there are no rigidities (e.g.: prices and wages inflexibility) the transfer would be carried out in a background of full-employment. But, in the short term, during the transition period, there are costs that can influence the labor market adjustment process. Here starts the concept of intra-industry trade, meaning the simultaneous export and import of products belonging to the same industrial category. The adjustments costs connected to a regional integration process or a commercial opening process would be lower when the decrease or elimination of the trading barriers led to an intra-industry specialization instead of an inter-industry one.

It arises from the previous point that although the inter-industry specialization (as predicted by the HO model) proves efficient in the long run it will necessarily produce serious effects on production and employment in the short run. Conversely, an intra-industrial specialization would lead to a smoother adjustment process[3]. Firstly, it would be easier for industries and production plants to stop producing a certain product line and produce a reduced range of products than moving to another kind of industry. Secondly, the variations in factor requirements inside the industries is lower than the one found among the different industries (Lucángeli; 1992). Thirdly, the changes in the distribution of income resulting from the process of free trade would not be so dramatic under the conditions of an intra-industry specialization (Behar, Jaime; 1991). Finally, regarding the reallocation of factors, the presence of intra-industry trade shows that a costly transfer would not be necessary when referring to training and labor adaptation time costs, because such resources are being transferred among the different products belonging to the same industry and the factors of production intra-sector mobility is higher than the inter-industry one.

It must be considered that the specialization -intra-industrial or inter-industrial- shall not necessarily occur in the same direction in all the sectors of the economy. In those sectors where there are strong comparative advantages, coming from, for example the possession of certain natural resources, an adjustment of the inter-industry kind will possibly take place. Instead, the presence of intra-industry trade is likely to occur in sectors where the presence of comparative advantages are not determining or which are otherwise compensated for example, by the upcoming of economies of scale in the production of differentiated products, originated in the broadening of the market.

[3] There is a general consensus among the different authors regarding the lower adjustments costs brought about by intra-industry trade, but we should not forget that every particular case shall greatly depend on the institutional characteristics that the product markets show and mainly the factors market (Greenaway, 1988).

III.2 Theoretical Background

The notion of intra-industry trade emerges before the Second World War as a theoretical need to explain the manufactured product by manufactured product trade that was taking place among industrialized countries. Since that time many authors have dealt with this matter and the outcomes are many and diverse[4].

The models that explain the presence of intra-industrial trade with a background of perfect competition in international trade are those that arise from derivations of the HO model family, since the simplest versions of these kind of models could not explain the empirical evidence of abundant intra-industrial trade between industrialized countries with similar factor endowments. An example of such derivations is the Heckscher-Ohlin-Ricardo model developed in Davis (1995), where they introduce the presence of technological differences between the countries into the HO model, similar to Ricardo model. In same cases, this would enable trading products between countries which have different factor endowments. In this regard, other authors introduce a certain amount of specific human capital in each country's industry which would mean a certain product differentiation which is generally expressed by higher quality and different price[5].

Also, based on different theories, like Vernon's product cycle (1966) we can justify the presence of intra-industrial trade, since in the initial stage, the production demands skilled workers for the development and improvement of the product, regarding the unskilled workers needed when the product matures and becomes standard. The comparative advantage may vary from a country which has plenty of skilled workers to another one which has plenty of unskilled workers and in this process intra-industry trade can take place.

Those models that hold imperfect competition in international trade are generally based on the hypothesis of the presence of economies of scale for the production of differentiated goods[6], where intra-industry trade may come from different groups of goods which can be classified - according to Lucángeli

[4] This section does not intend to carry out a deep review of the evolution of the theoretical development on intra-industry trade. We suggest those readers who are interested to consult the synopsis in Greeaway and Milner (1987) and in Greeaway and Torstensson (1997).

[5] It is usual to divide the intra-industry trade theory into two parts: "vertical" intra-industrial trade -where the goods merchandised show significant differences as regards price and quality; and "horizontal" intra-industrial trade where the trade is carried out on products which are basically equal. On this regard, it is commonly said that the adjustment costs in the presence of vertical intra-industry trade are usually higher.

[6] This argument was also held in the Grubel and Lloyd paper (1975), which is considered a pioneer in examining intra-industry trade between developed countries. Among other authors we can also mention Krugman (1980), where there is a model for countries with similar factor endowments which in the presence of economies of scale and product differentiation lead to intra-industry specialization in the production and marketing of those products.

(1993)- in: 1) goods with close substitute in use but with different supplies (e.g. wooden or metal furniture)[7]; 2) Products which are similar as regards the supplies but are not substitutes as regards their use (e.g. petroleum by-products); 3) Goods which are close substitutes and are produced based on similar supplies but which are different in design, quality or trade mark.

Another hypothesis is the presence of multinational companies whose organizational structure enables them to distribute their production or even components of one product in different geographical locations. This kind of trade is called intra-company. However, it must be considered that not every intra-company trade has the same characteristics of intra-industry trade since, although a vertical integration of production in the different plants of such company originates intra-company trade in intermediate products, it does not constitute intra-industry trade; while a horizontal integration of production (including the trade of different supplies between the plants) in a multinational company originates at the same time both kinds of trade. (Cantwell, J.; 1994).

Finally, other models explaining the presence of intra-industry trade are based in varied arguments such as the presence of transport costs, storage, merchandising or distribution, the presence of indivisibilities in the organization of production and the compensation of excess in supply and demand coming from the incompatibility between the requirements of demands before production.

III.3 Intra-Industry Trade Measuring Methodology

Before characterizing the different indexes for measuring the intra-industry trade, it necessary to solve the problem of the definition of the word "industry" which is being used. This is critical to know whether the intra-industry phenomenon being analyzed is a strictly statistical one or, on the contrary, it is a significant phenomenon at the time of explaining the trade patterns.

The definition of "industry" must be taken as how to divide all the production and consumption activities of one economy into adequate groups which are exhaustive and exclude each other. Following P. J. Lloyd (1989) and Lucángeli (1993) we can make the following distinctions.

From the point of view of demand, given any criterion to differentiate the goods it is necessary to define some goods substitution parameter that allows shortening the limits of the group. The definition of a group of "close substitutes" considers that the substitution partial elasticity within the group are larger that those between goods that do not belong to the group.

In terms of supply, the definition of industrial groups allows for various approximations, although an order which allows certain advantages considers that

[7] The presence of intra-industry trade for this kind of products is compatible with the HO model due to supplies differentiation.

the classification must go around the similarity of the materials used for their production.

As can be seen, to give a definition of the scope of the word "industry" is not that simple, but there is a consensus among the different authors who deal with this topic, that both aspects must be considered, that is, to consider both goods substitution as regards consumption and the similarity of the supplies needed for production.

In this regard, in order to measure the significance of this trade, the authors use an intra-industrial trade index taken from the SITC which in this paper is reckoned at a 3-digit level, because in said classification the compiling criterion considers the consumption substitution and the similarity of the supplies needed for production.

The index being used here to measure the intra-industrial trade level between Argentina and Brazil and the two blocks EU and NAFTA is the Grubel and Lloyd index[8], which is made up in the following way:

$$I_i = \frac{(X_i + M_i) - |X_i - M_i|}{(X_i + M_i)} \quad *100$$

Where X_i are the exports and M_i are the imports of each "industry i " respectively. The intra-industrial index ranges between 0 and 100. The latter corresponds to the full presence of intra-industrial trade, that is, the exports belonging to one title or industry are exactly the same as imports.

The addition of the G-L index in order to get a general total level at 1 and 2 digits in the SITC is carried out considering a weighted average of exports plus the imports of each title in relation to the general total exchange for each section and chapter respectively.

Although it is the most widely used index, it produces a deviation when comparing the outcome for the different years. Some of the difficulties appear when an increase in inter-industrial trade produces an increase of the G-L index although the increase in inter-industrial trade aimed at reducing the trading imbalance in the title considered (Thom and McDowel; 1999). Another difficulty posed by the traditional index is shown when two countries which have a certain intra-industrial trade level start a free trading relation as it can produce an equi-proportionate growth in the exports of each country and this will increase the

[8] A great deal of the literature on intra-industrial trade discusses the characteristics of the indexes used to measure the scope of intra-industrial trade. It is thought that they suffer a deviation when there is imbalance in the balance of trade, but there is not a general agreement whether an adjustment must be made or not and in case of needing the adjustment, the scope that it should have. In order to go deeper into the subject you can see Aquino (1978), Tornell (1986), and Greenaway and Milner (1981).

intra-industrial trade level shown by the G-L index, but the proportion in the balances of trade have not changed indeed (Hamilton and Kniest; 1991).

In order to pass over the stated difficulties which in this paper can be significant, since our goal is to study the trading flow during the 1986/96 period, we will also use an index known as "Marginal Intra-Industrial Trade Index" (MIIT), the version developed by Brülhart (1994). It is reckoned with the following formula:

$$A_i = 1 - \frac{|\Delta X_i - \Delta M_i|}{|\Delta X_i| + |\Delta M_i|}$$

where ΔX_i and ΔM_i are the variations in exports and imports at a 3-digit level in the SITC. The Marginal Intra-Industrial Trade index ranges between 0 and 1. The relations in high marginal intra-industrial trade levels are shown by values close to the unit; giving, in this way information about the direction and structure of the changes in exports and imports in different periods of time.

In this case the addition procedure used is the one suggested by Brülhart (1994), which consists of adding the weighted value of the *n* titles grouped in the general total level, the section or chapter respectively; that is,

$$A_w = \sum_{i=1}^{n} w_i A_i$$

where the weighted value w_i comes from:

$$w_i = \frac{|\Delta X_i| + |\Delta M_i|}{\sum_{i=1}^{n}\left(|\Delta X_i| + |\Delta M_i|\right)}$$

IV EMPIRICAL EVIDENCE

IV.1 Argentina-Brazil Exchange

Within in the high increase of the volume commercialized between Argentina and Brazil analyzed in Section II[9], intra-industry trade at a general level between both countries also showed a rising tendency and the G-L index moved from 22.36 in 1986 to 40.25 in 1996[10] (See Chart 5). These results also

[9] Argentina's exports to Brazil increased 848% and Brazil's exports to Argentina 672%.

[10] The G-L index does not have predetermined values to indicate from what values trade changes from inter-industry to intra-industry or viceversa, but among different criteria, G-L index values (calculated for 3 digits in the SITC) between 40 and 50 are considered to indicate

coincide with the high value shown by the MIIT index (0.405 at a general level for the period 1986/96, a level that is higher than the one shown in the commercial relation of each country with the commercial blocks analyzed in this paper) and prove a strong tendency towards an intra-industry specialization in the commercial relation between both countries, partners in MERCOSUR.

But the behavior of the different economical sectors is not homogeneous, and different behaviors among the different industrial branches can be distinguished. According to what is predicted by the HO models, in some sectors there is an inter-industry trade increase. Other sectors show an intra-industry trade increase and, taking into account their weight in the whole trade, lead to an increase in the G-L and MIIT indexes aggregated for all the goods traded.

The sectors in which an inter-industry trade specialization took place are those that belong to the following sections: Food Products (G-L 9.52), Crude Materials (G-L 10.04), Fuels and Lubricants (G-L 7.26) and Animal, Vegetable Oils and Wax (G-L 11.49).

Argentina mainly exports Petroleum and Petroleum products (chapter 33), cereals (chapter 04), especially wheat, rice and cereal products, dairy products (chapter 02), legumes and fruits (chapter 05) and textile fibers (chapter 26), especially cotton. Brazil exports to Argentina minerals and minerals remains (chapter 28), especially iron and products such as coffee, tea and cocoa (chapter 07).

The Beverages and Tobacco Section represents the highest intra-industry trade level in 1996 (G-L 85.1), but represented less than 0.5% in the trade between Argentina and Brazil in 1996. Section 6, corresponding to Manufactured Products according to Materials (in which Brazil has a considerable commercial surplus during all the years in the period analyzed) is the only group of remaining chapters to consider that does not have G-L index values higher than 50 points during the period analyzed. The section corresponding to Chemical Products and the section corresponding to Machines and Transport Equipment stand out because of their high significance in the volume negotiated and the high intra-industry trade indexes they show, especially the last one. In this case, the G-L index values were always about or above 50 but the significant increase in the volume of negotiated products helped the general index to grow during the period[11]. The MIIT index analysis shows almost the same results as the ones previously developed for the trade variation between both countries.

---

considerable intra-industry characteristics in the trade. It is important to highlight that these values will differ among the different tasks taking into account the aggregation level and the classification characteristics of the items (titles) used.

[11] Argentina increased Section 7 exports by 2684% and imports by 1333%. At a 3 digits classification level we can highlight item 784 that corresponds to Car parts and accessories and

In summary, in the Argentine-Brazilian trade flow evolution, there are two phenomena that stand out. On the one hand, there is a growth in the inter-industry trade of primary products according to the comparative advantages that each country has, for instance Brazilian exports of tropical products (coffee and cocoa) and Argentina's exports of warm areas crops (cereals, especially wheat). On the other hand, there is a high increase in the inter-industry trade of manufactured products in general. This fact can be seen in Chart 5, in which items from sections 5, 6, 7 and 8 (except chapter 68)[12] are together as manufactures, the G-L index added to this level shows that this one moved from 31.86 in 1986 to 58.35 in 1996. At a 2-digit level in the SITC, both indexes (G-L and MIIT) show that the inter-industry trade increase had a greater emphasis in Chemical Products and Transport Material and Equipment.

IV.2 Argentine trade with NAFTA and EU

From a general point of view, trade between Argentina and NAFTA was basically inter-industry trade during the period because the G-L index oscillated between 14 and 20 points, showing 14.91 in 1986 and 14.28 in 1996. We can reach a similar conclusion if we analyze the characteristics in the trade flow variations because the MIIT index for the whole period shows a 0.11 value (around ¼ of the value indicated by the trade flow between Argentina and Brazil variation index).

In Chart 5, at a deeper level, we can see that none of the sections shows a significant intra-industry trade character, and that the G-L index highest value in 1996 (23.73) corresponds to Section 2, Beverages and Tobacco. The G-L index added for all the manufactures (chapters in which Argentina is a net importer) shows a decrease in the intra-industry trade proportion because the G-L index decreased from 20.19 in 1986 to 13.46 in 1996. But, in the items that are not included in manufactures, the opposite occurs because the G-L index moves from 5.92 in 1986 to 16.69 in 1996.

The characteristics of the commercial relationship between Argentina and EU are similar to the characteristics between Argentina and NAFTA. The inter-industry character is stronger, the G-L index shows 9.90 in 1996 and is confirmed by the MIIT index that shows 0.096 for the period analyzed. At a deeper level, the structure is not homogeneous and the low value in both indexes at a general level is caused by the very low indexes indicated in Section 0 that corresponds to Food Products (3.20 points G-L, and represents 24.6% of the bilateral trade), and Section 7 that corresponds to Machines and Transport Equipment (5.58 G-L

item 731 that corresponds to Internal Combustion Engines in this section, because of their G-L indexes that are about 90 points.

[12] According to UNCTAD guidelines.

value, and represents 33.4% of the bilateral trade). Section 1, that corresponds to Beverages and Tobacco (mainly because of the Beverages exchange), has the highest G-L and MIIT indexes for 1996, with levels of 48.43 and 0.605 points respectively. In relation to Manufactured and Non-manufactured Products trade, their intra-industry characteristics show a slight increase, and their respective intra-industry trade indexes are around 10 points, in a 0 to 100 scale.

IV.3 Brazilian Trade with NAFTA and EU

The kind of trade held by Brazil with both regional blocks shows rather dissimilar aspects, and this differs from what happened with Argentina.

Intra-industry trade between Brazil and NAFTA has increased during the period. As an evidence of this, we can observe in Chart 6 an evolution in the G-L index (21.42 in 1986 and 30.29 in 1996) and in the MIIT index (0.193 for the whole period). In this sense, the manufactures trade evolution reflects that, even when the manufactures proportions in the total exports have increased (from 61% to 73%) and imports (from 72% to 83%), the intra-industry trade level in this kind of products showed a slight increase (from G-L index of 30.66 in 1986 to 33.21 in 1996).

At a deeper level, we can observe that, among the sections that correspond to manufactures, Section 7 (that corresponds to Machines and Transport Equipment) has a great significance (39% of the whole trade between Brazil and NAFTA) and the highest G-L index (42.02) in 1996.

The other items that are not included in the manufactures definition at a general level, show an increase in the intra-industry trade because the G-L index moves from 4.11 in 1986 to 19.26 in 1996. We must highlight that Section 2 (Crude Materials) has the highest MIIT index value (0.297) of all the sections, that means that the trade flow variation in this section was the most intra-industrial.

On the other hand, the commercial trade between Brazil and the EU is more inter-industrial, not only in the levels as it is indicated by the low G-L index value during the period (21.02 in 1996 and 19.23 in 1986) but also in the trade flow characteristics due to the MIIT index value (0.164).

The intra-industry character of the manufactures had a minor decrease since the G-L index for this classification level shows a decrease from 31.38 in 1986 to 28.04 in 1996. The same happens with the items that are not included in the manufactures: the G-L index moves form 8.46 in 1986 to 9.14 in 1996. It is important to highlight that the section with a higher intra-industry trade degree (Oils and Wax, with a 44.94 G-L index value in 1996 and a 0.683 MIIT index) is placed, at 2 SITC digits, among the items that are not included in the manufactures.

V CONCLUSIONS

The commercial opening and the regional integration process towards third countries carried out in the 90s by the governments of Brazil and Argentina, caused an important growth in the exports and imports of each country and a considerable growth in the bilateral trade between them, but it did not keep the former characteristics regarding the inter-industry or intra-industry characteristics of the trade between both countries and between each country with NAFTA and EU. While the bilateral relations between Argentina and Brazil in the first place, and between Brazil and NAFTA in a distant second place, indicated a growing flow and an interesting intra-industry trade level[13], the commercial relations between Brazil and EU and between Argentina and both economic blocks (EU and NAFTA), indicate an inter-industry specialization in which the Latin-American countries export primary products and import manufactured goods. This happens mainly in Argentina because, even when Brazil has low intra-industry trade levels, these levels are higher than Argentine levels and Brazil is also a net exporter of some manufactured goods, especially in Section 6 that refers to Manufactured Goods classified according to Materials, where it has a commercial surplus with EU in 1996.

The growing tendency towards a greater intra-industry trade between Brazil and NAFTA will constitute an authentic sign of the possibility of intra-industry trade existence between a developed country and a developing country. But we must take into account that this growth in the level and this change in the intra-industry trade flow is partially due to the increase of the G-L index for non-manufactured goods.

As regards bilateral trade between the two main MERCOSUR partners, we can see that the regional integration process with Brazil had different effects on the characteristics of the trade that became stronger between both countries. In some sectors, the comparative advantages of each country have prevailed and trade acquired inter-industry characteristics as it is shown by HO model.

But in most of the sectors, the intra-industry trade with Brazil had a growing behavior during the period analyzed. In this way, the index added to the whole economy has a strong increase. In this sense, there are some sectors that stand out such as the Chemical Industry sector and the Machines and Transport Equipment sector that show high G-L index values. As regards this aspect, we must highlight that the intra-industry trade is related to the growth of the

[13] In most of the situations analyzed, the conclusions we can draw from the annual analysis of the G-L index coincide with what is indicated by the MIIT index for the whole period. The reason for this behavior is that the variation in the trade flows in the countries and years analyzed is so significant that in the negotiations held before 1986 that are used as foundation do not have a great importance.

negotiated volume and the existence of high G-L index values in the Machines and Transport Equipment sector, especially the automotive sector as a consequence of the compensated exchange system with which said industry has been favored and that originates a substantial increase in the intra-company trade of multinationals with plants in both countries.

Finally, these facts highlight the interest in future research so as to identify with a greater precision the causes that originate (or not) the high intra-industry trade level between the countries analyzed (for instance, the importance of the economies of scale that make Brazil have higher intra-industry trade levels with NAFTA and EU than with Argentina) and the new policies implementation impact on the intra-industry trade evolution (for instance the implementation of a new automotive trade policy in MERCOSUR, that does not contemplate a compensated trade strictly). All these aspects and their consequences will play an important role in negotiations aiming at improving the relationship among MERCOSUR member countries and in future agreements between the regional integration processes analyzed.

REFERENCES

AMITI, Mary (1998): "Inter-Industry Trade in Manufactures: Does Country Size Matter?". Journal of International Economics, vol. 44 (2), pp. 231-255.

ATURUPANE, C., DJANKOV, S. and HOEKMAN, B. (1999): "Horizontal and Vertical Intra-Industry Trade between Eastern Europe and the European Union". "Measuring Marginal Intra-Industry Trade". Weltwirtschaftliches Archiv, vol. 135 (1), pp. 62-81.

BEHAR, Jaime (1991): "Economic Integration and Intra-Industry Trade: The Case of the Argentine-Brazilian Free Trade Agreement", Journal of Common Market Studies, Vol. XXIX, N° 4.

BROWN, D. and STERN, R. (1989). "Computable general equilibrium Estimates of the gain US-Canadian trade Liberalization". In Greenaway et al (edit), Economics Aspects of regional Trading Arrangements, Brighton.

BRÜLHART, M. (1994): "Marginal Intra-Industry Trade: Measurement and Relevance for the Pattern of Industrial Adjustment". Weltwirtschaftliches Archiv, vol. 130 (3), pp. 600-613.

CANTWELL, John (1994): "The Relationship Between International Trade and International Production". In Greenaway y Winters (edit.), Survey in International Trade, Basil Blackwell, 1994.

DAVIS, Ronald (1995): " Intra-industry Trade: A Heckscher-Ohlin-Ricardo Approach". Journal of International Economics, vol. 39, pp. 201-226.

DIAZ CAFFERATA, A. (1996): "Ajuste estructural y Desocupación de la Mano de Obra: Restricciones de Corto Plazo", XI Jornadas Anuales de Economía. Banco Central de Uruguay.

GREENAWAY, D and TORSTENSSON, J. (1997): "Back to the Future: Tacking Stock on Intra-Industry Trade". Weltwirtschaftliches Archiv, vol. 133 (2), pp. 249-269.

GREENAWAY, D. (1988): "Intra-Industry Trade, Intra-Firm Trade and European Integration : Evidence, Gains and Policy Aspects". In Dunnig , J y Robson, P. Multinationals and the European Community, Basil Blackwell, Oxford.

GREENAWAY, D. and MILNER, C. (1981): "Trade Imbalance Effects in the Measurement of Intra-Industry Trade". Weltwirtschaftliches Archiv, vol. 117 (1), pp. 756-762.

GREENAWAY, D. and MILNER, C. (1984): "A Cross Section Analysis of Intra-Industry Trade in the U.K.". European Economic Review, vol.25 (3), pp. 319-344.

GRENAWAY, D. and MILNER, C. (1987): "Intra-Industry Trade: Current Perspectives and Unresolved Issues". Weltwirtschaftliches Archiv, vol. 123 (1), pp. 39-57.

GRUBEL, H. and LLOYD, P. (1975): "Intra-Industry Trade". London: Macmillan.

HAMILTON, C. and KNIEST, P. (1991): "Trade Liberalization, Structural Adjustment and Intra-Industry Trade: A Note". Weltwirtschaftliches Archiv, vol. 127 (2), pp. 356-367.

HINE, Robert (1994): "International Economic Integration". ". In Greenaway y Winters (edit.), Survey in International Trade, Basil Blackwell, 1994.

JUAREZ DE PERONA, H. (1994): "Argentina en el MERCOSUR: Posibilidades de Complementación Industrial". FCE, IEF, Serie de Investigaciones, n° 64, 1994.

KRUGMAN, P (1980): "Scale Economies, Product Differentiation, and the Pattern of Trade". The American Economic Review, vol. 70, number 75, December.

LLOYD, P.J. (1989): "Reflections on Intra-Industry Trade Theory and Factor Proportions". In Tharakan, P.K.M. and Kol, J. (eds.), Intra-Industry Trade - Theory, Evidence and Extensions, Macmillan, London.

LUCANGELI (1992): "Integración Comercial, Intercambio Intra-industrial y Creación y Desvío de Comercio; El Intercambio Comercial entre Argentina y Brasil en los Años Recientes", Documento de Trabajo n° IE/01, Serie Integración Económica, Subsecretaria de Estudios Económicos - PNUD, Buenos Aires.

LUCANGELI, J. (1993): " La Presencia de Comercio Intraindustrial en el Intercambio entre Argentina y Brasil". Boletín Informativo Techint, n°275, july-september.

RODNEY, T. and McDOWELL, M. (1999): "Measuring Marginal Intra-Industry Trade". Weltwirtschaftliches Archiv, vol. 135 (1), pp. 48-61.

THARAKAN, P.K.M. (1984): "Intra-Industry Trade Between the Industrial Countries and the Developing World". European Economic Review, vol.26 (1-2), pp. 213-227.

TORNELL, A. (1986): "¿Es el Libre Comercio la Mejor Opción? Comercio Heckscher-Ohlin vs. Comercio Intraindustrial". El Trimestre Económico, july-september, pp. 529-559.

VERNON, R. (1966): "International Investment and International Trade in the Product Cycle", Quarterly Journal of Economics 80, n°2, pp. 190-207.

APPENDIX

Chart 1

ARGENTINE EXPORTS (Millons of US dolars)										
Sections	Exports in 1996	Share (%) of 1996 Exports	Exports in 1986	Share (%) of 1986 Exports	Share (%) of Selected Export Destinations					
					Brazil		EU		NAFTA	
					1996	1986	1996	1986	1996	1986
0-Food and Live Animals	9.235	38,8	3.220	47,0	21,8	11,7	29,7	34,2	6,6	9,7
1-Beverages and Tabacco	283	1,2	48	0,7	6,9	1,3	31,7	57,3	20,9	20,2
2-Crude Materials	1.941	8,2	905	13,2	12,4	1,9	47,9	62,2	9,8	7,1
3-Fuels, Lubricants	3.088	13,0	164	2,4	41,7	14,2	1,4	5,9	16,7	46,8
4-Annimal Veg. Oils, Wax	1.889	7,9	655	9,6	5,1	6,4	3,3	14,6	5,2	4,8
5-Chemical Products	1.349	5,7	321	4,7	32,0	14,7	11,8	17,1	9,1	27,9
6-Manufactured Goods	2.754	11,6	925	13,5	18,9	11,4	19,2	13,2	15,3	25,2
7-Machines, Transport Equip.	2.595	10,9	493	7,2	70,5	13,3	6,0	4,9	5,2	7,0
8-Misc. Manuf. Articles	675	2,8	116	1,7	26,8	15,8	12,4	11,9	21,5	32,4
TOTAL	23.808	100,0	6.847	100,0	27,8	10,2	20,1	29,4	9,7	13,0

Source: Owm estimates based on DATAINTAL-BID/INTAL data.

Chart 2

ARGENTINE IMPORTS (Millons of US dolars)										
Sections	Imports in 1996	Share (%) of 1996 Imports	Imports in 1986	Share (%) of 1986 Imports	Share (%) of Selected Export Destinations					
					Brazil		EU		NAFTA	
					1996	1986	1996	1986	1996	1986
0-Food and Live Animals	1.026	4,3	314	6,7	34,8	34,8	14,2	4,5	14,2	3,7
1-Beverages and Tabacco	89	0,4	6	0,1	22,5	18,2	42,9	35,9	10,8	15,5
2-Crude Materials	788	3,3	505	10,7	36,5	25,3	10,1	6,7	23,7	16,7
3-Fuels, Lubricants	864	3,6	423	9,0	5,9	0,2	22,7	1,4	10,3	11,8
4-Annimal Veg. Oils, Wax	46	0,2	6	0,1	34,2	18,7	27,3	19,8	8,9	32,1
5-Chemical Products	4.391	18,5	1.136	24,1	18,1	14,4	29,2	36,3	31,7	32,2
6-Manufactured Goods	3.414	14,4	530	11,3	37,1	20,5	24,1	43,8	16,0	10,6
7-Machines, Transport Equip.	10.931	46,0	1.523	32,4	20,7	10,3	34,4	44,5	24,1	20,6
8-Misc. Manuf. Articles	2.207	9,3	263	5,6	12,3	7,6	26,9	29,2	23,8	30,9
TOTAL	23.757	100,0	4.707	100,0	22,4	14,7	29,2	30,9	23,3	20,5

Source: Owm estimates based on DATAINTAL-BID/INTAL data.

Chart 3

BRAZILIAN EXPORTS (Millons of US dolars)										
Sections	Exports in 1996	Share (%) of 1996 Exports	Exports in 1986	Share (%) of 1986 Exports	Share (%) of Selected Export Destinations					
					Brazil		EU		NAFTA	
					1996	1986	1996	1986	1996	1986
0-Food and Live Animals	10.739	23,1	6.761	30,4	3,1	1,7	43,4	42,6	11,6	24,4
1-Beverages and Tabacco	1.636	3,5	428	1,9	4,9	0,2	41,0	50,0	20,1	28,1
2-Crude Materials	5.953	12,8	2.734	12,3	4,1	3,8	45,1	43,3	13,0	10,7
3-Fuels, Lubricants	421	0,9	704	3,2	8,4	0,1	15,0	4,4	30,7	45,2
4-Annimal Veg. Oils, Wax	881	1,9	262	1,2	1,6	0,4	9,6	18,0	4,5	11,3
5-Chemical Products	3.160	6,8	1.187	5,3	23,4	13,5	16,5	20,1	16,5	23,0
6-Manufactured Goods	11.164	24,0	4.469	20,1	10,5	2,4	19,6	17,5	22,9	28,7
7-Machines, Transport Equip.	9.522	20,5	3.824	17,2	24,3	4,5	13,3	14,2	30,9	40,7
8-Misc. Manuf. Articles	3.049	6,6	1.844	8,3	7,5	1,3	17,9	12,1	50,3	68,1
TOTAL	46.525	100,0	22.214	100,0	11,1	3,1	27,3	27,6	21,7	30,5

Source: Owm estimates based on DATAINTAL-BID/INTAL data.

Chart 4

BRAZILIANS IMPORTS (Millons of US dolars)										
Sections	Imports in 1996	Share (%) of 1996 Imports	Imports in 1986	Share (%) of 1986 Imports	Share (%) of Selected Export Destinations					
					Brazil		EU		NAFTA	
					1996	1986	1996	1986	1996	1986
0-Food and Live Animals	4.742	8,9	1.945	12,4	45,0	20,0	9,3	19,1	15,7	28,5
1-Beverages and Tabacco	255	0,5	43	0,3	7,1	0,9	42,6	82,5	31,3	2,9
2-Crude Materials	2.449	4,6	1.048	6,7	11,3	1,9	8,3	9,7	21,2	31,5
3-Fuels, Lubricants	6.897	13,0	3.548	22,6	17,9	1,5	4,5	1,0	11,3	10,5
4-Annimal Veg. Oils, Wax	379	0,7	126	0,8	28,8	41,1	31,2	33,1	4,0	15,7
5-Chemical Products	8.430	15,9	2.256	14,4	5,1	1,8	33,3	34,1	33,6	38,1
6-Manufactured Goods	5.325	10,1	1.032	6,6	9,9	10,5	31,9	41,2	26,0	27,8
7-Machines, Transport Equip.	20.559	38,8	4.890	31,2	8,9	1,6	35,2	32,6	30,8	40,9
8-Misc. Manuf. Articles	3.947	7,4	803	5,1	5,2	5,1	26,8	22,0	28,1	32,1
TOTAL	52.984	100,0	15.691	100,0	12,7	5,0	26,4	22,6	26,0	29,9

Source: Owm estimates based on DATAINTAL-BID/INTAL data.

Chart 5

Argentina's Intra-Industry Trade (all matched SITC 3-digit level)

Sections	BRAZIL			EU			NAFTA		
	G-L 1996[a]	G-L 1986[b]	MIIT[c]	G-L 1996[a]	G-L 1986[b]	MIIT[c]	G-L 1996[a]	G-L 1986[b]	MIIT[c]
0-Food and Live Animals	9,52	12,72	0,066	3,20	2,20	0,039	16,78	4,59	0,083
1-Beverages and Tabacco	85,10	73,76	0,856	48,43	8,17	0,605	23,73	16,09	0,251
2-Crude Materials	10,04	21,09	0,044	5,88	2,30	0,075	6,81	7,61	0,072
3-Fuels, Lubricants	7,26	0,32	0,073	35,67	66,43	0,345	22,67	7,22	0,137
4-Annimal Veg. Oils, Wax	11,49	1,33	0,144	33,16	2,19	0,195	2,14	2,21	0,004
5-Chemical Products	61,99	27,23	0,639	20,25	12,57	0,188	13,92	24,94	0,107
6-Manufactured Goods	44,02	7,90	0,470	18,71	13,71	0,125	20,33	13,48	0,180
7 Machines, Transport Equip.	63,12	53,22	0,628	5,58	6,52	0,058	9,78	19,81	0,077
8-Misc. Manuf. Articles	56,24	59,33	0,521	10,89	10,46	0,106	19,63	14,49	0,186
TOTAL	40,25	22,36	0,405	9,90	6,22	0,096	14,28	14,91	0,110
Manufactures[d]	58,35	31,86	–	10,98	9,89	–	13,46	20,19	–
Not - Manufactures[e]	10,08	13,39	–	8,10	3,15	–	16,69	5,92	–

Note: a) Aggregated Grubel y Lloyd index for 1996 b) Aggregated Grubel y Lloyd index for 1986 c) Brülhart's (1994) Marginal Intra-Industry Trade for the period 1986/1996 d) Weighted average of the G-L index over all the industries included in the sections 5,6,7y 8 (except Chapter 68) e)Weighted average of the G-L index over all the industries included in the sections 0,1,2,3, 4 and Chapter 68

Source: Owm estimates based on DATAINTAL-BID/INTAL data.

Chart 6

Brazil's Intra-Industry Trade (all matched SITC 3-digit level)

Sections	ARGENTINA			EU			NAFTA		
	G-L 1996[a]	G-L 1986[b]	MIIT[c]	G-L 1996[a]	G-L 1986[b]	MIIT[c]	G-L 1996[a]	G-L 1986[b]	MIIT[c]
0-Food and Live Animals	9,52	12,72	0,066	2,94	8,32	0,004	8,78	1,17	0,082
1-Beverages and Tabacco	85,10	73,76	0,856	5,95	1,59	0,002	11,27	0,73	0,151
2-Crude Materials	10,04	21,09	0,044	26,56	20,56	0,006	28,09	10,95	0,297
3-Fuels, Lubricants	7,26	0,32	0,073	33,88	58,61	0,003	28,44	4,38	0,011
4-Annimal Veg. Oils, Wax	11,49	1,33	0,144	44,94	2,22	0,005	9,55	1,85	0,199
5-Chemical Products	61,99	27,23	0,639	29,90	38,98	0,026	28,48	39,73	0,194
6-Manufactured Goods	44,02	7,90	0,470	33,59	33,09	0,037	28,30	22,67	0,149
7-Machines, Transport Equip.	63,12	53,22	0,628	26,94	25,08	0,069	42,02	36,24	0,273
8-Misc. Manuf. Articles	56,24	59,33	0,521	19,74	29,66	0,010	15,88	15,09	0,110
TOTAL	40,25	22,36	0,405	21,02	19,23	0,164	30,29	21,42	0,193
Manufacturas[d]	58,35	31,86	–	28,04	31,38	–	33,21	30,66	–
No - Manufacturas[e]	10,08	13,39	–	9,14	8,46	–	19,26	4,11	–

Note: a) Aggregated Grubel y Lloyd index of 1996 b) Aggregated Grubel y Lloyd index of 1986 c) Brülhart's (1994)Marginal Intra-Industry Trade for the period 1986/1996 d) Weighted average of the G-L index over all the industries included in the sections 5,6,7y 8 (except Chapter 68) e)Weighted average of the G-L index over all the industries included in the sections 0,1,2,3, 4 and Chapter 68

Source: Owm estimates based on DATAINTAL-BID/INTAL data.

Intra-Industry Trade of Argentina and Brazil in 1996 (G-L index)					
Sections and chapters	Argent-Brazil	Argent-EU	Argent-NAFTA	Brazil-EU	Brazil-NAFTA
00 Live animals	22,54	62,04	93,46	7,11	1,50
01 Meat, meat preparation	16,06	2,29	0,06	0,97	5,20
02 Dairy products, bird, eggs	2,89	8,08	41,59	2,76	1,06
03 Fish, crustaceans, molluse	8,55	4,16	10,46	15,95	3,69
04 Cereal, cereal preparat.	2,94	0,73	52,05	1,22	0,53
05 Vegetable and fruit	16,93	6,93	18,00	7,40	19,18
06 Sugar, sugar prep., honey	46,44	21,44	8,68	54,33	11,16
07 Coffee, tea, coccoa, spices	10,33	8,54	17,18	0,63	3,07
08 Annimal feed stuff	65,54	0,89	6,64	0,94	57,33
09 Micel. Edible products	49,23	41,78	21,29	12,01	14,19
0 Food and Live Animals	**9,52**	**3,20**	**16,78**	**2,94**	**8,78**
11 Beverages	76,76	90,09	82,25	12,14	32,04
12 Tobacco, tobacco manuf.	91,74	5,34	0,00	5,54	7,21
1 Beverages and Tabacco	**85,10**	**48,43**	**23,73**	**5,95**	**11,27**
21 Hides, skin, furnskins	0,00	46,37	0,22	14,03	55,88
22 Oils seed, oleaginous fruit	3,93	0,04	12,42	0,02	16,80
23 Crude rubber	15,53	95,08	22,65	86,49	30,38
24 Cork and wood	28,59	2,96	21,23	0,27	0,18
25 Pulpe and waste paper	80,56	4,02	0,00	0,68	55,85
26 Textile fibres	5,40	2,73	1,41	35,99	2,17
27 Crude fertilizer, mineral	72,43	49,22	4,45	24,96	23,93
28 Metalliferous ore	0,22	13,33	4,87	1,55	4,26
29 Crude animal, veget. material	30,22	52,73	10,55	84,97	62,51
2 Crude Materials	**10,04**	**5,88**	**6,81**	**26,56**	**28,09**
32 Mineral coal	0,00	0,00	0,00	0,00	0,00
33 Petroleum, petrol. products	7,54	35,87	23,46	36,55	48,88
34 Natural and manuf. gas	0,00	16,74	15,95	0,00	23,02
35 Electricity	8,90	0,00	0,00	0,00	0,00
3 Fuels, Lubricants	**7,26**	**35,67**	**22,67**	**33,88**	**28,44**
41 Annual oils	12,13	89,23	0,00	44,93	0,00
42 Fixed vegetable and oils	4,35	20,87	1,04	55,43	42,12
43 Annual Vet. fats, oils	64,88	88,14	51,08	86,74	45,02
4 Annimal Veg. Oils, Wax	**11,49**	**33,16**	**2,14**	**44,94**	**9,55**
51 Organic chemicals	59,16	27,24	22,69	34,43	34,30
52 Inorganic chemicals	71,56	12,67	3,94	60,64	56,99
53 Dyes, colouring materials	86,30	35,00	18,50	35,78	10,75
54 Medical, pharmac. products	77,83	17,95	14,66	12,95	10,16
55 Essentl. oils, perfume	52,22	15,65	25,81	26,43	32,04
56 Manufactured fertilizer	0,11	0,00	0,00	0,00	0,00
57 Plastics in primary form	52,24	19,18	3,54	24,26	21,62
58 Plastics, non-primary form	85,28	0,69	2,72	14,54	35,95
59 Chemical materials	50,02	16,15	21,28	47,74	35,98
5 Chemical Products	**61,99**	**20,25**	**13,92**	**29,90**	**28,48**
61 Leather, leather goods	6,86	1,62	1,18	4,65	18,53
62 Rubber manuf.	62,18	13,56	30,19	35,44	40,33
63 Wood and cork manuf.	62,76	36,13	51,01	7,04	2,47
64 Paper, paperboard, etc.	31,03	3,51	4,23	67,89	26,15
65 Textile, yarn, fabric	70,88	16,92	9,89	36,17	54,05
66 Non-metal mineral manuf.	47,78	16,19	25,94	42,65	42,87
67 Iron and steel	18,26	61,99	52,20	40,74	13,34
68 Non-ferrous metals	30,85	56,46	29,51	36,97	35,21
69 Metal manuf.	41,93	15,31	17,79	21,12	54,65
6 Manufactured Goods	**44,02**	**18,71**	**20,33**	**33,59**	**28,30**

Intra-Industry Trade of Argentina and Brazil in 1996 (G-L index) [Continuation]					
Sections and chapters	Argent-Brazil	Argent-EU	Argent-NAFTA	Brazil-EU	Brazil-NAFTA
71 Power generating machines	85,28	8,80	17,61	72,91	59,40
72 Special ind. machinery	16,98	1,76	2,55	13,42	40,72
73 Metal working machinery	36,92	0,43	15,90	10,82	71,41
74 General Ind. machines	64,18	5,76	9,73	26,07	64,43
75 Office machines	4,62	9,46	13,05	27,44	22,72
76 Telecomm, sound equip.	35,35	3,03	2,29	3,40	5,40
77 Elec. machin. appar, parts	35,00	5,83	3,16	24,54	24,19
78 Road vehicles	68,54	4,89	14,43	20,78	45,52
79 Other transport equip.	54,48	25,02	21,66	81,92	93,84
7 Machines, Transport Equip.	**63,12**	**5,58**	**9,78**	**26,94**	**42,02**
81 Prefab. Buildings	27,47	0,48	5,52	21,97	12,07
82 Furniture, cushions	47,73	26,22	55,82	42,08	63,53
83 Trunk, suit cases, bags	71,19	53,37	91,03	34,59	80,13
84 Clothing and accesories	40,28	16,84	25,98	46,29	58,58
85 Footwear	87,33	58,20	28,97	5,98	1,27
87 Scientific equip.	34,52	4,65	9,92	9,13	12,16
88 Photo appart	73,57	5,15	10,42	23,89	37,79
89 Misc. manuf goods	54,10	9,78	16,49	20,28	22,97
8 Misc. Manuf. Articles	**56,24**	**10,89**	**19,63**	**19,74**	**15,88**
TOTAL	**40,25**	**9,90**	**14,28**	**21,02**	**30,29**

Source: Owm estimates based on DATAINTAL-BID/INTAL data.

Marginal Intra-Industry Trade of Argentina and Brazil in the period 1986/96					
Sections and chapters	Argent-Brazil	Argent-EU	Argent-NAFTA	Brazil-EU	Brazil-NAFTA
00 Live animals	0,210	0,703	0,849	0,000	0,008
01 Meat, meat preparation	0,014	0,029	0,000	0,007	0,029
02 Dairy products, bird, eggs	0,028	0,076	0,003	0,012	0,002
03 Fish, crustaceans, molluse	0,060	0,058	0,149	0,000	0,007
04 Cereal, cereal preparat.	0,018	0,017	0,042	0,013	0,001
05 Vegetable and fruit	0,133	0,079	0,134	0,078	0,336
06 Sugar, sugar prep., honey	0,431	0,253	0,120	0,398	0,023
07 Coffee, tea, coccoa, spices	0,164	0,048	0,227	0,007	0,026
08 Annimal feed stuff	0,673	0,011	0,046	0,009	0,386
09 Micel. Edible products	0,435	0,000	0,000	0,000	0,000
0 Food and Live Animals	**0,066**	**0,039**	**0,083**	**0,019**	**0,062**
11 Beverages	0,770	0,910	0,840	0,143	0,283
12 Tobacco, tobacco manuf.	0,917	0,091	0,000	0,077	0,109
1 Beverages and Tabacco	**0,856**	**0,605**	**0,251**	**0,084**	**0,151**
21 Hides, skin, furnskins	0,000	0,000	0,000	0,000	0,000
22 Oils seed, oleaginous fruit	0,037	0,000	0,367	0,000	0,001
23 Crude rubber	0,161	0,045	0,839	0,991	0,543
24 Cork and wood	0,893	0,028	0,000	0,004	0,002
25 Pulpe and waste paper	0,546	0,025	0,000	0,008	0,712
26 Textile fibres	0,026	0,038	0,012	0,116	0,004
27 Crude fertilizer, mineral	0,204	0,560	0,060	0,135	0,069
28 Metalliferous ore	0,003	0,095	0,053	0,011	0,055
29 Crude animal, veget. material	0,380	0,634	0,066	0,806	0,602
2 Crude Materials	**0,044**	**0,075**	**0,072**	**0,078**	**0,297**
32 Mineral coal	0,000	0,000	0,000	0,283	0,000
33 Petroleum, petrol. products	0,076	0,351	0,144	0,222	0,000
34 Natural and manuf. gas	0,000	0,166	0,157	0,000	0,198
35 Electricity	0,089	0,000	0,000	0,000	0,000
3 Fuels, Lubricants	**0,073**	**0,345**	**0,137**	**0,205**	**0,011**
41 Annual oils	0,000	0,833	0,000	0,196	0,001
42 Fixed vegetable and oils	0,061	0,027	0,004	0,598	0,039
43 Annual Vet. fats, oils	0,696	0,934	0,000	0,921	0,438
4 Annimal Veg. Oils, Wax	**0,144**	**0,195**	**0,004**	**0,683**	**0,199**
51 Organic chemicals	0,726	0,273	0,147	0,312	0,194
52 Inorganic chemicals	0,440	0,115	0,015	0,382	0,222
53 Dyes, colouring materials	0,876	0,342	0,121	0,448	0,112
54 Medical, pharmac. products	0,710	0,187	0,112	0,060	0,070
55 Essentl. oils, perfume	0,539	0,074	0,238	0,204	0,275
56 Manufactured fertilizer	0,000	0,000	0,000	0,000	0,000
57 Plastics in primary form	0,579	0,143	0,045	0,204	0,212
58 Plastics, non-primary form	0,853	0,007	0,027	0,145	0,360
59 Chemical materials	0,420	0,192	0,239	0,336	0,315
5 Chemical Products	**0,639**	**0,188**	**0,107**	**0,237**	**0,194**
61 Leather, leather goods	0,016	0,018	0,023	0,003	0,011
62 Rubber manuf.	0,634	0,138	0,291	0,325	0,734
63 Wood and cork manuf.	0,599	0,312	0,428	0,091	0,029
64 Paper, paperboard, etc.	0,335	0,038	0,025	0,399	0,026
65 Textile, yarn, fabric	0,718	0,021	0,060	0,088	0,176
66 Non-metal mineral manuf.	0,442	0,207	0,213	0,396	0,464
67 Iron and steel	0,201	0,255	0,531	0,324	0,086
68 Non-ferrous metals	0,318	0,644	0,012	0,355	0,077
69 Metal manuf.	0,418	0,145	0,122	0,194	0,276
6 Manufactured Goods	**0,470**	**0,125**	**0,180**	**0,250**	**0,149**

Marginal Intra-Industry Trade of Argentina and Brazil in the period 1986/96					
Sections and chapters	Argent-Brazil	Argent-EU	Argent-NAFTA	Brazil-EU	Brazil-NAFTA
71 Power generating machines	0,866	0,106	0,161	0,602	0,346
72 Special ind. machinery	0,143	0,018	0,020	0,102	0,284
73 Metal working machinery	0,361	0,004	0,141	0,115	0,599
74 General Ind. machines	0,632	0,062	0,082	0,281	0,517
75 Office machines	0,021	0,000	0,127	0,226	0,198
76 Telecomm, sound equip.	0,196	0,025	0,024	0,008	0,031
77 Elec. machin. appar, parts	0,351	0,063	0,022	0,238	0,202
78 Road vehicles	0,687	0,053	0,003	0,160	0,364
79 Other transport equip.	0,548	0,262	0,216	0,430	0,052
7 Machines, Transport Equip.	**0,628**	**0,058**	**0,077**	**0,214**	**0,273**
81 Prefab. Buildings	0,275	0,005	0,025	0,219	0,029
82 Furniture, cushions	0,478	0,268	0,565	0,387	0,796
83 Trunk, suit cases, bags	0,712	0,529	0,663	0,000	0,000
84 Clothing and accesories	0,403	0,144	0,325	0,554	0,280
85 Footwear	0,861	0,533	0,575	0,084	0,037
87 Scientific equip.	0,341	0,054	0,094	0,081	0,029
88 Photo appart	0,323	0,049	0,001	0,273	0,000
89 Misc. manuf goods	0,539	0,088	0,142	0,095	0,117
8 Misc. Manuf. Articles	**0,521**	**0,106**	**0,186**	**0,168**	**0,110**
TOTAL	**0,405**	**0,096**	**0,110**	**0,164**	**0,193**

Source: Owm estimates based on DATAINTAL-BID/INTAL data.

COMPETITIVENESS AND EXTERNAL TRADE PERFORMANCE

Hada G. Juárez de Perona */

1. Introduction

The topic of competitiveness is particularly interesting in relation to the position held by the different industrial sectors of a country in the international markets. When talking about gaining foreign markets, the concept of competitiveness is always stressed, and considered as a necessary condition. However, it is not clearly defined how to quantify it.

An important aspect that should be taken into account is that many factors – related to public policies, company strategies and the tension between the public and private sectors – converge and interact within the general goal of competitiveness. Moreover, the interaction of such factors, creates a net of causalities which is not easy to interpret.

Therefore, it is necessary to consider both pure economic variables – such as technology, productivity, industry structure, demand conditions, inputs and costs – together with other variables more associated to management (business theory) – product quality, distribution channels and strategic alliances. All of them are essential to determine the degree of competitiveness in a globalized and fast changing world.

In the case of Argentina, competitiveness is particularly relevant to its agriculture and food industry. For this reason, the aim of this paper will be to outline a possible structure of analysis in order to be able to assess the degree of competitiveness of an agro-food industrial sector. Additionally, the comparison with other industrial standards would be insightful about the performance of Argentinean sectors. In this respect, the case of the dairy products industry will be analyzed, with reference to Brazil which is now the main recipient of national exports.

In the first part of this essay, some theoretical models that discuss the concept of competitiveness together with some attempts of measurement, will be presented. The second part deals with the dairy products industry, where the discussion will be centered around the several indicators designed to measure competitiveness. Finally, the last part suggests the limitations of the indicators

*/ We are grateful to Verónica García Seffino for her assistance with the processing of the statistical information.

considered to assess the degree of competitiveness of a specific branch of industry in relating to the external trade performance and the end conclusions.

2. The concept of competitiveness

The concept of competitiveness can be related to a company, a sector, or a country. In each case, there are different factors which become significant, being many of those factors of a qualitative nature. Nevertheless, research is generally restricted to quantitative factors – such as indicators based in the unitary value of exports and the unitary costs of labor – because they are easier to calculate.

Competitiveness is undoubtedly a notion of great importance for the aggregate productive sector of an economy. It is related to a vast number of agents and focuses on general variables, e.g. relative prices, production costs and the exchange rate. But for the competitive strategies of specific companies, product differentiation, quality, and management style, are also highly significant variables. Furthermore, in a context of globalization the study of competitiveness cannot be circumscribed to indicators associated with external trade, but should consider the penetration of markets through direct foreign investment, and technology exports.

2.a Theoretical models

In the specialized literature, various points of view are stressed when discussing the meaning of competitiveness, its limits and the indicators used to measure it, whose construction is usually preceded by the determination of a unit of outstanding relevance. In what follows, some of these ideas are reviewed:

1. **Competitiveness as performance:** It is based in the export performance of a company, an industry, or a country, being competitiveness associated with greater participation in foreign markets. Although it is a very broad notion, the expansion of exports involves numerous variables, which are constrained by both internal and external factors. These restrictions over variables determining export performance influence in turn the measure of competitiveness. Trade regulations, exchange rate policies or international agreements are examples of such constraints. Another restriction appears related to what is regarded as an ex post concept, so its use is being restricted with the purpose of setting policies that try to improve the competitiveness of a certain sector. However, reversing the argument, the loss of markets is definitely an indicator of the decline of competitiveness for the company, the industry or the country, respectively.

2. **Competitiveness as productive efficiency:** In this case, the company is the relevant unit of analysis, being competitiveness a structural characteristic of the productive conditions. Competitiveness is associated with lower costs, due to a favorable combination of inputs, given input prices. As a limitation, it should be pointed out that besides lower costs, there are other variables related to the ability to differentiate the product – such as delivery times – which determine that the product is not homogeneous from the point of view of consumers. It is also worth mentioning the technological and organizational aspects of production, which, among other factors, affect the competitiveness of a particular firm in the long term.

3. **Competitiveness as a multidimensional attribute of the company:** In this model, competitiveness is seen as a dynamic and multidimensional phenomenon, and it is associated to the industrial structure to which the firm belongs to (Bonelli,1992). As time develops, the company incorporates training and adopts strategies, by means of decisions which are subject to different restrictions, and which should change and adapt constantly, so that they become the sources of competitive advantages. These decisions can be identified with different levels of control. Segazio (1994) classifies the factors determining competitiveness in 'inner', 'structural' and 'systemic', according to the degree of control of the company. Among the first ones, most basic dimensions are found: costs, product quality, reliance in channels of distribution, capacity of innovation, and flexibility. Structural factors are related to the characteristics of consumer markets and industries, and the nature of competition. Finally, the systemic factors are external to the company, and correspond to the macroeconomic, political, institutional and regulatory environment.

4. **Competitiveness as an adjustment of the strategy of the company to a pattern of competition:** The study is carried out focusing on actions that are generated as a consequence of tensions occurring between structural and behavioral variables. The authors who agree with this approach, stress the fact that competitive strategies depend on the market structure in which the company develops. These strategies have different shapes, such as: price, quality, innovation, sale effort, publicity, etc. The problem that may arise is the lack of steadiness of the competence patterns in markets of fast technological changes that lead to the modification of strategies.

5. **Competitiveness as an adjustment to the internal organization and to the agricultural and food chain transactions**: It is clear that competitiveness is not a phenomenon restricted to a company or industry.

Instead, it is determined by the ability that companies – belonging to an agricultural or industrial chain – have, to adapt to changes in the economic environment. This flexibility depends on the capacity for the transmission of information, and on the existence of incentives and controls throughout the chain. Therefore, these agricultural and industrial chains become systems of vertical coordination of transactions among different structures of administration.

2.b Competitiveness indicators

From the former section, it can be concluded that there is not agreement respect to the indicators used to measure the degree of competitiveness. Different indicators can be constructed for different purposes or interests, and each of them will vary with the variables used for its computation, the geographic area it covers and the level of aggregation for the market and product involved, among others. They also diverge according to the math formula used and to the weight of the adopted patterns in the aggregation levels. We can thus consider a variety of indicators such as costs, competitive domestic prices, import penetration ratio, relative utility, not based on the prices etc.

In relation to what was previously expressed, it is possible to set up a structure of analysis, in order to study the competitiveness of a specific sector. To start with, it is necessary to deal with the factors that determine competitiveness which, according to Martin, Westgren and Van Duren (1991), can be classified into four categories:

- factors under the control of the company;
- factors quasi-controlled by the company;
- factors under the control of government;
- non-controlled factors.

The first company-controlled factors include company strategies, products, technology, costs, and chains of value. The quasi-controlled factors are basically given by demand conditions and input prices, The third category is formed by those factors derived from public policies, such as law and industrial policy, together with other factors related to the macroeconomic variables and the institutional structure, whereas the non-controlled ones, as their name indicate, refer to 'natural' conditions, such as the climate.

In this paper, several indicators related to market will be discussed, and then applied to a particular branch of industry. These indicators will be:

- rate of export participation in foreign markets by sectors and products;
- import penetration ratio in the domestic market;
- rate of risk of foreign competition;
- foreign prices versus export prices.

When the analysis focus on companies, the following indicators will be also taken into account:

- the export growth rate and the exporting specialization rate (Exp. /sales);
- the placing of capital bases in markets and the technological innovation;
- the trademark challenge and the strategic alliances;
- the productivity and costs.

The factors quasi-controlled by the firm will be analyzed in relation to

- the inputs
- the demand

3. Assessment of the competitiveness of a sector

The aim of this section is to analyze the competitiveness of a branch of the food industry and of the firms, which form this industry, given the framework of openness and integration characteristic of the modern world economy. To perform the analysis, the dairy sector has been selected in this study, a sector which is mainly oriented to Brazil within the Mercosur. To appreciate the significance of the dairy sector, it is worth mentioning that the world imports in 1985 amounted to USD 11,640 millions, a figure that increased 76% in 1990 especially due to a rise in prices, since the volume traded did not change significantly. In 1995, they reached USD 28,218 millions, declining till 1998 as a consequence of the fall in the average value of imports, whereas the volumes registered a steady growth (Figure 1a and 1b, in the appendix). Among the world producers of fluid milk, Argentina ranks 14th with a production of 9,450 millions of liters in 1998. World production, which is highly concentrated in developed countries, was around 548,000 millions of liters in the same year.

The starting hypothesis is that this branch of the food sector has undergone critical transformations affecting the determinants of competitiveness in all the segments of the chain of this agro-food complex. The external trade of the dairy sector grew significantly with the Mercosur – especially between Brazil and Argentina. The problems faced by the dairy sector are different for each of the two countries involved and, although this fact may generate uncertainty regarding the future of trade, the necessity of increasing competitiveness to win new markets represents at last, a point of convergence.

Therefore, the question here is how to evaluate the competitiveness of the dairy sector in Argentina, given that its participation in the world exchange is less than 1% and given the instability of the Brazilian market, which could be overcome through a greater diversification of foreign markets, escaping the dependence of exports from only one major destination.

3.a Factors under the control of the firm

3.a.1 In relation to market

i. Rate of participation in world markets

Changes in competitiveness should produce variations in export performance and in the share of markets. Figure 2 shows the evolution of the rate of participation of Argentinean exports in world markets (world exports/ imports). The percentage of participation is low but growing during the 1990s, both in export values – which doubled from 0.60 to 1.21% - and in volumes. The latter reached 0.96% in 1998.

The rate of participation is highly significant when measured with regard to the exports to Mercosur (Table 1). Furthermore, the coefficient reaches 47% if is calculated respect to Brazil, since Argentina destines 78% of its external sales to the neighboring country. It is important to notice that Brazilian imports seldom account for a 2% of world imports of dairy products. This leads to the conclusion that the growth of Argentinean exports is obviously associated to the broadening of market brought about by Mercosur, whereas the changing conditions of competition due to the liberalization of foreign markets, do not seem to have influenced the global positioning of the Argentinean dairy sector.

The analysis of competitiveness must be carried out not only in relation to the export performance of the aggregate sector, but also as a function of the performance of single firms within the different segments constituting the sector. Regarding the composition of the dairy sector outcome, Argentina produced 9,450 millions of liters of fluid milk in 1998. A 24% of this total was destined to domestic consumption whilst the remaining 76% was used as input for various industrial goods, in the proportion showed in Figure 3. There is a great diversity of products but, dry milk – a product which is traded as a commodity in world markets because of its use as a primary input by industry – is the one whose positioning in foreign markets is most well-established.

It is possible to observe that a double diversification has occurred in the case of dairy products. The consumer can choose among a larger variety of goods and moreover, among several qualities for each of them. From the point of view of competitiveness, this is showing that there are no major problems to increase diversification, which is permitted by the flexibility in production systems and the existence of economies of scope. The big issue here is positioning, that is, the place a particular good occupies within the range of similar goods offered by rival firms. The fixed costs associated to product development and marketing are important, and not always recovered through significant sales at the beginning, determining that scale economies due to high volumes of production are not secured. To be competitive it is essential to overcome this stage and when this is done, is still may happen that related to the growth in demand for the new product, many imitators will appear. It is at this point when positioning of trademarks and advertisement, become indispensable to keep the loyalty of consumers and to discourage the entrance of new suppliers.

Considering 20 dairy products, whose data for world exports are published by FAO, Argentina produces 11 of them but, in most cases, its share is inferior to 1%. The most important product is dry milk in its different versions, since its rate of export participation during 1998 amounted to 6.05%, which is substantially higher than the average rate for the sector (0.96%) and than the rate for other relevant products. Figure 4 shows the evolution of the rate of participation in world exports for the most significant products.

Regarding the exports to Mercosur, the rate of participation of Argentinean sales differs for each product. The average rate in 1998, was 46% and 62% for volumes and values exported, respectively. In the case of dry whole milk, those figures reached 80% and 86%.

To analyze the effects of competitiveness in a framework of integration, it is interesting to perform some comparisons with the Brazilian dairy sector, as long as Brazil is the prime importer of Argentinean products. The largest participation of Brazil corresponds to goods of lower value added, such as dry milk. This commodity goes to the neighboring country mainly from Argentina and competing in price with the Brazilian production, which was adversely affected by this fact.

ii. Rate of import penetration

This is a quantitative indicator of internal competitiveness. For each product, it is computed as a ratio between imports and domestic consumption, the latter obtained as a residual as the sum of production and imports, less exports. This indicator shows the degree of foreign competition for domestic markets.

$$TPM = M_j / C_j . 100$$

where M_j: imports of the j-th good C_j: consumption of the j-th good

The evolution of rates of import penetration is shown in Figure 5, for the central export products: dry whole milk, skim dry milk, fluid milk, cheese and butter.

In general, the data reveal a significant increase of the coefficient until 1992 and, from then on, there is a steady downward trend in the percentage of participation of imports in total domestic consumption. It is clear that the growth in imports at the beginning of the decade was a consequence of the increase in consumption and the instability in the supply of fluid milk in the short run, what was traduced in a rise in prices and stimulated imports, that were favored by strongly subsidized prices. From 1992 onwards, the export of dairy products stop being only circumstantial. The expansion in primary production, the growth in the common external tariff in Mercosur and the changes in international policies regulating subsidies, encouraged firms to follow a strategy based on exports. Particularly, this situation characterized the behavior of two commodities – skim dry milk and butter – for which the fall in import penetration was critical. In the case of the other products, the rate of import penetration remained oscillatory, albeit its peaks follow a decreasing trend.

To continue with the comparison with Brazil, it is worth noting that in the first five years of the last decade, the average coefficient of import penetration was 26.72% (dry milk), 45.25% (butter) and 8.62% (cheese). These percentages were lower for Argentina: 11.64%, 10.10% and 1.16%, respectively.

iii. Indicators of exposure to international competition

This indicator offers a quantitative measure of the degree of exposure of national production to international competition, as a percentage. Is assumes that both, exports and domestic production are subject to foreign competition, the latter in an extent given by the rate of import penetration. The indicator is computed as:

$$TE = X/P + (1 - X/P)\ TPM$$

Being X/P : exports (X) / production (P) * 100
TPM : rate of import penetration, as defined in the former section

The indicator is calculated in Table 2, only for the most relevant dairy products.

According to the table, by focusing on the values after 1993-1994, when exports were accelerated, the rate of exposure has decreased only in the case of non-fat dry milk. On the contrary, the rate of exposure doubled for dry whole milk in the same period, while it fluctuated for cheese and butter. However, in the latter case, the coefficient of exposure for butter registers a value in 1998 which is half of the corresponding figure in 1991.

Certainly, export dynamism varies with different products. Argentina ranks 7th among world exporters of dry whole milk and, in this commodity, the country presents a high rate of exposure to competition. On the other side, the trade of no-fat dry milk has been growing as a consequence of the sustained foreign demand and, in terms of the indicator considered here, this product is consolidating its degree of competitiveness.

Nevertheless, this statement should be taken with reservations, as long as special situations, such as conflicts between dairy farms and industry concerning the price of fluid milk, may appear. The emergence of such conflicts can induce big industrial firms in the sector to import dry milk to elaborate their products, as they did in fact during some periods. Of course, this strategy reduces competitiveness and affects the quality of dairy goods.

iv. Price indicators

By performing the comparison between international prices (minimum and maximum market price) and average export prices in Argentina, for the four main products exported by the dairy sector – non-fat dry milk, dry whole milk, butter and cheese – it is possible to derive some conclusions respect to the degree of competitiveness of those products in the world markets. The evolution of this indicator can be observed in Figure 6.

Using this indicator it can be inferred that, in terms of prices, the competitiveness of non-fat dry milk is not consolidated, since domestic prices do not present a tendency to stay below the maximum values for international prices, being in fact greater than this maximum value during the last three years of the period considered. This is also true in the case of dry whole milk. Despite Argentina ranks 7th in the list of world exporters, its average prices were always above the maximum value for international prices. While butter is better positioned [2], cheese can not be considered as a competitive product, when assessed through this indicator.

3.a.2 In relation to the firm

In order to measure competitiveness, it is necessary to take into account different dimensions of the problem. Computing the indicators already developed for the sector is important but rather limited. The analysis of the

[2] It is worth remarking that butter is one of the few dairy products whose exports are significant outside Mercosur. Nevertheless, it is characterized by a fall in world production and consumption.

competitiveness of a sector requires to take further steps, assessing factors more closely related to the firm and which are – although in different degrees – controlled by the firm.

i. Rate of growth and rate of exporting specialization

The dairy sector is characterized by oligopoly, a market structure that has been strengthened by openness and deregulation policies. To carry out the analysis, a sample of eleven firms whose exports amounted to 90% of the total exported by the sector during 1998, is considered. At the beginning of the 1990s only three of those firms were important from the point of view of the external markets, and continued to bear the leadership during the whole decade, not only in exports but also in overall sales. In turn, each of them is the market-leader for particular products: Sancor in non-fat dry milk and cheese; Mastellone in fluid milk, butter and yogurt; and Nestlé in dry whole milk and condensed milk.

As shown in Table 3.a., it is easy to differentiate the big multinational and national companies from the rest, based on their sales volume. When the three firms mentioned above are excluded, the sales of the remaining eight firms in the sample represented, in 1998, only 46% of the total sales of the former three.

In Table 3.b. the annual cumulative average rates of growth of exports are computed. In general, it is possible to observe an increasing orientation towards the external markets, especially Mercosur, although this conclusion varies for different firms, since some of them have chosen to consolidate their position in the domestic markets. The general fact that exports are growing for the whole sector is confirmed by the export-specialization coefficient that is, the ratio Exports/Sales which increased from 4% at the beginning of the decade to 12% in 1997.

All the indicators considered above are showing that a higher degree of competitiveness has been achieved. However, in view of some figures which seem to be negative, it must be recalled that in every process of economic integration a shifting of resources is taking place. For instance, the rate of growth of exports of Sancor and Milkaut – both leading firms in Argentina – are comparatively lower than the rest. But both companies have decentralized their sales and built their own sale centers in Brazil. Moreover, Milkaut has also decentralized its production since it has a subsidiary firm as well.

ii. Direct foreign investment and technological innovation

In a context of openness, integration and globalization, the search for competitiveness becomes a critical factor. Multinational companies penetrate all markets, introducing new products, technologies, habits of consumption and new organizational models while, at the same time, they benefit from the comparative advantages in local resources, such as labor, raw materials, etc.

During the period considered in this study, substantial structural changes took place in the dairy sector and in the main firms as well. Among these changes, it is worth remarking the important volume of investments, especially in 1995, directed towards the restructuration and expansion of productive capacity, association with multinational firms to incorporate and extend lines of production, direct investments in the country recipient of the final product (Brazil), together with direct investments in Argentina directly aimed at exporting. Between 1993 and 1998, the dairy industry invested around USD 1,300 millions to improve its competitiveness, both in the foreign and domestic markets. This is shown by the relationship between investment and trade for the different firms, particularly in the case of dry milk, cheese and yogurt, all of them products with very interesting possibilities in world markets.

Regarding technological innovation, it is important to distinguish primary production from the dairy industry. Milk production increased notoriously, in response to investments and changes in the organizational structure of dairy farms, whose minimum efficient scale increased, becoming dominant the medium and big farms. In turn, this expansion of primary production translated in lower costs for industry, with firms competing not only for their positioning in the different markets, but also for the sources of their primary input, milk. This fact, together with the arrival of high-technology transnational firms, determined that the dairy industry was subject to a strong process of technological innovation. Such innovations originated a remarkable growth in productivity, thereby reducing the costs of production. Moreover, they were of fundamental importance for trade and participation in foreign markets, since they permitted the introduction of new products, better quality and new varieties, essential to adapt to the preferences and tastes of foreign consumers. Without any doubts, the statement about the possibility of winning markets through foreign direct investment and technology transfers, is confirmed in the case of the Argentinean dairy sector but is very difficult to evaluate the significance of the indicators on the competitiveness level.

iii. Trademarks and strategic alliances

Trademarks are a critical factor for competitiveness in a globalized world. Argentinean firms in the dairy industry faced the challenge of preserving their own trademarks, while they expanded to second and third rank trademarks, to reach consumers with different purchasing power. Usually, when sales are declining, firms offer their products under the label of second rank trademarks, with lower prices. These trademarks are oriented to consumers whose main interest is the price of the product and firms competing in these segments win massive markets. Meanwhile, leading trademarks are oriented to selected markets, where the consumer cares about quality.

With respect to strategic alliances, during the years considered, there were some agreements between domestic and foreign companies, as a means of securing financial and technological support, in order to improve the market positioning, both in the domestic and foreign markets.

iv. Productivity and costs

It is not the intention of this study to analyze productivity and costs using primary information. In view of the scope of this essay, it is enough to consider the role of these two factors through references, taken from various sources.

Considering the whole chain for the dairy sector, the primary production of milk in Argentina has been characterized by high yields, estimated in approximately 3,833 lts/cow/year, a figure which is substantially greater than Brazil's. Being that country one of the largest producers of milk in the world, Brazilian yields only amount to 1,196 lts/cow/year . As a result of this difference in yields, the Argentinean dairy sector emerges with comparative advantages, which help to reduce the cost of milk as a primary input for industry. Just to illustrate, the USA and the European Union reported yields, are of 7,696 and 5,200 lts/cow/year, respectively.

This rise in productivity is associated with technological innovation, and has been accompanied by the growing profitability of dairy farms (see Table 4.a). It is worth remarking here the importance of distinguishing among different geographical regions, since productivity varies substantially for each of them.

Respect to the dairy industry, most indicators such as the average size, value of production per plant, average productivity – measured either as production per worker or added value per worker – are above the average value of the same indicators when the whole food industry is considered (Table 4.b.). In this case, it is also important to distinguish the sector as an aggregate from each of the particular firms within the sector. Productivity contrasts significantly between the three big leading firms and the rest, due to the remarkable differences in technology, scale of production and organizational structure.

Regarding the costs of production, fluid milk plays an important role, since it accounts for more than 45% of costs, this proportion varying for different products and varieties (Table 5.b.). Therefore, it represents an important element of competitiveness, which is relevant in the case of Mercosur. The average cost of production of a liter of fluid milk in Argentina are around USD 0.14 to USD 0.17, whereas this value reaches USD 0.21 for Brazil (Table 5.a). Of course these figures are only approximate, since there exists a multiplicity of costs and therefore, prices depend on the location of dairy farms, the volume of milk delivered, the volume of demand and the quality of milk.

To obtain a quantitative measure of competitiveness, it is also usual to rely on indices based on the unitary labor cost. However, this type of indicator should be carefully analyzed, since in most cases, it only considers the direct cost of labor used in production, excluding other relevant labor costs such as packaging and advertising costs. Table 5.c. provides an example, where those indirect costs represent as much as 11.5% of total costs.

With respect to non-labor inputs, their share in total costs may differ among countries and offset part of the comparative advantages derived from the cost of fluid milk. A paradigmatic example is given by electricity costs in Argentina, with non-uniform and high tariffs, whose share in the total costs of production is growing due to the introduction of new equipment, intensive in the use of energy. Table 5.b. shows that the item ‘electricity and fuel’ reaches 7% for some varieties of milk, while it accounts for another 7% of the direct cost of production of dairy farms.

As mentioned above, Argentina has comparative advantages in all those products using fluid milk as their main input, because of the high levels of productivity in the primary production, which positively affects the level of competitiveness. "Nevertheless, it is worth remarking the high sensitivity of costs to changes in production (see Table 6). This leads to the conclusion that in unfavourable periods of falling prices, it would be appropriate to increase the level of production, since this increment, via a reduction in costs, would prevent the fall in competitiveness".

3.b Factors quasi-controlled by the firm

3.b.1 Input Prices

At this stage, the relative control the dairy industry exercises over its primary input, fluid milk, must be remarked. It is not correct to take the average national price of milk as an indicator of competitiveness, because each firm has the opportunity of determining its own input price, through a process of direct negotiation with its suppliers. As a result, prices are not unique. Moreover, from the evolution of producer-prices of fluid milk and given the bargaining power that characterizes modern dairy farms, it can be seen that the greater productivity in the primary sector was hardly transferred to industry.

Another interesting aspect to consider in the analysis of competitiveness emerges from the correlation between the reduction in producer-prices of milk and the drop in domestic consumption which may be taken as a signal of the lack of consolidation of foreign markets. Neither international trade policies seem to be associated to the expected behavior of prices.

3.b.2 The demand side

To carry out an analysis of competitiveness, it is necessary to take into account the behavior of firms in relation to the different types of consumers, a segmentation which is directly associated to differences in income levels. In general, the demand of dairy products is characterized by a high income-elasticity, what in turn affects the quantity of dairy products actually purchased.

The world consumption of dairy products is growing, especially in the emerging markets, being the current average world consumption of 80 lts/person/year (liters are measured in an equivalent to fluid milk basis). This is good news for Argentinean production, where it is considered that internally, a maximum in fluid milk consumption (230.5 lts/person/year) has been almost reached. Fluid milk consumption in Brazil is around 140 lts/person/year. In both countries, the dairy sector followed a market-segmentation strategy and introduced new products to stimulate the demand, and thereby induce the growth of firms. Given the significant product diversification – observable through the great number of second and third rank trademarks that appeared as a result of firm strategies – this indicator appears of course as a positive symptom of competitiveness.

3.c Factors controllable by the government

When analyzing the competitiveness of a branch of industry, public policies should not be disregarded, since they may interfere by restricting the choice and/or implementation of firm strategies. Business are usually affected by taxes, rates of interest, exchange rates, and the like. Trade policies, R&D, education and training, governmental regulation; all these policies determine that the goal of competitiveness be achieved through a combination of public policies and strategies adopted by private firms. During the 1990s, several decisions adopted by government contributed to the enhancement of competitiveness in the dairy sector as well as in the firms within the dairy industry:

a) Deregulation of relationships between primary production and industry in 1991, that permitted the existence of direct arrangements between each firm and its suppliers.
b) Reduction of import tariffs which, in 1991, were set in 5% for dry milk, butter and cheese.
c) Increase in export drawbacks by the end of 1992, which rose from 5% to 7,5% (dry milk) and 10% (butter and cheese).
d) Institution of a common external tariff of 16% by the Mercosur partners, in 1995.

The existence of those preferential tariffs encouraged the export of dairy products to the Mercosur countries, especially dry milk, since the extra-Mercosur tariff set up by Brazil was above the 16% originally agreed upon, which represented additional stimuli for Argentinean exports. The opposite situation characterized the trade of cheese. Therefore, it is important for the discussion of competitiveness to be aware that, although tariffs were in general a positive variable in stimulating Argentinean dairy exports, they reduced but not impaired the subsidized imports from the European Union, that continued to keep the major proportion of the Brazilian market.

There are several other ways in which government can intervene to obtain growing levels of competitiveness in the firms of the sector, such as access to credit, labor-market flexibility and tax policies aimed at lowering costs. On the other hand, on occasion of low prices, the action of government is crucial to sustain the production level, in order to avoid a change in costs and consequently, in the level of competitiveness. This is e.g. the case of the dairy-fund credits, which would help to lessen the drop in international prices and/or the devaluation of the Brazilian currency.

3.d Non-controllable factors

Within this category of factors influencing the degree of competitiveness, those factors related to climate and weather conditions – whose effects on the primary production of fluid milk can negatively affect the price/cost relationship of industrial manufacturing – should be remarked. Such sort of negative externalities associated to the environment, might ultimately represent a competitive weakness.

4. Analysis of Competitiveness

Competitiveness is a phenomenon that occurs to firms and in the market. A sector is competitive whenever firms acting in such sector are competitive. And firms are competitive, when the strategies they adopt, are in accordance with international standards. In consequence, it is a requirement that all indicators used to measure competitiveness should be comparable, and that different factors could be weighted according to their degree of importance.

For every aspect of interest an indicator should be computed, which will depend on the variables considered for its computation and will be a function of the geographical area covered, and the aggregation level used for competitors, markets and products.

Two limitations in the indicators considered must be borne in mind when relating competitiveness to export performance: the aggregates that are used, and the lag between indicators and changes in the patterns of trade. For the former, a lower level of aggregation reveals a weak participation in sectors which have a strong external demand. With respect to lags, it is important to include them in the econometric analysis performed.

In the particular case of the dairy sector in Argentina, it was usually oriented towards the national market, whereas its exports represented the excess of production over domestic consumption. The processes of opening the current account together with economic integration introduced new dynamics into the sector which led to structural changes, such that, during the 1990s, the main recipient of exports is Brazil within the Mercosur. At present, the sector is facing the challenge of a greater diversification of markets, since production is growing and domestic consumption has reached its upper limit. Given such important changes taking place during the last decade in the sector, and the growth the sector has experienced in this period, could it be said that this branch of the agro-food industry is competitive?

From the indicators assessed it may be inferred that:

- According to its average rate of participation – 62% in export value and 46% in volume, both in 1998 – Argentina has the most competitive dairy sector within the Mercosur. This is true for the whole range of products, while the rate of penetration of imports is decreasing. However, it is not correct to talk about competitiveness when the process of integration has promoted almost exclusively only one market for the dairy products. It is not enough to associate competitiveness to performance and, in this sense, other indicators must be posed. Although Mercosur promoted efficiency and competitiveness of firms, it was not sufficient to permit the insertion of the sector in international extra-Mercosur markets.
- From the point of view of the strategy of product differentiation, it seems that not all products have achieved the same level of competitiveness, and only dry milk has succeeded outside Mercosur. This product then, scores the highest level of competitiveness based on its rate of expansion, despite it is not well established in relation to another indicator, export prices. In general, only one of the four products considered as the most significant ones, records international competitive prices during the last years. On the other side, each of the dairy products faces a different level of external competition and therefore, different competitive pressures in terms of varieties and marketing.
- It is not clear whether the characteristics of demand are a relevant determinant of competitiveness. Whereas in Argentina the average per capita consumption of milk has reached its limit, Brazil is far from this limit but, at the same time, Brazilian imports from Argentina are still marginal in relation to its national production. Moreover, the characteristics of demand are varied for the various dairy products and, given that demand (preferences) is a

variable very poorly controlled by firms, the correlation with the degree of competitiveness of the dairy industry is but very little. A thorough study of consumer patterns is required, to determine the quality and varieties to offer, and to develop packaging and trademarks able to succeed in different consumer markets.

- The size of firms in Argentina is smaller than Brazilian firms, as it is their investment in R&D and technology transfer. This fact has of course an impact over productivity levels. Nevertheless, in the case of the primary sector, the high yields of dairy farms in Argentina imply that in this country, industry faces lower costs. To what extent the concept of competitiveness based on economies of scale and technological innovations can be used to describe the dairy industry? Brazil presents technological advantages, while Argentina has comparative advantages in those products which require a greater percentage of fluid milk, the primary input. Due to its endowment of natural resources, Argentina produces milk at lower costs but these costs are highly sensitive to changes in production, a reason why it is necessary to guarantee a certain level of production in order to preserve the cost advantages.
- There are other components of costs – such as energy and financial costs – that are higher in Argentina, what may offset other competitive advantages. It is important to remember these costs, in the search for new markets, the achievement of certain levels of competitiveness might be restricted by those factors, which are not controlled by firms.
- Regarding the price/cost ratio, there may appear some problems when it is essential to sustain prices in order to ensure export profitability. If there is an upward pressure in export prices due to greater costs, the risk of loss of foreign markets increases. That is why, in the long-run, the relationship between export prices and prices of foreign competitors, should also be maintained at a stable level.
- The degree of concentration of supply is high, both in Argentina and Brazil, but this is not a limitation in a framework of economic integration. When the barriers to trade vanish due to integration, the firms enter a process of competition within the wider market.
- To be competitive, not only has a firm to be efficient from a microeconomic perspective, but also it must be surrounded by favorable conditions in its macroeconomic, sectoral and institutional environment, that present a positive influence to enhance competitiveness.

5. Conclusion

The aim of this study was to discuss the diverse factors that interact in the analysis and measurement of competitiveness and export performance of an industrial sector. In the present case, the essay focused on the dairy sector, for the period 1990-1998. Following, the main conclusions are stated.

- The concept of competitiveness is contentious and incorporate a great variety of factors co-determining it. The evaluation of competitiveness leads to the consideration of quantitative as well as qualitative indicators.
- One of the main conclusions derived from the discussion in the previous sections, is the loss of importance of prices and costs – two variables traditionally employed to assess competitiveness – relative to other indicators, such as innovation, trademark positioning, quality and packaging, among others.
- To carry out international comparisons, it is a key element to evaluate the competitiveness of a specific sector, together with the behavior of firms at different industrial segments within the sector considered.
- The process of globalization and integration characteristic of international trade relationships, is exposed to a high level of uncertainty and volatility, implying that it is difficult and sometimes impossible to forecast what will happen in the future. Therefore, export firms are subject to flexibility pressures to be able to adapt rapidly to changes in the environment, and to look for strategies that help reducing uncertainty.
- To establish the degree of competitiveness, it is necessary to take into account and to weight the different elements that are determining it. In this way, the causality network created by strategies adopted by firms, public policies that condition such strategies, and the structure of the industry to which those firms belong to, is made clear.
- Despite their usefulness, the indicators of competitiveness and their connection to the evolution of exports for a sector (or sectors) analyzed, are difficult to assess. Consequently, it is appropriate to perform a deeper analysis, capable of dealing with several indicators simultaneously.

References

Agénor, Pierre R. (1997) Competitiveness and External Trade Performance of the French Manufacturing Industry *Weltwirtschaflitches Archiv*- 133(1)

Bonelli,R./Fleury,P/Fritsch,W. (1992) Indicadores de Desempenho Competitivo ao Nivel da Firma - Río de Janeiro-BNDS,out.

Ferraz,J./Kupfer,D./Haguenamer,L.(1996) El Desafío Competitivo para la Industria Brasileña"- *Revista de la Cepal* No.58

GATT- The World Market of Dairy Products. Several years.

Gutman,Graciela (1999) La Industria Láctea en Argentina en la Década de los Noventa en Azpiazu/Gutman/Vispo *La Desregulación de los Mercados*- Grupo editor Norma-Flacso.

Juárez de Perona, Hada G. (1999) Estrategias de las Firmas Exportadoras Argentinas – CONICOR. Córdoba.

Krugman,Paul (1994) Competitiveness: a Dangerous Obsession- *Foreign Affairs* 73 (2)

Márgenes Agropecuarios : several numbers.

Martín,M./Westgren,R./van Duren,E. (1991) Agribusiness Competitiveness across National Boundaries. *American Journal of Agricultural Economy*- V73-No.5

Sagazio,G. (1994)Estudo da Competitividade Brasileira" *Revista Trevisan*, San Pablo.

SAGPyA (Secretaría de Agricultura, Ganadería, Pesca y Alimentación) La Industria Alimenticia Argentina. Buenos Aires (1999)

____________ Informe Estadístico de Leche y Productos Lácteos (1996).

____________ Revista *Alimentos Argentinos*: several numbers.

APPENDIX

Figure 1: World trade of dairy products
Figure 1a. (metric tons)

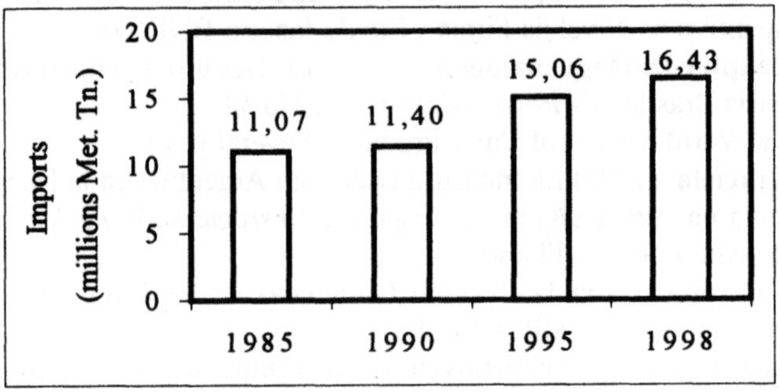

Figure 1b. (000 USD)

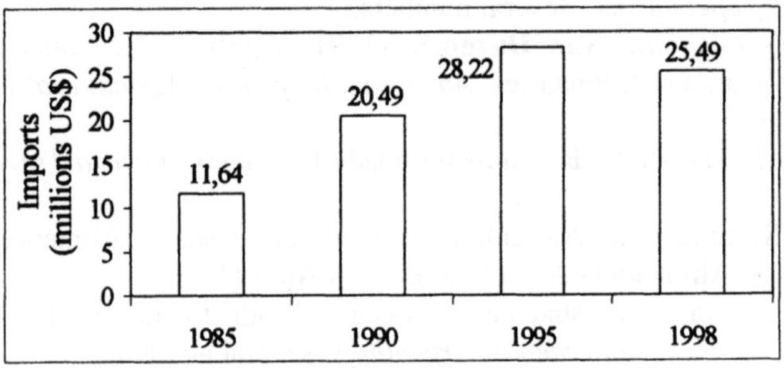

Source: FAO statistical database.

Figure 2: Evolution of the rate of participation in world markets
Figure 2a. (metric tons)

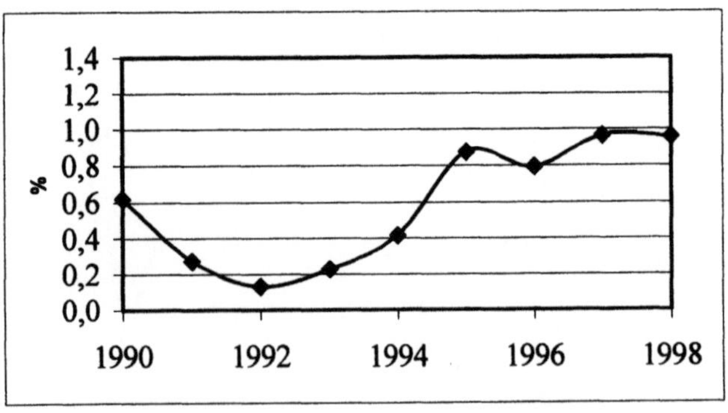

Figure 2b. (000 USD)

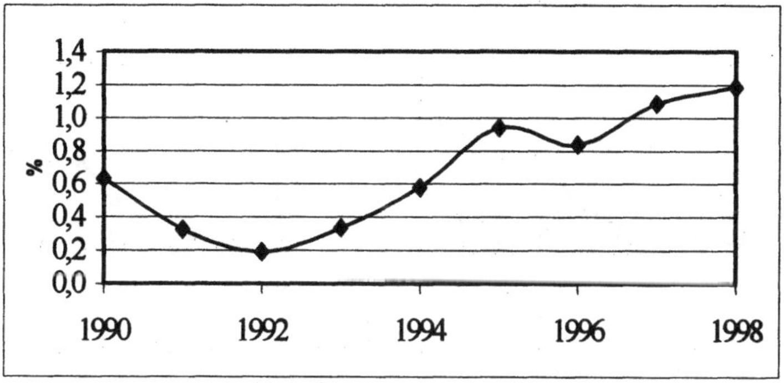

Source: FAO statistical database.

Figure 3. Composition of industrial uses of fluid milk, in 1998

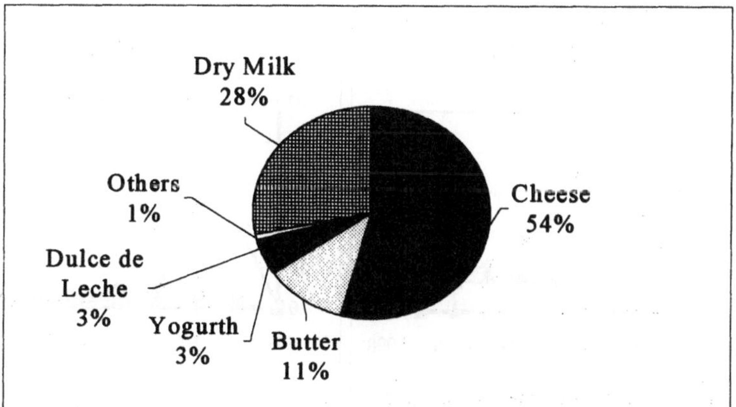

Source: SAGyP

Figure 4. Evolution of the rate of participation of selected dairy products in world exports

Figure 4a. (metric tons)

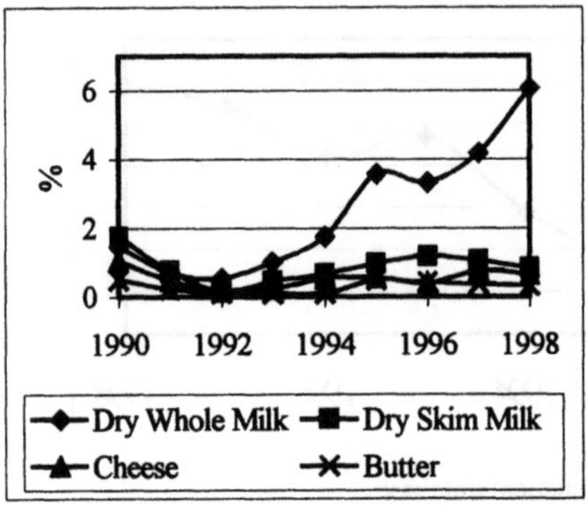

Figure 4b. (000 USD)

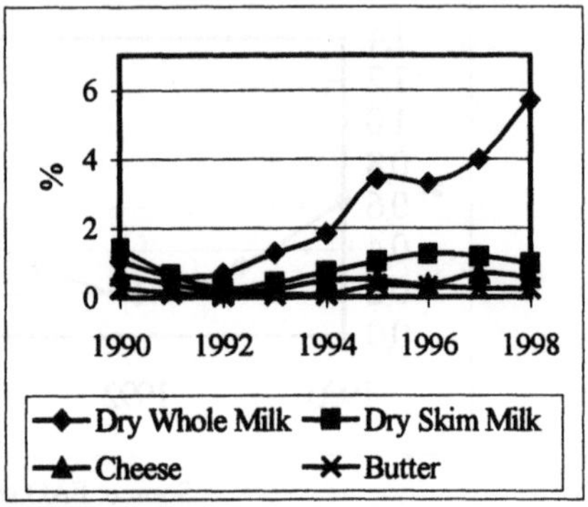

Source: FAO statistical database.

Figure 5. Evolution of rates of import penetration respect to domestic consumption

Figure 5.a

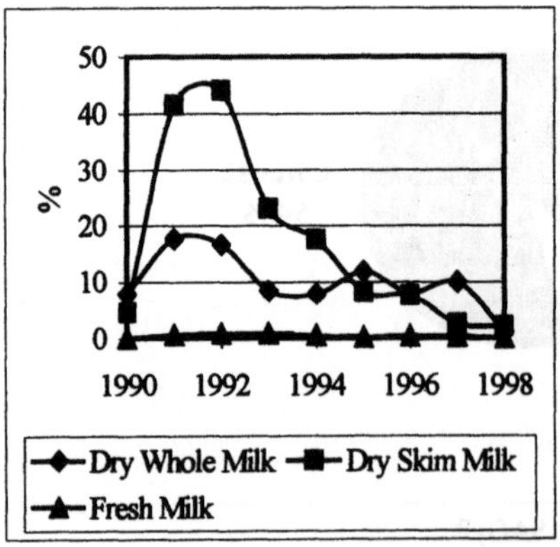

Figure 5.b:

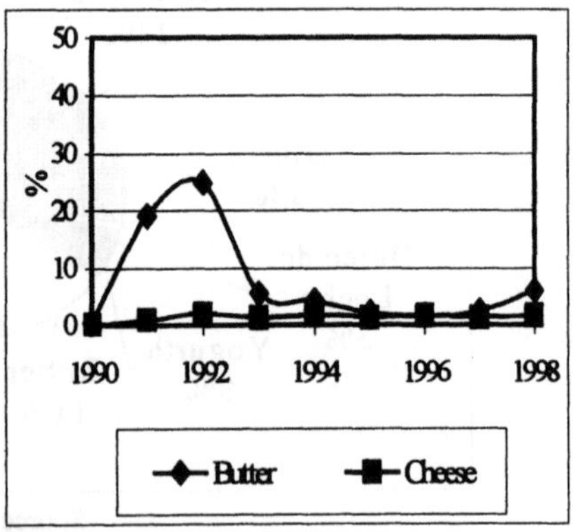

Source: FAO statistical database.

Figure 6: Evolution of international prices and average export prices in Argentina

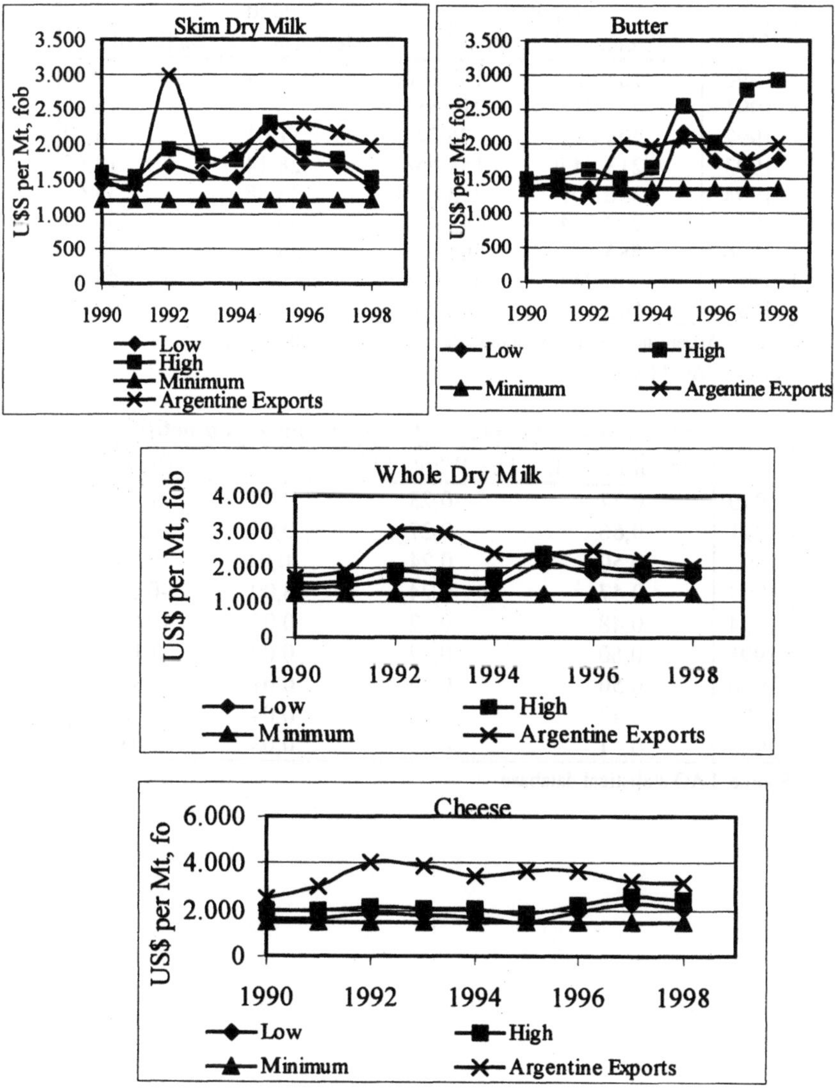

Source: USDA / GATT.

Table 1. Participation of Argentinean exports of dairy products in relation to imports, from Mercosur and from Brazil
(000 USD)

Year	Imports		Argentine Exports	
	Mercosur	Brazil	% Mercosur	% Brazil*
1990	185.610	168.706	-	37,34
1991	291.912	217.558	-	15,17
1992	208.811	76.344	11,01	5,24
1993	213.245	158.658	28,14	17,65
1994	346.501	273.813	33,88	33,60
1995	707.774	642.494	30,45	30,51
1996	585.118	509.033	39,21	40,27
1997	550.248	476.056	41,45	44,53
1998	563.113	506.735	46,39	47,16

Note: * Argentinean exports include dairy products, milk and eggs.
Source: FAO / INDEC.

Table 2. Rate of exposure to international competition

Year	Dry Skim Milk	Dry Whole Milk	Cheese	Butter
1990	0,77	0,23	0,08	0,17
1991	0,66	0,27	0,03	-0,09
1992	0,50	0,24	-0,01	-0,19
1993	0,47	0,24	0,00	-0,02
1994	0,48	0,32	0,02	-0,01
1995	0,60	0,57	0,02	0,11
1996	0,50	0,45	0,01	0,08
1997	0,43	0,46	0,04	0,08
1998	0,31	0,49	0,03	0,03

Source: FAO statistical database

Table 3.a: Evolution of sales for Argentine dairy products firms

Firms	1991	1992	1993	1994	1995	1996	1997	1998	Rate of Growth
Sancor	440,64	497,05	543,7	667,7	720,8	701,0	751,2	801,0	0,0776
Mastellone Hnos.	472,56	638,54	733,1	843,1	893,1	833,4	681,4	745,0	0,0586
Nestlé S.A.	195,28	362,17	365,3	403,9	400,1	459,0	453,0	435,0	0,1053
AUT (Milkaut)	56,10	112,56	90,6	110,1	126,9	147,0	112,0	181,7	0,1582
Suc. de A.	80,20	88,82	99,3	111,5	122,1	127,9	136,7	140,5	0,0726
Williner									
Manfrey Coop.			45,8	51,4	41,1	48,3	51,8	50,7	0,1228
Molfino Hnos.	26,17	40,80	41,2	49,4	55,7	60,5	64,7	69,0	0,1288
Abolio y Rubio	60,00	60,00	70,8	84,4	85,1	85,0	105,7	97,0	0,0619
Lactona S.A.			45,8	155,2	153,5	127,6	133,6	139,0	0,2033
COTAR	23,35		25,3	35,9	44,6	43,8	42,0	41,0	0,0729
Parmalat		12,5	50,1	60,1	s/d	75,0	s/d	200,0	0,4560

Table 3.b: Evolution of exports for Argentine dairy products firms

Firms	1990	1991	1992	1993	1994	1995	1996	1997	1998	Rate of Growth
Sancor	79,08	32,5	4,32	19,25	36,00	63,90	69,70	84,94	75,00	-0,0059
Mastellone Hnos.	14,90	s/d	s/d	s/d	16,17	34,41	30,63	39,08	83,22	0,2106
Nestlé S.A.	18,90	13,6	5,30	12,70	34,40	90,13	101,84	97,57	57,51	0,1316
AUT (Milkaut)		5,7	1,56	5,65	14,51	30,00	13,00	s/d	s/d	0,1473
Suc. De A.			3,81	5,04	6,31	13,76	18,04	14,17	16,00	0,2277
Williner										
Manfrey Coop.				1,39	2,14	7,79	9,78	3,31	4,43	0,2131
Molfino Hnos.					3,30	9,58	10,24	8,95	10,60	0,2629
Abolio y Rubio					2,41	2,37	3,84	3,49	3,75	0,0925
Lactona S.A.					2,03	2,26	2,03	5,70	7,55	0,3004
COTAR					1,97	5,30	9,15	6,17	2,20	0,0223
Parmalat						10,19	21,70	24,36	21,78	0,2091

Source: Based on data from Prensa Económica and Mercado.

Table 4.a: Indicators of productivity. Primary production

Indicator	1996	1998
Production (millions of lts)	8.700	9.450
Number of Dairy Farms	22.000	
Lts/Cow/Year	3.690	3.833
Productivity		
Kg. BF/ha/year	70,00	175,52
Rentability Margin		
Gross Margin (U$S/ha)	242,00	309,96
Gross Margin /Revenues (U$S)	41,90	43,29

Source: SAGPyA y Márgenes Agropecuarios.

Table 4.b: Indicators of productivity. Dairy industry

Productivity	1993	1994	1998
Sector			
Added Value/worker (000 U$S)	23,0		
Prod Value/ worker (000 U$S)	127,3		
Added Value /Prod Value(%)	22,5		
Firms			
Sales/worker (000 U$S)			
SANCOR	0,09	0,1	0,1
MASTELLONE	0,17	0,2	0,3
NESTLE	s/d	0,1	0,1
Rentability - Utilities/Sales (%)			
SANCOR	2,2	1,7	0,5
MASTELLONE	2,1	2,3	1,8
NESTLE	0,7	3,2	7,8

Source: Censo Nacional Económico, 1994 (INDEC), Prensa Económica y Mercado.

Table 5.a: Primary production costs

Items	$/Kg. BF	Per liter	
		U$S	%
Directs Costs	3.208	0,112	64,74
Structure Costs	1.245	0,044	25,43
Interests and Repayment	0,907	0,032	18,50
Profit Tax Recovery	(0.404)	(0,014)	(8,09)
Total	4.956	0,173	100,00

*/ Model of dairy farm of 380 ha. and 300 cows.

Source: Márgenes Agropecuarios.

Table 5.b: Cost structure for production in the dairy industry, 1995 (%)

Item	Product (%)			
	Dry Milk		Cheese (average)	Butter
	Whole (teen)	Skimmed (teen)		
Raw Materials				
Milk	49,8	48,3	52,6	77,9
Cool Down	11,2	10,4	10,4	
Inputs				
Package	19,5	19,1	2,5	8,8
Others			0,4	
Labor Force	2,9	3,1	11,8	6,8
Repayments	1,3	1,5	1,2	1,4
Power and Fuel	3,7	3,8	0,6	2,0
Structure Costs	11,6	13,8	20,5	3,1
Total Cost	100,0	100,0	100,0	100,0

Source: Gutman, E., "La Industria Láctea en Argentina en la época de los noventa".

Table 5.c: Average cost structure for the dairy industry (%)

Labor Force	Package	Administ.	Publicity	Transport	Others commercials	Raw Materials	Others
8,8	9,3	4,3	2,2	4,9	8,0	43,4	18,9

*/ Sample of firms.

Source: SAGPyA, Alimentos Argentinos, December 1998.

Table 6: Sensitivity of costs to changes in production (%)

Production	Costs	
	USD/Kg of BF	Per liter
Increase 10%	Fall 8,27%	Fall 8,09%
Decrease 10%	Rise 10,08%	Rise 10,40%

*/ Values for a dairy farm of 380 ha and 300 milk cows.

Source: Márgenes Agropecuarios.

THE ENVIRONMENTAL PROBLEMS OF AGRICULTURE: EUROPEAN UNION AND MERCOSUR EXPERIENCES

María Luisa Recalde, National University of Cordoba, Argentina
Michaela Kuhl, University of Giessen, Germany
María Cecilia Ganame, National University of Cordoba, Argentina

"With the aim of achieving sustainable development, the Parties shall encourage awareness of the issues of environmental protection and the rational use of natural resources in all fields of interregional cooperation".[1]

1. Introduction

Since the Rio Summit of 1992, governments all over the world have agreed to a world committed to the principle of "sustainability", which can be defined as development which meets the needs of the present without compromising the ability of future generations to meet their own needs. Agriculture is an important sector with respect to the economic, social and –of course- the environmental dimension of this definition[2]. The OECD describes sustainable agriculture by the four characteristics of "an ongoing economically viable agricultural production system, maintenance or enhancement of the farm's natural resource base, maintenance or enhancement of other ecosystems affected by agricultural activities and the provision of aesthetic qualities" (OECD, 1998b, p. 4). To bring this into reality is not an easy task as market failure through the existence of external effects and public goods as well as government failure are most evident in agricultural sectors in many parts of the world.

Over the last few years, the structure of consumer demand has changed. Consumers have increased their demand for goods with higher quality and more convenient packaging. This process has also shifted the demand in favour of goods which contain less chemical wastes. These developments may suggest that organic agriculture -based on the use of a minimum amount of chemical additives- will be an important theme in the future, leading to changes in

---

1 Article 17, No.1, of the Interregional Framework Cooperation Agreement between the European Union and its Member States, on the one hand, and the Southern Common Market and its Party States, of the other hand – Joint Declaration on political dialogue between the European Union and Mercosur (EU, Document 296S0319(02), 1996), which was approved on behalf of the Community in March 1999 (EU, Document 399D0279, 1999).

2 For example, 44% of the European land is agricultural area, that is, 138 million hectares (Pau Vall and Vidal, 1999, p. 1). Over 80% of EU land are rural areas (ISMEA, 1999, p. 9).

production technology and the institutional framework both within and across countries.

This article focuses mainly on the environmental aspects of sustainability; the relationship of agriculture with the environment and trade, and gives an overview of agri-environmental problems in the European Union and MERCOSUR, how they evolved and what kinds of policies were established to deal with them.

2. Agriculture, Environment and Trade: A Link

Agriculture is affected by two important policies: liberalised trade and environmental protection. There may be a conflict between these two policies. On the one hand, it is recognised that both trade liberalisation and proper environmental management may reinforce each other. With the implementation of effective environmental policies, trade liberalisation will provide the efficient allocation of resources, promoting economic growth and increasing welfare. However, in practice, neither complete trade liberalisation nor effective environmental policies are applied. There exist a regionalist phenomenon and heterogeneous policies among countries that impact differently on the environment depending on the country´s development. In this context, environmental protection might become a barrier to trade. On the other hand, environmental risk may emerge from the extension of agricultural production that comes from an increase in trade. Expanded trade induces complex shifts in the scale, composition and technologies of agricultural production that affect the environment.

A global empirical analysis of agricultural trade liberalisation and its effect on environment has concluded that a negligible effect on world output and a minor reallocation of production may occur. For example, through a complete removal of agriculture-support policies, some fraction of agricultural production will shift from some countries to others. Because the countries experiencing losses in production currently use more chemicals and practice intensive livestock production compared to most of those countries with increasing production, Anderson and Strutt hypothesise that global environmental pressure from agriculture will fall (Davin Ervin, 1997). However, due to the fact that developing countries do not have extensive environmental policies to protect against damages from their growth in agricultural production, this prediction might not occur. The environmental problems require other specific measures than agricultural and liberalised trade policies.

Specific measures have to be designed in a way that they do not harm trade expansion. Some agri-environmental programmes may limit production and trade without any benefit-cost analysis justifying such limitations. Traditional regulations also constrain production. A huge number of different and sometimes inconsistent regulations, for instance, may induce an efficiency loss and a reduction in competitiveness.

A new generation of environmental regulatory policies, such as tradable permits, offers the potential to reduce cost and trade impacts (Davin Ervin, 1997). This policy has not been applied in the agricultural sector yet due to implementation problems.

Another problem that emerges in the design of environmental policies is the substitution of environmental regulations by non-tariff barriers. As the World Trade Organisation (WTO) has eliminated some of the non-tariff measures in the Uruguay Round, countries may be tempted to use environmental regulations as a measure to protect their sensitive sectors.

Hence, the environmental policy design must be one that goes with liberalised agricultural trade. The increase in agricultural trade may increase welfare. By specialising in the production of goods which have a comparative advantage, each country allocates its resources efficiently, increasing national income and welfare. However, as the allocative market efficiency may generate negative pollution effects, increased income raises a social demand for environmental quality.

There exists a positive correlation between income and demand for environmental policy. Evidence from European countries shows that environmental quality is considered as a normal economic good (Kristom, 1994). Moreover, as the scarcity of rural environmental services may increase when development reduces their availability, a higher environmental protection may exist in high-income countries. This interpretation is consistent with the so-called "hump effect", which expresses that environmental degradation at first rises as a country's income grows before declining at higher income levels (Davin Ervin, 1997). Grossman and Krueger (1992) found evidence for this effect for the North American Free Trade Area.

Arrow and an important group of economists (1995) state that income growth might not induce sufficient progress to secure environmental sustainability due to the lack of remedy for the environmental damage and the efficacy of environmental policy responses that alter product composition and production technologies. They conclude that trade liberalisation and other economic growth policies are complementary to the environmental one.

With regard to environmental problems, agriculture is a prominent sector worth being looked at in more detail.

3. Historical Background

3.1 European Union

The first Environmental Action Programme was established in 1972 and was followed by three more programmes until the early 90s. The Fifth Environment Action Programme was adopted in 1992. It comes to an end this year and shall be succeeded by a sixth programme.

The fifth programme was prepared at the same time as the Rio Earth Summit and the debate on sustainable development. The integration of the environmental dimension into all major policy areas was seen as a key factor, and a wide range of instruments was seen as appropriate to come closer to sustainability such as legislation to set environmental standards, economic instruments to encourage the production and use of environmentally friendly products and processes as well as so called horizontal measures like information, education and research. Five "target sectors", to which particular attention should be given in terms of integrating environmental concerns, were covered by the strategy: Industry, the energy sector, transport, agriculture and tourism.

A report in 1996 on the progress of the programme concluded that progress was least apparent in agriculture and in tourism. Based on these conclusions the Commission aimed at speeding the process of moving towards a sustainable development in the EU.

3.2 MERCOSUR

Contrary to EU, in the MERCOSUR environmental matters were mentioned explicitly in the Asunción Treaty of 1991. However, they were explicit but not precise. The use of the expression "the most effective use of available resources" does not imply precisely the idea that resources must be assigned and managed according to economic optimisation criteria in the long run (Novara, 1994).

Inside the Common Market Group (CMG), ten Technical Sub Groups (TSG) were formed in order to make studies prior to the implementation of the Treaty. The objectives of these groups were to analyse the laws, regulations and other measures in the member states related to international trade. Examples are customs issues, technical laws, transport, industrial, technological and agricultural policies and the co-ordination of macroeconomic policies. However, the environmental issues did not receive special consideration. They were shared out between several TSG such as those of technical laws, industrial, agricultural and energy policies.

As the environmental problems extend the issues treated by sectors, it was necessary to co-ordinate the trade and economic expansion with the environmental problems that may arise from them. To deal with this objective, an "Environmental Specialised Meeting" was organised in 1993, two years after the first TSG started its work. This meeting, which established "the environmental base directives", was the main antecedent of TSG N°6 created in 1995. This TSG is in charge of the treatment of the environmental issues. The priority tasks of the subgroup are related to the analysis of restriction and non-tariff measures. One of the main aims is the harmonisation and/or elimination of such policies. However, the measures taken have been implemented as general rules and have not been targeted to the agricultural sector specifically.

4. The environmental effects of agricultural production

4.1 European Union

"Changes in technology, the financial situation of farmers, socio-cultural influences, agricultural and agri-environmental policy measures, and environmental regulations, all combine to influence the level, composition, location and practices of farmers that determine the environmental outcomes." (OECD, 1998a, p. 15)

For decades European agriculture was characterised by increasing specialisation[3] and intensification of production. However, in the 1980s more and more people became aware that the situation was not sustainable. This was not only within the scientific community, but also the public was alarmed by news about contaminated food and pollution of ground and surface water by pesticides and fertilisers[4]. Also adverse effects on biodiversity by high levels of fertilisation and application of crop protection products and the removal of semi-natural habitats became a topic. Further negative effects of agriculture were seen in air pollution and contribution to climatic change by emissions from agricultural production[5]. Last but not least, agriculture was blamed for in soil degradation by soil compaction and erosion. On the other hand, agriculture itself is influenced by industrial pollution, acid rain and climate change.

It was only quite recently that positive effects of agriculture like the maintenance of traditional landscapes, the preservation of habitats and

3 Table A1 in the appendix shows for the EU-9 that non-specialised farms in 1995 were only half the number they were in 1975 and their area reduced by a third. Also in EU-15 80% of farms with 78% of total area are specialised (Poiret, 1999b, p. 2).

4 E.g. in Germany, in 1992 3% of the national water sample showed a pesticide level of more than 0.1 microgramm/litre, three quarters of which are from atrazin, a herbizid ingredient (mainly used in maize production) which has been prohibited since 1991.

5 Agriculture accounts for about 9% of greenhouse gas emissions, but is the main source of methane and nitrous oxide emissions (see Sensi, 1999).

biodiversity, important contributions to a sustainable management of water resources and the provision of a carbon sink improved the picture the public had about agriculture.

The environmental problems of agriculture rooted in several developments (Poiret, 1999a, p. 2-3, 5-6):

- The expansion of animal husbandry and manure spreading and geographical concentration of animal holdings;
- Increasing intensity in input use;
- Reduction in the share of permanent grassland and a reduction in the number of crops grown in the crop rotations;
- Drainage and land clearance through the destruction of hedgerows, stone walls and ditches, which resulted in the loss of habitats for many species;
- Cultivation of environmentally sensitive land.

Some of these aspects are now looked at in more detail:

- A reduction in grassland results in a short-term release of nutrients following the decomposition of organic matter in the upper layers of the soil. After a meadow has been ploughed up, the nutrients in roots and leaves decomposing on the surface often run off or leach (e.g. nitrogen, phosphorus and potassium) (Poiret, 1999a, pp. 1-2). The use of maize for feeding has contributed to the loss in grassland. Maize demands more inputs (fertilisation, etc.) but has the advantage of higher flexibility (e.g. easy to store).
- The reduction in grassland and the shift from crops like barley, oats and rye to wheat and maize - which have higher yield potential and prices, and are more input intensive - has led to a loss of crop diversity. As Poiret (1999b, pp. 3-4) points out: "by putting all their eggs in one basket" (...) farmers increased their use of insurance systems. (...) This corresponds in general to an increase in, or stabilisation of, the yield, and involves the increased use of certified seed, fertilisers, pesticides, equipment, water and energy in order to guarantee maximum income with a yield optimising both the costs and crop production.
- The simplification of the land cover structure may disturb the normal physical flows of water, wind and earth and the biological flows of flora and fauna. It may also cause floods, drought, erosion (especially in row crops like maize and sugar beet) and the migration or disappearance of species (Poiret, 1999b, p. 6).
- Irrigation is used as a mean to achieve the stabilisation and increase in yields. With respect to irrigated areas, maize is the main crop to mention. However, problems of irrigation systems are an increased use of inputs like fertilisers

and pesticides on irrigated land, often leading to a loss of nutrients or pesticides into the environment (Poiret, 1999a, p. 3).

- Traditionally, crop rotation, regular fallow periods and the spreading of animal manure was used to recover the fertility of the soil. Today, mostly mineral fertilisers are used, although animal manure remains important especially in some regions with high animal density[6] (Pau Vall and Vidal, 1999, p. 1). To ensure that minimal environmental damage results from fertilisation, it is important that the fertilisers are applied in correct weather conditions (so run off losses can be avoided), at the right crop growth stage (i.e. at a time the crops can take up the nitrogen quickly) as well as in correct dosage. High nitrate surpluses can potentially result in high nitrate concentrations in water bodies. The estimated nitrate balance for all EU member countries is given in Figure A1 in the appendix.
- Livestock Units per hectare are good indicators for the intensity of husbandry. However, the environmental effects are different depending on the type of animals. Eutrophication[7] is often found in pig production areas whereas in areas with high sheep numbers soil degradation is the main problem (Boschma, Joaris and Vidal, 1999, p. 7).
- High concentrations of nitrogen in water can result in eutrophication of rivers and lakes, leading to proliferation of certain algae, depletion of oxygen, disappearance of benthic invertebrates and production of toxins with negative effects on animals and men. Also, excessive concentrations of nitrogen in the soil can lead to reduced oxygen, making it impossible for natural micro-organisms to function properly (Pau Vall and Vidal, 1999, p. 2). In the EU, mineral fertilisers are the main source of agricultural nitrogen input, followed closely by livestock manure. Commercial nitrogen fertilisers are particularly soluble to ensure an easy uptake by the crops. However, this characteristic increases the danger of run-off after heavy rains and the leaching to ground water. Excessive concentrations of nitrogen in ground water make necessary costly efforts to remove the nitrogen to be able to use it as drinking water.

Environmental stress was especially high in the 1980s with the high price policy still in place. On a regional basis, the most troublesome regions for Germany were:

---

6 Examples are Galicia (Spain), Brittany (France), Lombardia (Italy) and North West England, where in all four regions nitrogen inputs from animal manure are well above 100 kg/ha (Pau Vall, Vidal, 1999, pp. 4-5). Intensive husbandry can be found more often in regions close to the ports where feedingstuffs were imported, which substituted for expensive domestic cereals (Boschma, Joaris, Vidal, 1999, p. 7).

7 Eutrophication means an increase in nutrient supply in surface waters.

- Vegetable and wine areas in the Rhine plains, where high levels of mineral fertilisers and plant protection products are used;
- Livestock areas in the Northwest of Germany with high density of cattle, high quantities of manure and intensive production of arable land and grassland;
- Areas of intensive arable farming on highly productive soils (e.g. Hildesheimer Börde, Kölner Bucht, parts of Bavaria, eastern part of Holstein) with simplified land cover, high amounts of fertiliser and crop protection products used, crop rotations with only very few products ;
- Farming areas with high shares of cereals and maize and simple crop rotations (Northwest of Germany, parts of Bavaria) (Henrichsmeyer and Witzke, 1991, p. 205).

These environmental problems cannot be seen independently from policy influences as the minimum price system in the Common Agricultural Policy (CAP). High guaranteed prices resulted in incentives to intensify production, a shift in production to more intensive cultures, a higher capital intensity and the more complete use of land as well as land clearance. The unbalanced level of protection with high rates especially for cereals, sugar and milk supported the trend to specialisation. Through the stabilisation of prices, risk diversification was less necessary, thus allowing simple crop rotations.

Following the neo-classical production theory, the optimal situation is given with the value of the marginal product of a factor being equal to the factor price in each use[8]. An increase in output prices through market forces or policy interventions shifts the marginal revenue curve to the right, resulting in a higher level of input use.

Figure 1 (on the next page) shows these relationships in a stylised manner. The optimal level of crop protection can be found where the costs for further application are higher than the additional revenue through the further increase in yield.

Without the use of insecticides and fungicides, the maximum yields from nitrogen use are not attainable, so close relations between nitrogen and pesticides use exist. Theoretically, the use of herbicides can be substituted with labour; however this is not cost efficient in most cases.

While the use of fertilisers can be varied in quantity, pesticide use varies mainly through the number of applications.

Yields are increased through increased use of pesticides because of less damage from herbs, insecticides and fungus diseases. In addition, the use of crop

[8] This has to be modified for a situation with restrictions in the input use and with liquidity restrictions.

protection measures is a precondition for additional nitrogen use with a further increase in yield.

Figure 1: Production function with limitation relationships between nitrogen use and crop protection

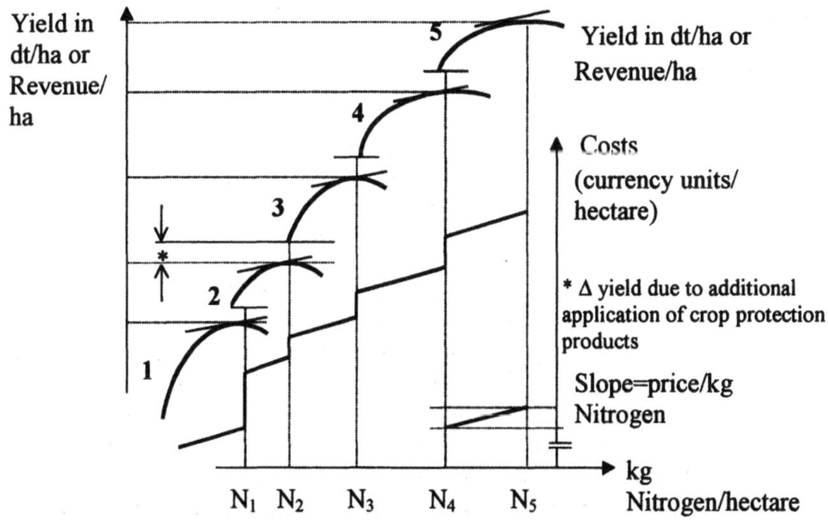

Source: modified from Schulte 1984, p. 113.

The EU experience shows that the use of phosphate and potash fertilisers has increased less than the use of nitrogen fertilisers over time (see Figures A2 and A3). The reason for this change in the structure of fertiliser use is that the maximum yield from use of phosphate and potash fertiliser is reached before the maximum yield from nitrogen use. The marginal product is declining relatively rapidly in the case of phosphate fertilisers. Another reason for the increase of fertiliser use until the end of the 1980s is an increase in the area with highly nitrogen-intensive crops like wheat and oilseeds. As Figure 1 shows, it cannot be seen independently from improvements in plant varieties and the use of pesticides (Pau Vall and Vidal, 1999, p. 3).

However, when input use has negative external effects[9] the quantity of inputs used for production might not reflect the optimal input level from the point of view of the society as Figure 2 (on the next page) shows.

9 Externalities are positive or negative spillovers which often occur in the production and consumption of goods and services. Externalities are not shown in the revenue and cost of

Figure 2: Optimal use of inputs with negative external effects

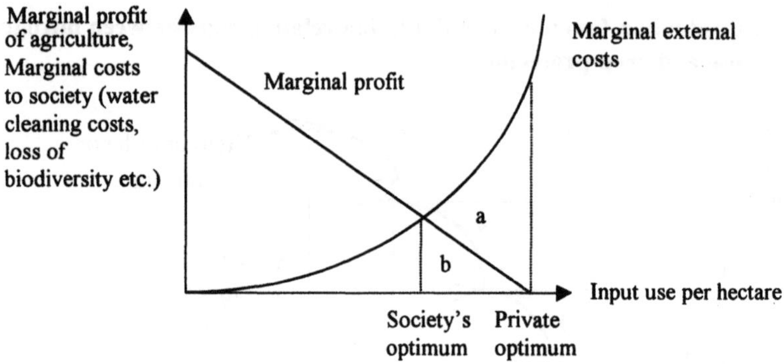

When only private costs and revenues are considered, the optimum is located where marginal profit from a further increase in fertiliser and pesticide use is zero. However, society's optimum can be found at the level where private marginal profit equals the marginal external costs. A reduction in input use down from the private to the social optimum decreases profits by area b but also reduces external costs by areas a and b, leaving society as a whole better off.

However, the use of pesticides in kg/ha does not necessarily reflect the impact on the environment as the method of application and other factors are also important. This shows a recent study by Frede and Bach (1999) who found that the main entry path of pesticides into water does not result from spraying on the fields but from cleaning the spraying equipment on the farm after use. Also, with regard to nitrogen, the leaching of nitrogen depends on geological, climatic and biological factors.

EU-pesticide sales in tons of active ingredients fell by 13% between 1991 and 1995. Although it increased again afterwards it is still well below the 1991 level now. Reasons are the introduction of low-dose pesticides, the produce price decrease, agri-environmental regulation and national policy developments (see below and Lucas and Pau Vall, 1999, p. 2-3)[10].

For a long time, environmental effects of agricultural production have played only a minor role. After World War II the increase in production capacity was the main aim of agricultural policy, and this aim was mainly targeted by a policy of high administered prices.

---

the producer although for society they represent real costs and benefits (OECD, 1998b, p. 5-6).

10 Fungicides accounted for 41% of total weight of active ingredients in 1996, herbicides 39% and insecticides 12% (Lucas and Pau Vall, 1999, p. 3).

In the 1980s a number of negative effects of agricultural production on environmental resources became more and more obvious. Today, even the European Commission acknowledges that: "the existence in Europe over several decades of an agricultural policy based on intervention to ensure high prices and unlimited and guaranteed outlets helped harness the productive potential generated by technological progress for agricultural intensification and specialisation. This had a negative impact on, among other things, the environment, the countryside and the quality of certain products offered to the consumer. To deny this, would be just as wrong as to place the blame for it exclusively in the common agricultural policy or on agricultural policy in general" (EU-Commission, 1999b, p. 2).[11]

However, since the 1992 reform (a significant reduction in administered prices and the introduction of hectare - or animal - based direct payments in combination with an obligatory set-aside scheme) farmers make less use of fertilisers and pesticides[12]. Also, effectively managed, the set-aside-area can be positive for environmental reasons, if a fairly dense cover of vegetation is given on the plots. Lower grain prices result in grain being more competitive for animal feeding, making cereal areas relatively more attractive for livestock farming, while before there was a locational advantage for farms near ports, where imported feed arrived.

On the other hand the reform had some negative impacts on the environment, e.g. when the cereal aid was extended to silage maize, giving a comparative advantage to intensive cattle rearing over extensive livestock rearing (Barthelmy and Vidal, 1999, p.5). Also the relatively high limit of two livestock units per hectare for premiums to the first two units made extensive rearing less attractive. To compensate this, a premium is paid for extensive rearing with only up to 1.4 livestock units per hectare. The "Agenda 2000" agricultural reform, agreed on in 1999, is a next step in continuing the reform efforts of 1992.

Since the Maastricht Treaty went into effect, the European Union is obliged to take into account environmental protection requirements when implementing policies. It is not only for the reason that half of the EU budget is used for

---

11 On the other hand, the price policy may have contributed to a continuation of farming in regions where it otherwise would not have been able to survive, resulting in negative effects for the environment, e.g. where low-intensity farming is succeeded by scub and forest, which can lower the level of biodiversity. However, the fact that price policy is not an efficient way to deal with these problems is nowadays acknowledged by most politicians.

12 Between 1985 and 1995 nitrogen fertilizer use in the EU decreased in volume and application frequency, with the highest decrease between 1989 and 1992. Although the level increased again afterwards, it stayed well under the level of 1991 (see Figures A2 and A3 in the appendix). In the years since 1995, the level of fertilizer use stayed approximately constant at the level of 1995 (Stat. JB ELF, p. 461).

agricultural purposes, it is also a vital requirement for agricultural production to take care of the natural resources. For a sustainable agricultural policy, therefore, the protection of the very basis for agricultural production is a precondition.

4.2 MERCOSUR

Agriculture is a vital sector in MERCOSUR countries because it not only provides the needed food but also generates the main export income.

The agricultural activity in Latin America has been developed by introducing farm modernisation, which promoted a technological-scientific dependency. This feature creates negative social and environmental impacts. The main cause is that the region has been exploited homogeneously, without considering the specific attributes of diverse ecosystems. Sometimes, technologies and their use for warm and wet zones were implemented in marginal (semiarid and tropical) areas of production. (Sammarchi and Lara, 1995)

The development of the agricultural sector was focused on the increment of productivity of the land in order to increase the exportable surplus. Hence, the short-run rather than the long-run efficiency was considered.

Another characteristic process has been the expansion of the agricultural frontier. This process was present in lands with climatic and edaphic limitations which led to a significant damage of ecosystems. As Jorge Morello (1985) pointed out, the expansion of the agricultural frontier is the process that mostly affects the natural resources of the continent, due to the fact that it causes a deterioration of forests and woods, soil erosion, sedimentation of watercourses, wild fauna destruction, biodiversity loss and climate transformations. Hence, the considerations of short-run efficiency in order to make farms profitable generated a very polarised activity: on the one hand, modern enterprises, and on the other, farmers with old strategies. These issues have a negative effect on the environment and society.

The production system is based on technological implementation that not only tends to make an intensive exploitation of natural resources but also to underemploy the environmental supply of such resources.

The main environmental problems of MERCOSUR are (Sammarchi and Lara, 1995):

- Erosion and fertility loss of soils.
- Blighting.
- Deforestation.
- Pasture degradation.
- Salinity of soil on irrigation schemes.
- Sub-utilisation of good quality arable land.

Some of these aspects will be analysed in more detail:

- Soil erosion is caused by the inadequate use of lands destined to crop or livestock and by deforestation. In Argentina it is estimated that erosion affects 20% of arable land [13].
- The blighting problem is basically focused in Argentina where more than 50% of the land is arid and semiarid. This process is taking place in the Patagonia and neighbouring areas, where natural dryness has grown in intensity and extension. The result is the loss of productive power and as a consequence a decrease in productivity. Deterioration was produced by the excessive use of grazing sheep land without the application of techniques aimed at the preservation of natural resources.
- In Latin America, deforestation has been rising since the 60's due to the increment of meat price in the United States, the national agricultural policies, the expansion of the agricultural frontier and the use of the agri-exporter model which emphasised mono-production. The increase of deforestation is very important in countries of the Amazonian basin.

  Paraguay was specially affected by the expansion of the agriculture frontier. During 1977 and 1989, the increase of the agricultural area caused a decrease of forest land of 27.7%. Since 1960, an important colonisation policy has been applied in this country. Between 1956 and 1989, the farming area increased 3.18 times. Most of the tropical jungle was burn after the extraction of the species that had commercial value. This fact caused eco-system deterioration of the area and intensive erosion of the soils. For this reason, the sub-tropical jungle of Paraguay is decreasing so speedily that it is estimated that after two decades the area will have disappeared (Kleinpenning Zoomers, 1990)[14]. Hence, the colonisation policy has resulted in calamitous deforestation.
- The expansion of livestock raising in tropical areas has, among other effects, the speedy degradation of pasture and a fall in livestock receptivity per hectare. In Argentina, the degradation process is reflected in a loss of production. As a consequence, it is estimated that in the Pampas, forage production has diminished by 50%.
- As regards biodiversity and biological inheritance, the main problems consist of the loss of the principal genetic resources, of the ecosystems and of their ecological functions with respect to the support of life and habitability, and the sub-utilisation and over-exploitation of the ecosystems and species.

---

13 The world average is 17%, South America 14%, North and Central America 8% and Africa, Europe and Asia is 20%.

14 Quoted in Sammarchi and Lara, 1995.

One aspect related to the deforestation of rain forests is the loss of species which are unknown and/or have not been studied yet. Besides, diversity loss and the genetic erosion of the crops constitute the main problems that arise from the deforestation process. Biodiversity is the basis of a functioning ecosystem and its loss, apart from its value as an economic resource, represents a threat to the ecological regulatory capacity in the region.

It is worth mentioning that the Latin-American germplasm is used to treat agricultural pest. The increment in agricultural crop returns depends on the genetic resources of the plants in as much as 50%. Hence, genetic improvement and the biodiversity conservation are important not only for ecological but also for economic reasons.

Considering the consumption of different kinds of fertilisers, as can be seen in Figures A4 to A7, the situation of MERCOSUR member countries has been very different from that of the European Union. While in MERCOSUR consumption has increased from 1985 to 1995, in the European Union this consumption has diminished, as was mentioned above. The increment in MERCOSUR may be explained by the economic openness, which has improved the relative input-product prices. However, the levels of consumption per hectare in MERCOSUR are not so high as those in the European Union. This fact is due to the predominance of extensive farming among MERCOSUR members.

5. Agri-environmental policy

5.1 European Union

As was already mentioned in Section 4.1, agricultural policy reforms since 1992 had been characterised by a shift from market-support towards budgetary-financed measures and efforts to decouple support from production[15]. Also, governments had increased more stringent regulations requiring farmers to put more emphasis on environmental aspects. One example is the German fertiliser use regulation requiring German farmers to use fertilisers in accordance with the so called "good agricultural practice", i.e., in a way nutrients can be used by the plants to the highest extent possible thus avoiding nutrient losses as far as possible (through time of application, research on the fertiliser needs of each area, maximum quantity of nitrogen per farm from manure, etc.). However, there are concerns that the reform efforts might lead to abandonment of land to the detriment of the environment. These, as well as the generally increasing demand for pro-environmental activity, have led to the formulation of new policy areas: the agri-environmental programmes.

---

[15] While the share of direct subsidies in agricultural net income was 20% in 1992, this figure increased to 37% in 1997 (Barthelemy and Vidal, 1999, p. 1).

In Regulation 2078/92, the EU accepted the possibility to pay farmers a premium, if they:

- Reduce substantially, or maintain a reduction, in the use of fertilisers and/or plant protection products, or adopt or continue with organic farming methods;
- Change to, or maintain, more extensive forms of crop production, or convert arable land into extensive grassland;
- Reduce the stock rate of cattle and sheep per hectare;
- Rear animals of local breeds in danger of extinction or plants endangered by genetic erosion;
- Maintain abandoned farmland or woodland for reasons of environmental protection;
- Set aside farmland for at least 20 years for environment-related purposes, in particular for the establishment of biotope reserves or natural parks;
- Manage farmland for public access and leisure activities.

The farmers can sign contracts over at least five years (set-aside: 20 years) and a premium is paid to compensate for the loss in income and an additional incentive of up to 25% of this loss. Both the EU and the member states contribute to the financing of the annual premia. The share of EU co-financing is 50% (75% in the so called objective-1-regions, i.e., in Ireland, Portugal, Greece, East Germany as well as some regions in Italy and Spain).

The importance of different environmental problems varies widely across the EU countries. However, the programmes themselves are designed on a more regional level reflecting the EU principle of subsidiary. For example, in Germany the programmes are designed, administered and evaluated by the 15 Bundesländer. The programmes reflect different priorities within the EU, stemming from different environmental pressures, different environmental assimilative capacities and different preferences of the society.

These differences resulted in having some member countries targeting their programmes to specific habitats (e.g. the UK) while others support specific measures like extensive farming systems (which sometimes already were in place before and are only maintained) on a broad-based scale, (e.g. Austria, France and the German Länder of Bavaria and Baden-Württemberg). While only specific farms were eligible in the specific territory approach, in the member countries with a more general approach almost all farmers have the possibility to participate in the programmes. Further differences among the countries exist with respect to political priorities, problems in certain administrations, difficulties in certain states or regions to provide the necessary part-financing, and higher profits in some regions when intensive farming is continued compared to when the farms take part in the programmes. While, on average, 20% of farmland area in the EU and 1 out of 7 farms participate in the programmes[16], the participation is –for the above mentioned reasons- quite unequal. Finland, Austria, Sweden (each over 50% area coverage in 1998), Luxembourg (76%) and Germany (39%) as well as Ireland (24%) and France (23%) participate on a level above average while Belgium, Denmark, Greece, Spain and the Netherlands fall much below[17] (Fay, 1999, p.3). This is also reflected in the different shares the countries have in total EU-financing for agri-environmental measures with Germany, France and Austria having the largest share. However, also within a country, different regions receive very different amounts of money. For instance, in Germany, the two Länder Baden-Württemberg and Bavaria (from 15 Länder altogether) get 57% of financing (1993-1997). Also, three of the ‚New Länder' (Sachsen, Thüringen and Brandenburg) account for another 25% (Niendieker, 1998).

The total budgetary expenses of the EU for agri-environmental programmes in 1999 are about 1.9 Million EURO, which, however, it is still only 4% of the European Agricultural Guarantee and Guidance Fund's (EAGGF) Guarantee Section. In the Agenda 2000 the maximum amount of money for co-financing agri-environmental programmes was increased by 20%.

The Agenda 2000 supports the idea that –not on an EU but on a more regional basis- a certain basic level of environmental practice can be defined which can be regarded as "good agricultural practice" and the farmers be urged to produce at least in an environmentally friendly manner as this norm suggests. However, for efforts beyond this "good agricultural practice", society should pay the farmers, e.g. through agri-environmental programmes. (Agra-Europe 47/99; EU-Commission, 1999a, p. 1). Below this norm "the polluter-pays-principle" shall be in effect.

Several aspects seem to determine the success of agri-environmental programmes, making them effective when (OECD, 1998a, p. 21):

- Environmental goals are clearly specified;
- The required actions are closely linked to the goals;
- The land accepted in the programmes has a high conservation value;
- Measures were adapted to the environmental, economic and social situation in the area;

---

16 For example, organic farming has been increasing its share to 1% of the farms and 2% of agricultural land in the EU today. German experiences show that organic farming has lower input use and concentration of nutrients, leading to reduced leaching into water and less emissions into the atmosphere. It can therefore be a good contribution to the safety of the environment. However, organic farming is not enough to protect biodiversity. Special measures like the establishment of biotope areas and structural features are also important (Fay, 1999, p.5).

17 In Belgium, Greece and the Netherlands the rate of participating area is below 2% (Fay, 1999, p.3).

- Compliance was monitored;
- Training and advice were provided.

Critics say that the present agri-environmental programmes are a step in the right direction; however, they are not enough to achieve an agriculture standard respecting a minimum level of agricultural production on an EU-wide basis (Eggers and Hagedorn, 1998). It is also criticized that in regions with high participation rates, e.g, in the German Länder Baden-Württemberg and Bavaria, this is done mainly because of attractive premiums with only very moderate rules for changing production methods. Therefore, many programmes can be regarded more as a general measure for transferring money to the sector than bringing real environmental improvement, while contracts for nature conservation on specific areas through a prohibition of fertilisers, rules concerning the time of cuts, etc., and organic farming have only low shares in the financial funds (see e.g. Bioland, 1999)[18].

With more targeted programmes, on the other hand, the following expectation might become a reality: "Considering the ongoing debates surrounding budget issues, it is safe to predict that tensions between environmental issues and income support will be a recurrent theme in the future" (ISMEA, 1999, p. 10).

5.2 MERCOSUR

In most member countries, the environment-related agriculture laws are extensive but as they are not supported by accurate research findings, there has been very little impact on environmental quality. In general, they do not constitute a coherent set of acts for environmental defence due to the fact that these laws have been drawn up to avoid conflict among users instead of establishing the basis to preserve natural resources. It is worth mentioning that these laws were created when natural resources were so abundant that they were considered redundant.

Besides these failures, as there has been no efficient control of the application of these laws, there has been no significant impact on environmental quality. For instance, in Argentina the Law of Soil Conservation Encouragement and in Uruguay, the Law that controls the introduction and production of pesticides, were not efficient. In Paraguay, there is a permissible law, which allows "a rational exploitation of the land" without a precise definition of these terms. This fact has allowed the rise of non-sustainable agriculture practices and

18 However, in Germany the conversion of conventional farming to organic farming methods is now supported with 300 DM/hectare compared to 250 DM/hectare before (Agra-Europe 40/99).

the commercial exploitation of forests followed by artificial pastures, which has led to a loss of large quantity of wooded areas every year.

Another important aspect to consider is that the conservation of natural resources has an international dimension, which exceeds the national and regional policies of MERCOSUR. Besides, it is very important to consider the relationship with the world economic-financial market and the implementation of protectionism in almost all developed countries.

For example, it should be stressed that in the last two decades, there have been evident relations among economic growth, foreign debt, protectionism and conservation of the natural resources. The over-exploitation of natural resources in developing countries arises as a consequence of the pressure for the payment of foreign debts and the protectionism of the agricultural markets (Sammarchi and Lara, 1995).

Therefore, the drop in international terms of trade and the over-exploitation of natural resources are not only "natural" risks but also effects of the behaviour of developed countries, which should be reviewed in the new international context (Obschatko, 1992).

Within the MERCOSUR framework, the last advance in this area was the Protocol of the Environment written in 1999. In this Protocol the objectives and principles of the environmental policy are established such as:

- To encourage the incorporation of the environmental issue in other sectoral policies.
- To consider the dimension of environmental problems in member states, the way and opportunity to resolve them as well as the tools and resources available.
- To promote sustainable development based on the co-operation of member states and the economic and environmental policies that complement them.
- To encourage environment harmonisation legislation among member states, considering the jurisdictional instruments and its effective implementation.

In its chapter VI, the Protocol which refers to the instruments of environmental management, establishes that each member can use its own criteria, regulations, laws and instruments in order to achieve the objectives stated in the protocol. Each member state should promote procedures and instruments such as the training of human resources; environmental audits; application of sanctions for non-fulfilment of the laws; etc.

As can be seen, these objectives and principles do not incorporate the specific tools to achieve them. Rather, they express an intention to encourage solutions to the environmental issue but do not provide for the implementation of specific measures to ameliorate the environmental quality in the MERCOSUR area.

6. Some aspects concerning trade liberalisation and the environment

After a compromise within the EU was reached[19], negotiations for liberalising trade between the European Union and MERCOSUR are supposed to start on July 1, 2001.

What a more liberalised trade regime between these two blocs might mean for the environment in the participating countries depends on a number of factors:

"..., trade liberalisation can contribute to enhancing environmental performance by improving the efficient allocation of resources, promoting economic growth and increasing welfare, provided effective environmental policies are also implemented." This view of the OECD (1998a, p.28) is quite optimistic not only with respect to market results but also with respect to the ability and the will of politicians to formulate and implement efficient environmental policies to accompany more liberal trade relations. In general the effects of trade on the environment depend on three main factors (USDA, 1997, pp. 12-14):

- A "scale effect" (activity and pollution levels)
- A "composition effect" (reflecting comparative advantage)
- A "technique effect" (change in production methods)

How these effects will work in the case of trade liberalisation between the EU and MERCOSUR has not yet been formally studied. To do so will not be an easy task for economists and ecologists as "the art and science of carrying out environmental assessments of trade agreements .. (is) still at an early stage of evolution" (OECD, 1999, p.2).

However, several EU-Commissioners are concerned that expanding trade with MERCOSUR might lead to more competition for EU farmers. They expect this increased competition to be especially high for products like sugar, meat, cereals, fruits, soya and wine. Member countries also express this fear, mainly France. However, agriculture *has* to be included in the negotiations as this is in the vital interest of the MERCOSUR Countries (EU-Commission, 1999c).

---

19 While Spain wanted the negotiations to start as soon as possible, France suggested waiting until the end of a new WTO round (Agra-Europe 26/99).

7. Concluding Remarks

The Cooperation Agreement between the European Union and MERCOSUR places explicit emphasis on environmental protection and the rational use of natural resources in all fields of cooperation. With agriculture being one of the sectors with most intensive trade relations between the two economic regions and likely being one of the politically most sensitive sectors, the paper focuses on how agriculture contributes to environmental stress in the two regions and what kind of policies to put into effect.

As was mentioned above, the main environmental problems of the EU are the reduction in grassland, the simplification of the land cover structure, the irrigation problem, the increased use of inputs such as fertilisers and pesticides, the degradation of the soil, the high concentration of nitrogen in water, etc. It is mainly with respect to biodiversity that major agricultural threats result from the observed polarisation, characterised by intensification in some areas and marginalisation of land use in other areas.

In MERCOSUR, there are some similar environmental problems such as reduction in grassland, land blighting and erosion of the soil. However, there are others that are typical of the MERCOSUR area, such as deforestation, the salinity of soil under irrigation and the sub-utilisation of agricultural land of good quality.

The reasons for the different problems not only lie on the relative scarcity of land and the different natural environmental conditions like climate and soil type, etc., but also on different political influences on incentives for intensive or extensive production methods. Generally, with the on-going liberalisation process, more efficient agricultural production will evolve. However, expecting globalisation to increase welfare and therefore the demand for environment and environmental quality is a suboptimal strategy. Not only is some environmental damage irreversible (and therefore future generations are not able to decide on the use of the particular environmental good, e.g. in the case of distinction of certain animals) but the degree of the environmental stress might not even be efficient for the current generation as far as externalities exist and result in welfare losses. Political efforts to internalise these effects will only be efficient if measures are implemented as close as possible to the origin of the externality and to the most appropriate degree. Considering the different situations not only between MERCOSUR and the EU but also within the regions, political answers to environmental problems in agriculture cannot be uniform.

Overall, it can be expected that trade liberalisation among the blocs should improve the environmental situation provided that agri-environmental policies are applied efficiently in MERCOSUR countries. The liberalisation of trade might increase the production of the agricultural sector in MERCOSUR members with more extensive production practices compared to the EU. However, this increase in production will aggravate the environmental problems in MERCOSUR countries if the liberalisation process is not accompanied by efficient environmental policies.

References

AGRA-EUROPE 26/99, Grüne Welle für Abkommen mit Drittländern. EN 8-9.

AGRA-EUROPE 40/99, Neue Förderschwerpunkte in der Gemeinschaftsaufgabe. LB 41-43.

AGRA-EUROPE 47/99, In der Agrarumweltpolitik wird die gute fachliche Praxis maßgebend. EN1-2.

ARROW, K.; BOLLIN, B.; COSTANZA, R.; DASGUPTA, P., FOLKE, C. HOLLING, C; JANSSON, B.; LEVIN, S.; GORAN-MALER, K.; PERRINS, CH. AND PIMENTEL, D.; (1995). "Economic Growth, Carrying Capacity, and the Environment". Science, Vol. 268, April 28.

BARTHELEMY, P. A. and C. VIDAL, (1999). "A Dynamic European Agricultural and Agri-Foodstuffs Sector". Environmental Report of the EU-Commission. Brussels, www.europa.eu.int/comm/dg06.

BIOLAND, Erklärung des Bioland Landesverbandes Hessen, Thüringen, Sachsen-Anhalt zur Neuausrichtung der Agrarumweltprogramme (Agra-Europe 32/99, LB 22-24).

BOSCHMA, M., JOARIS, A. and C. VIDAL, (1999). "Concentration of livestock production". Report of the EU-Commission. Brussels, www.europa.eu.int/comm/dg06.

EGGERS, J. and K. HAGEDORN, (1998). "Umwelteffekte und agrarumweltpolitische Ansätze der Agenda 2000". Agrarwirtschaft, Vol. 47, No. 12, p. 482-491.

ERVIN, David, 1997. " Agriculture, Trade and Environment: Anticipating the Policy Challenges". Organization for Economic Co-operation and Development, OECD.

EUROPEAN COMMISSION, (1999a) Preface. "Environmental Report of the EU-Commission". Brussels, www.europa.eu.int/comm/dg06.

EUROPEAN COMMISSION, (1999b) "The challenge of integrating environmental requirements into the common agricultural policy". Environmental Report of the EU-Commission. Brussels, www.europa.eu.int/comm/dg06.

EUROPEAN COMMISSION, European Dialogue: May-June 1999c. Issue 3: EU in the world. www.europa.int/comm/dg10.

FAY, F., (1999). "Impact of agri-environmental measures". Report of the EU-Commission. Brussels, www.europa.eu.int/comm/dg06.

GROSSMAN, G. AND KRUGER, A. (1992). " Environmental Impacts of a North American free Trade Agreement". Discussion Paper, John M. Olin Program for the study of Economic Organization and Public Policy, Princeton University, February.

HENRICHSMEYER, W. and H. P. WITZKE, (1991). "Agrarpolitik", Vol. 1. Stuttgart .

ISMEA, (1999). "The European Agro-Food System and the Challenge of Global Competition". Rome.

LUCAS, S. and M. PAU VALL, (1999). "Pesticides in the European Union". Report of the EU-Commission. Brussels , www.europa.eu.int/comm/dg06.

MORELLO, J. (1985). "Temas para el Conocimiento de la Naturaleza y su Manejo en Sudamérica". Avances en la interpretación ambiental del desarrollo agrícola de América Latina. Santiago de Chile, Naciones Unidas.

NIENDIEKER, V., (1998). "Zur Finanzierung der Agrarumweltprogramme gemäß der VO (EWG)". Nr. 2078/92. Agrarwirtschaft, Vol. 47 , No. 2, p. 123-125.

NOVARA, JUAN (1994). "Integración Económica, Comercio Internacional y Medio Ambiente" Enseñanzas para el MERCOSUR. IEERAL y Fundación Konrad Adenauer.

OBSCHATKO, E. (1992). "Argentina: Agricultura, Integración y Crecimiento". Buenos Aires, Instituto Interamericano de Cooperación para la Agricultura (IICA).

OECD, (1998a). " Agriculture and the environment. Issues and Policies". Paris.

OECD, (1998b). "Agricultural Policy Reform: New Approaches. The Role of Direct Payments". Paris.

OECD(1999). "Methodologies for environmental assessment of trade liberalisation agreements". Report of the OECD Workshop held on 26-27 October 1999. COM/TD/ENV(99)92/FINAL. Paris.

PAU VALL, M. and C. VIDAL, (1999). "Nitrogen in Agriculture". Environmental Report of the EU-Commission. Brussels , www.europa.eu.int/comm/dg06.

POIRET, M., (1999a). "Crop Trends and Environmental Impacts". Environmental Report of the EU-Commission. Brussels , www.europa.eu.int/comm/dg06.

POIRET, M., (1999b). "Specialised holdings and more intensive practices". Report of the EU-Commission. Brussels, www.europa.eu.int/comm/dg06.

SAMMARCHI, M. And LARA, A, (1995) "Sector Agropecuario/Forestal en el MERCOSUR. Rol, Situación Actual y Pautas para su Desarrollo Sustentable". Revista de la Universidad del SalvadorSIGNOS Universitarios. MERCOSUR II. Año XIV, No 28, Julio-Diciembre.

SCHULTE, J., (1984). "Begrenzter Einsatz von Handelsdüngern und Pflanzenschutzmitteln". Publication Series of the German Federal Ministry for Food, Agriculture and Forestry. A: Applied Science (Angewandte Wissenschaft), No. 294. Münster-Hiltrup.

SENSI, A., (1999). "Agriculture and climate change". Report of the EU-Commission. Brussels, www.europa.eu.int/comm/dg06.

USDA, (1997). "Exploring the linkages among agriculture, trade and the environment". Washington.

Table A1:
Concentration of the Europe of Nine's agricultural production (in 1,000 and 1,000 ha)

	Holdings (1,000)		Difference (holdings)	UAA (1,000 ha)		Difference (UAA)
	1975	**1995**	**%**	**1975**	**1995**	**%**
Specialised	**3,943**	**3,595**	**-9**	**58,869**	**68,159**	**16**
Field crops	1,049	1,021	-3	17,678	26,055	47
Horticulture	125	106	-15	390	415	6
Permanent crops	1,098	1,192	8	4,585	4,560	-1
Grazing livestock	1,584	1,205	-24	35,766	36,183	1
Poultry	86	70	-19	449	946	111
non specialised	**1,892**	**833**	**-56**	**27,680**	**18,928**	**-32**
Mixed cropping	619	339	-45	5,475	3,763	-31
Mixed livestock	464	126	-73	6,626	2,766	-58
Crops – livestock	808	368	-54	15,579	12,399	-20
TOTAL	**5,835**	**4,428**	**-24**	**86,549**	**87,088**	**1**

Source : Eurostat; taken from Poiret 1999b.

Figure A1: Estimate of nitrogen balance for EU countries*, 1995 (kg/ha)

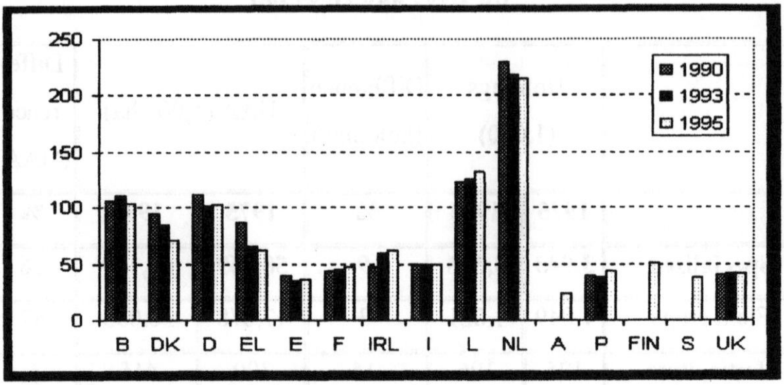

*Area refers to agricultural area which includes: arable land, permanent crops and permanent meadows and pastures

Source: Eurostat , taken from Pau Vall and Vidal, 1999.

Figure A2: Apparent Consumption of mineral fertilizers in EU15

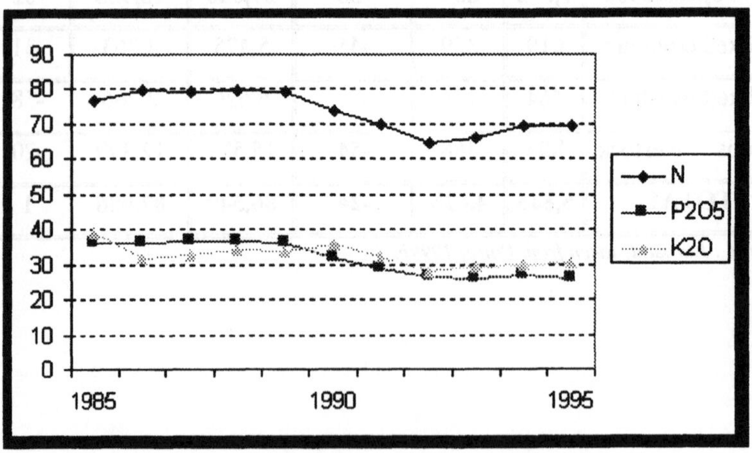

Figure A3

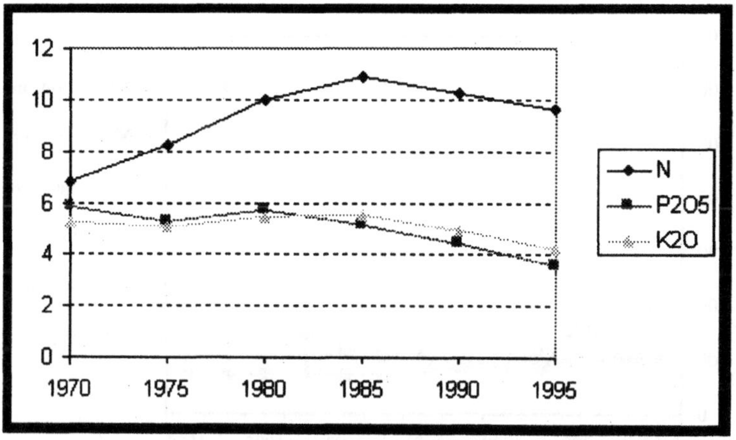

Apparent Consumption in Volume (,000,000 tonnes) Application rate (kg/ha)

Notes: "Apparent consumption" is not necessarily equal to "use by farmers". It refers to deliveries made to wholesalers by domestic producers and importers, which is used as a proxy, in the absence of real data on fertilizer use by farmers.

Up to 1990, "Germany" refers to West Germany prior to unification.

Source: FAO and Eurostat, taken from Pau Vall and Vidal, 1999

Figure A4: Consumption of Phosphate Fertilizer-Index

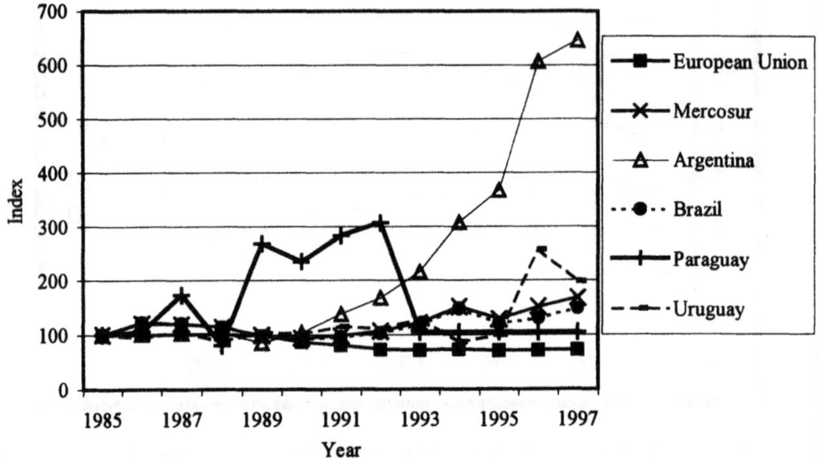

Figure A5: Consumption of Nitrogenous Fertilizer-Index

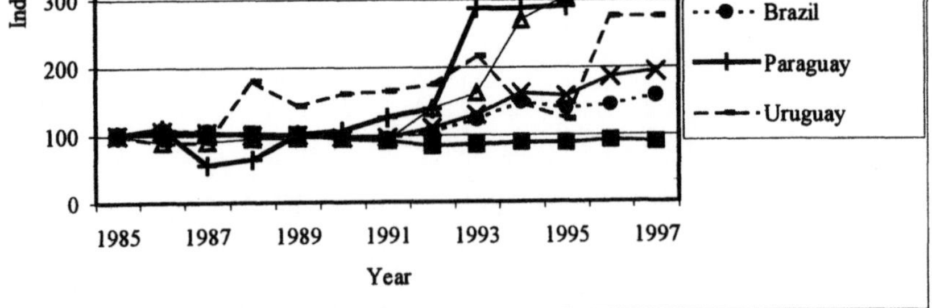

Source: Authors' calculations based on FAO Database.

FigureA6:Consumption of Potash Fertilizer-Index

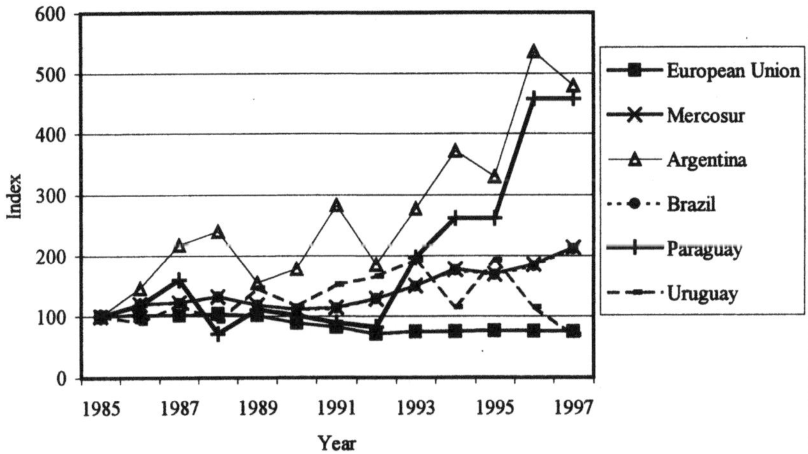

Source: Authors' calculations based on FAO Database.

FigureA7: Total Consumption of Fertilizers-Index

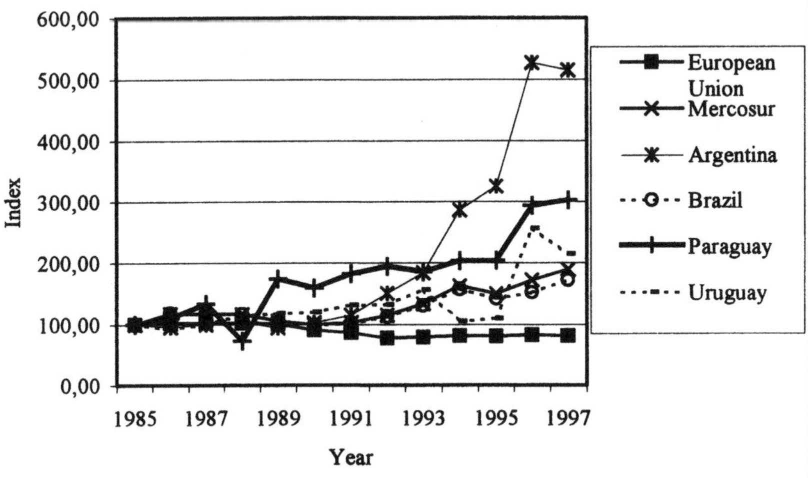

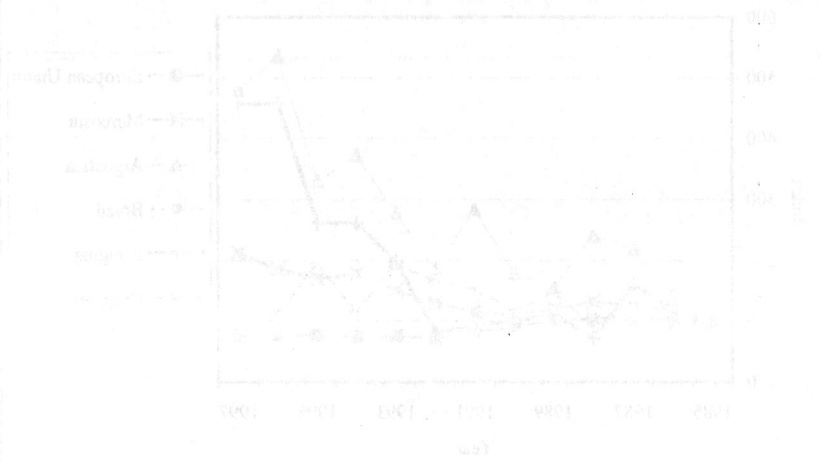

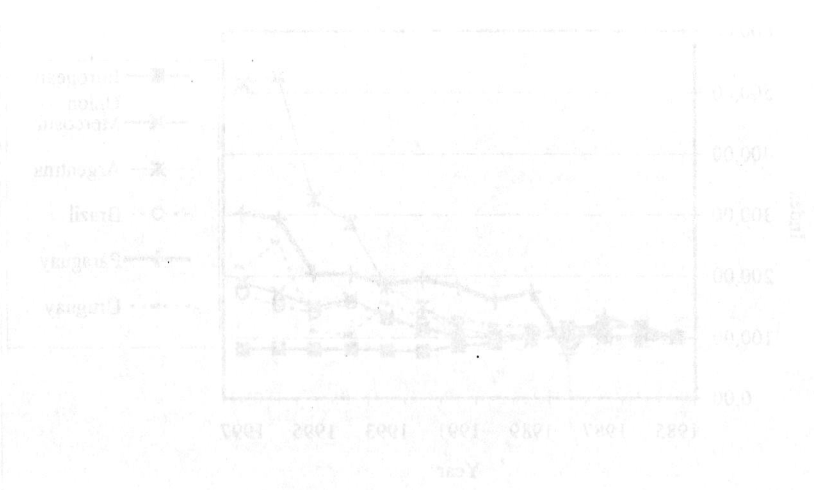

Information Technologies: International Aspects

TELECOMMUNICATIONS MARKET: REGULATION FOR COMPETITION IN ARGENTINA AND BRAZIL

Rinaldo A. Colomé*, Á. Enrique Neder and Carlos Ceballos Ferroglio*****

I. Introduction

In today's world, important transformations in the structure and corporate productive firms as well as in human behavior and the economy at large are being generated by telecommunications.

To a greater or lesser extent, everybody feels the impact of telecommunications both individually and collectively. No access to them means not being able to fit into the so-called "information society".

The role of telecommunications in business is all-important; it has become a strategic resource. It is through them that productive, administrative and commercial activities are coordinated; considerable cost savings are achieved because less capital and labor are needed to reach equal or even higher production levels. The telemeasuring systems used in the natural gas and mining industries are good instances to illustrate this case. Also, the greater the information flow that is generated, the greater the control over logistics. Communication with customers and suppliers is enhanced, project and business administration becomes more efficient and the best way to make a product reach consumers is achieved.

Wireless telecommunications -cellular phones, personal communications systems (PCS), trunking, paging and satellite systems- have contributed to greater efficiency. In the desire to reduce costs, the trend has been to change from voice communication to data services because the latter have fallen some 1000% while voice services have gone down only 10%. (Petrazzini, 1996).

Telecommunications also generate investment. Shaw (1998) points out that the greater the information flow, the greater the need for the most advanced telecommunications infrastructure. The new technologies generate new information as well as the need to spread it. The telecommunications sector is in

*Instituto de Economía y Finanzas, Fac. de Ciencias Económicas, UNC. E-mail: racolome@eco.uncor.edu

**Depto. de Economía y Finanzas, Fac. de Ciencias Económicas, UNC. E-mail: eneder@eco.uncor.edu

***Instituto de Economía y Finanzas, Fac. de Ciencias Económicas, UNC. E-mail: cfceba@eco.uncor.edu

permanent expansion and will be faced with an ever-growing demand; important investments in research and development will be generated.

Telecommunications also favor market integration and this means a direct impact on income levels and market efficiency. Technological advancements make it possible[1].

Macroeconomically, telecommunications have created new employment. Although technologically the sector is highly developed, the generation of employment is not related only to the very qualified skilled employees in this sector. High qualifications are demanded by the sector itself, but there are demands in the non-technical or non-specialized areas for which a particular training is not required. Very especially, this kind of employment helps to fight off youth unemployment and shows the so-called "tertiary effects" of various orders. A first order effect is found when sales and maintenance agents are wanted after a new service has been implemented. There can also be a second-order effect and more, not all of them with a positive impact. It may well be that the introduction of a new communications system means the elimination of another[2].

Consumers are after the services telecommunications make possible in order to optimize their time, improve their welfare, increase productivity or to stay competitive. There are "virtual offices", teleworking, "intelligent cards" or debit cards, direct purchase orders, e-commerce[3], telephone operations and e-banking, videoconferencing, distance learning. The range of choice is made wider for consumers: from the "yellow pages" "to surfing" the net, there are many options that allow consumers to maintain their "consumer" sovereignty.

It is by means of telecommunications that the way we work, live and play, the way we do business, get organized and interact are being transformed (European Community Commission, 1994). And therefore, the mechanisms to generate the adequate regulation of the sector are necessary in order to foster (not prevent them) the changes that telecommunications themselves bring about

---

[1]Very especially with respect to information flow. Tourism and finance increased their productivity in communications quite considerably. This makes such activities boost efficiency in the country because they are exposed to international competition.

[2] With technological progress and to the extent important cost reductions take place wireless telephony will replace paging and trunking and the Internet telephony might easily replace traditional services.

[3] E-commerce on the Internet in the USA and in Europe amounted, in 1998, to about US$ 5,100 m , and it could reach between US$ 1,8 and US$ 3,2 trillions the world over towards 2003 (Forrester Research, 1998). In Argentina, there are some 220,000 Internet subscribers - about 6‰ of the population and 9.7% of the total computerised population- (Moreyra and Moreyra, 1998). Although there is a large potential market, there may also be the case banks do not accept Internet operations; then, doing business on the phone would be more expensive.

in the economy. More competition must also be introduced to create a favorable environment for both consumers and business companies.

The main objective of this paper is to analyze to what extent the regulatory system recently enforced in Argentina favors the development of a competitive market.

The various aspects of the telecommunications market in Argentina and in Brazil are dealt with in Section II. Section III analyses the economic regulation of telecommunications, while Section IV shows the factors that account for distortions and the slowdown in developing competition. Section V analyses Decree 264/98 about the transition towards competition in Argentinean telecommunications. The conclusions are found in Section VI.

II. Telecommunications in Argentina and in Brazil

II.a Privatization and Structure of the Telecommunications Market

II.a.1 Argentina

The privatization of Empresa Nacional de Telecomunicaciones (ENTel) started in 1990. The company was divided into:

- ✓ Two licensed companies to provide local and long distance domestic wired telephony[4].
- ✓ A licensed company to provide international services.
- ✓ A licensed company to provide competitive services (domestic data communication, domestic telex, and maritime mobile radio services).

The country was divided into the North Region and the South Region in the case of the local and long distance wired communications. The exclusive right was allowed to Telecom Argentina S.A. (Telecom) in the North Region and to Telefónica Argentina S.A. (Telefónica) in the South Region. The term to exercise the exclusive right for urban services initially held until November 1997 but was later extended until October or November 2000.

Cellular telephony started servicing a year before the privatization of ENTel. In fact, privatization is not exactly the case with this service since a state-owned company before had not provided it.

International communications and the competitive services were allocated to Telecomunicaciones Internacionales de Argentina S.A. (Telintar), and to Startel S.A., respectively. When both these companies obtained the license, they

[4]Decree 62/90, Annex I, point 8.1, defines basic telephony as the provision of fixed relays that are part of public telephony or are connected to it, and the provision of local and long distance voice telephony through them.

were part of the wired services provider and had equal shares in it. The exclusive right to international communications held until November 1999 after the extension in 1997. The international service is also now in competition. On the other hand, the competitive services, which had been offered by ENTel, have entered competition with other companies although they have been allocated to a license holder (Startel). However, it is worth noticing that the companies with license to operate and provide this kind of service in the international segment had to make use of the Telintar relay.

Wireless communications were allocated to Compañía de Radiocomunicaciones Móviles S.A. (Movicom) which obtained the license in November 1989 to operate in Área Múltiple Buenos Aires (AMBA) and its extension (later Área II of mobile telephony). In March 1993, Miniphone started operations in this same area (in competition with Movicom). Miniphone belonged to the two licensed wired service providers with equal shares. In November 1993, Compañía de Teléfonos del Interior (CTI) obtained the license to operate in both the North and the South Areas established for wireless services. Later, in 1996, the corresponding Telecom (Telecom Personal S.A.) and Telefónica (Unifon) subsidiaries started to operate, the former in Área Norte (Área I) and the latter in Área Sur (Área II).

Finally, the personal communications system (PCS)[5] was offered in public tender in 1997 to allocate licenses in AMBA and its extension (Área II). This process was suspended by law, and in June 1999 three licenses were allocated to the then mobile telephony players.

Public telephony, telecommunications services on a public net offered to the general public by installing, operating and exploiting public telephone booths, also meant a step forward in the sector´s competition. Decree 264/98 established that the exploitation of call boxes would be open and in full accordance with Reglamento General de Telefonía Pública (Public Telephony Regulations) as from the day after said decree was made known, and different companies were given the permission to operate.

Both Telecom and Telefónica were allowed "to encroach or cross the lines" mutually.

The structure of the telecommunications market as shown in Chart 1 (in the appendix) is characterised by competitive services and by exclusive rights. Concerning the latter, since Decree 264/98 (analysed in Section V), more deregulation has been taking place.

[5] According to Resolution 60/97 of Secretaría de Comunicaciones, it is wireless multiple service telephony that uses access digital technology and makes possible the communications between two or more users or between such users and other networks or systems either to receive or to generate communications.

As seen in the Chart 1, the structure of telecommunications is mainly competitive. Nevertheless, there is margin for more competition in wired telephony while still maintaining regulation, which would be a crucial element in making competition more transparent. Interconnection charges and providing the so-called universal service are essential for the development of a competitive market.

II.a.1.i Investment, Productivity Changes and Consumer Benefits

There have been big important transformations since the privatisation process was started in 1990 in Argentina's telecommunications sector. The benefits for the whole of the Argentinean society have also been significant, and they refer to telephone lines availability, lower costs and improved services. For instance, when ENTel was privatised, a telephone line cost some US$ 1500 while today it is a maximum US$ 150. Likewise, to eventually obtain a line would take some years literally while it only takes a few days now.

The economy at large was also favoured. The accumulated investment value of wired telephony in the period 1991-1995 was close to US$ 10,000m, and a similar figure was forecasted for the next 1996-2000[6] five-year period. Such investments have proved especially good to increase not only corporate income but also consumer standards since the economy can count on a greater teledensity[7].

Table 1[8] shows the ratio investments-corporate net income, including comparisons with foreign companies.

Those companies operating in Argentina, if compared with the companies quoted in Table 1, allocate larger portions of their income to investment, which shows the decision of preparing for the arrive of competition, and not in yardstick competition as today[9].

If investment figures are compared to teledensity, it will be seen that the sector's investments in relation to corporate income are bigger as teledensity decreases, in developing economies which should also show a good performance in their economy's evolution.

Employment and productivity are further elements to consider. Table 2 shows employment and productivity levels with reference to the license holders of wired telephony in Argentina. Although employment diminishes over the years, what in fact can be observed is the low productivity before privatisation.

[6] See Secretaría de Comunicaciones (1998).

[7] Teledensity is understood to be the number of telephone lines operating per one hundred inhabitants.

[8] All tables are in the appendix.

[9] Note that the United Kingdom started deregulation in 1988, New Zealand at the start of the '90s and Chile in 1984.

The reduction of personnel in the wired telephone companies was also the result of outsourcing different services, and the new subsidiaries of the license holders became such services providers. In turn, productivity shows significant growth levels. The positive variation between pre-privatisation and the following five years is striking (187%). Over the last years, productivity increases are between 16% and 30%.

Table 3 shows a comparison of productivity between different companies. Productivity increase in Argentinean companies is very clear. Not only the fact that there were more lines in operation but also personnel reduction account for such increase.

II.a.1.ii Telephone Rates

Rates are another important element in the analysis of the telecommunications market evolution toward competition in Argentina.

The price cap system was established with privatisation. As soon as the private companies started operating, they were allowed (they were not demanded) a monthly rate updating according to the Consumer Price Index of Argentina (applied in Buenos Aires, the Capital City), and to corrections in the exchange rate due to the inflationary and hyperinflationary processes that the country had had to suffer. After the Convertibility Law was passed, the rates were nominated in US dollars, fixing the cost of the dialling mode (set in pulses) in dollars, with adjustments in April and October annually, according to changes in CPI in all items of the USA, and officially published by the Department of Commerce.

In the period analysed, the cost of the pulse grew at an average rate of 2.5% annually along with very small increases of the inflation rate; this meant important hikes in real terms. It must be noted that the charge the consumers observe, without considering taxes, is not only the cost of the pulse but also the rate pacing, that is to say, the number of seconds that compose a pulse. Therefore, when comparing the charge per minute, the average length of the call must be borne in mind[10].

The last of the important changes introduced in Argentina's telecommunications rates took place at the beginning of 1997 when rates were restructured. There were alterations in the cost of the minimum monthly charge and of the local, domestic and international long distance services. Significant increases were the case with minimum charges: the family billing grew over 40% while professional and business categories rose 38% and 14% respectively. (Neder, 1997).

[10] This is a situation made clearer by the per minute rate implemented by the phone companies.

The local rate increased because the rate pacing changed: four minutes instead of six for overnight rates. A new time slot called "rush hours" (and later suppressed) was created: Monday to Friday from 10am to 1pm and from 8pm to 10pm. Additionally, for consumers residing in the territories not in the Capital District, enjoyed the privilege of paying the local rate for calls within the area not farther than 30 km away.

Long distance rates –domestic and international- were reduced considerably, although the reduced long distance rate (Monday to Friday from 6pm to 8pm) was eliminated, and prime time was extended until 10pm. The considerable reductions in the international services –particularly with the USA- took place because it was a segment under strong competition in the system known as call-back[11].

The present rate structure is compared with one in other countries where the telephone networks have different degree of maturity, in order to consider if there are cross subsidies between services.

Table 4 shows comparisons of the different connection charges, minimum fee and per minute rates in family and business services. The data provided in Table 4 help to establish the excess ratios in connection charges and business over family minimum monthly charge, and the differences between the per minute domestic long distance rate and the per minute local rate. Table 5 shows the different percentages. Countries analyzed do not show differences between the business and the family connections except for Canada and Uruguay. However, important differences are observed between such connections with respect to minimum charges except for Spain and Chile. The minimum fee means the charge needed to maintain the line; then, a bigger communication flow could be thought of which would demand more maintenance. Technological progress very quickly does away with such assumption and makes the mentioned difference meaningless.

When comparing local and domestic long distance rates, the differences are very big in the cost per minute. Bridging distance by technological advances (Cairncross, 1997) leads to think such differences allow considerable cross subsidies[12] which are the result of the obligation to provide the service in non-profitable areas.

[11] An international call was put through by means of operators outside the territory of Argentina, and communication was reached as if it were domestics call but ruled by international rates.

[12] A detailed analysis should include a thorough knowledge of the demand elasticities of each service plus the cost of providing the services. There are as many figures as analyses made in Argentina.

II.a.2 Brazil

Over the last decade, like in Argentina, Brazil has undergone restructuring in the telecommunications sector. In general terms, the process presents three stages: first, the state-owned enterprises are privatized; then, the private companies enjoy the exclusive rights in the provision of services, and the provision is rendered, in some cases, by private duopolies and, in others, by oligopolies; in the last stage, total market liberalization allowing free entrance to potential competitors is introduced[13].

The objective pursued with such transformations in the telecommunications sector is to make the market competitive. Nevertheless, it is advisable to keep in mind that completely doing away with the legal barriers to entrance alone will not generate competition; competition encouragement and promotion policies to that effect are necessary.

Before privatization, two large state companies provided the telecommunications services: EMBRATEL (EMPRESA BRASILERA DE TELECOMUNICACIONES) for long distance services and radiobroadcast, and TELEBRAS (TELECOMUNICACIONES BRASILERAS S.A.) which gathered 27 state dealers in one national holding that covered the domestic services.

The telecommunications services provision by state companies that were administratively and financially independent was the instrument to implement a national telecommunications system, and the expansion of teledensity the cause for greater service efficiency and the protection of the imports substitution industry. The well known regulator-regulated conflict within the same entity, then, arose.

Following Tavares de Almeida (1999), the state services provision started to cause problems in the 1970s when the state control over the state enterprises was part of the macroeconomic anti-inflationary policies. Control over prices and budget allocations of the firms along with cross subsidies and administrative inefficiency contributed to weaken reinvesting in the companies. Such investment fall was the cause of a considerable lag of the sector, the service provision deterioration and the failure to meet claims.

According to Pastoriza (1999), the main features of Brazilian telecommunications before privatization were: a) poor quality and high congestion; b) a small network and many unserviced areas; c) high cost and long waits to get new lines; d) not enough provision of value added services.

Different types of influences intervened in the Brazilian telecommunications privatization. On the one hand, the internal pressures that saw the need to improve the sector's efficiency and to transform the

[13]This final stage of market liberalisation had not yet been completed, neither in Argentina nor in Brazil, at the time this study was beeing conducted.

telecommunications market -to change from monopoly to competition- given the technological advances. On the other, external pressures originated in the need to unify regulatory policies in the light of economic globalization and the agreement signed with WTO.

Following Linhares Pires (1999), the Brazilian telecommunications restructuring was a six stage process that ended with the privatization of Telebras. We will briefly analyze each of them, and greater attention will be paid to Telebras transformation.

1. *Constitutional Amendment Nº 8 (1995)* removed the exclusive rights the state companies enjoyed. The Constitution ruled that telecommunications had to be serviced by a state monopoly. This amendment was aimed to making the state monopoly flexible to allow Brazil to keep the monopoly power but also to allow the private companies the license to provide the services. This bidding mechanism for the rights to operate in monopolist conditions in certain services provision is known as the Demsetz Competition, and the main purpose with it is to introduce competition for the market as a substitute for competition within the market.
2. *Minimum Telecommunications Act (1996)* established the bases for obtaining licenses for the services provided by state companies, but was an economically attractive possibility, such as wireless telephony, band B.
3. *Telecommunications Act (1997)* defined the sector's institutional model, created ANATEL (Agencia Nacional de Telecomunicaciones), defined their scope and power, fixed a different rate system[14], introduced a new classification for the telecommunications services[15], and established non exclusivity for licenses. Non exclusivity licensing is essential in the legislation because it allows regional duopolies for the service provision.
4. *Geral de Outorgas Plan (1998)* traced the general lines for competition and defined the exploitation areas.
5. *Telebras deep restructuring*. The company was divided into three holdings of wired telephony licensing to serve each of the areas defined by the Geral de Outorgas Plan.
6. *Public offer of authorization to operate "mirror" companies[16]* in each area; the characteristic of the licenses was non-exclusivity.

[14] It was a rate rebalancing that reduced cross subsidies.

[15] The services were classified into restricted interest and collective interest services; the former to be provided under a private regimen and the latter under a mixed private and public regimen. The difference between private and public being that the latter is subject to rate control, the obligation to universalise the services and the obligation of network penetration, while the former does not present obligations. A clear asymmetry is, then, observed.

[16] These companies and the incumbent hold the market.

II.a.2.i Telebras restructuring

This mechanism for privatization consisted of regional duopolies to provide local services in three areas of similar interest and economic benefits. The international and interregional services would be provided by another duopoly made up by Embratel and a possible competitor.

Telebras holding dealers were grouped in a sole company to serve the three areas the country was divided into. The regions were distributed so that little economic attraction and high profitability were both possible in the same area. The pulling together of different companies into one allowed cross subsidies from profitable areas with low operating costs, with economies of density to areas with difficult access and high cost. Additionally, with large companies, the idea was to generate their own investment resources, diminish the information asymmetry and make comparison and state control easier.

In the operating area of each of the initial four companies, competition in the form of the so-called "mirror" company is a possibility.

A salient characteristic of the privatization process was the presence of pro-entrant asymmetries. The way such asymmetries were implemented imposed the initial companies network expansion obligations, universal service financing and provision and rate control by means of fixing price caps. The entrant companies were exempted such obligations with very few exceptions.

The mentioned asymmetries allow potential competitors entrance in profitable market segments thanks to the fact that the incumbents have the obligation to adopt cross-subsidy policies in order to provide universal service in non-profitable areas. This is how short-term efficiency was sacrificed in favor of entrance assurance.

Each company or consortium interested in participating in the process could only compete in the name of one of the four companies being offered. Concentration was thus prevented and yardstick competition favored (cream-skimming policy).

The duopoly per area system will hold until 2003; thereafter, the market will be completely open. It is to be noticed that the system adopted could give way to collusive practices between the incumbents and the entrant company, which would allow, after total market openness, accumulated profits to be used to discourage possible entrants.

II.a.2.ii Interconnection rules

Great stress on the interconnection regulation is laid in Brazil to create a pro-competitive atmosphere in the telecommunications market, in the light of the international experience. Since the incumbents have access to end users, interconnection agreements are wanted so that the new firms can enter the market. The non-mandatory condition of interconnection would make the economies of scope of the demand reinforce the initial monopolist situations. Also, if duplicating the networks were possible, the cost of such provision for the users would mean entrance refusal for the new competitors.

According to Linhares Pires (1999), general interconnection agreement norms are added to the obligations in order to suppress the following practices: a) cross subsidies; b) omission of relevant technical information and c) obstructing, coercing or any other abusive demand to celebrate the interconnection agreement.

With respect to cross subsidies, if the interconnection charges are high enough, they represent entrance barriers for the segment under consideration and for other services provided by the company. To illustrate, if there are two firms that have signed an expensive interconnection agreement to cover domestic long distance services, a third one wishing to enter that market would be prevented from doing so by the barrier created. In turn, if that third company withdrew from the domestic long distance service and wished to enter the local calls segment, there would also be a barrier. This last barrier is born because the incumbents, seizing the chance to skim the cream, may considerably reduce the cost of communications.

The interconnection charges for wired telephony were established in the licensing agreements, and the criterion adopted is the cost of using the local network. All network operators have the obligation to offer unbundling services to competitors. All the local service providers must offer consumers the possibility to choose the long distance provider of their preference.

II.a.2.iii Universal service

The obligation to provide universal service is found in the licensing agreements in accordance with the General Plan Objectives for Universal Services. This plan sets the expansion obligation to offer individual and collective access and call boxes plus servicing rural areas, the disabled and the schools and hospitals (Linhares Pires, 1999).

In Brazil, the universal service is an instrument of pro-entrant asymmetries that cause rate distortion due to cross subsidies.

The Telecommunications Act allows a wide margin for further objectives to cover cases the licensed companies have no obligation to serve (under 100 people areas).

The Telecommunications Act created Universal Service Fund in case the cost of providing the universal service could not be recouped.

If there is an expansion of universal service objectives, the licensed companies might implement cross subsidies between services or between user segments. Besides, they can charge an additional cost above rate boundaries imposed on interconnection charges, which might mean a new entrance barrier and a threat to neutrality in universal service provision related to competition.

In a few words, Brazil's telecommunications privatization policy is characterized by a pronounced pro-entrant asymmetry whose final consequence means sacrificing efficiency in the short term and introducing marked distortions. If this situation persists, it would ultimately hinder instead of encouraging competition.

III. Telecommunications Regulation

The regulation of telecommunications should be independent, just like in the case of other services, for both the service players and the daily implementation of the governmental telecommunications policy (Melody,1999).

The regulator must exercise control over the policy implementation to be observed by the players; the regulator must also settle disputes arising between competitors or between consumers and the service providers. The regulator must balance the effects of technological advances and the changes in relative prices, and must also allow companies to make the best out of bigger productivity while, at the same time, transfer it, at least in part, to the customers. Regulation must become the support for markets to work more efficiently. Politically, an important feature of regulation is income distribution.

Why regulate public services? The answer is that they are services that must possibly reach the whole community in quantity and in quality, and because there are monopolies and oligopolies in the sector although technological advances reduce their influence. Another reason is the desire to protect the " consumer's sovereignty" ; that is to say, consumers enjoy the exclusive right to decide what, which and how to consume at the same time that the influence exercised by the companies should be reduced to a minimum (Neder, 1999).

There may be two different approaches to the analysis of the regulation process: the positive and the prescriptive. The former is referred to the creation of regulating bodies and their performance once they have been established and are in operation. The main point in the prescriptive approach is when a natural monopoly should be regulated. An evaluation of the impact of regulation on welfare, and a clear way to measure it, is necessary to this effect. The measure will be given by the consumer's and by the producer's surplus.

The objective will be to set the price that maximizes the net economic benefit, in order for the firm to remain economically viable, guaranteeing the provision of the service.

The two cases of natural monopoly will be analyzed: economies of scale (traditional definition), and subadditivity of costs.

Let us assume a firm producing a single product with constant prices of factor for production, and that is not able to price discriminate.

III.a Economies of scale

Let us assume the traditional notion of natural monopoly. This is based on economies of scale throughout the relevant range of production. Economic principles set that Pareto-efficient solution is achieved at Q_e (see Figure 1) where the service is provided to all the consumers who wish to pay, at least, the marginal cost of producing the commodity.

Figure 1

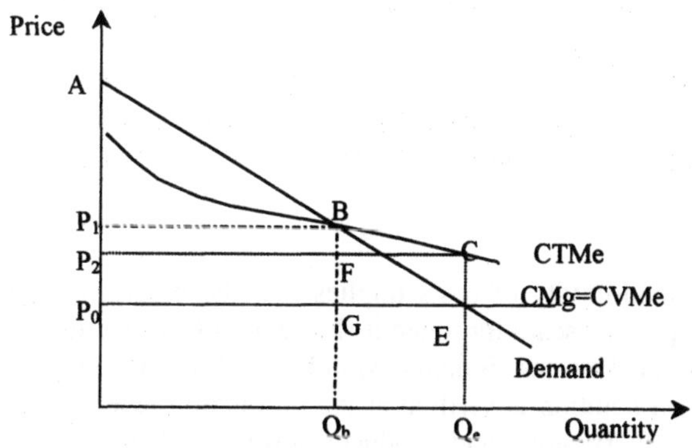

Let us assume a total cost function with the structure

$$C(Q) = F + mQ$$

If the regulatory authority forced the company to set a price equal to marginal cost (first best), Q_e is the production level that verified the Pareto-efficient condition[17]. However, monopolist will be operating at a loss equal to fixed costs (F) showed by the area P_0P_2CE and equivalent to the area P_0P_1BG, since total fixed costs are constants for any production level. In order for the firm to remain economically viable (and to guarantee the provision of the service), the authority should give the company the corresponding subsidy[18].

[17] Consumers' surplus is P_0AE, while the producers' surplus (total income less total variable costs) would be nul.

[18] The net economic benefit of fixing a rate equal to marginal cost would be $P_0AE - P_0P_1BG$, or $P_1AB + GBE$.

However, this is not the only possible solution to increase efficiency with respect to the monopoly solution: a viable alternative is to set a price equal to average cost (second best).

As shown in Figure 1, the net economic benefit generated by such a solution is the sum of the P_1AB area (consumer's surplus) and P_oP_1BG area (producer's surplus). This solution increases the net economic benefit and, at the same time, avoiding to subsidize the firm. The firm reaches a breakeven point but consumers loss P_oP_1BG area (which is transferred to the firm) and the GBE area (deadweight loss).

So, there is a trade off between the Pareto-efficiency loss (deadweight loss) and the possible welfare losses in other markets that could be taxed in order to provide revenues necessary to keep the firm viable.

Fixing a tax to subsidize the firm would not generate a deadweight loss in the case of perfectly inelastic market demand. Nevertheless, it would reduce consumer surplus in the amount of the collected tax.

Despite economists are prone to favor first best solution, in this case the second best -despite causing the deadweight loss- increases net economic benefit, and keeps the firm viable (guaranteeing the provision of the service).

III.b Subadditivity of costs

The concept of subadditivity of costs implies that the natural monopoly need not exhibit economies of scale throughout the range of production in the market (Braeutigam, 1989). This case is analyzed in Figure II (on the next page).

The Pareto-efficient solution is verified at the production level Q_e, where consumer surplus is the P_oAE area, and producer surplus is P_2P_0EC. At this production level the firm gets a supernormal profit equal to the area P_1P_0EF, and the net economic benefit with respect to the monopoly solution is that the deadweight loss (efficiency loss caused by monopoly) is recoup.

If the monopolist were forced to set a price P_3 equal to average costs, the production level would be Q_b, greater than Q_e. Consumer surplus would be now P_3AB, and producer surplus would be P_4P_3BG. We can see that consumer surplus has risen in P_3P_0EB, while producer surplus has decreased in P_3P_0EH (transfer to consumers), and in P_2P_4GC, and has risen in IHBG. The net effect on the producer surplus is the decrease in the supernormal profit (since the fixed costs are the same for every production level).

The final effect is a benefit showed by HEB area that is part of the increase in the consumer surplus. This solution brings an improvement with respect to the solution given by setting price equal to marginal cost.

Figure II

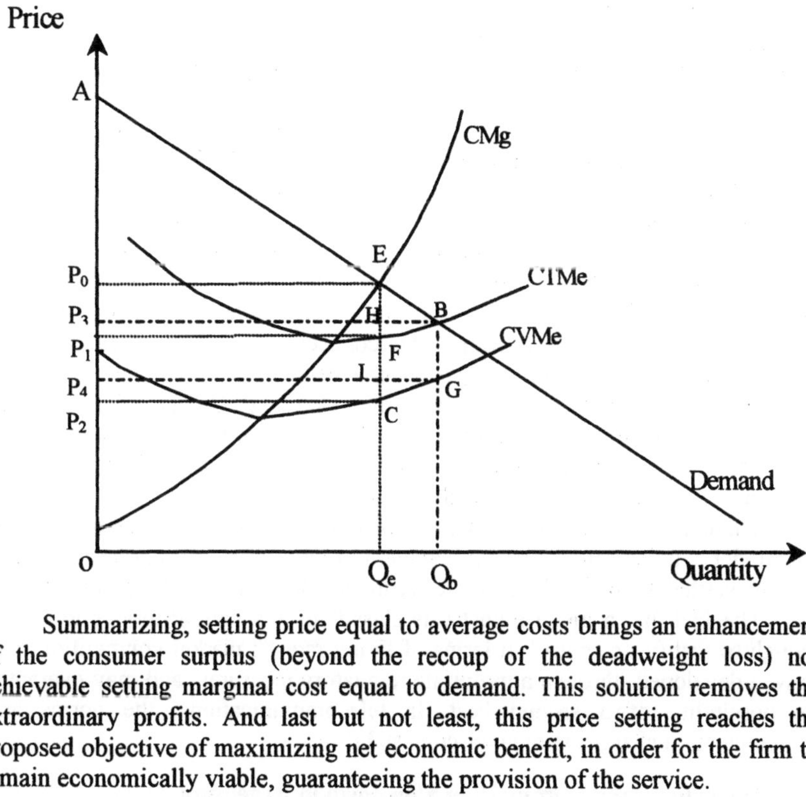

Summarizing, setting price equal to average costs brings an enhancement of the consumer surplus (beyond the recoup of the deadweight loss) not achievable setting marginal cost equal to demand. This solution removes the extraordinary profits. And last but not least, this price setting reaches the proposed objective of maximizing net economic benefit, in order for the firm to remain economically viable, guaranteeing the provision of the service.

III.c Competition for the market

According to Braeutigam (1989), there are different alternatives to introduce competition in a market characterized as a natural monopoly. As was seen before, competition in a market where large economies of scale operate is not possible; however, it is possible to develop some competition for the rights to operate in that market and the resulting solution would be quite close to second best. This is known as Demsetz Competition[19].

[19] The Demsetz Competition is possible if the following conditions are satisfied: a) production inputs should be available to all competitors in open markets and at competitive prices; b) the collusion cost between the different bidders should be high to guarantee that the result of exercising the right to operate in the market is the competition of the different bidders.

However, appealing the Demsetz Competition may be -it allows the possibility of competing even in monopolist markets- it may be seriously deficient because the winner in the public bid may be motivated to adopt a strategy of providing the service at the lowest possible level of quality. It could achieve a considerable cost reduction and, consequently, increase benefits.

An important failure of the Demsetz Competition occurs when the companies can offer more than just a single service to consumers; in such a case, it is not possible to determine who the winner will be. The Demsetz Competition does not offer the base to choose between two rate vectors and no domination could be established.

Another way to introduce competition where natural monopoly is the case is constituted by the concept of contestable markets. The idea behind contestability is that a greater competition is achievable even in markets with subadditive cost functions. A proper interconnection could transform a natural telecommunication monopoly in a contestable market.

The main difference between the Demsetz Competition and the contestable markets in order to obtain P=AC is that in the latter the approach does not require the authority to be the arbiter in the bidding process. Equilibrium is achieved automatically without intervention.

There is a third way known as Chamberlin monopolist competition or intermodel competition to develop competition in the type of market dealt with here. Nevertheless, it is difficult to verify in the telecommunications sector.

The fact that a given industry is classified as a natural monopoly is not enough to justify its control in terms of fixing rates[20]; market competition may be well developed -through appropriate regulatory measures- and may guarantee the possibility of a second best. In telecommunications, the norms and interconnection charges may favor contestability.

IV. Distortions and Competition Slowdown in Argentina

Telecommunications generated great changes in Argentina's national economy along with important investments and benefits for consumers and business. There are still serious distortions that prevent the introduction of fuller competition. If such distortions are not corrected, openness to more competition will not generate the desired results. Distortions in the sector are observed in the different rates, the universal service, the consumer inertia and, particularly, in the interconnection of the networks.

[20] Regulation is also necessary in different aspects that concern the quality of the services provided.

IV.a Rate Distortion

Before rate restructuring (Decree 92/97), the local minute rate was "supposedly" some 21.43% below marginal cost while the domestic long distance minute rate was 160%, 279% and 253% over marginal cost for short, medium and long distance respectively[21]. After restructuring, assuming the same costs, such distortions are still present. The local minute rate is still some 18% below marginal cost and the domestic long distance minute rate (smaller percentages than pre-rebalancing) stays some 43%, 32% and 55% over marginal cost for short, medium and long distance respectively.

Although they were reduced, Decree 92/97 did not remove the implicit rate cross subsidies. They still hold, together with subsidies between services, cross subsidies between customers (the minimum monthly business charge is 31% higher than the one for the professional category, and 156% higher than the family charge in AMBA). Between areas, the minimum business charge in AMBA is 11% higher than in the rest of the country. The connection fee is the same all over the country in spite of the differences in teledensity between provinces.

It can, then, be inferred that the domestic long distance service and the differences between categories and regions as shown in the minimum monthly charge figures subsidize the local service provision and the universality of the service. The openness to a bigger local service competition would be limited: if a given low cost company considers it is profitable to enter densely populated urban areas, the "business cream" the incumbent would get for providing long distance service would make it possible to avoid competition. It could displace the entrant by means of a predatory rate policy that can be seen as the "investment" by the incumbent in building a bar entrance. Depending upon success in a "price war", it may be possible to attract "partners" to finance such policy[22]. Thereby the need to simultaneously verify long distance competition so that local rates reductions may be constant and effective.

Can the proposed long-distance rate reductions be seem as a consumer benefit? It will depend on the service "packages" offered by firm. It may occur that consumers can obtain certain services at lower rates but, at the same time, have to consume some minimum time or buy from the same company other services with a wider margin. This could give way to the persistence of cross subsidies and repetition of a predatory corporate policy.

---

[21] See *Considerandos* in Decree 92/97. Boletín Oficial n. 28576, 1st section, p. 8, Jan. 31, 1997.

[22] A bank, for example. However, an entrant could also get it.

IV.b Interconnection and Competition

Cost and quality are the aspects to consider when dealing with the influence of interconnection on competition. If the interconnection cost is low enough with respect to the service marginal cost, the incumbent in the very profitable segments might offer the entrant a low quality interconnection[23]. This would discourage the customers of the latter, which would mean strongly barring entrance or a predatory practice. Instead, in segments without the threat of customer loss or where attracting new customers would mean large investments, the incumbent would be ready to maintain the good quality interconnection to the extent marginal cost is included.

When quality is assured, the cost of interconnection becomes the issue. According to the annex to Art. 4 of Decree 266/98, the interconnection cost for both local access and local transmission are the following:

Validity	Local Access	Local Transmission
From Nov 9, 1998 to end of exclusive rights[24]	US$ 3,50 cents (plus 30% in under 10,000 people areas)	US$ 1,50 cents
From end of exclusive rights to Nov 8, 2000	US$ 3,15 cents (plus 30% in under 10,000 people areas)	US$ 1,00 cents
From Nov 9, 2000 on	US$ 2,15 cents (plus 30% in under 10,000 people areas)	US$ 1,00 cents

Regulations establish that entrants and incumbents must agree on interconnection charges. If no agreement is reached, Secretaría de Comunicaciones (Telecommunications Secretariat) will decide on the corresponding figures. If art. 23 of the Regulations -long-term incremental cost method will be used- cannot be applied, then art. 24 may be applied -interconnection charges are calculated as the average of the figures in the selected countries- or the referential values can be used. If the cost turned out to be high, then it would be a barrier to entrance and would induce incumbents not

[23] Congestion might be the cause of poor quality. Although quality is a requirement, the obligation to comply with it may be lessened because a satisfactory global percentage of answered calls is demanded. But Reglamento General de Interconexión aims at adequate control.

[24] Convenios de Interconexión (Interconnection Agreements) between Telecom and Telefónica do not show differences with respect to the figures in the former table.

to celebrate interconnection agreements with entrants, whenever Secretaría de Comunicaciones applied referential values.

Despite the fact that referential values are higher than a local-call rate, incumbents (read Telecom and Telefonica) have signed agreements on interconnection charges equal to the referential values. This can be seen in the following table:

Traffic	Local Access	Local Transmission
Local in the Greater Buenos Aires Multiple Area (GBAMA)	US$ 0,035 per minute or fraction	
Rest of the Country-GBAMA	US$ 0,035 per minute or fraction	
GBAMA-Rest of the Country	US$ 0,035 per minute in over 10,000 people areas, and plus 30% in under 10,000 people areas	According to Anexo I. E.G.: over 240 km ⇒ US$ 0,.27 per minute
Rest of the Country-Rest of the Country	US$ 0,035 per minute in over 10,000 people areas, and plus 30% in under 10,000 people areas	According to Anexo I. E.G.: over 240 km ⇒ US$ 0,.27 per minute
Ended in co-operatives	US$ 0,035 per minute in over 10,000 people areas, and plus 30% in under 10,000 people areas	According to Anexo I. E.G.: over 240 km ⇒ US$ 0,.27 per minute
Provider in GBAMA - Third Provider		US$ 0,015 per minute or fraction.

Source: Authors´ based on licensees agreements.

Given that interconnection agreements should not discriminate, these agreements should be applied for entrants. These access charges will not favor new entrants since losses will be present. Nevertheless, those access charges do not harm the incumbents. This is because both companies have similar traffic between them. This constitutes a bar entrance for new comers.

IV.c Universal Service

The obligation to provide this service implies the need to regulate it to generate competition. There should be some compensation mechanism to reach regions or sectors of the population that produce very low or negative profits. Under the assumption that what the universal service includes is known, then, who should provide it is the real issue. In principle, all companies that offer basic telephony -both entrants and incumbents- must provide it. This would prevent outsized advantages for entrants, particularly with reference to the local service. However, if competition were free and total, an entrant company could offer service in urban areas without the need of universal service. In such a case, compensating for such inequality would mean charging that company a differential rate on their income to finance the universality of the service.

Financing the whole universal service would be possible with the corresponding payment by the service users and a rate on the income of the sector's players. Then,

$$\left[\frac{\sum_i c_i \cdot l_i}{\sum_i l_i} - p\right] \cdot \sum_i l_i - t \cdot \sum_j Y_j^e = 0,$$

where $\frac{\sum_i c_i \cdot l_i}{\sum_i l_i}$ is the weighted average cost of the universal service,

c_i the service cost in region i, l_i the eligible customers in each of the i regions,

$\sum_i l_i$ the total universal service users, p the average to collect from eligible customers, $\sum_j Y_j^e$ the expected j players' income and t the rate to be applied on this income (Colomé et al., 1998).

There should be a t>0 rate in case of deficit when providing the universal service when the expected income is not enough.

IV.d Consumer Inertia

There may be different causes for this inertia, such as the cost when changing the provider, the absence of dialing parity or number portability. These factors limit competition because of the decisions made by users rather than inaction on the part of the service providers.

Although openness to competition has taken place, the desired results may not be easy to obtain if the existing distortions and problems do not meet a solution.

V. Decree 264/98: Legislating for Competition?

Of all the telecommunications sector norms and regulations, Decree 264/98 is the most relevant one for the future of both the licensed companies and the consumers. This decree, quite a long one, introduced the need for competition in telecommunications: openness to competition to exploit public telephony, instructing Secretaría de Comunicaciones to enforce the universal service regulations, liberalization of transmission of Mercosur data, instructing Secretaría de Comunicaciones to enforce restrictive practice regulations in competition and cross subsidies, fixing the parameters for regulating rates in the transition towards competition, granting two new licenses to operate local basic telephony, point to point relaying and international data and telephony as from November 1999, and new licenses for long distance calling[25] (domestic and international) as from November 1999 as well.

Needless to say, the most controversial aspect in this decree is the very few new licenses granted to operate the basic domestic long distance calls service. The question arises whether this is the way to bigger competition or simply is a small openness of the existing regional monopolies. If art. 5 of this decree is recalled, it is found that it establishes that the two players to be appointed must be players in " ...phone services with quality levels similar to those in Red de Telefonia Pública Nacional (National Public Telephony Network) -Servicios de Radiocomunicaciones Móviles Celular- (SRMC) and Servicio de Telefonía Móvil (STM)-, whose stockholders show international experience in wired telephony, *having resided in the country...*"[26] and, also, " ... operating physical networks in television broadcasting (CATV) covering a minimum five(5) cities with over a hundred fifty thousand (150.000) inhabitants or a minimum one hundred thousand (100.000) users either individually or collectively." Other existing " ...players in telecommunications services with already installed physical networks" will be able to provide service as well.

As may be inferred from the conditions in the mentioned decree, bigger competition to promote technological and financial improvement is ruled out. It is expressly stated that, no matter technological advances, " ... the international experience shows a marked inclination to concentrate the companies..." that provide basic telephony. Nevertheless, such an idea is not altogether accurate in the sense that today technology and capital are available to those interested in

[25] Although not specified in the decree, 3 (three) is the predicted number.
[26] Emphasis in italics by the authors.

entering the market. This is made possible by means of corporate and administrative models that reduce the incumbents' advantages and achieve a competitive standing in the sector. Also, the fast technological advances contribute to eliminate natural barriers to entrance. Wireless telephony and personal communications systems are a clear example: they do away with the barriers of scale that building parallel networks would imply.

A large size may not be an advantage in the future to the extent small players may offer a wider range of services or even use some "niches" thanks to being closer to their users. This is the case with videocable where fiber optic technology would be in condition to simultaneously provide television, basic telecommunications, e-mail and Internet.

The real technological problem is interconnection, rather than any other aspect of the sector, which demands strict regulation. It may be a lot more simple to regulate interconnection agreements between a few companies than when a great number are implied. But this would mean to ignore how the market works. It is generally expected that the greater the number of competitors, the fewer the anticompetitive practices. This does not imply everything is left to market regulation. Regulation should still be necessary, but only to seek agreements or fix values when free negotiations were not successful (as established by Reglamento General de Interconexión – Interconnection General Regulations). Additionally, to guard against the possibility of collusive agreements, it would also be feasible to have yardstick competition. In fact, regulation should favour interconnection agreements beneficial to companies (in cost and quality), and should likewise transfer the benefits to the users of the phone services.

VI. Conclusions

If the effects technological progress caused in the telecommunications market are added to the explosive demand expansion of said services, then, it can be inferred that the market is not near monopoly. In some countries, it is still the case that a single company provides the services, but this is due to legal limitations rather than to the technical impossibility for competitors to enter the business.

Two further factors contribute to consider doubts with respect to the existence of a natural monopoly:

1) In densely populated urban areas the explosive demand expansion might allow and make duplication of installations profitable.

2) By means of interconnection charges fixed fairly (considering long-term incremental cost), duplicating the telecommunications networks might be unnecessary.

With respect to the telecommunications market contestability in Argentina, from the technological point of view, the different technologies used by the providers and the potential competitors should be checked so that free market entrance and exit is guaranteed at no cost. As Train (1991) states, free entrance refers to the fact that possible competitors do not have to incur in cost that the incumbent does not face; that is to say, the entrant should not be at a cost disadvantage with respect to the incumbent. By exit at no cost is understood the possibility a company that operated in the market has to withdraw and recoup the investment made; that is to say, the possibility to sell installations, equipment and other at the market value minus depreciation.

Fast technological progress is removing the entrance cost through the fall of fixed costs, use of common resources or other means. In relation to the exit[27], costs are also reduced through factor specificity reduction, fall of sunk costs and others.

It must be said that certain elements are generating cost disadvantages for entrants, and they must be eliminated if a greater degree of market competition is to be achieved. Such elements are absence of number portability, no dialing parity, consumer inertia, cross subsidies, and, particularly, interconnection charges.

Contrary to the case of Argentina, the telecommunication policy of privatization in Brazil is characterized by a strong pro-entrant asymmetry. The effect of this kind of policy is the introduction of distortions, and could provoke an efficiency loss for the society.

Finally, it may be held that technology and demand evolution are making the telephony market a lot more competitive, but still there are problems that the regulatory authority must solve in order to maintain and reinforce the competitive spirit.

[27] This very technological advancement may cause the opposite effect. The reason is that such a speedy development could make a company wishing to leave the market find that their installations have become obsolete or even useless to provide similar services.

References

Braeutigam, Ronald R. (1989). *Handbook of Industrial Organization.* Volume II. Edited by Richard Schmalensee and Robert D. Willig. North-Holland. Amsterdam

Cairncross, Frances (1997). *The Death of Distance. How the Communications Revolution Will Change Our Lives.* Orion Publishing Group, Ltd. U.K.

Colomé, Rinaldo Antonio (1993). "Las telecomunicaciones en Argentina. Especial referencia al servicio básico telefónico". *Actualidad Económica.* Año III, N° 16, septiembre, pp 13-18.

Colomé, Rinaldo Antonio (1995). "La Regulación de los Servicios de Telecomunicaciones en la Argentina". *Actualidad Económica.* Año V, N° 28, sep-oct.

Colomé, R. A.; Á. E. Neder y C. S. Valquez (1998). "Interconexión, servicio universal y competencia en las telecomunicaciones en Argentina". *Anales.* XXXII Reunión Anual de la Asociación Argentina de Economía Política. Mendoza, Argentina. Noviembre.

Comisión de las Comunidades Europeas (1994). LIBRO VERDE SOBRE LA LIBERALIZACIÓN DE LAS INFRAESTRUCTURAS DE TELECOMUNICACIONES Y REDES DE TELEVISIÓN POR CABLE. Primera Parte. Principios y Calendario, Bruselas, 25.10.

Forrester Research (1998). "Forrester Estimates Worldwide Internet Commerce Will Reach As High As $3.2 Trillion In 2003". Dirección de *Internet*: www.forrester.com; 22/12/1998.

IERAL (1999). "Las regulaciones en la Argentina" ***CAPÍTULO V:* BARRERAS A LA COMPETENCIA EN TELECOMUNICACIONES: UN ESTUDIO COMPARADO. *ABA*, Reunión Anual 1999. Buenos Aires, Argentina.**

Linhares Pires (1999). "Políticas regulatórias no setor de telecomunicações: a experiência internacional e o caso brasileiro". *Textos para Discussão 71*, Rio de Janeiro, DEPEC-BNDES.

Melody, William H. (1999). "Telecom reform: progress and prospects". *Telecommunications Policy*, Vol. 23, No. 1, February.

Moreyra, Álvaro y Martín Moreyra (1998). "Un año de expectativas". *Apertura*, noviembre, pág. 14-23. Buenos Aires, Argentina.

Neder, Ángel Enrique (1997). "La nueva estructura de las tarifas telefónicas". *Actualidad Económica.* Año VII, N° 36, enero-febrero.

Neder, Ángel Enrique (1999). "Regulación de los servicios públicos: un ente para Córdoba". Publicado en *La Voz del Interior*, domingo 21 de marzo de 1999, pág. 11A bajo el título "Y en Córdoba ¿para cuándo?".

Pastoriza, Florinda (1996). *"Privatizacao na Indústria do Telecomunicacões: Antecedentes e Licões para o Caso Brasileiro".* Textos para Discussão 43, Rio de Janeiro, DEPEC-BNDES.

Petrazzini, Ben (1996). *Global Telecom Talks: A Trillion Dollar Deal.* Institute for International Economics. June. Washington, DC.

Secretaría de Comunicaciones (1998). "Evolución de la industria de las telecomunicaciones local". Dirección de *Internet*: www.secom.gov.ar; 03/12/1998. Argentina.

Shaw, James (1998). *Telecommunications Deregulation.* Artech House. Boston. United States of America.

Tavares de Almeida, María Herminia (1999). *La Política de la Privatización de las telecomunicaciones en Brasil.* Departamento de Ciência Política, Universidad de São Paulo.
www.cienciapolitica_usp.br/docentes/almeida/a_papers.htm

Train, K. (1991). *Optimal Regulation.* The MIT Press, Cambridge.

CHART 1
Structure of Argentina´s Telecommunications Market

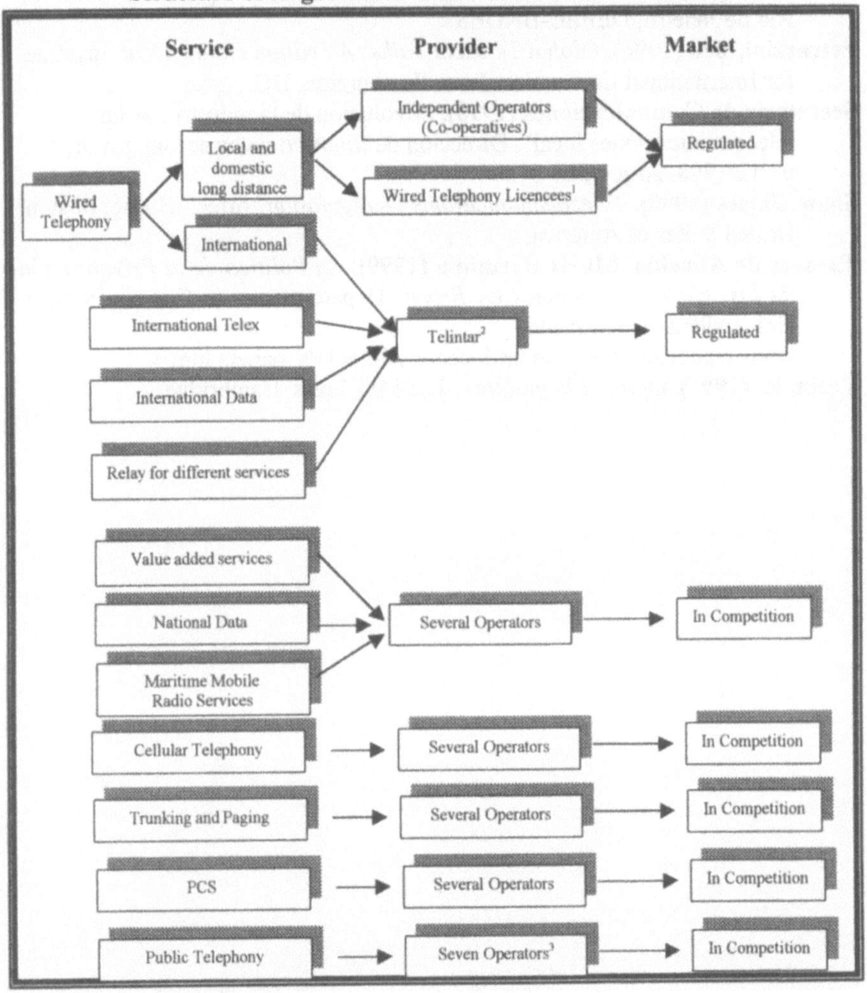

[1] There are two new operators in long distance from november 1999, and since then the Telecom and Telefonica´s exclusivity was eliminated. Up to november 2000, Telecom and Telefonica will enjoy the exclusivity only in local telephony.
[2] The exclusivity of Telintar was eliminated in november 1999.
[3] Telecom, Telefonica, and five new operators.

Source: Authors based on Colomé (1993) and Colomé (1995)

Table 1

Investment to Income Ratio (%)

Company	1995	1996	1997	1998
Telecom (Arg.)[1]	s/d	47,17	31,06	29,59
Telefónica (Arg.)[1]	44,38	39,57	28,22	25,46
British Telecom (UK)	18,25	17,31	18,88	19,87
Telecom (New Zealand)[2]	16,21	19,56	22,57	17,27

Source: Authors, using Companies' balance sheets.

1. To September annually.
2. To March annually.

Table 2

Wired Telephony, Employment and Productivity in Argentina

Year	Employees	Lines***	Productivity (lines/employees)
1989*	44.339	2.926.374	66,00
1995**	29.690	5.622.474	189,37
1996**	27.264	6.226.625	228,38
1997**	23.105	6.852.086	296,56
1998**	21.234	7.323.205	344,88

*Belonging to Empresa Nacional de Telecomunicaciones.

**Belonging to Telecom and Telefónica.

***To September 30 annually.

Source: Authors', using Companies' balance sheets.

Table 3
Wired Telephony Compared Productivity

Company	1995	1996	1997	1998
Telecom (Arg.)[1]	188,54	217,51	276,60	330,74
Telefónica (Arg.)[1]	190,09	238,27	315,20	357,77
British Telecom (UK)[2]	196,89	208,86	216,10	
CTC (Chile)[3]			347,01	221,74
Telecom (New Zealand)[2]		186,30	206,90	375,33

[1]To end of September annually.
[2]To end of March annually.
[3]To end of December annually, except 1998 whose data corresponds to end of September.
Source: Authors´, using Companies´ balance sheets.

Table 4
Rates (US$)

Country	Connection fee		Minimum monthly charge		cost per min.(local) (Mon - Fri)		cost per min. (domestic) long distance (Mon-Fri)	
	Business	Family	Business	Family	Prime	Off-Prime	Prime	Off-Prime
EUROPE								
U.K.[1]	166,69	166,69	20,96	12,71	0,0566	0,0212	0,1133	0,0598
ITALY[2]	170,29	170,29	14,31	9,19	0,0195	0,0107	0,1909	0,0859
SPAIN[3]	144,30	144,30	9,79	9,79	0,1081	0,1081	0,3718	0,2717
FRANCE[4]	44,66	44,66	15,36	9,95	0,0406	0,0212	0,1660	0,0830
LATIN AMERICA								
ARGENTINA[5]	150,00	150,00	33,39	13,02	0,0462	0,0462	0,5700	0,4100
BRAZIL[6]	44,58	44,58	17,99	12,00	0,0694	0,0174	0,4166	0,2083
URUGUAY[7]	263,68	169,99	15,87	6,95	0,0483	0,0161	0,3869	0,2321
CHILE[8]	119,13	119,13	10,29	10,29	0,0317	0,0050	0,1700	0,1200
OTHERS								
CANADA[9]	46,36	33,60	32,59	12,26	na	na	na	na
AUSTRALIA[10]	108,56	108,56	12,55	7,31	0,1569	0,1569	0,1380	0,1318

See notes on the next page.

[1]Data to Sept. 1998. Prime time: Monday to Friday-8am/6pm. Off prime: M. to F.- 6pm/8am.
[2]Data to April 1998. Domestic long distance: over 30km away. Prime: M. to F.- 8am/6.30pm.
[3]Data to Sept. 1998. Prime: M. to F.-8am/5pm. Off prime: M. to F.-5pm/10pm. Minimum charge included.
[4]Data to Sept. 1998. Domestic long distance: over 52km away. Prime: M. to F.- 8am/7pm.
[5]Data to Aug. 1999. Local. Prime: M. to F.-8am/8pm. Off prime: M. to F.-8pm/8am. (the pulse was the reference although its duration varies according to the case: 120 sec. In prime time and 240 sec. off prime). Domestic long distance: 240km or over. Prime: M. to F.-8am/10pm. Off prime: M. to F.-10pm/8am.
[6]Data to June 1998. Local. Prime: M. to F.-6am/12pm. Domestic long dist.: over 300km away. Prime: M. to F.-9am/12am and 2pm/6pm. Off prime: 7am/9am, 12am/2pm and 6pm/9pm.
[7]Data to Sept. 1998: Domestic long distance: over 100km away. Local prime: M. to F.-11am/2pm and 4pm/6pm. Off prime: M. to F.-9am/11am and 6pm/9pm. There is an intermediate rate from M. to F.-2pm/4pm. Domestic long distance prime time: M. to F. 9am/9pm.
[8]Data to June 1998: Domestic long distance: between 100km and 800km Local prime: M. to F.-7am/7pm. Domestic long distance prime: M. to F.-8am/8pm.
[9]Data to Feb. 1998.
[10]Data to June 1998. Prime: M. to F.-7am/1pm. Off prime: M. to F.-1pm/7pm.
Source: Telecom Argentina using the data from *Tarifica on CD-Rom*

Table 5
Differences Among Rates

Country	Conecction Fee business/family	Minimum charge business/family	Cost per minute Mon. to Fri. local/domestic long distance	
			Prime	Off Prime
EUROPE				
U.K.	0%	65%	100%	182%
ITALY	0%	56%	879%	703%
SPAIN	0%	0%	244%	151%
FRANCE	0%	54%	309%	292%
LATIN AMERICA				
ARGENTINA	0%	156%	1134%	787%
BRAZIL	0%	50%	500%	1097%
URUGUAY	55%	128%	701%	1342%
CHILE	0%	0%	436%	2300%
OTHERS				
CANADA	38%	166%		
AUSTRALIA	0%	72%	-12%	-16%

Source: Authors, using Table 4.

MODELING INTER-ORGANIZATIONAL WORKFLOWS FOR INTERNATIONAL COOPERATION

Kirsten Lenz, Andreas Oberweis[1]

1. Introduction

Due to the fast growth of internet-based electronic business, languages for modeling as well as methods for analyzing and executing distributed business processes are becoming more and more important.

Efficient inter-organizational processes in the field of e-business require the integration of electronic document interchange and inter-organizational processes: from the document point of view, there is a need for electronically interchanging structured documents and data between the involved organizations. From a process-oriented perspective, modeling, analysis, and automated execution of distributed workflows gain importance. Moreover, the advantages of workflow driven electronic document interchange are also relevant for the intra-organizational process management, especially with the emerging integration of mass data in databases and document management.

Special problems arise when business processes involve international participants of one or more organization. These problems result from different languages, laws, or different cultures: e.g. documents have to be translated into another language, the same business process is executed differently in different countries, or information has to be added to a document to satisfy country specific legal requirements.

This paper proposes XML nets, which are a new kind of high-level Petri nets. XML nets are a formal, graphical modeling language that allows to model both the flow of XML documents and the business process. They are based on GXSL, a graphical XML schema definition language, and the XML query language XManiLa. XML nets can be directly executed by a workflow engine and therefore allow for a detailed analysis and simulation of processes. Additionally, XML nets support the identification of relevant process fragments, assigning them to the appropriate organizational units in different countries, and thus help deriving an improved, process-oriented organizational structure.

[1] Institute of Information Systems, University of Frankfurt/Main, P.O. Box 11 19 32, D-60054 Frankfurt/Main, Germany, phone: ++49-69-798-22997|28998.
email: {lenz|oberweis}@wiwi.uni-frankfurt.de.

Global international workflows can be modeled as XML nets. With some extensions, the workflow can be partitioned into workflow fragments for the involved countries. Moreover, the flexibility of XML nets allows for necessary country specific modifications of the fragments.

This paper is structured as follows: first, we give a brief introduction into XML, Petri nets, and workflow management. In the following section, we present a graphical XML schema definition language and a graphical XML manipulation language. We propose XML nets for the intra- and inter-organizational workflow driven document interchange. In the next section we discuss aspects of executing international workflows by a workflow management system. Then we give examples for problems that arise especially for international workflows and describe how XML nets are able to cope with these problems. We finally present the stepwise modeling and distribution of international workflows.

1.1 Extensible Markup Language

The Extensible Markup Language (XML) [W3C00] is a document description standard proposed by the World Wide Web Consortium (W3C, http://www.w3.org/) as a simplification of generic Standard Generalized Markup Language (SGML, ISO 8879). The document type definition (DTD) of XML allows to model a document type as a classification of XML documents that are valid for this specific DTD, i.e. follow the document design rules. Figure 1 shows a simple DTD for an employee document with personal information, a list of projects she or he works in and a list of the skills. A corresponding valid document for the employee Mary L. Miller is shown in Figure 2.

1.2 Petri nets

For the modeling of business processes several more or less formal description languages have been proposed. In contrast to other languages, Petri nets [BRR86, Rei85] combine the advantages of the graphical representation of processes with a formal definition. As well as visualization of processes Petri nets allow for the analysis and validation of business processes [DeE00].

A simple example of a low-level Petri net is shown in Figure 3. It describes the following process: first, a planned project is initialized. Afterwards, employees can be assigned to the project. The beginning of a project transforms the project into a running project and has influence on the department which is responsible for the management. After finishing the project, the employee information must be updated: new skills learned in the project have to be added, whereas the project has to be removed from the list of projects the employee works in.

High-level Petri nets such as predicate/transition nets (Pr/T-nets) [Gen86, Obe96] or nested relation/transition nets (NR/T-nets) [ObS96] integrate behavior- and object-related aspects of workflows. In Pr/T-nets or NR/T-nets the places represent relation schemes according to which the marking of the net assigns a relation to each place. A transition represents a class of operations on the relations in the adjacent places. When a transition occurs, the respective tuples are removed from its input places and inserted into its output places according to the edge inscriptions.

1.3 Workflow management

Workflow management supports business process management: business processes can be modeled by more or less formal or graphical modeling languages like event-driven process chains [ScN00] or Petri nets. The workflow itself, i.e. a concrete process execution, can be interpreted as an instantiation of the workflow model. The main tasks of workflow management are the specification of the workflow model, its analysis and verification, the execution of the workflow by a suitable workflow architecture, and the development of workflow applications [Jab00].

Petri nets are well suited and frequently proposed for workflow modeling [JVW00]: they provide a restricted number of graphical modeling concepts and possess at the same time formal semantics. Their formal foundation enables the application of theoretical analysis techniques (e.g. analyze whether a certain system state can be reached or not) and the model-driven execution of the workflow. Moreover, they integrate data and behavior aspects and therefore meet the need to model for example inter-organizational workflows based on electronic document interchange. The use of Petri nets of different formalization levels allows for a stepwise workflow modeling process. A survey of Petri net based business process and workflow management can be found for example in [ADO00].

2 Graphical languages for XML document management

In this section, we introduce the main concepts of the graphical XML schema definition language (GXSL) for graphically specifying XML schemas that represent DTDs. XManiLa, an extension to the graphical XML schema definition language, is proposed for the retrieval and manipulation, especially insertion and deletion, of XML documents.

2.1 XML schema definition with GXSL

The XML document type definition represents a grammar for object classification. Unfortunately, this grammar is textual so that the DTDs for complex objects often may become quite unreadable: the advantages of a graphical schema definition language (like the entity/relationship model for the database design) are missing. Therefore, we propose a graphical schema definition language based on the Unified Modeling Language (UML) [BRJ99] for the design of XML document types which we call *graphical XML schema definition language* (GXSL). From a *Graphical XML Schema* (GXS) modeled with GXSL a DTD can be unambiguously derived.

The main principles of XML DTDs are classification of documents with comparable structure and aggregation of document elements. The definition of a document type allows for the characterization of a class of valid XML documents that have to obey certain rules for the composition of XML markups. Moreover, the structure of a DTD is hierarchical, i.e. recursive element definitions are not allowed. In the following, the main GXSL concepts are explained. A more detailed description of GXSL can be found in [LeO01].

- **Simple element declaration:** In general, element type declarations of the XML DTD are represented by classes in GXSL. By simple element types we understand element types without children (i.e. they are not composed of other element types), namely the empty-element type for elements without content and the any-element type for arbitrary elements (see Figure 4 for the GXSL representation).
- **#PCDATA-element declaration:** The #PCDATA-element type describes elements that consist of a sequence of *parsed character data*, i.e. they do not contain other elements (see Figure 5). Like the simple element types, the #PCDATA-element type cannot be nested.
- **Attribute lists:** A DTD can include attribute declarations for element types. In GXSL, the attribute list for an element *ename* is added to the element class with the attribute name *aname*, the attribute type *atype* and an optional default value *default* (see Figure 6). With a full attribute specification, the GXS becomes very detailed. However, it is possible to restrict to the attribute name or even to omit the attribute list of the element types in a survey diagram.
- **Nested element types:** Element types in XML can be nested (i.e. the element type declaration refers to other element type declarations of the DTD) by composition, represented by a filled diamond in the GXS, or aggregation, represented by an open diamond. GXSL allows for assigning cardinalities of the element types (see Table 1) that describe the occurrence of child elements for the relevant element type. For example, the element type declaration for

the qualification of an employee consisting of a set of skills has the GXS in Figure 7. Furthermore, GXSL allows for cascading nesting of elements where the cardinality of a nested element type can be written above the respective branch (see Figure 8).

- **Choice, sequence:** In order to model a choice of elements with GXSL we introduce a constraint between the alternative subclasses (see Figure 9a)). Within a document which is valid for this DTD there must appear either an element $ename_2$ or an $ename_3$ element inside the $ename_1$ element (and must not appear both). A sequence of elements that have to appear in a predefined order within another element can be expressed in GXSL by ordering the respective element types (see Figure 9b)). In valid XML documents, the elements must appear in the same order as the respective element types of the corresponding GXS, i.e. for example the element of type $ename_1$ before the element of type $ename_2$.
- **Referential integrity:** GXSL allows for explicit referential integrity constraints between attributes of different element types by {ref}-dependencies (see Figure 10). {ref}-dependencies are labeled by the referencing and the referenced attribute.

We are now able to construct a GXSL-schema which is equivalent to the employee DTD of Figure 1. Compared to the textual representation the graphical representation in Figure 11 gives a better survey about the defined elements and the logical structure of a valid employee document.

2.2 Manipulation of XML documents with XManiLa

We use GXSL with some extensions for querying and manipulating XML documents. The GXSL-based XML manipulation language is called XManiLa [see also LeO01]. A GXSL-schema can be seen as a template for a set of XML documents that describes conditions on the structure as well as on the content of the "matching" documents. For example, we may want to search for all female employees that have a first name followed by an initial and the last name "Miller". The GXS template of Figure 12 describes this query. The content of relevant document elements can be stored in variables that are assigned to the respective element name.

The abstract no-name element type can be used in order to model explicitly the element order of the matching document. I.e., the template in Figure 12 describes only documents with the employee name followed by arbitrary elements, but not documents with elements before the employee name. Whenever the element order is unambiguous (for example when the DTD is known), abstract classes can be omitted in most cases.

XManiLa is not only suited for document retrieval but also for insertion and deletion (and thereby also for updating). Insertion and deletion operations either concern a whole document or elements on lower hierarchy levels. The level of elements to be inserted or deleted are depicted by a solid line on the left side of the element's rectangle. The insert- and delete-qualification is inherited by all subtypes. Examples of insertion and deletion operations on the employee documents are given in Figure 13.

3 Inter-organizational workflows

The interchange of XML documents between organizations can be handled in different ways: the XML document can be sent to another organization without any DTD, the DTD can be stored within the document or stored as an independent file (see for example [Eck99] or [Har99]). In the following, we suppose the set of process relevant DTDs being known to all participants of the business process.

3.1 XML nets

XML nets, a new kind of high-level Petri nets, are a formal, graphical modeling language that allows to model both the flow of XML documents and the underlying business process. The static components of XML nets (i.e. the places of the Petri net) are labeled by graphical XML schemas which represent a DTD. Places can be interpreted as a container for XML documents which are valid for the corresponding DTD. The initial marking assigns to each place of the XML net a set of valid XML documents.

The flow of XML documents is defined by the occurrences of activated transitions which thereby manipulate (create, change or delete) documents of their adjacent places, i.e. places that are connected with the transition by an edge. The decision whether a transition is activated depends on the documents of these places, the edge labels and the transition's inscription:

- Documents that are to be deleted must be available.
- Documents that are to be created must not already exist.
- Documents that are to be manipulated, i.e. some of its elements have to be deleted or new elements have to be inserted, must be available.

Moreover the documents have to match the extended GXS (constructed with the graphical XML data manipulation language) that labels the edge from the respective place to the transition. The assignment of variables to document elements within the extended schemas allows for ensuring equality of certain parts of the documents (for example the project number being the same in two documents) as well as for the declaration of restricting conditions (for example that the new budget of a project does not exceed a certain limit).

Activated transitions indicate a possible system behavior which can but does not have to take place. When the transition occurs, it changes the state of the system by deleting, creating or changing the documents: it removes the matching documents or parts of the documents as specified by the edge label from the places in the preset of the transition and inserts new documents into the places in the postset of the transition or new elements into the matching documents.

To continue the example of Figure 3, we can now assign to each place a GXS and to each edge an extended GXS as edge label. Figure 14 shows the schemas for planned, running and finished projects, the department, and the lessons learned and Figure 11 that for the employee. Besides the definition of all process relevant document definition types, the behavior of the XML net has to be specified in detail for all transitions.

- *initialize project*: A new document of type *planned project* is created.
- *assign employee*: The assignment consists of inserting the employee ID as team member for the project and the time required for the task execution together with the project ID for the employee.
- *start project*: When a project is started, a responsible department is chosen for the project. This is only possible for departments with an identifier that differs from the default identifier 0. The document of type *planned project* is deleted and a new document of type *running project* including the department ID created. The project ID is added to the department's list of running projects.
- *finish project*: Delete the respective document from the list of running projects and create a new document with the information about the finished project. Moreover, delete the project ID from the department document. Create a new document that contains all information about the skills that an employee has learned from the project.
- *update employee*: Finally, the information about project participation is deleted in the employee document. At the same time, the new skill is appended to his or her list of skills.

The XML net corresponding to the simple Petri net of Figure 3 is shown in Figure 15. For the sake of readability, we omitted the GXS place labels and no initial marking is specified.

3.2 Fragmentation of XML nets

The globalization of companies and the development towards distributed business processes and international cooperation require the application of geographically distributed information system technologies. Workflow distribution implies a distribution of the workflow management system on the execution level and on the design level methods for the fragmentation of global international workflows. The fragmentation of predicate/transition nets as a kind of Petri nets is described in [GLO98] and can easily be transferred to XML nets. A global XML net can be decomposed into several local net fragments that can be allocated to different execution locations together with the allocation of the process relevant and possibly replicated documents to the corresponding fragments.

For our workflow example for the project execution we can identify three different organizational units which are concerned with the execution of the workflow: the management, the department that is responsible for the execution of the specific project and the human resources department (see Figure 16). The arcs describe the document flow and thus describe the interdependencies between the workflow fragments. For example, fragment 2 depends on fragment 1, i.e. the project department needs documents from the management for the execution of their part of the workflow (the running project document).

For the execution of a distributed workflow based on a Petri net several architectures are conceivable, with the degree of distribution ranging from centralized to completely distributed. Organizational structures, the distribution of workflow relevant data and documents, as well as technical restrictions are crucial criteria for the allocation of the workflow fragments. The workflow engine may run in a central place, may be installed at all process participants' sites, or may be sent to the execution site on demand (together with the workflow fragment).

4 Workflows for international cooperation

Compared to nationally distributed business processes, business processes for international cooperation induce supplementary problems:

- Documents must be available in *different languages*. For example, an order from an organization in France is sent to a supplier who is located in the United States: the French order document must be translated into English. The international process therefore contains a sequence of activities (translating the document, then sending it) where the national process simply consists of one activity (sending the document). Moreover documents that are needed by process participants in different countries must be available in different languages, that is, they must be replicated and translated. For this purpose an effective replication management is needed in order to avoid inconsistencies within this set of documents with identical content but in different languages: for example, the simple comparison of the content of two documents fails to decide whether these documents are replicates due to their different language.

- *Different laws* in different countries can influence the process relevant documents and/or the process execution. For example, some information must be added to a certain document to fulfill the legal requirements of a certain country. In this case, the replication management is even more difficult because of the different structure of the document replicates. Moreover, the execution of parts of the global process might be correct for most countries, but violate the law of one country. In this case, the workflow fragment for this process has to be modified for this country under the condition that the interfaces with other workflow fragments will not be changed. This implies that the country specific variant of the workflow (with different behavior) produces the same output documents from the given input documents.
- International workflows usually involve process participants with *different cultures*. A different cultural background may have an impact on the execution of a business process. Whereas one country has detailed rules for example for the process of a negotiation, the negotiation in another country takes place during a dinner party and is with respect to the workflow rather a 'black box' although the result of the negotiation is the same in both countries.

Therefore, a flexible workflow management system for international workflows must tackle with two completely different aspects of global cooperation: on the design level, it must allow for the modeling of the global international workflow and for the integration of country specific aspects (variants of workflow fragments and additional fragments between the workflow interfaces). On the execution level, it is necessary to localize the workflow management system for the countries that are involved in the relevant global business process.

4.1 Execution of international workflows

In order to assure acceptance of supporting the business process by a workflow management systems, it is crucial to pay attention to the following problems:

- The cost of participation must be as low as possible (so that not only participants from highly developed countries can be involved into the process). This can be achieved when the workflow engine is realized for example as a platform independent applet, that runs within the window of an internet browser.

The necessary workflow fragments can be sent to the participants on demand and executed either locally or on a server with connection to the local documents.

- The workflow must be designed in a way that the process participants can understand the workflow model and accept the prescribed execution order. This implies a localization of the workflow itself. One country is able to adapt the reference workflow fragment to its own requirements and execute the resulting variant of the workflow fragment.
- The process participants accept to work with the workflow management system, i.e. the workflow management system has to fulfill certain ergonomic requirements. Especially for cross-cultural workflows, it is important to pay attention to this aspect and to localize the workflow management system.

A discussion of the problem of localization in e-commerce can be found for example in [Chr00].

4.2 Modeling international workflows with XML nets

The use of XML nets is well suited for the modeling and execution of international workflows: the world wide acceptance of XML as platform independent document description standard proposed by the international World Wide Web Consortium is growing. XML allows for easy document interchange over the internet and can even serve as an application independent interchange format for application specific files (like for example Microsoft-Word documents). Moreover, XML nets integrate behavioral aspects and the process relevant XML documents and can be subject to distribution. For international workflows, a criteria for the fragmentation of the global workflow should be that a workflow fragment is only executed by participants of one country. In this case, the interfaces between the workflow fragments might indicate international document transfer or document sharing.

In the following we give some examples how XML nets are able to cope with some of the problems of international workflows sketched before.

4.2.1 Translation of a document

A document has to be translated into another language: the place of the XML net that contains this document is part of the interface between two fragments which are executed in different countries with different languages. For example, the corresponding place in one workflow fragment contains all documents in German whereas the place in the other workflow fragment contains the documents with the same structure (and DTD) in English. The workflow fragment in Figure 17 shows a supplementary process part for the translation of the documents.

The process of translation is not described in detail, but it is possible to model an XML net as suitable refinement of the transition *translate document*.

4.2.2 Restructuring of a document

Although the structure of a document type differs in two countries due to different laws, the documents must be available for both workflow fragments because of mutual fragment dependency, i.e. the documents flow from one fragment to the other and vice versa. Figure 18 shows a supplementary process part for the restructuring of the document, so that each document is available for both fragment 1 and fragment 2. In contrast to the translation example in Figure 17, the restructuring transitions do not delete the document in the respective place, but create a new document (if this does not already exist) as a restructured copy of the original document. Thus all documents are available in both fragments and for each fragment correctly structured. Note that this simple workflow fragment does not encounter the problem of managing the document replicates. For example, changing the document in one country would not affect the respective document replicate in the other country. Nevertheless, this example shows the basic idea of document replication.

4.2.3 Variation of a workflow fragment

A workflow fragment can be replicated and allocated to several locations in different countries that want to execute this part of the business process. If the process is executed differently in one of these countries, the respective process fragment can be modified as long as the fragment interface remains the same. I.e. the process variant must start with the same input documents and produce the same output documents like the other workflow fragment and therefore has the same behavior with respect to the workflow interface. In Figure 19, two replicates for the evaluation of a list are shown. The original process consists of the creation of a result from a list. The modification describes the process more precisely: the list must be evaluated first, then the result is composed. Note that both replicates have the same places *list* and *result*. Moreover, the definition of the pre-result does not have any influence on the result of the evaluation (so that the result differs from that of the other workflow).

4.3 Distribution of international workflows

In addition to the distribution of the original workflow fragment, the supplementary fragments of the global international workflow must be integrated into the global workflow and considered for the allocation of the workflow fragments to the process participants. Thereby, two possibilities are conceivable:

- The new process part is added to one of the existing fragments. For example, the document is translated in one country before being sent to another country. The transition *translate* in Figure 17 would be added to fragment 1.
- The new process part becomes a new fragment which can either be allocated to one or all involved process participants. This is an adequate solution e.g. for the restructuring of documents because this could be done automatically in each country.

Finally, we can identify several steps for the modeling and distribution of international workflows with XML nets:

Step 1: Modeling of the global international workflow. There is no essential difference to the modeling of national workflows. However, localization aspects can already be anticipated.
Step 2: Fragmentation of the global workflow. Choose fragmentation so that no two participants from different countries are responsible for the execution of a single fragment.
Step 3: Allocation of the fragments to the relevant process participants. Replicate the workflow fragments if necessary.
Step 4: Inspection of the supranational fragment interfaces. Take a closer look at fragment interfaces of two fragments that are assigned to different countries and identify if there is a need for translation or restructuring of documents or replication of document translations.
Step 5. Modeling and integration of supplementary process parts if necessary.
Step 6: Modification of fragments for alternative processes without changing the interfaces.

For national workflows, the global workflow can easily be reconstructed from the distributed workflow fragments simply by merging the interface places. For the global international workflow this is not the case because supplementary fragments have been added or fragment replicates have been changed after fragmentation. Therefore, the following aspects have to be taken into account when reconstructing the global international workflow:

- Several variants of one fragment exist. Which workflow fragment should be used for the reconstruction of the global workflow: the original fragment or a workflow fragment that summarizes all fragment variants? Should this artificially constructed fragment describe the behavior that is common to all fragment variants or describe completely the behavior of all fragment variants. Anyway, a repository of workflow fragment variants is needed.

- A supplementary workflow fragment exists. It is possible to omit this fragment and reconstruct the original global workflow. On the other hand, it is interesting to extend the original workflow by the workflow fragment which describes explicitly behavior that results from international cooperation. In this case, the additional fragment can be inserted between the interfaces of the respective fragments.

5 Summary

In this paper, we have introduced XML nets for the modeling of international workflows, which integrate behavior- and document-related aspects. Research on GXSL and XManiLa, the presented languages for XML document management, is still ongoing. Additionally, we are implementing a prototypical simulator for XML nets based on a native XML database system. This tool will be used to simulate and validate distributed workflows which are modeled as XML nets.

With respect to international cooperation, we have shown, that XML nets are able to cope with the requirements of international workflows: problems of the international document interchange like document translation and country specific variations of a process part can be modeled as workflow fragments and added to the distributed workflow. Furthermore, localization of the workflow engine helps support the acceptance of the workflow management system. Finally, the cost of participation are relatively low for workflow management based on the execution of XML nets because of the interchange of platform independent standardized XML documents and the workflow execution within an arbitrary internet browser.

References

[ADO00] van der Aalst, W.; Desel, J.; Oberweis, A. (eds.): *Business Process Management – Models, Techniques and Empirical Studies*, Lecture Notes in Computer Science, Vol. 1806, Springer-Verlag, 2000.

[BRJ99] Booch, G.; Rumbaugh, J.; Jacobson, I.: *The Unified Modeling Language User Guide*, Addison Wesley, 1999.

[BRR86] Brauer, W., Reisig, W., Rozenberg, G. (eds.): *Advances in Petri Nets, Part I*, Lecture Notes in Computer Science, Vol. 254, Springer-Verlag, 1986.

[Chr00] Chroust, G.: *E-Commerce und Lokalisierung*, in: Jasper, H.; Küng, J.; Vossen, G. (eds.): *Informationssysteme für E-Commerce*, Linz, November 2000, pp. 11-27 (in German).

[DeE00] Desel, J.; Erwin, Th.: *Modeling, Simulation and Analysis of Business Processes*, in [ADO00], pp. 129-141.

[Eck99] Eckstein, R.: *XML Pocket reference*, O'Reilly, 1999.

[Jab00] Jablonski, S.: *Workflow Management Between Formal Theory and Pragmatic Approaches*, in: [ADO00], pp. 345-358.

[JVW00] Janssens, G.K.; Verelst, J.; Weyn, B.: *Techniques for Modeling Workflows and Their support of Reuse*, in: [ADO00], pp. 1-15.

[Gen86] Genrich, H.J.: *Predicate/Transition Nets*, in [BRR86], pp. 207-247.

[GLO98] Guth, V.; Lenz, K.; Oberweis, A.: *Distributed Workflow Execution Based on Fragmentation of Petri Nets*, in: Traunmüller, R.; Csuháj-Varjù, E. (eds.): Proc. 15th IFIP World Computer Congress 'Telecooperation – The Global Office, Teleworking and Communication Tools', Vienna, Budapest, September 1998, pp. 114-125.

[Har99] Harold, E.R.: *XML bible*, IDG Books Worldwide, 1999.

[LeO01] Lenz, K.; Oberweis, A.: *Modeling Interorganizational Workflows with XML nets*; in: Proc. 34th Hawaii Conference on System Sciences, Maui (HI), January 2001.

[Obe96] Oberweis, A.: *An Integrated Approach for the Specification of Processes and Related Complex Structured Objects in Business Applications*, in: Decision Support Systems, 17, 1996, pp. 31-53.

[ObS96] Oberweis, A.; Sander, P.: *Information System Behavior Specification by High-Level Petri Nets*, in: ACM Transactions on Information Systems, 14(4), 1996, pp. 380-420.

[Rei85] Reisig, W.: *Petri Nets: an Introduction*, EATCS monographs 4, Springer-Verlag, 1985.

[ScN00] Scheer, A.-W.; Nüttgens, M.: *ARIS Architecture and Reference Models for Business Process Management*, in [ADO00], pp. 376-389.

[W3C00] *Extensible Markup Language (XML) 1.0, Second Edition*, World Wide Web Consortium Recommendation, Technical Report, 6-October-2000. (http://www.w3.org/TR/2000/REC-xml-20001006)

Appendix

Table 1: GXSL cardinalities for XML occurrence operators

GXSL cardinality	Element occurrence is...
1 (default value)	... mandatory
0..1	... optional
*	... zero or more times
1..*	... one or more times

Figure 1: Document type definition for employee documents

```
<!-- DTD for an employee document-->
<!ELEMENT employee (empname, work_in_proj*, skill*)>
<!ATTLIST employee    empid ID #REQUIRED
                      sex (male|female) "female">
<!ELEMENT empname (title?, (firstname|initial)+, lastname)
<!ELEMENT title (#PCDATA)>
<!ELEMENT firstname (#PCDATA)>
<!ELEMENT initial (#PCDATA)>
<!ELEMENT lastname (#PCDATA)>
<!ELEMENT work_in_proj (#PCDATA)>
<!ATTLIST work_in_proj          projid IDREF #IMPLIED>
<!ELEMENT skill (#PCDATA)>
```

Figure 2: Employee document which is valid for the DTD of Figure 1

```
<?xml version="1.0"?>
<!DOCTYPE employee SYSTEM "http://...empdoc.dtd">
<employee empid="0815" sex="female">
      <empname>
            <firstname>Mary</firstname>
            <initial>L.</initial>
            <lastname>Miller</lastname>
      </empname>
      <work_in_proj projid="328">20</work_in_proj>
      <work_in_proj projid="85">10</work_in_proj>
      <skill>Java</skill>
      <skill>C++</skill>
      <skill>Oracle 8</skill>
</employee>
```

Figure 3: Simple Petri net for the process of project execution

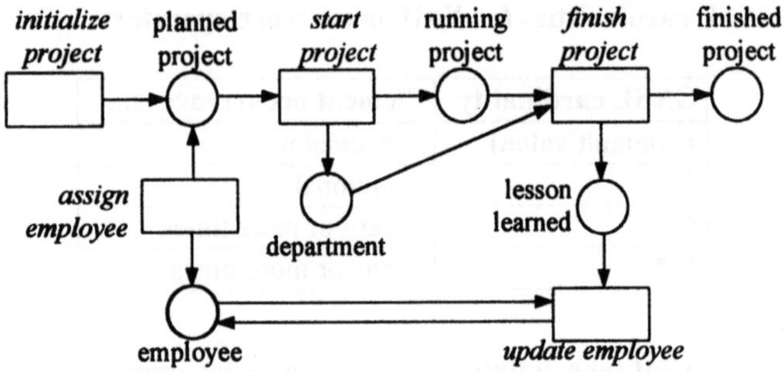

Figure 4: GXSL class representation of the ANY- and EMPTY-element type declaration

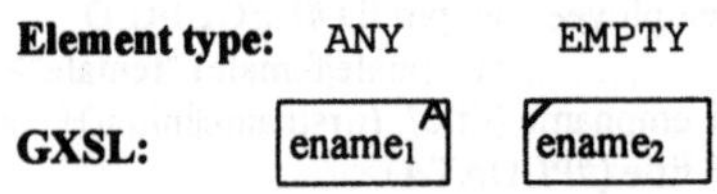

Figure 5: GXSL class representation of the #PCDATA-element type

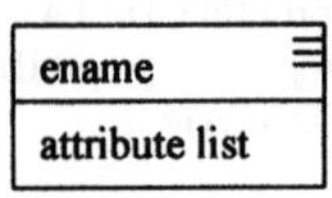

Figure 6: Element class with attribute list

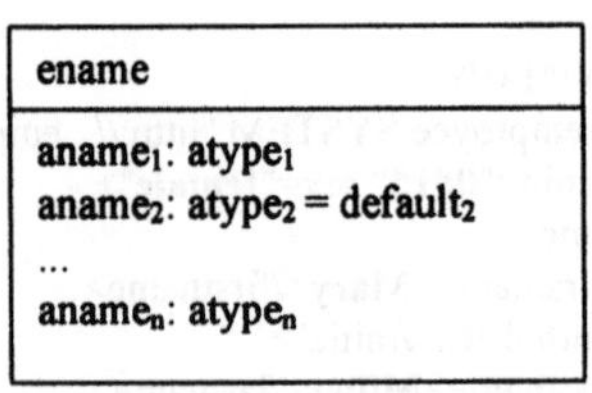

Figure 7: GXS for a nested element with occurrence operators

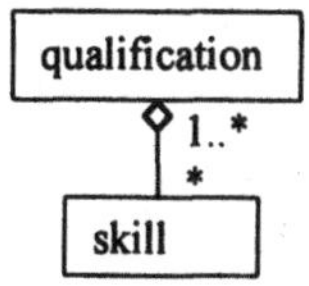

Figure 8: GXS for a nested element type consisting of a composition of three element types

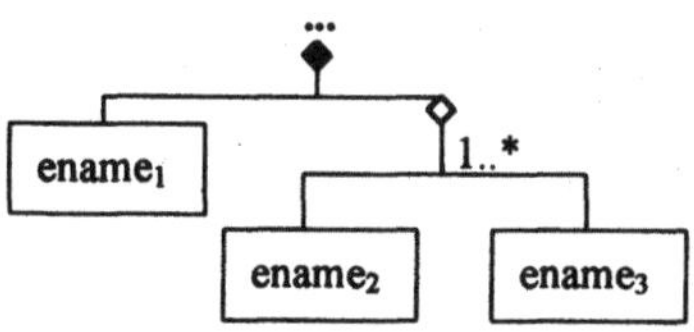

Figure 9: GXS for alternative and for sequential element types

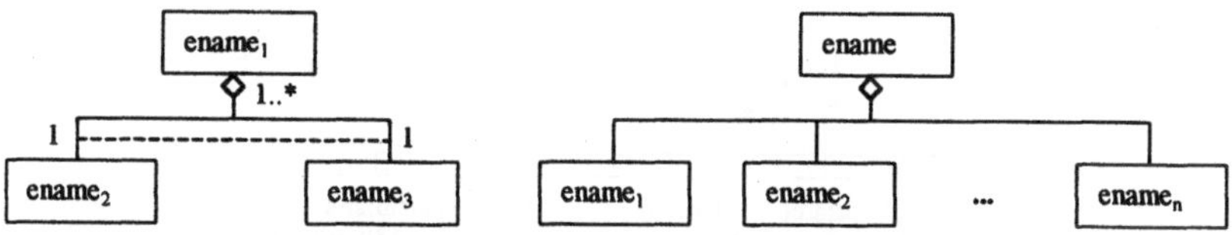

a) alternative element types b) sequential element types

Figure 10: GXSL dependencies for referential integrity constraints

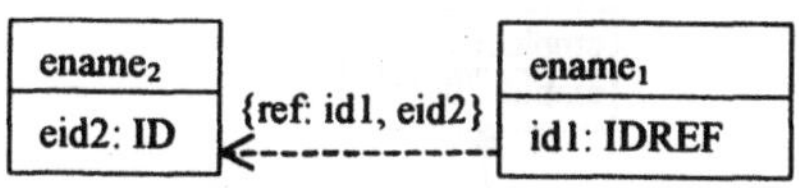

Figure 11: GXSL-schema for the employee DTD of Figure 1

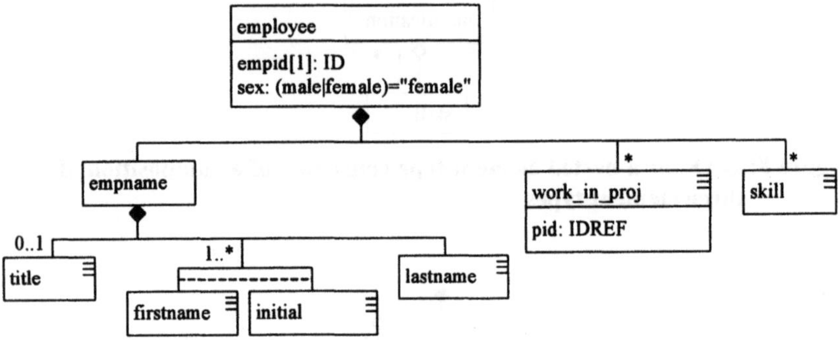

Figure 12: Female employees named Miller with a firstname followed by an initial

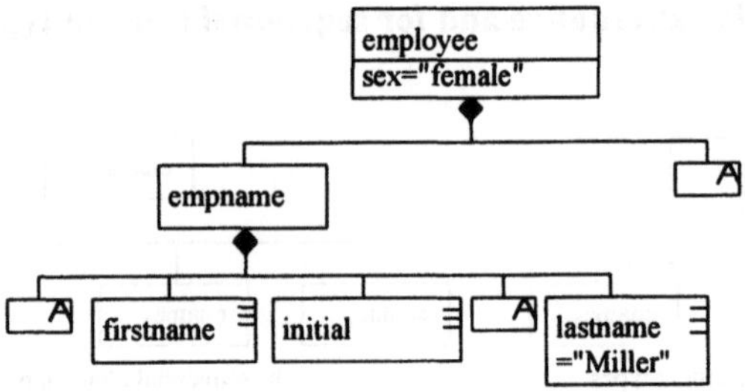

Figure 13: Insertion and deletion operations on the employee documents

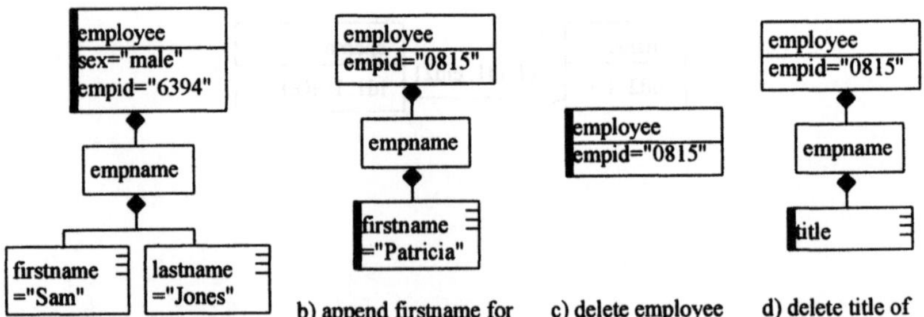

a) create new employee b) append firstname for employee 0815 c) delete employee 0815 d) delete title of employee 0815

Figure 14: Graphical XML schemas for the project execution

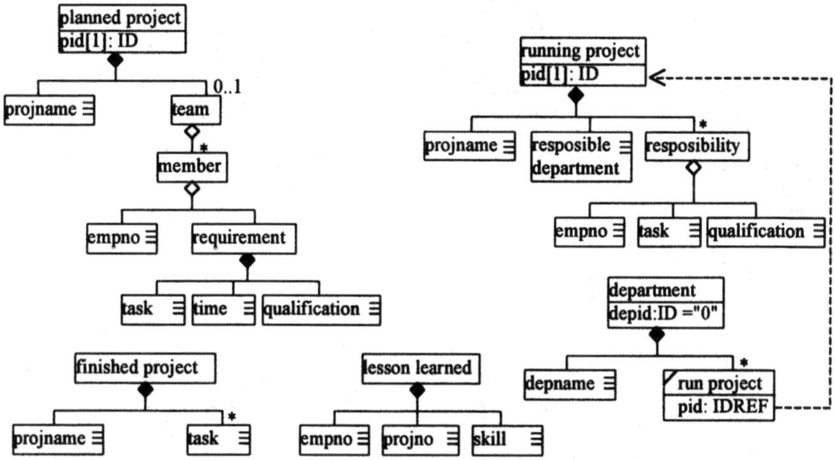

Figure 15: XML net for the process of project execution (see next page)

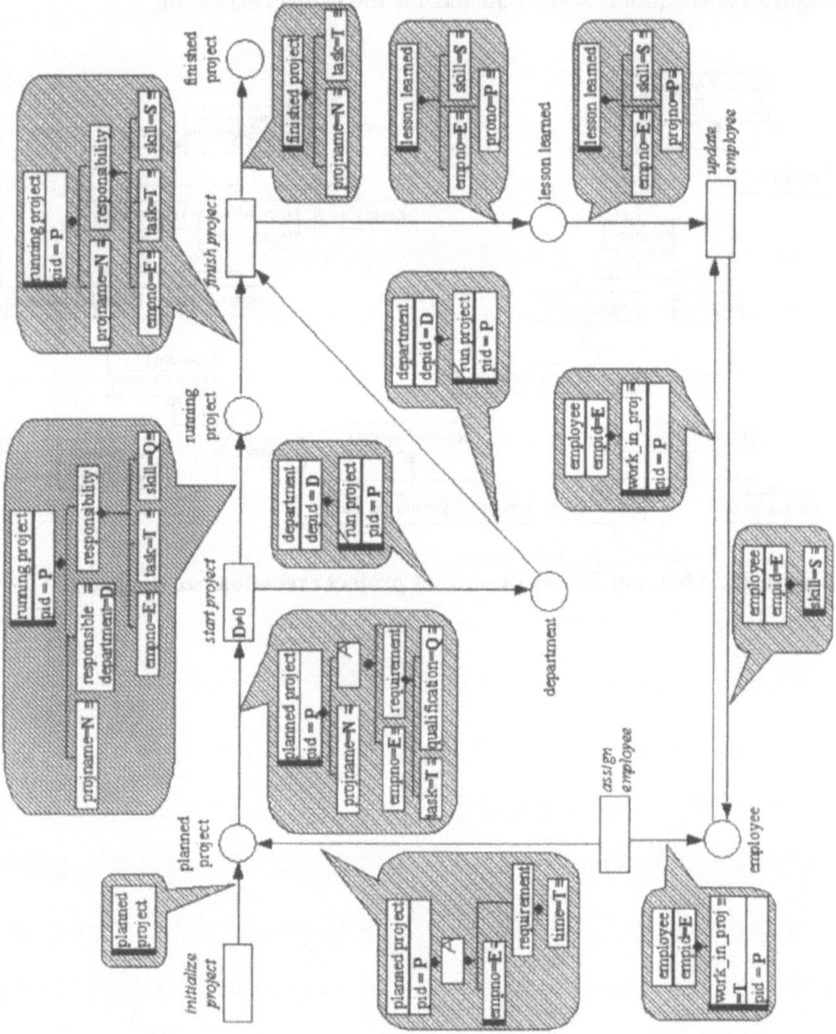
initialize project
planned project
start project
D≠0
running project
finish project
finished project
department
lesson learned
update employee
assign employee
employee

Figure 16: Workflow fragments for the distributed project execution

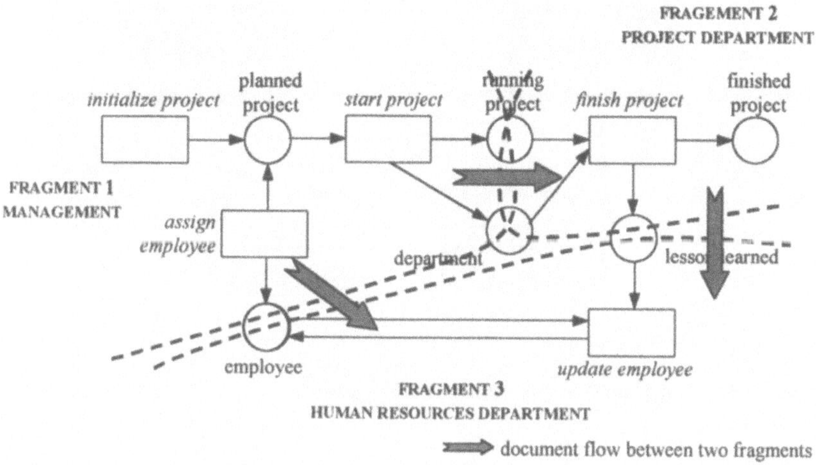

Figure 17: Translation of documents

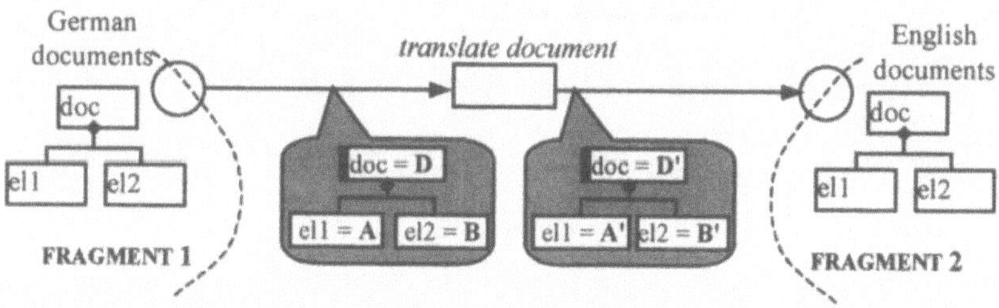

Figure 18: Mutual restructuring of documents

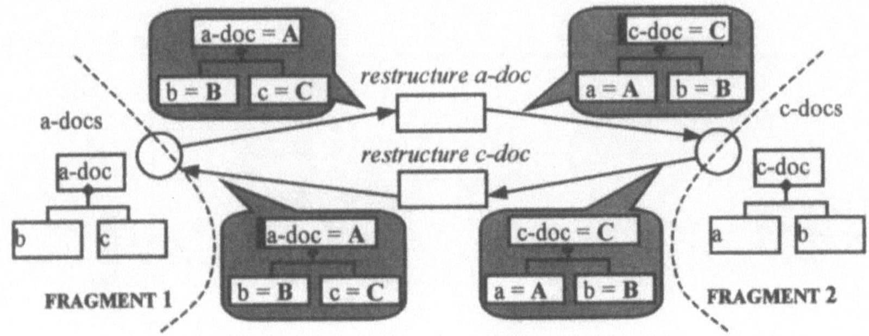

Figure 19: Modification of a replicated fragment

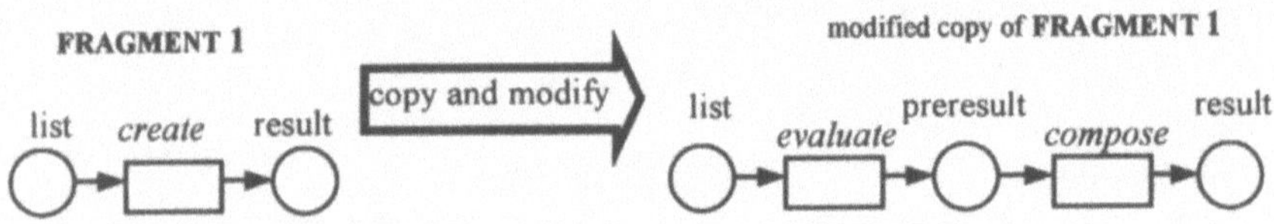

FROM THE INTERNET-UNIVERSITY TO E-COMMERCE AND TO THE UNIVERSITY OF THE FUTURE

Ulrich Peter Ritter[1]

I. The Internet-University: an Actualization of Former Propositions

At the Arnoldshain III- Seminar in São Paulo in October 1998, I presented a paper with Marta Podzun de Buraschi and Claudia Bremer called "The Internet University in Argentina, Germany and USA. An International Comparison."[2] In that paper I was responsible for the part on the US and held the position, that the Internet-University presented an important challenge to traditional universities. In this paper I will discuss, in how far this hypothesis can be upheld or must be modified in view of the developments, which occurred during the last two years. I will look at the meaning of these developments for our universities and will then present some ideas on the model of a university of the future.

Let me start by explaining what I mean by "Internet University". It can be described by the answers to the questions:

- Where?
- What?
- How?

1 Where is The Internet University?

As to where the Internet University can be found, my answer is: "It is literally nowhere and everywhere. **It is present everywhere**, where somebody has a computer and a modem and thus access to the internet independently of whether she or he is in the Sahara or the Gobi desert or in the center of New York or Frankfurt. Also the answer would be correct, if you said: **it is nowhere**. There is no definable location, where this university has its seat. Principally an internet-teaching offer can be made from every location in the world, which fulfills the technical conditions. With satellite-communication there is

---

[1] Johann Wolfgang Goethe-University, Institute of Economics, 60054 Frankfurt am Main, Germany, e-mail: ritter@wiwi.uni-frankfurt.de

[2] Bremer, Claudia; Buraschi, Martha; Ritter, Ulrich Peter (1998): The Internet University in Argentina, Germany and USA. An International Comparison. In: Basilia Aguirre: III. Arnoldshain Seminar, Argentine, Brazil and Germany: Comparative studies in structural transformation. São Paulo, Brazil.

practically no location, which does not fulfill these technical preconditions. Thus, a guru in an oasis of the Sahara is as much a potential professor as a wise man of the Inuit in Alaska or a world famous chemist at Harvard or BASF."

2 What is The Internet University?

The Internet University can be described by a URL[3] and a bibliographical reference:

Figure 1: The Internet University

http://www.caso.com/ until September 1998 and since then: www.newpromise.com

Corrigan, D.: The Internet University: College Courses by Computer, Cape Software; several editions since 1996 and since March 1999: Caso's Internet University. Your Guide to Online College.

This means, it is essentially a homepage in the Internet and a study guide. The homepage contains listings and links of providers of internet courses: community colleges, colleges and universities as well as information on the programs, requirements, costs of courses etc. It was provided by the author of the book "The Internet University" and now by the firm "New Promise, Inc" in Cambridge, Mass.

3. How does the Internet University work?

I explain this in the following way: The home page of The Internet University has the following structure (see figure 2 in the appendix).

If you click on "New Promise" on the home page you are informed, that New Promise is dedicated to convenient, quality online education; that it was founded by preeminent educators associated with Harvard University and MIT and that it has its seat in Cambridge, Mass.

On this home page three browsers are offered. Under "Find a Course" you can search for courses offered by discipline, by providers, by course title and by cue words. From here you can click your way directly to the providers or sign up for a course.

[3] Universal Resource Locator; internet address.

You can also find the way to the providers through the browser "Search by School". Here you find the list of the colleges und universities and the courses each one is offering. There are further browsers for those who are looking for possibilities to acquire a certain degree or a certain certificate. Under "Quick Search" your can find offers attending to special interests. The criteria for a course to be offered through this platform was that it had to be possible to get credit for this course by offering it completely on- line.

Until last year for me The Internet University or „New Promise“ was the paradigm of on-line university education. I was very much impressed by this model because I saw the chances for traditional universities to enter this field by having an increasing part of their courses offered globally through this channel. Today, I must modify this view:

1. What I have said about the internet university is, of course true for all online-education.
2. The market for online education is continuing to grow and diversify in a rapid process
3. New Promise may not become, as it intended to be, the main gateway to US Online university education
4. New Promise is changing from 'The Internet University' to one participant of many in a huge market of training and education, which is changing into one more sector of e-commerce, online courses and online education being negotiated like other products.

Let me explain these hypotheses in a more detail.

II. Some quantitative considerations

Let us first take a look at quantitative developments and start again with New Promise. During the last years I have spoken of the take – off[4] of The Internet University and illustrated it by the following statistics. As can be seen in table 1 the number of providers increased from 27 in 1996 to 112 in 1998, this representing an average annual growth rate of 125 %. In the same time period, i. e. two college years, the number of courses had increased from 705 in 1996 to 3463 in 1998 i. e almost 500 %. In 1999 we see another impressive increase. If we look at New Promise, now Mind Edge in the year 2000 the number of online courses has increased to 4529 (as of August 22).

[4] The term take-off was used as an analogy to the take-off of an airplane to describe the phase of development preceding self-sustained growth by W. W Rostow in his book Stages of Economic Growth.

Table 1: Course providers and number of courses offered 1996 and 1998

	1996	1998	Increase	July 1999
Number of Providers	27	112	315%	126
Number of Courses	705	3.463	391%	3826

Source: Corrigan, D.(1996): p.190 and http//www.caso.com September 1998; new promise.com July 4, 1999

The number of providers has increased in the meantime to 121 and. the number of courses offered to 3932. The web-site is visited daily by 2.300 people. An innovation in August was the creation of a membership which is free. In the future this membership will give access to a number of services such as an e-mail address, discussion forums and the sale of books. This membership program allows 'New Promise' to know more about its visitors. 55 % are women; the average age is 35. The lowest age is 11 and the oldest 78 years. Since August, 4 1999 membership is increasing daily by 100 and was 8.570 on the date of my visit, October, 11. Almost 7.900 members come from the United States, 100 from Canada and 570 from all parts of the world. In October 102 countries were represented.

Another interesting figure to know concerns student enrollment. Unfortunately we are not able to give any exact numbers here. We know that the number of participants per course varies between ten and several hundred. If one calculates an average of 30 students per course and an average of 1.5 courses per student, the number of students of The Internet University could be calculated to be 50 000. The real number, however, could be far higher. The fact that the Internet Book Store Amazon.com claims to have sold more than 74 000 copies of Corrigan's book by the summer of 1998 speaks for this possibility.[5]

What about prospects for the future? From here on I will speak in more general terms, not limiting myself to The Internet University but referring more generally to "academics in the internet", thus including virtual universities as well as other forms of academic internet teaching and learning which we will see in the future.[6]

[5] http://www.amazon.com

[6] There are sure to be such new forms about which we can only offer guesses. But two forms I can mention here, because I have encountered them in the net: 1. Professionals and experts offering courses with the backing of some professional association. 2. Mixed courses, in-ternet students participating in regular classes at some university.

At present we cannot say how the development of academics in the internet will continue to develop. Will we see a slow tapering off of the growth rate or will present growth rates continue or even increase? Optimists foresee a continuation of present trends as pictured in figure 3. They predict that by the year 2000 50 % of the market of academic learning will be provided through the internet.

Figure 3: Projected percentage of academics conducted online

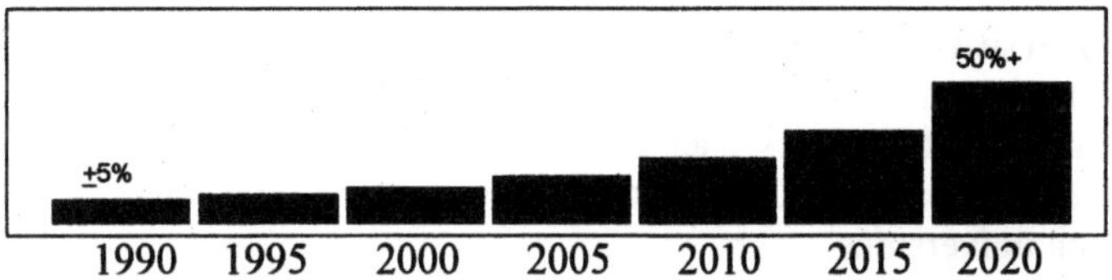

Source: Corrigan, D.(1996): p.4

Nobody knows, how many students actually are studying online. Evidence is, at best ambivalent. The fact, that student numbers are not published and certain comments of persons active in or knowledgeable of the field indicate, that expectations of the optimists may have been too high. Initial success may have been due to the fact that there was a backlog of people who jumped on this opportunity to finish their education and obtain a university degree. Also the dropout rate may have been high and thirdly some online courses may not have met peoples' expectations.

However, there are also other observable trends which speak for a continuing boost to online education. One is technical: the number of people having access to the internet is continuing to increase dramatically.

Another is the development of new didactic models for internet instruction and of staff development programs aimed at preparing staff for teach in online and developing online courses. A third indicator is the increasing number of books and articles on online teaching as well as the increasing attention this topic is attracting on national and international conferences on education. Thus at the 25. International Conference on Improving University Teaching and Learning, which took place in July 2000 in Frankfurt am Main 25% of the contributed papers, 50 % of the theme sessions and the opening Address were dedicated to this topic.

Lastly a boost is expected when the so called Net or N-Generation becomes interested in the online market. They are now 12 - 17 years old and about 65 % if them subscribe to online services or have access to them.

III. Education Brokerage and E-Commerce

Formerly New Promise was to me the paradigm of the internet university. Today I look at the internet university, which I have described above, as only one example and maybe only a small agent in what is rapidly becoming a very differentiated market for teaching and learning in tertiary education in general and specifically in the on-line market for academic education. In this market, New Promise is only one of many providers as the following list shows:

- **Individual universities with an online campus:**
  Many universities have turned their extension-services i.e. their long distance divisions into internet universities, such as the Berkeley and Los Angeles Extensions of the University of California. Hungry mind lists and offers twenty-nine such universities.
- **Associations of Universities:**
  Some universities have formed associations to offer common programs in the internet such as the University of Phoenix or cooperate in their telecommunication activities as the Western Cooperative for Educational Telecommunications
- **Online – Universities:**
  More and more universities are being founded as internet universities from the beginning such as Bill Gates' International University in Paris.
- **Corporate Universities:**
  Many firms have turned their training services into so-called corporate universities of which there are supposed to be more than one-thousand in the U.S. Many of these offer online-courses and more and more of these offer their courses not only to their own employees but on the general public.
- **Distance Universities:**
  Many distance-universities have turned themselves into internet-universities or at least added an online-campus such as the United States Open University.
- **Commercial Education Enterprises:**
  More and more commercial firms offer training and education programs online. Some of these are the big providers of software or hardware or specialists in certain fields.
- **Education brokers:**
  This new development shall be explained more in detail below.

IV. Education Brokers

Let me take New Promise, Inc.[7] as an example of the latest development of what is going on in the academic market place in the US. 'New Promise'[8] is now a shareholder company. Shares are owned by the Prof. Quinn Mills of the Harvard Business School, some other members of the board and the 11 employees.

Up to now 'New Promise' required an investment of 1.000.000 Dollars, which is comparatively low in comparison to its competitors such as 'Hungry Mind' and 'Training Net'. It is said, that 'Hungry Mind' has a budget of 50 Mio. for this year.

At present, 'New Promise' is in the red. In the future, it hopes to generate income through the following sources:

1. A small percentage of the tuition fee of students who subscribe to a course.
2. Banner advertising on the Home Page.
3. A bookstore
4. Target group advertising addressing people interested in certain courses, such as computer courses or marketing courses or management.
5. Agency of loans to students

To write black numbers and make profits New Promise plans to enlarge its activities. The internet university will continue under the heading of 'nothing but'. This will list courses which are exclusively taught through the internet.

Aside from this there will be offers of direct teaching and mixed teaching. For this purpose the offers are bundled, because New Promise thinks, that there is a strong demand for direct teaching which should be satisfied within a diameter of 10 to 30 miles of the interested person.

An enlargement of activities is expected by the widening of offers to training. New Promise is offering its platform to corporate training programs as well as cooperate universities and to commercial firms specialized in the sector of training.

Summing it up, we can say, that New Promise is turning from the internet university of the world to an e-commerce business dedicated to education brokerage. This is underlined by the fact that two of its most important members are Jesse Jacobson, who taught the first internet course of E-Commerce at MIT five years ago and a second person who was managing director of a corporate university in the metal industry.

[7] In the meantime the name has changed to "Mind Edge".
[8] The data presented here were collected during a personal visit Oct. 6-11, 2000.

I report this not without a note of sadness. Of course I understand the dynamics of the firm and its people. It is normal, that they want to apply their know-how to more profitable and growing businesses, such as the corporate training market. On the other hand, I think, that even when they continue their activities in the academic field the idea of the internet university, which I have so much admired, will loose. However, as the large competitors of New Promise show with their efforts to build up their own platforms in this field, this is where the tide seems to be going.

However, many questions remain open. Many respected universities are still in a hold or stand-by position offering no or only a few courses just to be present in the market and keep in touch with developments, such as the University of Michigan with 7 and Harvard with one course in 1998. Skeptics give several reasons for the stand-offishness of many universities: they are afraid to sap students from their face-to-face programs or fear for the prestige of the degrees which they are offering etc. Nevertheless many institutions such as the prestigious Harvard Business School are poised to start or have started with MBA programs. Some have immediately acquired a prestigious clientele such as the Duke University MBA-Program in International Management. These programs provide for a mix of learning situations and learning experiences such as face to face tutorials, learning and project groups, weekend seminars and workshops to keep up motivation and to enable students to develop social, research and discussion skills. The "virtual" students, who have communicated only electronically with their teachers and fellow students may remain deficient in theses skills.

In the author's opinion much can be said in favor of the argument, that in the US academics in the internet will neither be a "temporary fad" nor a "niche product" but rather a type of " revolutionary innovation". The following list of arguments lead to the conclusion that for the US and very likely soon in other states as well for the following reasons we are dealing with an innovation, which has come to stay:

1. It is entering the scene in accordance with some broad societal developments which favor its diffusion such as
   - the break up of the "three houses": education is no longer limited to youth but becomes just as necessary during the life phases of work and elderliness;
   - the relative decreasing importance of basic education in comparison with continuing education and
   - the preference for those solutions in our society which increase the number of options;

2. Innovative offerings in education are demand led. The motor is the increasing demand from students for internet courses to update their knowledge as well as the demand from firms for education and training
3. An important motor and motivational factor for both professors and institutions is the tuition fee. It makes it interesting for universities to offer courses in the internet and it is attractive for students, because cost per credit hour and per degree such as B.A. or a M.A. is lower than in the traditional university or college. For students these costs include not only room, board, and transportation but also opportunity costs in the form of giving up a job or forsaking opportunities for part-time work.
4. Course offers in the Net are directed towards the growing and economically interesting expanding market of adult, part-time students, who are neither in need of nor interested in the university experience.
5. Transaction costs are low. Faculty and students can be recruited on a world wide scale.
6. The offer of courses is extremely flexible and can meet both broad and very specialized interests.
7. There exists great transparency in all respects.
   Competition is intense. It will increase even more as more and more providers enter the market.

V. The University of the Future

As to the University of the Future I do not want to pretend that I am a prophet who foresees the future. However, from recent developments we can deduct certain conclusions:

1. The future landscape of the academic marketplace, i. e. the market for university training will be marked by pluralism and variety.
2. Traditional universities will continue to lose their share of the market unless they make a special effort to modernize
3. There could be a specialization and division of labor.

What should universities do? Here I have three postulates:

1. Universities must wake up. They may not continue to sleep and just let things happen.
2. They must take an active role in deciding on their future role in the education world and produce the necessary adjustments and changes.
3. The following general options are still open to them:
   - Specialize on the university experience. At the last IUT conference in Frankfurt in July of this year one participant described this as the four Ls:

Living, Liquor, Love and (very little) Learning, in Greek tradition this was described as the right of every person to have two academic years for personal growth and development. No doubt, this is a very important social task.

- training and continuing education
- research and elite training.

Still universities have the comparative advantage that they can offer face to face contacts to researchers and academic staff on different levels of teaching. This should be used to develop competitive programs.

The option, which is not open in my view, is to just sit back and wait and to continue as one has always done unless one is reconciled with the fact of the universities continuously loosing ground to other institutions in their field. There will be continuous and increasing pressure on universities to change and to answer to the challenges and demands of society. What is beginning now with the demand for IK specialists and competition in the internet on the one side and increasing financial bottle necks on the other is only a first taste of what is going to come. But, as many experts say in Germany:„ In education and training the money is lying on the street – you just got to pick it up“ The question is if and how the universities will pick up this money.

References

Bremer, Claudia; Buraschi, Martha; Ritter, Ulrich Peter (1998): The Internet University in Argentina, Germany, and USA. An International Comparison. In: Basilia Aguirre: III. Arnoldshain Seminar. Argentine, Brazil and Germany: Comparative studies in structural transformation. São Paulo, Brasil.

Bremer, Claudia: How to go Online: Considerations of Designing an Online Course - Technical Options, Didactical Methods and the Students. In : Contributed Papers, 25th. International Conference on Improving University Teaching and Learning, Frankfurt am Main, 2000, pp. 481-487.

Bremer, Claudia; Ritter, Ulrich Peter (1997): Internetgestützte Hochschulveranstaltungen speziell am Beispiel Virtueller Tutorien, in: Das Hochschulwesen 4/97, pp. 203-210

Caso's Internet University. Your Guide to Online College Courses; The Cyber Classics Editors 1999

Caso's Internet University: http://www.caso.com

Corrigan, D. (1996): The Internet University. College Courses by Computer, Cape Software:

Gillett, Max: Staff Development for On-Line Teaching and Learning in Universities: Identifying Specific Needs, Principles and Initiatives. In : Contributed Papers, 25th. International Conference on Improving University Teaching and Learning, Frankfurt am Main, 2000, pp. 183 - 188.

Greyling, Liz (E.S.G.): On Determining the Instructional Quality of Online Courses: A Case Study. In : Contributed Papers, 25th. International Conference on Improving University Teaching and Learning, Frankfurt am Main, 2000, pp. 211-216.

http://www.amazon.com

http://www.hungrymind.com

http://www.internet-architect.com

http://www.internet-university.com

http://www.mindedge.com

http://www.newpromise.com

http://www.sln.suny.edu

Kanuka, Heather A.: Creating a Learner Centered Environment with Web Based Instruction: Going the Distance. In : Contributed Papers, 25th. International Conference on Improving University Teaching and Learning, Frankfurt am Main, 2000, pp.: 494-499.

van Eijl, Pierre, Pilot, Albert, de Jong, Yvonne, de Voogd, Peter, Janssens, Tosca: A Model for a Website Supported Course. In : Contributed Papers, 25th. International Conference on Improving University Teaching and Learning, Frankfurt am Main, 2000, pp. 223-228.

Lenaghan, Donna D.: PLUG IN OR OUT: The Quentiscent Question for the Learner Centered University. In : Contributed Papers, 25th. International Conference on Improving University Teaching and Learning, Frankfurt am Main, 2000, pp. 378-382.

Oberprieler, Gudrun: Learning to Choose - Choosing to Learn: On-line Computer Literacy Training as Part of a Foundation Course Package for 1st Year Humanities Students. In : Contributed Papers, 25th. International Conference on Improving University Teaching and Learning, Frankfurt am Main, 2000. pp. 168-173.

Pillay, Hitendra: Emerging Attributes of Pedagogy and Curriculum for Universities of the Future. In : Contributed Papers, 25th. International Conference on Improving University Teaching and Learning, Frankfurt am Main, 2000, pp. 133-139.

Ritter, Ulrich Peter (1997):Lernen im Netz - Hochschuldidaktischer Traum oder Alptraum? in: Das Hochschulwesen 4/97, pp. 201 – 202.

Ritter, Ulrich Peter (1999): Die Internet-Universität, virtuelle Universitäten und die Zukunft der europäischen Universitäten in: Das Hochschulwesen 4/99 pp. 102-107.

Ritter, Ulrich Peter (1999) The Take-off of The Internet University: in 24th. International Conference on Improving University Teaching and Learning, Brisbane, Australia, 1999.

Ritter, Ulrich Peter (2000): Learning through Research in Mass Education in: Proceedings of the 25th. International Conference on Improving University Teaching and Learning, Frankfurt am Main, 2000.

Turrisi, Patricia A. and Albert, A. Midori: A Case Study of Online Course Development: Emphasizing Learner-Centered Pedagogy through the Team Approach. In : Contributed Papers, 25th. International Conference on Improving University Teaching and Learning, Frankfurt am Main, 2000, pp. 402 - 406.

Western Cooperative for Educational Telecommunications (www.wiche.edu/telecom).

Wright, Donald and Pan, Alex: A Working Model for Web-Enhanced Instruction. In : Contributed Papers, 25th. International Conference on Improving University Teaching and Learning, Frankfurt am Main, 2000. pp. 412-417.

Figure 2: The Homepage of New Promise[9]

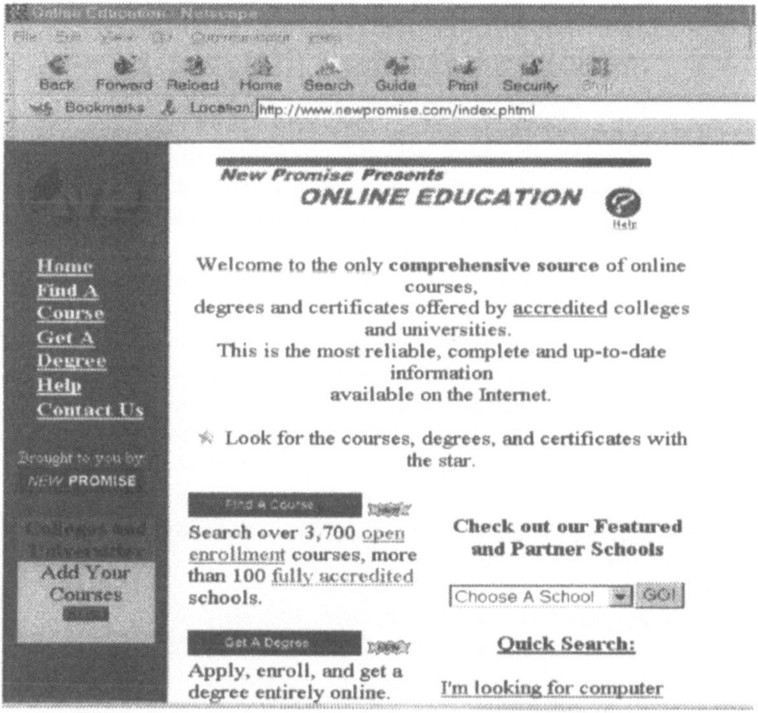

[9] Since August 1999 this homepage has been redesigned and restructured.

Consequences for Labor Markets

INTEGRATION AND REGIONAL RESTRUCTURING

Alberto M. Díaz Cafferata, Alberto J. Figueras, José Luis Arrufat *

Members of the Research Team: **Ricardo Descalzi, Mauro Roca**

1. Introduction. About trade liberalization and regional economic restructuring

The '90s have been a period of substantial economic changes in Argentina, caused by domestic trade liberalization policy, exogenous trade shocks (the fall in the terms of trade) and the Mercosur regional association, as well as domestic policies leading to reduced government intervention.

These changes in the institutional organization of the country and trade are likely to have regionally differentiated impacts on economic activities and welfare.

Our working hypothesis is that "Regional economic restructuring" in Argentina is an ongoing process, with substantial welfare effects. And it must be emphasized that a precise perception of current and future evolutions is required, for an appropriate approach to regional economic policy.

Remarkable regional unemployment disparities in Argentina during the last two decades are perhaps the most immediate and striking signal of this spatial impact of the new trade regime. Thus, we regard the labor markets in the different urban agglomerates a useful indicator of how the economic forces are operating the process of regional restructuring (Díaz Cafferata and Figueras, 1999; Arrufat, Díaz Cafferata and Figueras, 1999).

Even when there is an intuitive perception of these processes, there is also scanty systematical statistical evidence organized to provide a coherent picture of regional phenomena in Argentina, useful for economic analysis and theorizing. Even the basic macroeconomic data on regional value added are not highly reliable and have to be used with caution.

There is also a lack of theoretical and empirical research on the effects of Mercosur, specially on the spatial impacts of the agreement, on which policy recommendations may be founded.

*Instituto de Economía y Finanzas. Facultad de Ciencias Económicas. Universidad Nacional de Córdoba. Av. Valparaíso s/n. 5000 Córdoba. República Argentina.
Ph.: (54-351) 4334089/90. Fax:(54-351) 4334092
E-mail: diazcaf@eco.uncor.edu, alfi@eco.uncor.edu, jarrufat@eco.uncor.edu.

Welfare gains from integration. A geographical dimension

The welfare effects of policy changes is the key problem of economic analysis in the issue of integration. Concern for the distribution effects shall not be confined to the effects among countries, but also must take account of impacts within countries. A prominent policy problem is the regionally differentiated welfare effects brought about by integration. The current integration process is in its initial steps since the Asunción Treaty[1], signed on March 26, 1991. The most significant phenomenon in this initial period has been the rapid growth of trade between Argentina and Brazil. The continuity of this increased exchange, and the expected participation of Chile and Bolivia, will require investment in infrastructure, further driving towards a new pattern of allocation of production and population. The magnitude, direction, and consequences of these movements, are certainly a priority subject for research in Latin America.

Further progress in integration will demand that conflicting regional policies at the national level be abandoned. And a consensus shall be found to contrive a new continental regional policy.

Robson, 1998, notes that beyond the issues addressed in the traditional theory of regional integration agreements, the "analysis of the distributional aspects of integration in its spatial dimension, largely ignored in the orthodox theory, has become an important component of the subject". He also points out that "integration may affect the location of production and through this and other channels may have important implications for the geographical distribution of the gains from integration". He concludes that "an analysis of the effects of international economic integration must therefore extend far beyond the traditional theory of market integration".

A natural reference point is the European experience. In particular, he remarks that "at the time of its first enlargement the EC decided to introduce its own regional policy, which was designed to complement national policies and to contribute to a reduction in economic disparities within the Community"[2].

A risky but inevitable task for economists is to talk about the future. When significant trends can be assessed the degrees of freedom of many variables are reduced and more reliable scenarios may be built. New significant evolutions in the economy of the Latin American countries relevant for the transformation of its spatial structure, are: (i) the next steps in trade integration, the question of "when and how Mercosur should 'broaden' by adding new members", with the likely participation of Bolivia and Chile, and (ii) the process of "deepening

[1] The English text of the Treaty, as well as complementary material may be obtained from the Web Site of the Organization of American States: http://www.sice.oas.org/trade/mrcsr

[2] Robson, 1998, p. xiv, 6 and 10.

integration" with efforts concentrated on institutional infrastructure, including areas like security, geopolitics and ecology[3].

Substantial impacts of these processes may be expected. We are concerned here with the identification of the geographical areas that are likely to be more severely affected in the short and medium "transition" run (and the implications as regards the convenience of the Mercosur for Argentina). Our a priori hypothesis is that some poor "peripherical" areas will bear the heavier burden of the changes. On the one hand because of the negative economic impact (specially if the agglomeration forces, as some historical experiences - like the Italian integration in the XIX century - show, prevail). On the other, because the same more vulnerable locations are the less likely to generate (current and future) local or external savings flows to finance substantial investment required for a strategy of "positive" adjustment[4]. This perspective puts the issue of distribution and regional policy on the top of the agenda. And introduces the need to define the direction and magnitude of redistribution, as well as the coordination of regional policies, both at the national and supranational level.

From the fiscal perspective the spatial issue also appears to be related to the need for advancing co-ordination and convergence of national budgetary policies. Fiscal federalism is today a prominent issue.

Regional economic restructuring involves the consideration of institutional processes. Specifically, attention must be given to the current process of formation of new regions in Argentina, created through agreements among provinces, in order to evaluate the optimality of this process in terms of economic efficiency and to explain why a particular actual regionalization was agreed on.

We approach the problem with the following working hypothesis: trade liberalization and integration provide incentives for the reallocation of resources (both sectoral and spatial) and will generate a pattern of spatially distributed effects in the Mercosur countries. The contribution of this paper is to provide a characterization of the Argentine economy useful to establish stylized facts and presumptions on the spatial effects of integration.

With this purpose indicators of the spatial pattern of economic activity in Argentina along the 20th century will be presented, to provide a historical perspective. On this basis, some insights into the forces that are likely to influence the future regional restructuring process in Argentina and Mercosur as

[3] Cfr. Roett, 1999

[4] "Positive adjustment" is meant to indicate actions to reinforce regional advantages with accumulation of social capital like infrastructure and education. Choices have to be made, like with the design of the corridor Atlantic- Pacific between Brazil and Chile through the Argentine territory. "Defensive adjustment" would be oriented to avoid the loss in production activities and population.

a whole are offered. As useful references, international experiences on regional restructuring and alternative approaches to regional policy will be discussed briefly.

The rest of the paper is organized as follows. Section 2 discusses the main domestic and international economic forces that in the last two decades are driving economic restructuring in Argentina, and our prior hypothesis on how it manifests as regional economic restructuring and on which economic phenomena have to be examined to provide objective evidence of the process. This interpretation is summarized in Figures 1 and 2, which suggest how domestic openness, and the modern closening of ties between the economies of the world, have an impact on regional allocation of resources and regional development. Section 3 assesses a concept of "spatial economic structure" and the statistical indicators that provide objective evidence of both the pattern and the degree of stability of such structure. In Sections 4 and 5 we report the calculation of statistical indexes that provide "stylized facts" of the regional dimension of the Argentine economy, and discuss such evidence. The last section summarizes the stylized facts and provides a synthesis and concluding remarks.

2. *International trade and regional economic restructuring in the 80's and 90's: a framework*

Trade and current economic restructuring

The internationalization of goods and financial markets and the revalorization of the liberal ideology of economic society had impacts in the world economic space. Our interest is the particular class of problems created by the ways in which this modern phenomenon of global structural transformation has been transmitted to the interior economic spaces of nations. Figure 1 provides a general scheme of the international and domestic forces that account for the substantial reforms in the last two decades in Argentina, especially at the beginning of the nineties. The two boxes at the top of the figure indicate the driving determinants of the reform process during the nineties. It is worth noting that both are related to international trade: (i) The **collapse of the import substitution strategy** of economic development; (ii) The change in the economic organization required to keep pace with **the new dynamics of the international markets**. The "external sector" was, in fact, the key factor of structural transformation.

The question we address is: what happens to the regions as a consequence of this process of structural transformation? On the one hand we postulate that there are **"direct (spatial) impacts"**, related mainly to the local *industry mix*, i.e. regional specialization. On the other hand, the Argentine economy underwent a broad range of substantial **institutional reforms** (both structural reform policies and macroeconomic policies) to recover basic resource allocation rules, after half a century during which "rent- seeking" and printing money were at the heart of economic policy.

We want to understand how, as a result of regional integration, domestic reforms, and the necessary accommodation to the challenges posed by the generalized world economy transformation (a series of interrelated features sometimes summarized by the term "globalization"), alter the economic space in Argentina, Mercosur, and the rest of Latin America.

Trade liberalization (generalized tariff reductions) and the Mercosur were central to structural reforms in Argentina. These changes were accompanied by a broad range of domestic institutional reforms that include a still incomplete revision of the rules governing the labor market, privatization of state enterprises providing public services, reform of the financial system, transfer of education and health services from the national state to the provinces, to name just a few. Those socio- economic processes can be expected to alter the frontiers of the **"natural regions"**.

Two points are useful to state on this matter. **Firstly**, the presence of the phenomenon (Figueras, 1996) is not easily quantified due to the paucity of reliable regional data and, in any case, the short period for the consequences of the process to fully develop. We are in fact in the transition period, and new institutional adjustment can be expected. **Secondly**, as discussed by Bennett, 1997, the "economic space" is not identical with the "administrative space". The technical administrative ideal is, he explains, for a functional or activity space, to be matched by administrative boundaries ("truly bounded"). More commonly, administrative structures are "under bounded": the functional activity space crosses over many local government boundaries. It is "over bounded" when the functional activity space is a part of an administrative division[5].

To sum up: The confluence of diverse spatial effects of trade liberalization and integration alter the "natural economic regions" (NERs). Of course NERs **exist as a real phenomenon**, whether its existence and characteristics are politically or institutionally recognized or not. The changes in the economic conditions at the interior of those NER´s, and the change in their frontiers, is perceived in different degree by economic agents. At the **individual** level they adjust to the new conditions through actions such as shifting technologies or moving resources from one sector to another. There are also **collective actions** of which the spontaneous formation of new institutional sub-national areas.

On the one hand there is, beyond the national frontiers, an exogenous globalization process operating as a powerful conditioning force. On the other hand, at the interior of the national territory, municipalities and provinces are

[5] Díaz Cafferata, 1997.

engaged in a dynamic process of regional institutionalization, local alliances, and a reshaping of roles.

A "new territorialization" is certainly, in Argentina, a most significant issue. New "political" regions have been formally created recently: the "Región Centro" with the participation of Córdoba, Santa Fe and Entre Ríos; the "Región Cuyo" with Mendoza, San Juan and San Luis. The provincial governments have, in each of the above cases, agreed to coordinate actions to improve the efficiency of economic policies.

Are the newly formally created sub-national territorial clusterings efficient to attain the objectives of development and increasing welfare? Or, on the contrary, the operative solution in the current circumstances would be a centralized national organization of government actions? This particular question should not be taken lightly, and different arguments must be taken into account. But a key point to argue for decentralization is the necessary speed of response in a rapidly changing economic (and political) environment.

A few key questions shall be posed concerning these **tendencies to institutional regional restructuring** with the definition of "new territories". (a)Is an internal division of the national state in powerful regional states a likely outcome of current tendencies in the Mercosur countries?; (b) Would this be efficient as an economic organization?; (c) Which is the degree of decentralization that is politically desirable?

A response to the emergence of these new scenarios is a change in the "regional episthemology" (Boisier, 1994: Cepal, 1952). A new typology is suggested by Sergio Boisier: he distinguishes "regiones pivotales", "regiones asociativas" and "regiones virtuales". They are differentiated from each other by the degree of flexibility in the association, the degree of voluntarism, and the permanence.

Similar issues were discussed independently in Díaz Cafferata and Figueras, 1999. It appears to us that the coincidence is a similar intellectual perception of current territorial evolutions in Latin America. And the need to build an analytical apparatus useful to understand them. We were not aware at that time of this particular publication by Boisier, a recognized authority in the area of regional economics.

It was said above that the first problem a researcher finds to give a response to the above mentioned questions is the lack of precise quantitative facts on regional phenomena in Argentina. It is the purpose of this paper to contribute on depicting new perspectives that help build a more complete perception of the issue.

International comparisons. European Union and Mercosur.

It is worth devoting a few paragraphs to state some relevant coincidences and differences between Mercosur and the EU, as well as economic features of the constituent countries, as regards the objectives and possibilities of local adjustment to spatial restructuring processes, and the alternative solutions to regional disparities. We have in mind for future comparative research Argentina, Brazil, Germany, and Spain. Despite the very significant differences in wealth, income, and structure of production, it is interesting to note that in the regional dimension there are some similarities that provide useful basis for comparison.

The first of them is, for our present purposes of studying the spatial restructuring effects of regional economic agreements, that all these economies, two South American countries, two European countries, participate in regional economic agreements.

A second interesting point is that these countries have undergone processes involving some sort of institutional regional restructuring. The most significant of them occurred when the Federal Republic of Germany (FRG) and the German Democratic Republic reunited formally with the approval of Article 23 of the Constitution on October 3, 1990. But also Spain underwent changes with the organization of "regiones" and "comunidades autónomas". In Argentina some of the provinces have responded to the strains of globalization with the formation of new regions. Brazil experiences the growing weight of municipalities. In Argentina there is an ongoing process of new regions formation.

On the relations between local and national governments, it is worth noting that they are federal countries. Argentina is federal. Germany is the Federal Republic of Germany, and Brazil official name is Federal Republic of Brazil.

The new balance of forces may be a hindrance to the efficiency to the efficiency of economic policy when conflicts between national and local objectives exist. Also, a mechanism to solve the conflicts between regions of different countries at the supra-natural level must exist to prevent what has been called "wars between regions". In spite of this general idea that induce the researcher to try to make useful comparisons, an empirical approach is plagued with difficulties[6].

[6] Mancha Navarro, 2000, has pointed out that there are very substantial differences among regions in the European Union itself. There are, for example, regions with an area of 215.000 Km^2 in central Spain as opposed to Brussels, Belgium, whose area is of the order of 200 Km^2. Another basis of comparison is given by population. Ile de France is inhabited by 10 million people whereas Valle de Aosta has only 115 thousand inhabitants. It is also likely that we should pay more attention to institutional factors, in so far as they have a bearing on economic performance. Mancha Navarro regards Germany and Belgium as examples of federal states,

To sum up, there have been substantial institutional reforms concerning the roles and relations between different levels of government. They have undergone a process of economic reform and regional restructuring in the last two decades.

In addition to this, it is also the case that the European countries, as opposed to the Latin American countries we are considering here, have developed formal arrangements for the coordination of regional policies and may be rightly regarded as being several steps ahead in the way in which they can jointly deal with regional challenges.

Identification of common and differential features in each of them might prove helpful to highlight the central mechanisms of spatial restructuring.

Empirical perspective: Evolution of regional labor markets in Argentina as indicators of regional restructuring

It is worth pointing out that the economic changes are not homogeneous across the national geography. This is understandable under the circumstance that the economic space itself is indeed, heterogeneous, previous to the shocks. Two kinds of empirical outcomes of regional restructuring were pointed out in the discussion of Figure 1 and Figure 2. One of them is the differential impact **on regional labor markets** which find striking expression in the regional unemployment disparities. Another, albeit limited, indicator of regional economic restructuring that we shall explore below is the location of **"economic gravity centers"** as they evolve in time. Other features are also considered in connection with measures of specialization and concentration.

It is useful at this point to summarize the present authors' empirical findings in connection with regional labor markets. The regional behavior of the rate of unemployment in Argentina is an indicator of spatially differentiated impacts of structural changes. National unemployment has steadily grown after the debt crisis in 1982, reaching 18.6% in 1995. Some regions have suffered from this process more severely than others: the standard deviation of local unemployment rates climbed from 2.4 in 1990, to 4.7 in 1995 in Argentina. As a consequence, the pattern of regional unemployment has markedly differential local features. It is also worth emphasizing that the highest rates of unemployment in the mid nineties were observed for those urban centers showing the lowest levels in the previous decade.

Spain and Italy as regional states, the United Kingdom, Ireland, and Luxembourg, as examples of more centralized states. There are still other types, like France and Portugal, which have some sort of political and administrative regionalization.

Similar features can be observed in other countries, as has been reported in Armstrong and Taylor, 1999; Arrufat, Díaz Cafferata and Figueras, 1999; Díaz Cafferata and Figueras, 1999. From the discussion in Díaz Cafferata and Figueras, 1999, about the stylized facts of regional unemployment in Argentina, the following central points can be stated:

It must be recognized that there exists not a single but alternative concepts and objective statistical measures of regional unemployment disparities, among others the variance, standard deviation, coefficient of variation, and an index of regional unemployment disparities.

Persistence: the degree of change in the regional pattern of unemployment is identified as "persistence". The degree and sign of convergence of regional unemployment rates when national unemployment changes are useful indicators of the existence and characteristics of spatial heterogeneity.

Response to shocks: it is of special interest to find whether regional unemployment rates converge or diverge in periods of acceleration of nation wide unemployment as in 1977-82, or 1991-95 in Argentina.

Three alternative explanations are provided for a differential regional unemployment impact: (a) the *industry mix* explanation; (b)differences in the *socio-economic* characteristics of the workforce; (c) *constraints on the interregional mobility of labor*. A related question is why spatial disparities of unemployment persist.

Trade and unemployment

The effects of trade on labor market developments are usually modeled assuming that the economy is a homogeneous space. The Harris-Todaro type models provide an interesting basic framework for regional unemployment analysis, but the understanding of regional unemployment disparities they offer is still limited. Differential regional effects can be established in the line of the "industry mix" explanation of the effects of "large trade policy shocks". In Díaz Cafferata, 1997, a theoretical explanation of how structural changes generate unemployment, emphasizes the role of obsolescence of capital and capacity limits. Under those conditions labor demand curves become inelastic with respect to the wage rate and labor dismissed in shrinking sectors find it more difficult to get a job in expanding sectors. Given such restrictions, the industry mix hypothesis argues that a regional concentration of distressed sectors will generate a regional unemployment problem.

Pressures for government involvement to smooth out the adjustment process arise. Apart from the general problem of government intervention, the regional dimension has implications for the formulation of unemployment policies. The key issue is to determine whether the optimal response should be at the federal or provincial level of government.

Is there a general rule? When is an intervention to modify the operation of the market justified? There is a growing interest in the policy consequences of regional unemployment disparities (RUD). It has been noted that "regional policy exists primarily because of the persistence of regional unemployment disparities. Unemployment has been the main criterion for designating areas in the United Kingdom since the early 1930s, and it is unemployment disparities which are invariably referred to in discussions of the "regional problem" (Armstrong and Taylor, 1993).

The practical definition of regional frontiers

Empirical analysis of economic activity from a spatial perspective, poses the problem of territorial aggregation. The literature on regional economics discusses the definition of "region" but empirical studies typically use data gathered following just administrative lines, contrary to the desirable property of being related to the economic behavior (Arrufat, Díaz Cafferata y Figueras, 1999 a).

In the future we intend to explore the conceptual and operational regional demarcation in order to understand the **phenomenon of the formation of "new economic spaces"** and **"new administrative spaces"**, but these points will not be pursued further here. For the moment we merely state here that from the viewpoint of economic policy making it would be useful to define homogeneous areas or regions in order to address specific problems like, for example, unemployment. A particular example of this line of approach is given in Arrufat, Díaz Cafferata and Figueras, 1998, in which use is made of cluster analysis. This would facilitate policy making because in this way one would be able to tackle particular problems in each region. Whereas it might be argued that there is some force to this argument in connection with specially severe policy problems, it is also evident that it cannot be used as a general means of regionalization. This particular approach would entail the need for devising as many different regional structures as there are economic problems to address as policy objectives, a clearly demanding and probably hopeless task. As a result of these considerations, a practical solution calls for what we call a "basic regionalization" which takes into account not only one, but several important features which are thought to be relevant for policy making purposes.

3. *Our approach explained*

In this section we spell out what we shall be doing in the rest of the paper to deal with the spatial effects of trade liberalization and regional economic integration in the following steps:

i) We start by recognizing as a key concept to approach the research the notion of "spatial economic structure" (and a hypothesis about the forces that make it change). We are interested in the concept and measurement of "regional economic structures", and on the economic mechanisms that make it change. We have to start with an appropriate concept of what is a regional economic structure, and then select indicators that are fit for objectively detecting changes in the RES of a given economy. As regards economic mechanisms of change, and economic policy problems, in the next section we will briefly comment, as a convenient reference, on the experience in the formation and the characteristics of the spatial economic structure in different countries (especially in the USA and the EU).

ii) The identification of objective statistical indicators of spatial structure. As a starting point for an empirical assessment of the **degree of stability (or change) of a regional economic structure**, appropriate objective (quantitative) indicators of the process have to be defined. Following Hallet, 1999, in sections 4 and 5 indicators with a sectoral emphasis ("concentration"), and a geographic perspective ("specialization"). Also "gravity centers" are identified. Other indicators of "regional structure persistence" and of "regional restructuring" can be mentioned as possibilities for further quantitative research: usual measures of dispersion, input output analysis, correlation coefficients (Armstrong and Taylor, 1999). A recent branch of the literature approaches the problem from the perspective of the existence, and mechanisms of regional convergence.

iii) Calculation of indicators for Argentina (and Mercosur countries when comparable data are available).

iv) A presumption of the spatial restructuring effects of Mercosur, based on the kind of ongoing and expected changes in the economic environment and current spatial structure.

Spatial economic structure and driving forces of regional restructuring.

What is a "Regional Economic structure"? Regional economic structure alludes here to the spatial pattern of location of the goods and services markets, the location of the product, and the exchange network. The pattern of location, in turn, includes both the geographical location of economic activity and relative sizes, and these characteristics are the result of a history of optimizing behavior of economic agents. A few relevant variables that condition economic behavior, and have space structuring effects are:

(a) What is called in the theory "path dependence". That is, a historic event determines the future of a particular regional economy. Harry Richardson, used the term “location constants”, nodal points which form a conditioning territorial hierarchy.

(b) The location, the dimension and the qualities of demand.

(c) The technical characteristics of the productive processes (i.e.) productive processes which generate a loss of weight in the transformation, in which case the location near the source of raw materials tend to be more convenient.

(d) The characteristics of factors of production and technology, such as: d1- The degree of spatial specificity or the cost of mobility makes the spatial pattern more heavily dependent on the size and structure of demand for final goods; d2- If factors are highly mobile, location of production is driven by the location of the market; d3- Production and transportation technology interaction with these forces.

To close this discussion we might formulate a few hypotheses about conditions that provide stability to the spatial economic structure. (i) the more location specific are the factors of production (minerals, agriculture, fishing) and the less substitution is possible in sectoral production functions; ii) the higher the variety of the industry mix; iii) the more advanced (and complex) is the local economy; iv)the more closed the economy is.

Economic efficiency and regional policy

It is a common occurrence that despite the well known inertia of spatial structures, a “resistance” feature that makes transformation efforts frequently disappointing, the governments try to correct the regional disparities and to mitigate the adverse effects of exogenous shocks. It is often the case that the usual conflict between efficiency and equity appears in the application of regional policies. In terms of regional economics the conflict is between national global efficiency and local growth.

As an alternative response to regional problems, the constitution of new administrative regions is being suggested as an instrument to strengthen local prospects. A couple of questions arise. Which is the role of institutional regions? Do they contribute to the efficient allocation of resources? The general theoretical framework includes elements of location theory, the economic analysis of migrations (and the concept of "spatial equilibrium"), fiscal federalism, political economy (the action of regional lobbies).

The issues a policy approach addresses are: (a) differences in regional wealth and income per capita; (b) regional heterogeneity of exogenous shocks and of national policies; (c) the design of regional policies.

Some policies are of a general scope, such as the development of poor regions or undesired local side effects of aggregate policies (like monetary policy.). Some other are more specific, like regional unemployment disparities.

Spatially-specific economic problems ask for the efficiency of national regional policy and of local policies, and the necessary coordination among different levels of government. Regarding distributional conflicts, policy problems that arise from the large gains for some and losses for some other regions or local communities, stemming from structural changes, shake political national agreements and cohesion.

Well known contemporaneous examples are the recurrent discussions about the separation of Québec in Canada, and the events taking place in the former socialist countries. Germany devoted large amounts of resources to prevent this danger to alter the recent reunification and to prevent that the incentive of spatial differentials in real income provoke massive movements of population from East to West. Finally, due attention paid to the regional inequalities in the EU is the basis for the Cohesion Funds.

Efficiency, the national interest, and solidarity are three traditional principles to harmonize in the design of regional policy. Regional integration adds a new international dimension to the issue.

4. *Statistical indicators of spatial structure for Argentina.* [7]

Before moving to the particulars of the empirical application in this paper it is worth remembering that a regional approach to economic problems faces the difficulty that the quality of the data is critically low. Certainly much lower than those available for the national aggregates. A first reason is the lack of internal tariffs on which a register of interregional trade could be kept. To make the best use of the limited statistical information available, we calculate indexes that are useful to get a first approximation to the spatial economic structure .

On this context the concept of "Economic Gravity Center" will be used, as well as indicators of specialization, concentration and clustering (Hallet, 2000).

4.1 Center- periphery systems, and economic gravity centers

The concept of a center- periphery spatial structure is useful to describe relevant features of the Mercosur economies from the spatial point of view. This approach suggests a characterization of regional restructuring that distinguishes the changes in the center and the transformations in the periphery, and examining the exchange between them. Two cases that appear as convenient

[7] Because of space constraints the Annex included in the original paper presented in the Fourth Arnoldshain Seminar, containing the data utilized to calculate the indicators, is not published here. The Annex tables may be requested to: ricdes@eco.uncor.edu.

points of references are those when there is not a displacement of the center, and those when the center changes. We can name these two cases:

a) Peripheric spatial restructuring, with a fixed center.
b) Global spatial restructuring, with displacement of the center.

In previous work we have shown evidence of significant spatial heterogeneity in the behavior of economic variables in Argentina during the last two decades.

Our general hypothesis is that the phenomenon is a consequence of the structural transformations generated by trade liberalization, the change in the role of the state and regional integration in Mercosur. We cannot however provide at present a formal general model, neither are some of the analytical pieces amenable to be formally tested due to the serious lack of reliable regional data for Argentina.

We find an early assessment of the process in Figueras, 1996. He argued that Brazil and Argentina show each, historically, an own economic gravity center. Each is the progressive outcome of a succession of historical events, and the pattern resulting form the closing strategy since the 50 ´s. It was suggested that the economic gravity center in Brazil was likely to be in the triangle Belo Horizonte- Rio- Porto Alegre. The center in Argentina was intuitively located in the area of the "Balcón del Litoral", the industrial corridor La Plata-Buenos Aires-Rosario (together with some Mediterranean "islands" such as the city of Córdoba).

The author added that the regional integration in Mercosur which dilutes progressively the economic frontiers (while the national economies are themselves opening), can be expected to alter the location of "gravity centers". The hypothesis is that the gravitational center of Mercosur was likely to be found at some point in the area NE of Argentina –SW of Brazil. In other words, we might "a priori" tentatively fix it in the wide space of the Paraná – Santa Catalina- Río Grande states (together a surface of about 562.000 sq. Km., an area similar to the three economically larger Argentine provinces: Buenos Aires, Córdoba, Santa Fe). This spatial shift of the "central point" towards the South in Brazil, towards the NE in Argentina, would alter the pre-existing optimal locations, and was therefore likely to generate changes in the allocation of resources, with the accompanying costs that reallocation would bring about.

A somewhat similar preoccupation is present in the empirical research by Haddad and Azzoni, 1999, who using Brazilian data construct a computable general equilibrium model and use it to predict the new locations of the economic gravity centers brought about by new trade policies.

The next paragraphs present different indicators of Argentine spatial economic structure. They include measures and discussion of gravity centers in Mercosur as well as regional specialization, concentration, and measures of clustering. Finally some indication is provided with regard to the likely effects on economic activities from a regional point of view as a consequence of the Brazilian devaluation of January 1999.

4.2 The economic gravity center in Argentina during the 20th century

The concept of gravity centers

In order to gain an understanding of some important features of geographical dispersion of economic activities, however rough that understanding may be, calculations of gravity centers have been carried out. In keeping with the usual definition of a gravity center one takes into account both the latitude and the longitude data referring to specific locations where, for example, people live, generate output, use electricity or are unemployed. The calculation of the gravity center then calls for an appropriate weighting mechanism to be applied to such magnitudes, which takes into account how important each of them is in relation to the overall value of the magnitude being measured across the total space. Some calculations reported refer to Argentina whereas some others have been carried out for Brazil, Paraguay, and Uruguay and for Mercosur as a whole.

- **Argentina. Gravity centers based on Population data**

To begin with, gravity centers for Argentina will be reported. As shown in Table 6.1, population-based gravity centers were calculated for the years 1895, 1914, 1947, 1960, 1970, 1980 and 1991, which are the years for which census data are available. This period spans a little less than a century. In all cases calculations have been performed according to the following conventions:

(i) Population is measured at the provincial level (taking into account present-day definitions, there are now 23 provinces in Argentina, and the City of Buenos Aires which is the Argentine federal capital).
(ii) The latitude – longitude figures applied are those describing each of the province's capital city, the underlying assumption being that that particular city is itself the gravity center of the province. This will not in general be true, but it is merely used for convenience, as is commonly used in the literature. In fact, some calculations carried out by taking cities, and not provinces, into account for 1991 show that gravity centers calculated in the simplified way are very accurate. It goes without saying

that the simplified calculations are much more easily carried out given that they alleviate significantly the burden in terms of data availability.

(iii) Each capital city latitude – longitude data is weighted by the proportion that the province it represents has in the total Argentine population for a particular year.

A very striking feature, certainly one that the authors did not expect, is that there appear to have been only minor changes in the values of the population-based gravity centers for Argentina for a long period of nearly one century, in a large territory. To further elaborate on this point, notice that the gravity center is shifted from Sastre (in the Province of Santa Fe), in 1895, to the region of San Lorenzo – Rosario, also in the Province of Santa Fe, in 1991. The distance between the two centers of gravity is of the order of only 165 km.

This feature, however, should not be taken as meaning that provincial shares in total population have not experienced any significant changes throughout those years. For example:

(i) The City of Buenos Aires had 16.05% of the total population in 1895, in 1991 it only accounted for 9.09%, the minimum in the series. In 1914 the City achieved its historical record by having 19.98% of the total Argentine population.
(ii) The Province of Buenos Aires, on the other hand, had a share of 22.28% of total population in 1914 which by 1991 had risen to 38.62%.
(iii) The Province of Córdoba, in turn, in 1914 had a share of 12.85% whereas in 1991 that share went down to only 8.1%.
(iv) A totally different picture emerges for the Province of Mendoza. In fact, its share of total population went up from a mere 2.81%, in 1895, to a 4.33% in 1991, an increase of roughly 50%.

Given the very significant importance of the Buenos Aires, both the City and the Province, in terms of population (bear in mind that together they account for nearly 50% of total Argentine population in 1991), it was thought interesting to carry out a sensitivity check. This useful additional exercise was carried out in two different ways. For the first one, we do not include the City of Buenos Aires nor the Province of Buenos Aires. The second exercise was performed not taking into account City of Buenos Aires, the Province of Buenos Aires, the Province of Córdoba and the Province of Santa Fe. These last two provinces are the second and third largest.

If we refer to 1991, the year for which the last Census is available, the result of the second exercise above shows that the population-based gravity center is shifted North West by a distance of approximately 300 Km. The center moves from an area in the vicinity of San Lorenzo – Rosario (Province of Santa Fe) when all provinces are taken into account, to a place named Cañada de Luque, located on the Western side of Laguna de Mar Chiquita (Province of Córdoba).

- **Electricity consumption and Geographical Product**

Two alternative sets of calculations were carried out with regard to gravity centers. The first rests on the use of overall electricity consumption at the provincial level, i.e. takes into account residential as well as industrial use of electric energy and also street lighting. The second, in turn, uses Gross Geographical Product on a provincial basis. The gravity center results obtained by the use of these two alternative methods are reported in Table 1 and 2.

Summing up, we observe a very small spatial displacement of the gravity center both in the case of a long period for the exercise performed with population, and when use was made of either the Gross Product or the total energy consumption (the last two cover a very short time-span of five years). The GC is always located within a rectangle of about 150 km wide and 300 km long, whichever the variable used for the calculation or the moment in time.

- **The gravity centers for the Mercosur area**

With a view to having a broader picture, gravity-center calculations were carried out for Brazil, Paraguay, and Uruguay, Argentina's partners within Mercosur. In order to ease the understanding of the basic results obtained, gravity centers based on population figures were independently calculated first for each of the four Mercosur countries. For the purposes of this calculation we resorted to very detailed regional level population figures for Brazil and Uruguay (state and provincial level, respectively). Unfortunately, we did not have access to information with the same level of disaggregation for Paraguay and we, therefore, calculated this country's gravity center by resorting to data covering the population of only the most important cities.

Having obtained each one of the Mercosur country's gravity center, we proceeded, in the second stage, to calculate the Mercosur gravity by using the appropriate weights based on the population of each member country. Please notice that Brazil's population, amounting to roughly 157 million people, accounts for 78.2% of the Mercosur population, and therefore the resulting gravity center is located well within the borders of that country. Argentina's share in total Mercosur population is 17.5%, which added to the Brazilian share in total population gives a very significant 95.7% for the two major partners within Mercosur. Paraguay and Uruguay's share of total Mercosur population are 2.6% and 1.6%, respectively. The results are shown in Table 3. Given that

Argentina and Brazil are the major partners within Mercosur, the following considerations arise:

We have not been able to compute the Mercosur gravity center using the Gross National Product of each country. This is due to our lack of reliable regional data which should be used to calculate each of the member countries' gravity centers. It is to be expected, however, that the influence of Brazil will be, once again, extremely significant and stems from the fact that this country accounted for 69.69% of total Mercosur output in 1997, followed by Argentina with 27.65%, Paraguay and Uruguay trailing far behind with 0.87% and 1.70%, respectively.

As regards the whole territory of Mercosur, we can say that there did not exist a common Argentinean- Brazilian economic gravity center before the nineties. During the 80´s and 90´s the Argentine economy moved, after ninety years, again towards a more open trade regime. But the geographical structure of direction of exports is rather different from that prevailing at the beginning of the century. Empirical evidence also points to a view that the new pattern has been influenced by the constitution of Mercosur in Asunción on March 26, 1991. For example, in 1989 Argentine exports to Mercosur and Nafta countries amounted to 1428 and 1387 million dollars, respectively. In 1996 the equivalent figures were 7925 and 2327 million dollars. That is to say that in a period of 8 years whereas exports to Mercosur grew by 455%, those going to Nafta grew by a mere 68%.

A clear picture appears that a new market is in the making. It is also true that the degree of openness of the Argentine economy is about 9%, an almost constant fraction that did not change much despite the liberalization taking place during the nineties. One third of this are exports to Brazil. Again a regional perspective provides a richer picture. In Section 5 it is shown that there are provinces with a substantially higher concentration of activities with the Brazilian market. As a consequence, they are considerably more vulnerable to adverse evolutions in economic activity taking place in the partners.

The Brazilian population GC is located near the Bambuí - Arcos area, two towns in the SW of the State of Minas Gerais.

The Mercosur GC is driven, given the weight of Argentina, towards the area of Barretos, on the North East of the State of Sao Paulo (about 400 km from the city of Sao Paulo). Economic integration that dilutes the frontier between the partner countries, would "displace" the Brazilian gravity center by only 250 km in the SW direction in relation to the own Brazilian gravity center.

By way of contrast, please notice that the own Argentine GC was near the city of Rosario. It is therefore the case that the Mercosur GC is located at 1700 km towards the NE (and far beyond the national frontiers).

All this suggests that optimal locations are likely to be altered. In this case, regional economies in Argentina may be very much affected. It is rather difficult to make precise long run predictions, but we can see that Catamarca, for example, was at a 700 km straight-line distance from the Argentine GC, before integration. Now, after integration, it is about 2000 km straight-line distance from the newly created area's GC, GCM, namely three times farther away from the operating GC. It is to be expected that this new state of affairs will have a significant impact on that province's economy, perhaps potentially of a more harmful than beneficial nature vis-à-vis to that what one expects to happen to other Argentine regions like, for example, Buenos Aires.

5. *Other indicators of spatial economic structure.*

Regional specialization and concentration. Regional effects of the Brazilian devaluation on Argentina.

For the empirical calculations GDP data for Argentina in 1994 were used. This particular year was chosen because it reflects the situation prevailing in the country before the Mexican devaluation of December 1994, a time that may be regarded on a priori grounds as a candidate for a structural break to have occurred. It is a pity, however, that so far we have not been able to obtain more recent data to either confirm or reject this initial hypothesis. We should point out that, in our view, this kind of regional data are not highly reliable. Anyhow, there are no other statistical sources that we could find.

Regional Concentration

Using the data sources referred to above, we calculated measures of concentration taking into account what percentage of a given sector national production is attributable to each province. This calculation was carried out for each of the Great Division sectors, as follows: 1. Agriculture; 2. Mining; 3. Manufacturing; 4. Electricity, gas, and water; 5. Construction; 6. Commerce; 7. Transportation; 8. Financial Services; and 9. Services.[8]

One important result is that there exists a high degree of concentration in almost all great divisions. The greatest concentration area for most sectors is made up of the city of Buenos Aires, the province of Buenos Aires, as well as by two neighbouring provinces, namely Santa Fe and Córdoba. The only exception is the great division Mining for which the Patagonian provinces, because of its weight in the oil production sector, add to 69%.

[8] The full results we obtained are available from the authors. We highlight here only the most striking features.

GD1- Agriculture. Province of Buenos Aires: 43% (+ Córdoba + Santa Fe: 65%).

GD2- Mining. Neuquén 29% (+ Chubut + Santa Cruz: 69%).

GD3- Manufacturing. Province of Buenos Aires + City of Buenos Aires: 67% (+ Córdoba + Santa Fe: 81%; +San Luis: 85%).

GD4- Electricity, gas, and water. Province of Buenos Aires + City of Buenos Aires: 66% (+ Córdoba + Santa Fe: 78%)

GD5- Construction. Province of Buenos Aires + City of Buenos Aires: 51% (+ Córdoba + Santa Fe: 64%)

GD6- Commerce. Province of Buenos Aires + City of Buenos Aires: 60% (+ Córdoba + Santa Fe: 79%)

GD7- Transportation. Province of Buenos Aires + City of Buenos Aires: 67% (+ Córdoba + Santa Fe: 81%)

GD8- Financial Services. Province of Buenos Aires + City of Buenos Aires: 71% (+ Córdoba + Santa Fe: 87%)

GD9- Services. Province of Buenos Aires + City of Buenos Aires: 56% (+ Córdoba + Santa Fe: 71%)

Analyzing the Gross Geographic Product, we find that the city of Buenos Aires together with the province of Buenos Aires sum up 61%; adding to these Santa Fe (8%) and Córdoba (7.6%), we find a concentration of 76.6% in the three more important provinces (it reaches 80% if Mendoza is included).

Of course we know that the secondary and tertiary sectors in all the divisions have a concentration of more than 50% in the Federal Capital and the Province of Buenos Aires (71% in financial services). Since the primary production uses land intensively such a concentration is not possible. In any way, the province of Buenos Aires concentrates 43% of agriculture (the first position) and 2,5% of mining (the seventh position) followed by the non-Patagonian provinces.

Regional specialization in Argentina.

Following Hallet, 2000, a specialization index was calculated using the formula[9]:

$$S_i = \frac{1}{2}\sum_{k=1}^{K}\left|y_i^k - \bar{y}^k\right|$$

[9] Krugman (1992) uses a similar measure.

where S_i stands for the specialization index for region (province) i, y_i^k stands for the sectoral share of industry k in region i, and, finally, $\bar{y}^k$ represents industry's k national average.

It should be borne in mind that i = 1 to 24, and K= 9, that is there are 23 provinces in Argentina plus the Capital Federal and we only have GDP data referring to the so called Great Divisions.

It may be seen in the formula above that the index takes on a value of zero whenever a region's output composition is identical to that of the country as a whole. In the light of this line of reasoning this implies that a region having a very large value for the index, has an industry mix so dissimilar to the national average, so as to make the region much more likely to be differentially vulnerable to shocks affecting the economy.

On the basis of these indicators, together with the numbers in Table 4 that reflect the degree of specialization (provinces of Buenos Aires 0.13; Santa Fe 0.12 and Córdoba 0.085), we can put forward a few ideas at the level of hypothesis.

To begin with, the less diversified areas are more likely to be more vulnerable to idiosyncratic shocks. Going one step further, we might point out that the most specialized provinces, like Neuquén or Santa Cruz, bear the higher risk, since an idiosyncratic shock on their production have less possibility for factor reallocation in the spatial area. One would expect Buenos Aires, Córdoba, and Santa Fe to be less fragile than Santa Cruz, La Pampa, Formosa, and Neuquén, all of which have a specialization index in excess of 0.35.

It must be said that this general argument is not a conclusive indicator of local sensitivity to structural shocks. Note that while unemployment figures are collected by Index in urban centers, the production data are reported at the provincial level. Since the provincial capitals have a large weight, an association can be made (tentatively) of both kind of data. In our previous research on regional and employment disparities (Díaz Cafferata and Figueras 1999; Arrufat, Díaz Cafferata and Figueras, 1999), we have found that the agglomerates most heavily affected in the second half of the nineties were located in the less specialized provinces. A possible explanation is that we are talking about the agglomerates in which the import substitution process had enabled manufacturing sectors to grow, even with a low level of international competitiveness.

More precise conclusions would require: a) to examine more recent data in order to identify the characteristics of regional restructuring; b) further disaggregation of data on sectoral economic activities; c) to identify the loss of employment at the level of great division on each region (recognizing that it is very unlikely that statistical data will be available in the near future).

Clustering

Following Hallet, 2000, we calculated an index of clustering for sector k according to the following formula:

$$C^k = \frac{\sum_i \sum_j \frac{y_i^k \cdot y_j^k}{\delta_{ij}}}{\sum_i \sum_j \frac{y_i \cdot y_j}{\delta_{ij}}}$$

where k indexes sector I, and j indexes province (region), y_i^k stands for the share of sector k in total output of region i, y_i denotes the share of region i in output for the country as a whole, and finally, δ_{ij} measures the distance in kilometers between the provincial administrative capital cities of regions i and j. In the formula above, one does not of course use i = j because δ_{ii} is equal to zero.

The clustering index is based on the gravity model by adding up the distance-weighted production of all pairs of regions. It thus measures the degree of "economic cohesion" or agglomeration potential.

From the formula above it is straightforward to realize that other things being equal, the closer the regions are to one another the greater the value of the coefficient. On the contrary, the more widespread production is across the country, the smaller the value of the clustering index for that sector. In Table 5 we report the calculated values of the clustering index for each of the sector using data for 1994.

The most remarkable features of this table are the following. First, the mining sector has an index of only 0.217. Second, financial services, on the other hand has an index of 1.225.

6. *Regional effects of the Brazilian devaluation of January 1999*

One of the main problems which the economic policy in Argentina must address is that of the impact of the evolution of the Brazilian economy may have on the provinces. An interesting case to analyze is given by the Brazilian devaluation which took place in January 1999.

A recent paper by the Dirección Nacional de Políticas Económicas Regionales[10] contains an assessment of the likely impact of the devaluation. The approach is basically the following. That paper only takes into account the main export products which the Argentine provinces sell to Brazil, which account for 85% of total exports to this country. For each province, a calculation was made of: a) the likely sectoral loss stemming from drop in direct sales; b) the expected risk level. This is a sectoral indicator which measures the likely drop in national exports to Brazil.

Then an Index of Provincial Impact was calculated. This index is a ratio of the exports loss to provincial geographical product of tradable goods. In their tabulations they consider the 5 intervals ranging from the "very low" impact (index less than 5) to "very high" (index greater than 25). A remarkable feature is that the degree of vulnerability to the Brazilian devaluation does not depend on: a) which region a particular province belongs in; b) the level of provincial development; c) the geographical proximity to Brazil.

On the basis of this index, the three provinces which appeared to be more vulnerable are Córdoba, Buenos Aires, and Chaco, in that order.

Key features for the province of Córdoba are: its degree of openness, defined as the ratio of exports to gross geographical product, is 10%, a full percentage point above the national average. Besides this, even though the ratio of exports going to Brazil over total exports is roughly similar to the national average, a significant proportion of them is concentrated in the car making industry, which has a high sectoral risk.

With regard to Buenos Aires, the following points are worthy of notice. Its degree of openness to foreign trade is as high as 11%, that is 20% higher than the national average. Its share of Brazil-bound exports to total exports is also higher than the national average. It is also the case that a significant share of its exports are concentrated in the car making industry. Other important sectors include wheat, plastic products, textiles, fishing, rubber tires, onions, and dairy products.

The province of Chaco, in turn, has a degree of openness of nearly 8%, which is slightly lower than the national average. Its main crop is cotton which accounts for over 60% of the total area devoted to agriculture. Brazil is the destination of 65% of total exports, of which cotton makes up 92%.

So far we have just summarized the analysis carried out by the Secretaría de Programación Regional. It is not possible to fully trace the line of reasoning used in that paper because the procedure is not spelled out in detail. For example, the definition and quantification of risk used by the authors of that paper is not explicitly discussed. To get a better understanding of this topic, we present a very simple table in which we report the degree of external openness

[10] Argentina. Dirección Nacional de Políticas Económicas Regionales, 2000.

(XT / GGP), the amount of total exports to Brazil as a percentage of total exports (XBRAZIL / XT), and the product of these two ratios, which gives us the ratio of total sales to Brazil as a proportion of GGP. To aid a better understanding we also include the main export product which is likely to experience a "very high risk" of being affected by the Brazilian devaluation, according to the Secretaría de Programación Regional.

Our results imply that the ratio of total sales to Brazil to GGP is not very high, probably with the exception of Santa Cruz with 14%. Even though we do not know the values of the appropriate multipliers in each one of the regions, the total impacts do not appear to be very big. For example, if we take the case of Córdoba, even assuming that the exports of the car making industry dropped by 70%, a mere drop in 1.6% is to be expected at the level of the provincial GGP. This figure comes out of the following exercise: a 70% drop in the exports of the car making industry, multiplied by 78% (the share of the car making sector in Córdoba exports to Brazil), times 3%, which is the ratio of total exports from Córdoba to Brazil to the GGP of Córdoba.

7. *Synthesis and concluding remarks. Stylized facts: synthesis of statistical results on the spatial structure of Argentina.*

Unfortunately, the short time period that has elapsed since the trade policy changes were enacted (less than a decade for the Mercosur, a somewhat longer period for the progressive opening of the economy) does not provide an adequate perspective for a clear understanding of the economic forces at work. There are however a few things that can be said.

On the one hand, there is a high degree of inertia, as shown by the minor displacement of the national EGC. On the other hand, there are substantial changes across the Argentine territory which do not alter the national EGC because the regional economies have a small relative weight; but the understanding and political decision on how to manage these changes are nonetheless a central piece of a regional policy strategy. Stylized facts of spatial structure emerge as a synthesis of the calculations performed in the paper. They offer us an understanding of the forces that are likely to operate on economic location patterns in Argentina and the Mercosur in the next years, as a response to a progressive removal of barriers to the movements of goods and factors of production. It would be necessary to follow the spatial structure indicators of the Argentine economy through time, in order to more fully understand the dynamic response to the new economic conditions. For the time being, we only have the purely static approach we have been able to adopt in the present paper which shows a very high degree of concentration along the Rosario – Buenos Aires corridor. Obviously, the economic structure appears to be mature enough so as to take a long time to be altered by current events, and therefore, to be amenable to be measured. In the light of this, we offer now a conjecture on the future likely impacts brought about by economic integration within Mercosur. Will this process lead to more concentration? Given the current data limitations we have calculated the **Mercosur gravity center (MGC)** and in our view, it is very likely that new investments will favor the Sao Paulo area, which will obviously bring about further changes in the location of the gravity center. Historically, in the context of international economic relations with trade partners in USA, and Europe, the geographical distribution of economic activity in Argentina was dominated by location forces near the operating border (the port of Buenos Aires). During two centuries the center of the domestic market became gradually concentrated along the Rosario – Buenos Aires corridor. As a consequence of this, the closing of the economy brought about during the import substitution period did not change the Argentine gravity center, since domestic industries were already located near the main consumption center. In Argentina the consolidation of the prominent relative size of the center (Greater Buenos Aires, or more broadly the Rosario – Buenos Aires corridor) during the import substitution period, makes it difficult that new location stimulus in the periphery (the interior provinces), originating in trade liberalization and fresh trade channels in the Latin American, be strong enough so as to generate a "spatial structural transformation" with a significant displacement of the center in the next decades in the Argentine territory. From a different perspective, new investment in activities that serve the Mercosur market are likely to receive a differential stimulus to locate closer to the new **"operating" common gravity center** of the integrated bloc (the new economic space of the Mercosur economy), near Sao Paulo. Several questions emerge with a sense of urgency. What does all this say about the future growth of the Argentine economy? Do we face a somber prospect? Are regional income differential going to increase? Which new activities might substitute for those that are driven towards the Brazilian territory and may be favored by the present trade regime? A final word on institutions is in order. New regions are being formed in Argentina as a response to the economic challenge of the internationalization of the economy. As we have discussed elsewhere (Arrufat, Díaz Cafferata y Figueras, 1999a; Díaz Cafferata y Figueras, 1999) a word of caution is in order, since it is not clear at all that this organization drives to efficient allocation of resources or improves regional economic policy. On the other side, there are regions in competition in the wide space of Mercosur; but there are not clear multinational rules of the game, situation that ask for a solution: either a multinational regional policy will be required to arbitrate the regional conflicts between regions in different countries, or at least a consensus multinational framework for regional policies will have to be found. The response to all these questions is critical to assess the perspective of survival of the Mercosur society.

References

Argentina. Dirección Nacional de Programación Económica DNPE, 2000. "Impacto Provincial de la crisis Brasileña".

Armstrong Harvey and Jim Taylor, 1999. The Economics of Regional Policy. Edward Elgar Publishing Limited, Cornwall.

Armstrong Harvey and Jim Taylor, 1993. Regional Economics and Policy. Harvester, Comwall. Wheatoheaf. New York.

Arrufat JL, AM Díaz Cafferata and AJ Figueras, 1998. "Regional unemployment time series. Argentina & Germany in the ´80 and ´90´s ". IIIrd Arnoldshain Seminar. U. Sao Paulo. October.

Arrufat JL, AM Díaz Cafferata and AJ Figueras, 1999a. " Apertura, integración y tendencias regionales de la desocupación en Argentina". Seminario Integración Económica y Convergencia. Universidad de Alcalá y Cátedra Banco de Santander Central Hispano. Mayo. Forthcoming.

Blomström M. and A. Kokko; 1997. "Regional integration and Foreign Direct Investment". Policy Research Working Paper. N° 1750. The Word Bank, April.

Boisier, Sergio, 1996. " Modernidad y Territorio". Ilpes. Santiago de Chile.

Boisier, Sergio, 1999. Teorías y metáforas sobre desarrollo territorial. Cepal. Santiago de Chile.

Cuadrado Roura, J.R.; 1998. "Divergencia versus convergencia de las disparidades regionales en España". *Eure, Vol. XXiV, N°72, pp.5-31. Santiago de Chile.*

Cuadrado Roura, J.R.; 1998. "Integracao economica e regionalismo competitivo: a experiencia iberica no contexto da Uniao Europeia". En **Debates: Competitividad Internacional e desenvolvimmento das Regioes.** *Konrad Adenauer Stiftung.*

Cuadrado Roura, J.R. y T. Mancha Navarro; 1999. "Política regional y de cohesión". En Economía de la Unión Europea, tercera edición, Civitas Ediciones,.

Díaz Cafferata, Alberto, 1997. "Globalization and the international experience on regional unemployment: implications for federal administration policies". **XXX Jornadas de Finanzas Públicas**. Universidad Nacional de Córdoba.

Díaz Cafferata and Figueras, 1999. La desocupación en Argentina. Una visión regional. Edición Centro de Estudios Científicos y Técnicos (Cecyt). FACPCE. Buenos Aires.

Figueras, Alberto J., 1996. "El rol del Economista en el Mercosur". Conferencia el XVI Simposio dos Conselhos de Economía Do Brasil, Gramado (Rio Grande), Publicado en La Gaceta, CPCE de Córdoba # 51, Octubre.

Funke, M. and H. Strulik; 1999. "Regional growth in West Germany: convergence or divergence? **Economic Modelling**. Vol. 16, N° 4, pp.489-502.

Haddad, E. and C. Azzoni, 1999. "Trade Liberalization and Location: Geographical Shifts in the Brazilian Economic Structure". Seminario Integración Económica y Convergencia. Universidad de Alcalá y Cátedra Banco de Santander Central Hispano. Mayo. Forthcoming.

Hagood, M. J.; 1943. "Statistical Methods for Delineation of Region Applied to Data on Agriculture an Population". **Social Forces**. Vol. 21.

Hallet, Martin, 2000. "Regional Specialization and concentration in the EU". **European Commission Economic Papers**. N 141. March.

Krugman, Paul, 1992. Geography and trade.

LeSage, J., 1999. Spatial Econometrics. Department of Economics, University of Toledo. http://www.rri.wvu.edu/WebBook/LeSage/wbook.pdf.

Mancha Navarro, Tomás, 2000. "Convergencia y Heterogeneidad regional: un análisis de la experiencia europea". I Congreso de Economía de la facultad de CC.EE. Universidad de Málaga.

Martin, R.; 1999. "The New "Geographical Turn" in economics: some critical reflections". **Cambridge Journal of Economics**. Vol. 23, pp. 65-91.

Porto, Guido, 1996. "Las economías regionales en la Argentina". GEL, Bs. As.

Ponce, Carlos, 1999. *"Cambio estructural y desempleo"*. En **El futuro del empleo.** Fundación de Empresas, Córdoba.

Table 1

Argentina. Population-based gravity centers. 1895-1991. Census years.

City*	Province	Population 1895		Population 1914		Population 1947		Population 1960	
		hab.	%	hab.	%	hab.	%	hab.	%
Buenos Aires	Cap. Federal	663854	16.05	1575814	19.98	2981043	18.76	2966634	14.83
La Plata	Buenos Aires**	921168	22.28	2066948	26.21	4273874	26.89	6766108	33.81
Córdoba	Córdoba	531223	12.85	735472	9.33	1497987	9.42	1753840	8.76
Mendoza	Mendoza	116136	2.81	277535	3.52	588231	3.70	824036	4.12
Santa Fe	Santa Fe	397188	9.61	899640	11.41	1702975	10.71	1884918	9.42
S.M. de Tucumán	Tucumán	215742	5.22	332933	4.22	593371	3.73	773972	3.87
Total Argentina		4134911	100.00	7885237	100.00	15893827	100.00	20010539	100.00
Gravity centre	Latitude	31.86		32.46		32.48		32.61	
	Longitude	61.35		60.89		60.80		60.70	

City*	Province	Population 1970		Population 1980		Population 1991	
		hab.	%	hab.	%	hab.	%
Buenos Aires	Cap. Federal	2972453	12.72	2922829	10.46	2965403	9.09
La Plata	Buenos Aires**	8774529	37.56	10865408	38.88	12594974	38.62
Córdoba	Córdoba	2060065	8.82	2407754	8.62	2766683	8.48
Mendoza	Mendoza	973075	4.16	1196228	4.28	1412481	4.33
Santa Fe	Santa Fe	2135583	9.14	2465546	8.82	2798422	8.58
S.M. de Tucumán	Tucumán	765962	3.28	972655	3.48	1142105	3.50
Total Argentina		23364431	100.00	27947446	100.00	32615528	100.00
Gravity centre	Latitude	32.77		32.78		32.78	
	Longitude	60.63		60.70		60.79	

Source: Own Calculations based on Censo Nacional del Población y Vivienda.
* Coordinates used as the provincial gravity centre.
** Does not include Capital Federal.

Table 2

Argentina. Alternative calculations of gravity centers. 1895-1991. Census years.

Population	Coordinates	1895	1914	1947	1960	1970	1980	1991	1992	1993	1994	1995
Population, all provinces (without Capital Federal)	Latitude	31.86	32.46	32.48	32.61	32.77	32.78	32.78				
	Longitude	61.35	60.89	60.80	60.70	60.63	60.70	60.79				
Population, interior provinces: Without Buenos Aires (city and province)	Latitude	30.09	30.54	30.60	30.57	30.74	30.80	30.91				
	Longitude	63.33	63.21	63.02	63.15	63.20	63.26	63.29				
Population, small interior provinces: Without Buenos Aires (city and province), Córdoba and Santa Fe.	Latitude	29.29	29.930	30.07	30.07	30.31	30.43	30.63				
	Longitude	63.68	63.79	63.41	63.56	63.64	63.69	63.69				
Energy consumption	Latitude							34.46	34.36	34.37	34.33	34.33
	Longitude							61.07	61.00	61.00	60.95	60.90
Gross Geographical Product	Latitude				33.47	33.58	33.83	33.88			33.88	
	Longitude				60.24	60.17	60.13	60.32			60.30	

Source: Own calculations based on (i) Population, the same as Table 1; (ii) Energy, Secretaría de Energía; (iii) Gross Geographical product, Consejo Federal de Inversiones.

Table 3
Gravity Centre of MERCOSUR

Country	Population in 1996	% Pop in 1996
Argentina	35219612	17.5 %
Brazil	157070163	78.2 %
Paraguay	5291020	2.6 %
Uruguay	3163766	1.6 %
Total	200744561	100.0 %
Gravity Centre	Latitude	20.55
	Longitude	48.16

Source: Own calculations based on individual countries' gravity centers. Population data refer to 1996, except for Paraguay (1998). The latitude – longitude figures reported in the table are those of the gravity center.

Table 4
Specialization index of Argentinean regions

Province	Specialisation Index
Neuquén	0.45
La Pampa	0.45
Formosa	0.37
Santa Cruz	0.36
Tierra del Fuego	0.36
San Luis	0.36
Chubut	0.34
Corrientes	0.29
Sgo del Estero	0.27
Entre Ríos	0.27
Jujuy	0.26
Río Negro	0.24
Tucumán	0.21
Chaco	0.21
C. de Buenos Aires	0.21
La Rioja	0.18
Catamarca	0.17
Misiones	0.16

Province	Specialisation Index
Salta	0.16
Buenos Aires	0.13
Mendoza	0.13
Santa Fe	0.12
San Juan	0.11
Córdoba	0.09

Source: Author's calculations based on Ministerio del Interior data.

Table 5

Sector	Clustering Index
Agriculture	0.401
Mining	0.217
Manufacturing	0.937
Electricity, gas, and water	0.782
Construction	0.603
Commerce	1.022
Transport	1.116
Financial Services	1.225
Services	0.922
Total	1.000

Source: Own calculations based on Provincial Gross Geographical Product. The distances δ_{ij} between provincial administrative capital cities were taken from http://www.vialidad.gov.ar.[1]

[1] For some strange reason the city of La Plata, capital of the Province of Buenos Aires had not been included in the tabulations. Given the fact that the distance between Buenos Aires and La Plata is 70 Km, we proceeded to compute the distance between any capital and La Plata as the appropriate distance to Buenos Aires plus 70 Km.

Figure 1

A general scheme of modern regional economic restructuring: causes and evidence

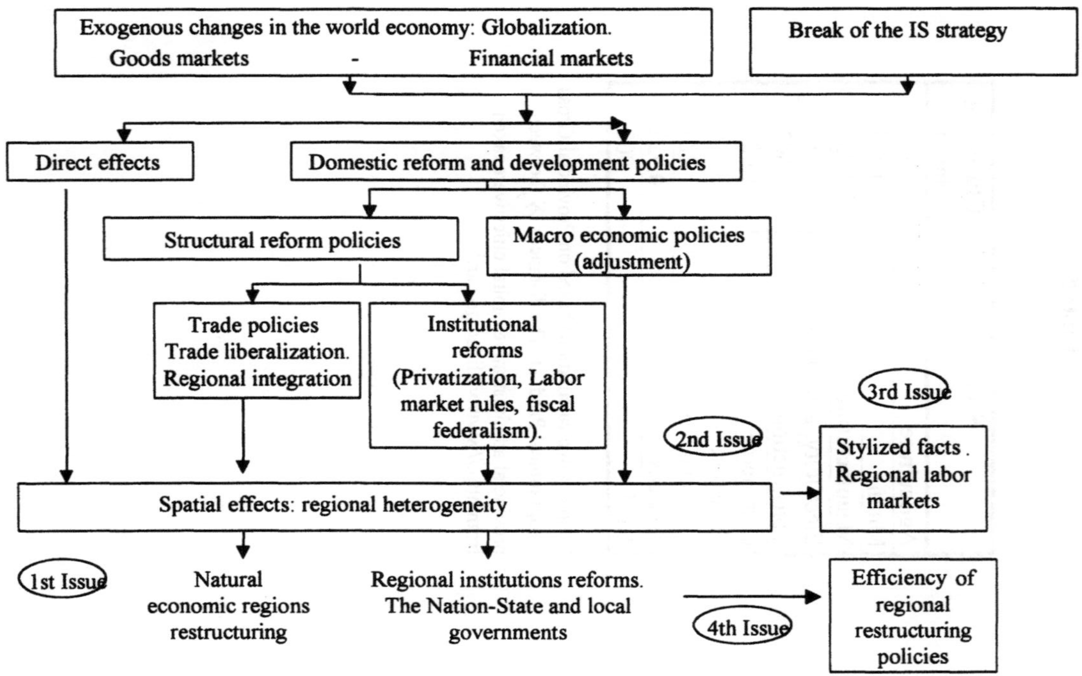

Figure 2
Focusing on international trade and regional restructuring

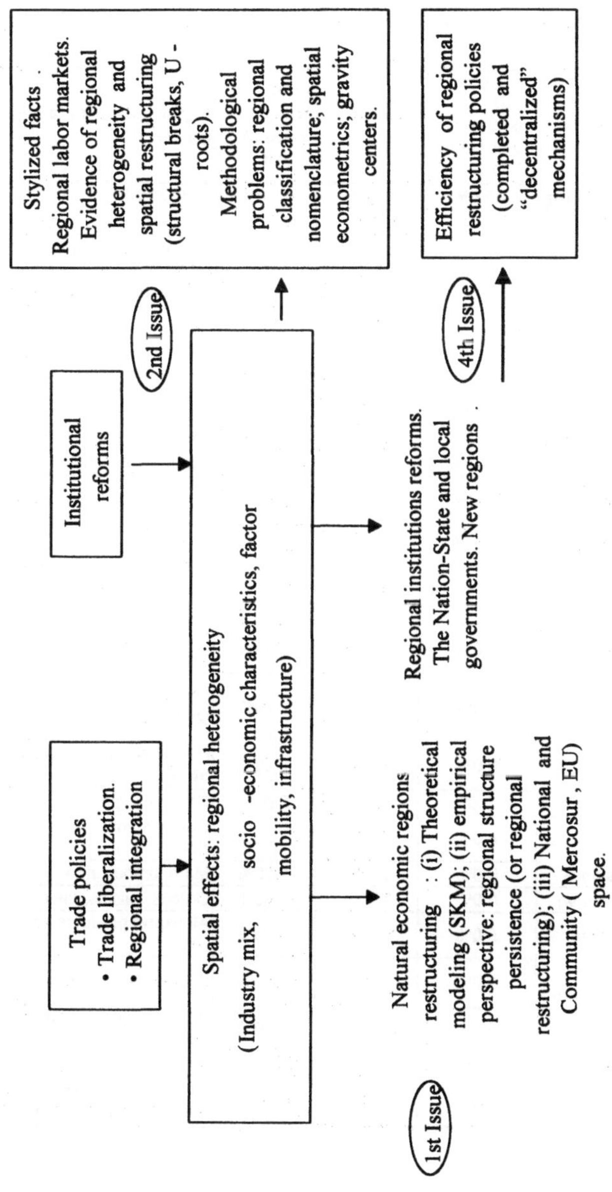

Impacts of the Brazilian devaluation of January 1999. Provincial level

Province	**Foreign trade openness coefficient (FTOC)**	**Sales to Brazil**	**FTOC times Sales to Brazil**	**Export products facing greater risk**	**Main export product to Brazil**
Santa Cruz	35.0%	40.0%	14.0%	Fillet of fish	Oil (98%)
Chaco	8.0%	65.0%	5.2%	Cotton spinning and weaving	Cotton fibre (92%)
Buenos Aires	11.0%	40.0%	4.4%	Car-making, synthetic textiles, rubber products, plastic materials, onions and **fish**.	Car-making (54.5%), wheat (12.6%)
Tierra del Fuego	7.0%	60.0%	4.2%	Machinery and electric appliances	Oil(75%), machinery (21.0%)
La Rioja	10.0%	40.0%	4.0%	Garlic and **olives**	Olives(71%)
Chubut	25.0%	16.0%	4.00%	**Fish**	Fish (84%)
Entre Ríos	8.0%	40.0%	3.20%	**Rice**	Rice (60%)
Córdoba	10.0%	30.0%	3.00%	Car-making (70%)	Car-making (78%)
Río Negro	10.0%	30.0%	3.00%	Onions, plums and **apples**	Pears (51%), apples (34%)
Neuquén	12.0%	25.0%	3.00%	Apples	Oil (87%)
San Luis	8.5%	35.0%	2.98%	Mayonnaise, plastic materials, electric machinery, synthetic textiles	Paper and cardboard (38%)
Salta	7.0%	40.0%	2.80%	Cotton fibre, beans (all of them with average risk)	Beans (69%)
Tucumán	9.0%	30.0%	2.70%	Cotton spinning and weaving, shoes, **car-making**	Car-making (45%), shoes (40%)
Mendoza	8.0%	30.0%	2.40%	Plums, onions, apples and **olives**	Garlic (24%), olives (18%)
Santa Fe	20.0%	10.0%	2.00%	Car-making and **rice**	Car-making (22%)
Corrientes	4.0%	50.0%	2.00%	Cotton spinning and weaving, **rice**	Rice (82%)
Misiones	6.0%	30.0%	1.80%	Mate, timber, **rice**	Paper pulp (65%)
San Juan	5.0%	30.0%	1.50%	Onions, raisins, olives	Insecticides (38%)
La Pampa	5.0%	20.0%	1.00%	All export products have **low risk**	Wheat (40%)
Santiago del Estero	6.0%	15.0%	0.90%	Cotton (average risk)	Cotton (50%)
Jujuy	5.0%	10.0%	0.50%	Beans, steel bars (average risk)	Beans (28%)
Formosa	3.0%	10.0%	0.30%	Cotton spinning and weaving	Cotton fibre (50%)
Catamarca	6.0%	5.0%	0.30%	**All export products have either low or very low risk**	-

REGIONAL UNEMPLOYMENT IN GERMANY: HIGH RATES AND PERSISTENCE OF DIFFERENCES

Roland Eisen[1],
Dimitrios Gotsis, André Kolodziejak

I. Introduction

Two of the key concerns in recent economic research and political debates have been and still are the high rates and persistence of unemployment following some initial adverse shocks, such as the increase in oil prices in 1973 and again in 1979, the counter-inflationary policies of the 1980s and the 1990s. Nevertheless, different countries have reacted in different ways and have shown different capabilities to absorb these shocks (see Table 1 and Figure 1[2]).

In recent economic research some major factors have been identified as very important in determining the *height* and *persistence* over time in *national* unemployment rates: real wage resistance, fluctuations in aggregate demand, mismatch between demand for and supply of labor, degree of unionization, the income replacement rate of unemployment insurance, cumulative effects of long-term unemployment on skill levels, and capital stock constraints.

However, the overall unemployment figures hide substantial *regional disparities*: Disparities at the regional level within one country are often wider than those at the national levels between the countries. According to Table 1, unemployment rates range e. g. from 3.1 to 11.9 on the national level (in 1995) or from 4.1 to 12.3 (in 1998), while the range is from 5.0 to 13.5 for Germany or even from 5.7 to 22.2 for Italy (1995) on the regional level (see Table 2). The figures for 1997 (shown in Figure 2) show a very similar picture: While the average unemployment rate varies between 3% (for Luxemburg) and 21% for Spain, the variation of the minimum and the maximum rate of unemployment is between 5% and 20% for Germany or between 4% and 21% for Italy.

Furthermore, while regional disparities shrank or have shown a slight cyclical pattern until the second half of the 1980s, this pattern changed in the second half of the eighties and especially in the 1990s (see OECD, 2000). In Germany, only part of this change is due to the large differences between the new and the old Bundesländer (see Figure 3 and Table 4 for Germany; see also Pench et al., 1999).

There are several reasons to focus on regions rather than on countries. First, as economic integration becomes a reality for European countries,

[1] Institute of Economics, Faculty of Economics and Business Administration, Johann Wolfgang Goethe-University, Frankfurt a. M., Germany, eisen@wiwi.uni-frankfurt.de

[2] All tables and figures are in the appendix.

economic and social disparities within Europe become more apparent, and, consequently, region-specific developments become more prominent. And - as remarked by Collier (1994, p. 145) - "the very forces which generate integration will widen those disparities, and hence set up processes which threaten the achievement of integration itself." The argument relies on the polarization effects of regional competitiveness after the protection of non-tariff barriers has been removed. And a good measure for regional disparities are regional unemployment rates, which give a clearer indication of welfare differences within and between regions than regional income disparities. Therefore, we will concentrate on the explanation of different levels of regional unemployment and their persistence, changes of the macroeconomic environment notwithstanding.

Second, region-specific or industry-specific shocks may initiate different adjustment mechanisms than nation-wide shocks. For instance, one would expect substantially more migration within countries or between neighboring regions than between nations.

Third, as elaborated already by Lipsey (1960), it is necessary to know not only the level of unemployment but also "*its distribution between the various markets of the economy*" (p. 19, emphasis in the original). In other words, the national labor market dynamics are a fairly arbitrary aggregation of very heterogeneous regional labor market dynamics. Therefore, analyzing regional labor market dynamics should provide more interesting results.

In this paper, we first draw attention to the macroeconomic features of unemployment in Germany via a small model and cross-sectional study. We try to identify the major factors responsible for the fluctuations over time in *national* unemployment rates. With these factors in mind, we then discuss factors that may be expected to influence *regional* or *spatial disparities* in the unemployment rate *within* any given national economy over time. Then, we investigate for Germany in how far the "unexplained differences" are due to industrial or sectoral variations. In the end we investigate to what extent year to year changes in unemployment have been common to all regions in Germany. The goal here is to identify the determinants of the *persistence* of spatial differences.

II. A Bird's Eye View of National Unemployment in Germany

The national unemployment rates (UR) for some OECD countries are shown in Figure 1 and Table 1. There are mainly two different approaches of analyzing unemployment. The first concentrates on long-term labor market equilibrium. Movements of unemployment over time are then considered as random variations around this long-term equilibrium rate, the "natural rate of unemployment" or NAIRU[3]. The second approach stresses the adjustment problems and states that the unemployment rate tends to "get struck" at whatever its current rate happens to be. Every unemployment rate can be a long-run rate and the effects of temporary labor market shocks persist.

Both approaches seem to be extremes or polar cases to explain unemployment dynamics, but nevertheless they both stress almost the same factors responsible for unemployment. E. g. to explain the picture shown by the national UR, the (long-run) equilibrium approach has to consider also changes in the supply side of the labor market, called "structural changes", to account for "changes in NAIRU": The nontransitory part of unemployment has risen because of "worsening structural factors" such as increasing trade union power, increases in replacement ratios of unemployment benefits, the wedge between (real) total labor cost to employers and (real) take-home pay for employees (due to taxes and social security contributions and the discrepancy between consumer and producer prices), and mismatch of unemployed workers to available jobs.

On the other hand, the "hysteresis approach" stresses more the factors responsible for the high degree of persistence in any national labor market, such as institutional and other features, e.g. the degree of centralization of its bargaining structure (see Calmfors/Driffill, 1988). In this light, a rigid distinction between these approaches is impossible, because the "bargaining structure" is evidently a "structural" factor, which affects both the long-run equilibrium level as well as the persistence of unemployment.

Table 3 shows some differences between Argentina, Brazil, Germany, Italy, USA and the United Kingdom in the institutional arrangements for bargaining and union coverage. Calmfors/Driffill (1988) e. g. have argued that countries with highly centralized bargaining systems or highly decentralized systems tend to have low unemployment rates while countries with a mixed system, such as the United Kingdom, experience relatively high unemployment rates. However, Soskice (1990) suggested that the degree of employer co-ordination may be more important in determining unemployment than the bargaining system. Furthermore, Table 3 shows the (income) replacement ratios of unemployment benefits and assistance, and their duration.

Given the importance of these "structural factors", they may account for the different levels of national UR. However, since the "structural factors" change only gradually and to a limited extent (see e. g. for Germany van der Willigen (1995) and Eisen (1997)), there remains the need to explain the high correlation over time in the time series data.

However, also the long-run implications of the "hysteresis approach" seem to be at variance with empirical facts: if unemployment were to depend on its

[3] Some authors prefer the notion of QERU for “quasi-equilibrium rate of unemployment” (see e.g. Lindbeck, 1992).

past value, the coefficient in the auto-regression estimates the degree of persistence. But, if this value is near unity (implying a unit root plus a random error), then the variance of unemployment would clearly be unbounded. This means, that unemployment would eventually hit 100 percent or zero with certainty (Henry/Snower, 1997b, p. 8).

Nevertheless, the large differences in *regional unemployment* shown in Tables 2 and 4 as well as in Figures 2 and 3 remain to be explained.

III. Regional Unemployment: Dispersion and Persistence[4]

III.1 Some Methodological Issues

In recent years various studies discussed different aspects of regional labor markets in Europe and the USA[5]. We follow this approach to get a better understanding of the factors responsible for the differences and persistence of unemployment, because national structural factors explain only part of the picture.

In the literature various methodologies are used to reveal different structural factors or dynamical features of regional labor markets. Blanchard/Katz (1992) construct first a simple model with full employment, so the development of relative wages and of employment is determined only by the interaction of labor demand and supply. (Technological) shocks are permanent and hence - for a given wage - the derived demand for labor follows a random walk with drift.

To account for unemployment, Blanchard/Katz (1992) add to their model two new characteristics: First, they assume that the relationship between unemployment and employment depends upon the wage rate, so that e.g. part of the initial response to an adverse shock in (labor) demand shows up as an increase in unemployment. Second, they assume that labor immigration depends negatively upon unemployment and positively upon the wage rate. As a first approximation, they suppose that migration between firms is independent of unemployment (given the wage rate). It results therefore that relative wage rates and unemployment are negatively related. I.e. a positive drift in the relative labor demand, which leads to a positive relative trend in employment, in turn leads to higher than average wages and to lower unemployment.

Although there is a trend in the development of (relative) employment, Blanchard/Katz (1992) do not believe in a deterministic trend, rather they assume a unit-root process. Nevertheless, they test for every state of the USA the following equation:

[4] We thank Cambridge Econometrics Ltd. for the data set.

[5] See e.g. Blanchard/Katz (1992), Decressin/Fatás (1995), Taylor/Bradley (1997) and Obstfeld/Peri (1998).

(1) $\Delta u_{i,t} = \alpha_{1i} + \alpha_{2i}(L)\Delta u_{i,t-1} + \alpha_{3i}u_{i,t-1} + \alpha_4 T + \eta_{i,t}$,

where $u_{i,t}$ is the logarithm of employment in state i in year t minus the logarithm of total employment in year t; T=time and $\eta_{i,t}$ is white noise. Simultaneously, four lags are allowed in $\alpha_{2i}(L)$ (inclusive of a time trend to allow for a deterministic trend under an alternative hypothesis).

The Augmented Dickey-Fuller test, which considers the t-statistic of α_{3i} (the coefficient of the lagged variable), is mixed: In all states the coefficient of the lagged level is negative, but only in three states the coefficient is significant at the 5 percent level. Hence, the authors postulate the "unit root" characteristic in relative employment. However, as Robert Hall (1992, pp. 62 sqq.) critically remarks, the "long-run" is very long, leading to a lower frequency of the state level compared to the national level. I.e. a regional cycle of approximately 5-years-frequency is "tilted over" the quicker national cycle. The explanation for this result is relatively simple: Labor supply in each region is perfectly elastic in the long-run. Every shift of labor demand on the regional level causes a movement along a horizontal labor supply curve. And labor supply increases, as long as there is a wage differential.

A further critic advanced by Eichengreen (1992, pp. 65 sqq.) points to the existence of hysteresis, i.e. "there are reasons why a one-time shock to labor demand might have permanent effects on the level of unemployment. Some of these arguments might be adopted to explain persistent differences across regions in the growth of employment" (p. 65).

However, to bring this picture to a clear front, one has to allow for different regional trends. This produces less persistence than restricting the trend in the unemployment rate to be the same for all regions, as was postulated in Obstfeld/Peri (1998).

Therefore, we follow here the procedure of Decressin/Fatás (1995) and start with an analysis of "common labor market disturbances", i.e. we identify e.g. whether the elasticity of regional unemployment changes with respect to economy wide unemployment changes equals unity or not.

III.2 Persistence of Regional Unemployment

As stated in Decressin/Fatás (1995, p. 1631) "the main purpose of this section is to evaluate the extent to which labor market disturbances" in Germany "are distributed symmetrically across regions". Furthermore, we want to isolate the region-specific evolution and analyze this in more detail.

Table 5 shows as a first step the correlation between national unemployment rates for 15 EU-countries with Germany: Normally the correlation is quite high, ranging from 0.98 for France and 0.89 for U.K. to 0.32 for Portugal (see column 3 in Table 5). The (unweighted) average of R^2 is 0.84, i.e. 84 percent of the movement of the unemployment rates on the national level are common to all EU-countries. Table 5 also clearly shows the power of the European integration process before and after 1970, and not only for unemployment, but also for GDP and factor prices.

In the next step we carried out an analysis for the German "Laender" with relation to the German (national) unemployment rate. The tested equation is of the following form:

$$(2) \quad \ln u_{ri} = \beta_{ri} \ln u_d + c_i + \varepsilon$$

where u_{ri} denotes the regional unemployment rate and u_d the German (national) unemployment rate. The results are as follows:

The overall picture with NUTS 1 (level of "Laender") is that 47% of the differences in regional unemployment can be explained by the German average unemployment rate (see Table 6). The differences between the "Laender" are visible: the relationship is weakest for the northern "Laender". Furthermore, the dispersion pattern shows a clear tendency measured by the coefficient of variation. For the first period (1983-89) the coefficient of variation is 0.34, in the second period (1991-1996) it is 0.29 (see Table 4).

For the regional level (we use the so-called NUTS2 - Classification in Regierungsbezirke) of Germany we get the following results (see Table 6): While the correlation seems to be less strict for the regional level than for the state level (Laender), the co-movement (or the movements which are common across regions) is still high, i.e. 47 percent of the year to year changes in regional unemployment are shared by all regions in Germany.

The pattern becomes clear, when we single out the four highest and lowest regional unemployment rates (see Figure 4): Even a cursory look at this figure reveals that the correlations between the regions represented by the upper lines and those represented by the lower lines are rather strong. To analyze this problem deeper, we looked at the unit-root tests for variable Amplitude 2 (i.e. the interval between the average unemployment rate of the four regions with initially the highest unemployment rates and those of the four lowest). The Augmented Dickey-Fuller regressions show that the null hypothesis of a unit root clearly cannot be rejected (see Table 7). This indicates that the variable Amplitude 2, is not changing systematically over time. Therefore, the dispersion of regional unemployment shows a high degree of persistence. This conclusion turns out to be independent from the exact way in which an amplitude of the interval or the dispersion is calculated.

Despite this fact, a substantial portion of the variance in regional unemployment changes cannot be explained. Therefore, the question still can be raised: which factors can explain the large differences in the levels of regional unemployment whose pattern seems to be highly persistent. The basic trends are clear (see Figure 5): If we compare the regional unemployment rates in 1984 and 1994, the regression line has a slope of 0.71 and the R^2 equals 0.65. We conclude from this: the differences in unemployment rates between regions are rather persistent. Those regions with a high (low) unemployment rate in 1984 continue to have high (low) unemployment rates in 1994.

Clearly, with substantial regional differences in industry structure, the dynamics of unemployment at the regional level will differ from those we can observe at a higher level. And as specified in equation (2), we allow for different cyclical sensitivities of the regional unemployment rates to changes in the aggregate rates. The next section, therefore, deals with structural factors behind this persistence of different levels of unemployment.

III.3 Dispersion of Regional Unemployment

In the analysis sofar we have seen that regional unemployment rates move to a large extent with the national unemployment rate. It has also been shown that co-movement of unemployment rates is quite high in the European Union. These correlations cannot explain the relative level of regional unemployment. What they do implicate however is, as has also been shown by comparing 1984 and 1994 regional unemployment levels, that the dispersion of regional unemployment is rather stable: The amplitude measuring the difference between the unemployment level of the four NUTS 2 regions with the highest and those with the lowest rates has a unit root. Therefore this section attempts to identify the determinants of the persistence of spatial disparities in the unemployment rate within Germany.

A particular and challenging problem in the analysis of structural determinants of relative regional unemployment rates for Germany is of course given by the specific effects of reunification. In principle, these effects should increase the degree of regional unemployment rates by structural factors. For former Eastern Germany however data are only available for about half a decade and simply are included as from 1991.

Turning to structural determinants of relative regional unemployment rates (variable UNEMPLOY) we have tested[6] the influence of (a) the per capita income level (INCOMPC) and (b) the distribution of employment among five sectors: Agriculture, forestry and fishing (RELAGRI), industrial production (RELINDUST), trade and transport (RELTRADE), commercial services (RELCOMSER) and non-commercial or state services (RELNCOMSE):

[6] Unlike Taylor and Bradley (1997) we do not use a one equation approach but rather a step-wise approach towards explaining regional unemployment levels.

$$(3) \quad UNEMPLOY = \alpha_0 + \alpha_1 INCOMEPC + \alpha_2 RELAGRI + \alpha_3 RELINDUST + \alpha_4 RELTRADE + \alpha_5 RELCOMSER + \alpha_6 RELNCOMSE + \varepsilon;$$

Table 8 contains the estimated correlation matrix of these variables. The numbers clearly indicate that the relative income level and the sectoral employment structure are capable to explain the dispersion of regional unemployment rates to a large extent.

Regions with a high relative per capita income level and relative high employment in the trade and commercial services sector tend to have low relative regional unemployment rates whereas regions with relatively high employment in agriculture, forestry and fishing as well as in non market services show high relative unemployment levels. The influence of the relative position of industrial production in regional employment is not determined, i.e. it is mixed depending to some extent on the kind of industry.

These findings stress the importance of the regional specialisation pattern in explaining the "residual" regional unemployment dispersion. It is therefore no surprise, that these results are stronger than those of Taylor/Bradley (1997).

A major drawback of the Taylor/Bradley analysis was that the results for different countries were far from pointing in the same direction. Following from our stepwise approach this outcome is very doubtful for reasons of logic given the high degree of national and international co-movements. Thus international comparison of the German persistence pattern can indeed be fruitful in terms of e.g. the effects of globalization on the level and persistence of unemployment.

However, our results need some further elaboration with respect to the causal relationship. We therefore tested - as Taylor/Bradley (1997) have done - (nominal)[7] unit labor cost (ULC). In contrast to Taylor/Bradley (1997, p. 235ff.) our results are weak. When we regressed the German UR over total compensation divided by detrended gross value added (GVA), the R^2 was 0.0247; when we took a lag in the UR, R^2 increased to 0.3803. Furthermore, on the NUTS-1 level the results range between R^2=0,0002 (for Nordrhein-Westfalen) and R^2=0.5604 (for Berlin), and the coefficient is sometimes even negative.

One reason maybe, that there is a difference between "living" and "working regions", therefore there is a lot of commutation between regions, a factor we could not control for. Furthermore, there is little variance in the distribution of (nominal) unit labor costs among Länder.

Given the phenomenon of globalization, the sluggish response of regional industry structure and employment patterns needs explanation. One reason put forward in the international debate about unemployment rates and persistence is

[7] We could not use real unit labor cost because it is impossible - at the moment - to get regional NUTS2 inflation rates.

the „real wage resistance“ of some countries, in particular Germany. However, most of the factors used in explaining this phenomenon rely on structural factors, such as wage bargaining, government regulation and social security systems (see e.g. Steiner/Boockmann/Peters, 2001). Since these factors are relevant for the *national* level, we still do not have an explanation for the great dispersion of regional UR.

Hence, to elaborate our problem further, we turned to the employment side: Maybe that the dynamics of labor markets are more strongly influenced by changes in employment than by changes in unemployment. Employment growth is a necessary condition for decreasing regional unemployment, it is, however, not a sufficient condition. Or formulated in a different way: A fast growing population needs more work places ("capital widening"), and while keeping unemployment constant or even increasing, employment can increase. Despite an increasing employment ratio, in a fast growing population, the UR can increase. While the correlation between employment ratio and UR for Germany is very high (-0.9), the figures for the Laender (NUTS 1) and for NUTS 2 are inconclusive (see table 9, column 1&2).

Therefore, in explaining regional unemployment we have to take into account not only changes in industrial composition of labor demand, but also changes in labor supply, see e.g. Wasmer (1997). Changes in labor supply can result not only from population growth or migration-induced population change, but also from adjustments in participation rates. Figure 6 shows the female employment ratios (FER) for German (old) Laender (1975-1996): While the average of FER is increasing from 0.37 to 0.43, the dispersion itself is shrinking from 0.25 to 0.06. Furthermore, the relationship between the (national) unemployment rate and FER is very high: almost half of the (variation of) national unemployment can be explained by the (variation of) FER (see the first figure in column 3 of table 9). This strong relationship "disappears" however on the regional level; here the results are very differentiated.

However, the FER is not an exogenous variable but reflects the changing industry structure. Therefore, we tested the co-movement of regional FER and relative employment in commercial services. This relationship is relatively strong (see Table 9, column 4) for the "old Laender", but weak or negative for the "new Laender". The co-movement of regional UR and regional FER is weak and "differentiated", and the co-movement of regional FER and regional RELCOMSER is even reversed for the "new Laender".

Both these results can be explained in the following way, taking into account the very different original positions in services and female employment: The great expansion of commercial services in the "new Laender" has not led to a higher FER - just the opposite. However, in the "new Laender" the FER was at the time of reunification very high (compared to the level in the "old Laender"), while the commercial services sector was very small. Hence, the rapid development in the commercial service sector in the "new Länder" has - in the first line - absorbed the male unemployment while "setting free" a large part of the female labor force[8].

IV. Summary

The aim of the research reported here was to find an answer to the following question: what can we learn while explaining national unemployment rate differences - in persistence and dispersion - for regional unemployment rate differences? Or to put it the other way round: what can we learn while explaining regional differences - in persistence and dispersion - in unemployment for the difference of national unemployment rates?

Hence, in the first step we analyzed unemployment and UR on the European level - as a proxy for an international comparison of the development of unemployment. It is our conviction that, despite large differences in the level of unemployment, the persistence of these differences should be explained, too. We found a strong relationship between the national UR. That means, external (real) shocks hit all of the chosen countries in almost the same manner. There is also a strong positive relationship between the year-to-year volatility of the UR and the trend rise in unemployment. This leads to the following conclusion: a temporary boost in unemployment caused by an adverse economic shock may in many cases contain elements which contribute to a rise in trend unemployment (as reported in Elmeskov/MacFarlan, 1993, p. 81). Or put otherwise: On the national level we find lasting effects of shocks due to hysteresis. However, we could explain only a small part of the national UR differences by this approach.

In the next step we therefore looked at the regional differences in unemployment rates in Germany: While part of the unemployment fluctuations can be explained by "Europe wide" shocks, hitting all countries in a similar fashion, the reaction of different countries must be analyzed. This is the now familiar research area of the "structuralist approach" (see e.g. Layard/Nickell/Jackman, 1991). However, there are various arguments in favor of going one step further down, namely on the regional level. And here, our result is that "nation-wide" shocks can also explain almost half of the regional unemployment variations, but only half. We therefore went one step further to analyze some structural factors we thought to be "responsible" for the remaining part of unemployment.

[8] Compare the results of the study by Kahrs, Lo, Dunn (1998).

The tests support this hypothesis: A large part of the remaining unemployment dispersion in regions can be explained by the following structural factors: the relative portions of commercial services and trade, non-commercial services, and agriculture in GDP.

Despite the normal prejudice, the (nominal) unit labor costs explain only a small part of unemployment. Therefore, we investigated the following hypothesis: It is possible that variations on the demand side are not so important as variations on the supply side. And one factor which is clearly visible, is the change in the female labor market participation. Taking the female employment ratio (FER) into account gives the following strong results:

First, on the national level almost half of the (variation of) national unemployment is due to the (variation of) FER. Second, however, on the regional level the results are "inconclusive": For the old Laender the relationship between relative employment in the commercial services and FER is positive and relatively strong while for the new Laender this relationship is negative! Furthermore, also the co-movement of regional FER and relative employment in commercial services is relatively strong for the "old Laender", but it is reversed for the "new Laender". These results show that for strong conclusions the very distinct original positions in the relative importance of the service sector as well as the FER have to be taken into account. This is certainly also true for international comparisons.

References

Blanchard, Oliver and L. Katz (1992), Regional Evolutions, in: *Brookings Papers on Economic Activity 1*, 1-61.

Calmfors, L. and J. Driffill (1988), Bargaining Structure, Corporatism and Macroeconomic Performance, in: *Economic Policy* 6, 14-61.

Collier, Jane (1994), Regional Disparities, the Single Market, and European Monetary Union, in: J. Michie and J. Grieve-Smith (eds), *Unemployment in Europe*, London et al. (Academic Press), 145-159.

Decressin, Jörg and Antonio Fatás (1995), Regional Labor Market Dynamics in Europe, in: *European Economic Review* 39, 1627-1655.

Eichengreen, Barry (1992), Comments to Blanchard/Katz, in: *Brookings Papers on Economic Activity 1*, 65-70.

Eisen, Roland (1997), Reformüberlegungen zur Arbeitslosenversicherung, in: R. Hauser (ed.), *Reform des Sozialstaats* I, SVSP 251/I, Berlin (Duncker & Humblot), 45-75.

Hall, Robert (1992), Comments to Blanchard/Katz, in: *Brookings Papers on Economic Activity 1*, 62-65.

Henry, S.G.B and Dennis J. Snower (eds) (1997a), *Economic Policies and Unemployment Dynamics in Europe*, Washington (International Monetary Fund).

Henry, S.G.B. and Dennis J. Snower (1997b), The Dynamics of European Unemployment, in: Henry/Snower (1997a), 1-38.

Kahrs, Katrin, Vivien Lo and Malcolm H. Dunn (1998), Woman-Labor Force in a Changing Economy, ms.

Layard, Richard, Stephen Nickell and Richard Jackman (1991), *Unemployment,* Oxford, University Press.

Lindbeck, Assar (1992), Macroeconomic Theory and the Labor Market, in: *European Economic Review* 36, 209-235.

Lipsey, Richard G. (1960), The Relation between Unemployment and the Rate of Change of Money Wage Rates in the United Kingdom (1862-1957): A Further Analysis, in: *Economica* 27, 1-31.

Nickell, S. (1997), Unemployment and Labor Market Rigidities: Europe versus North America, in: *Journal of Economic Perspectives* 11, No.3, 55-74

Obstfeld, Maurice and Giovanni Peri (1998), Regional Non-adjustment and Fiscal Policy, in: *Economic Policy* 26, 207-247.

OECD (1997), *Employment Outlook*, Paris.

OECD (1999), *Economic Outlook*, Paris.

OECD (2000), *Employment Outlook,* Paris.

Pench, Lucio R., Paolo Sestito and Elisabetta Frontini (1999), Some Unpleasant Arithmetics of Regional Unemployment in the EU. Are there any lessons for EMU?, *Economic Papers,* No. 134, European Commission Directorate General for Economic and Financial Affairs, April.

Soskice, David (1990), Wage Determination: The Changing Role of Institutions in Advanced Industrialized Countries, in: *Oxford Review of Economic Policy* 6, 36-61.

Steiner, Viktor, Bernhard Boockmann and Ralf-Henning Peters (2001), Social Security, Real Wage Resistance, and Employment in Sweden, the UK and West Germany, in: David F. Milleker (ed.), *Beschäftigungspolitik in Europa*, Bad Homburg (Frankfurter Institut – Stiftung für Marktwirtschaft und Politik), 89-101.

Taylor, Jim and Steve Bradley (1997), Unemployment in Europe: A Comparative Analysis of Regional Disparities in Germany, Italy and the United Kingdom, in: *Kyklos* 50, 221-245.

van der Willigen, Tessa (1995), Unemployment, Wages, and the Wage Structure, in: R. Corker et al. (eds), *United Germany: The First Five Years - Performance and Policy Issues*, IMF Occasional Paper No. 125, Washington/D.C., 21-40.

Wasmer, Etienne (1997), Can Labor Supply Explain the Rise in Unemployment and Inter-group Wage Inequality in the OECD? *IIES Seminar Paper* No. 629, Stockholm.

Table 1: Unemployment Rates in Major OECD Countries 1970-1998

	1970	1975	1980	1985	1990	1995	1998
Canada	5.6	6.9	7.5	10.5	8.1	9.5	8.4
France	2.4	4.0	5.8	10.1	9.0	11.7	11.7
Germany	0.5	3.3	2.6	7.2	4.8	8.2	9.4
Italy	5.1	5.5	7.1	8.5	9.1	11.9	12.3
Japan	1.1	1.9	2.0	2.6	2.1	3.1	4.1
United Kingdom	2.2	3.2	6.2	11.5	7.1	8.7	6.3
United States	4.9	8.5	7.2	7.2	5.6	5.6	4.5
unweighted average	3.1	4.8	5.5	8.2	6.5	8.4	8.1
standard deviation	1.9	2.2	2.1	2.8	2.4	2.9	3.0
variation coefficient	0.6	0.5	0.4	0.3	0.4	0.4	0.4

Note: 1) Standardized unemployment rates. For EU countries Eurostat definition from 1985 onwards.
Source: OECD (1999).

Table 2: Regional Disparities in the Unemployment Rate. Average of 1st and 4th quartiles, 1985-1995[9]

	1985-1st q.	1985-4th q.	1990-1st q.	1990-4th q.	1995-1st q.	1995-4th q.
Belgium	8.2	14.4	3.8	10.0	5.9	14.2
Denmark	5.5	10.1	5.4	9.7	5.2	9.6
Finland	1.8	6.0	1.5	5.5	13.4	18.5
France	7.4	12.1	6.6	11.2	9.0	14.5
Germany	4.3	9.9	2.8	7.3	5.0	13.5
Greece	5.6	10.0	4.1	8.1	5.3	11.1
Ireland	13.5	18.0	11.2	15.0	10.6	13.5
Italy	6.5	13.2	2.5	17.3	5.7	22.2
Netherlands	8.0	10.7	6.5	8.5	5.9	7.8
Portugal	4.4.	12.0	2.4	6.3	5.7	9.6
Spain	16.0	28.1	11.8	24.2	17.0	30.0
Sweden	0.8	1.6	1.0	2.0	7.4	10.4
United Kingdom	7.0	15.7	3.2	11.5	5.7	11.9

Source: OECD (1999), own calculations.

[9] All regions are divided into quartiles according to their unemployment rate.

Table 3: Some "Structural Factors" for Unemployment Rates

Country	Co-ordination of Wage Bargaining	Union Density in 1995	Replacement Ratio of		Duration (in years)	
			UI	UA	UI	UA
Argentina	high		80/30% *	-	1**	-
Brazil	high					-
Germany	moderate	29%	63%	56%	1	Indef.
Italy	low	39%	20%	-	0.5	-
United Kingdom	Zero/low	34%	38%	-	1.0	-
USA	Zero	16%	50%	-	0.5	-

*The replacement ratio is 80% but with a maximum benefit of 250 Pesos, while the average wage rate was 840 Pesos by the end of 1993.

** Only for those with more than thirty-six months of tenure at the last job.

UI = Unemployment Insurance, UA = Unemployment Assistance.

Source: Adapted from Taylor/Bradley (1997, Table 1), Nickell, S. (1997, Table 4) and OECD (1997, p. 71)

Table 4: Dispersion of NUTS 1 [Länder viz. Alte Bundesländer] Unemployment Rates for Germany, 1983-1996

Year	1983	1984	1985	1986	1987	1988	1989	1990	1991	1992
Average Rate	7.44	7.82	8.27	7.63	7.41	7.24	6.63	5.69	4.66	4.58
Standard Dev.	1.95	2.35	2.71	2.60	2.80	2.62	2.54	2.19	1.75	1.45
Variation Coef.	0.26	0.30	0.33	0.34	0.38	0.36	0.38	0.38	0.38	0.32

Year	1993	1994	1995	1996
Average Rate	6.06	7.33	7.03	7.58
Standard Dev.	1.61	1.81	1.74	1.83
Variation Coef	0.27	0.25	0.25	0.24

Source: OECD (1999), own calculations.

Table 5: Development of correlation vis-à-vis Germany of year to year changes in GDP (y), in unemployment (u), in consumer prices (p_c), in private wages (p_l) and in long-term interest rates (p_k) in Member-States of the European Union 1958-1997

	1958-1997					1958-1970					1970-1997					
	Y	U	p_c	p_l	p_k	Y	U	p_c	p_l	p_k	Y	U	p_c	p_l	p_k	p_k[10]
GER (1958)	1,00	1,00	1,00	1,00	1,00	1,00	1,00	1,00	1,00	1,00	1,00	1,00	1,00	1,00	1,00	1,00
BEL (1958)	0,73	0,91	0,74	0,64	0,61	0,64	0,62	0,11	0,07	0,79	0,70	0,85	0,75	0,87	0,54	0,87
DK (1973)	0,62	0,84	0,71	0,73	0,57	0,56	0,10	-0,21	0,36	0,83	0,48	0,73	0,76	0,80	0,49	0,77
GR (1981)	0,56	0,71	0,22	-0,19	-	0,30	0,62	0,47	-0,20	-	0,50	0,91	0,08	0,11	-0,06	0,23
ESP (1986)	0,56	0,96	0,51	0,45	-	0,26	0,44	0,16	-0,45	-	0,48	0,94	0,48	0,68	0,72	0,77
FRA (1958)	0,68	0,98	0,68	0,55	0,61	0,55	0,32	-0,11	0,27	0,74	0,66	0,97	0,70	0,67	0,55	0,80
IRL (1973)	0,09	0,89	0,70	0,51	-	0,05	0,31	0,20	0,57	-	0,09	0,82	0,72	0,66	0,52	0,73
ITA (1958)	0,50	0,94	0,63	0,44	0,41	-0,43	0,30	0,29	0,19	0,69	0,61	0,91	0,63	0,66	0,28	0,85
LUX (1958)	0,64	0,91	0,70	0,58	-	0,75	-	0,20	0,52	-	0,59	0,85	0,71	0,73	0,33	0,68
HOL (1958)	0,76	0,82	0,81	0,82	0,77	0,75	0,71	0,01	0,21	0,80	0,79	0,67	0,89	0,95	0,77	0,97
AT (1995)	0,71	0,90	0,87	0,76	0,76	0,45	0,37	0,21	-0,02	-0,03	0,73	0,95	0,89	0,91	0,79	0,95
POR (1986)	0,58	0,32	0,31	0,16	-	-0,15	-0,13	0,08	0,46	-	0,67	0,59	0,23	0,44	0,30	0,48
FIN (1995)	0,29	0,83	0,69	0,49	0,37	0,63	0,57	-0,76	-0,23	0,46	0,09	0,77	0,76	0,75	0,26	0,69
SWE (1995)	0,45	0,75	0,56	0,26	0,35	0,48	0,76	0,31	-0,26	0,84	0,27	0,73	0,55	0,43	0,15	0,76
UK (1973)	0,34	0,89	0,67	0,39	0,61	0,25	0,33	0,15	0,68	0,62	0,32	0,82	0,67	0,60	0,57	0,86

Note: The period 1958-1970 is about the period in which the original six EEC Member-States were on the road to a customs union and the monetary dimension was largely determined by the Bretton Woods System; the period 1970-1997 is about the period of the European Customs Union followed by the Internal Market (1993) in which four new Member-States joined the European Community (1995). Starting year of Community or Union Membership between brackets. Source: Own calculations, based on EC database.

[10] Long-term interest rates for the period 1981-1999 which is about the period of Exchange Rate Mechanism as well as the period of reduced capital movement controls.

Table 6: Regression of the German regional UR on national unemployment

$$\ln u_{ri} = \beta_{ri} \ln u_d + c_i + \varepsilon$$

	Period	Coefficient β_{ri}	constant c_i	R^2	Actual $u_{ri}(1989)$	estimated $u_{ri}(1989)$
R1 GERMANY						
R11 Schleswig-Holstein	1983-1996	0,284	1,329	0,07	6,6	6,2
R12 Hamburg	1983-1996	-0,032	2,134	0	8,9	7,99
R13 Niedersachsen	1983-1996	0,537	0,979	0,26	7,3	6,79
R13A Braunschweig	1983-1996	0,703	0,758	0,59	7,7	7,28
R13B Hannover	1983-1996	0,484	1,066	0,21	7,4	6,76
R13C Lüneburg	1983-1996	0,401	1,067	0,15	6,1	5,85
R13D Weser-Ems	1983-1996	0,537	1,027	0,18	7,6	7,13
R14 Bremen	1983-1996	0,264	1,833	0,08	11,2	9,92
R15 NRW	1983-1996	0,504	1,061	0,29	7,7	6,96
R151 Düsseldorf	1983-1996	0,49	1,14	0,35	8,2	7,35
R152 Köln	1983-1996	0,523	0,957	0,35	7,4	6,48
R153 Münster	1983-1996	0,3	1,451	0,07	7,9	7,2
R154 Detmold	1983-1996	0,652	0,602	0,29	6	5,69
R155 Arnsberg	1983-1996	0,564	1,028	0,32	7,9	7,48
R16 Hessen	1983-1996	0,992	-0,3	0,7	4,4	4,18
R16A Darmstadt	1983-1996	1,127	-0,684	0,71	4	3,61
R16B Gießen	1983-1996	0,978	-0,187	0,78	4,9	4,57
R16C Kassel	1983-1996	0,76	0,401	0,52	5,5	5,63
R17 Rheinland-Pfalz	1983-1996	0,845	0,06	0,43	4,8	4,64
R171 Koblenz	1983-1996	0,741	0,216	0,27	4,6	4,52
R172 Trier	1983-1996	0,382	1,01	0,07	5,9	5,35
R173 Rheinhess.-Pfalz	1983-1996	1,016	-0,257	0,69	4,9	4,56
R18 Baden-Württemberg	1983-1996	1,426	-1,38	0,85	3,2	3,03
R181 Stuttgart	1983-1996	1,672	-1,947	0,87	2,9	2,64
R182 Karlsruhe	1983-1996	1,063	-0,549	0,72	4	3,69
R183 Freiburg	1983-1996	1,452	-1,398	0,85	3,2	3,12
R184 Tübingen	1983-1996	1,424	-1,439	0,83	2,9	2,84
R19 Bayern	1983-1996	0,988	-0,434	0,46	3,7	3,63
R191 Oberbayern	1983-1996	0,87	-0,367	0,34	3,5	3,16
R192 Niederbayern	1983-1996	0,899	-0,231	0,41	3,6	3,81
R193 Oberpfalz	1983-1996	0,634	0,503	0,19	4,9	5
R194 Oberfranken	1983-1996	1,076	-0,456	0,5	4,1	4,14
R195 Mittelfranken	1983-1996	1,164	-0,657	0,57	4,2	3,95
R196 Unterfranken	1983-1996	1,099	-0,603	0,63	3,9	3,73
R197 Schwaben	1983-1996	1,283	-1,12	0,57	3	3,06
R1A Saarland	1983-1996	0,552	1,106	0,26	8,4	7,92
R1B Berlin (West)	1983-1996	0,918	0,409	0,79	7,1	7,46
R1C Brandenburg	1991-1996	0,922	0,802	0,87	14,7	11,15
R1D Mecklenburg-Vorp.	1991-1996	0,49	1,776	0,27	17,4	13,9
R1E Sachsen	1991-1996	0,971	0,663	0,8	14,6	10,57
R1F Sachsen-Anhalt	1991-1996	1,134	0,47	0,81	17,2	11,57
R1G Thüringen	1991-1996	0,815	1,018	0,57	15,8	11,48
Average Nuts 1 Regions		0,723	0,72	0,47		
Average Nuts 2 Regions		0,807	0,306	0,47		

Source: Own calculations.

Table 7:Unit root tests for variable AMPLITUD2

7.a: The Dickey-Fuller regressions include an intercept but not a trend.

	Test Statistic	LL	AIC	SBC	HQC
DF	-1.7764	-5.4533	-7.4533	-7.6505	-7.0277
ADF(1)	-2.1653	-3.7448	-6.7448	-7.0407	-6.1064
ADF(2)	-1.9471	-3.7335	-7.7335	-8.1279	-6.8823
ADF(3)	-1.6458	-3.6803	-8.6803	-9.1734	-7.6183
ADF(4)	-2.0262	-2.0417	-8.0417	-8.6334	-6.7649

95% critical value for the augmented Dickey-Fuller statistic = -3.2698

7.b: The Dickey-Fuller regressions include an intercept and a linear trend.

	Test Statistic	LL	AIC	SBC	HQC
DF	-.43684	-4.9957	-7.9957	-8.2915	-7.3572
ADF(1)	-1.0955	-3.7368	-7.7368	-8.1312	-6.8856
ADF(2)	-.34832	-3.7330	-8.7330	-9.2261	-7.6690
ADF(3)	-.49711	-3.4907	-9.4907	-10.0824	-8.2139
ADF(4)	0.88837	-1.8676	-8.8676	-9.5579	-7.3779

95% critical value for the augmented Dickey-Fuller statistic = -4.0816

Notes: LL = Maximized log-likelihood AIC = Akaike Information Criterion

SBC = Schwarz Bayesian Criterion HQC = Hannan-Quinn Criterion

9 observations used in the estimation of all ADF regressions.

Sample period from 1988 to 1996.

Table 8: Estimated Correlation Matrix of Variables

	UNEM PLOY	INCOME PC	REL AGRI	REL INDUST	REL TRADE	REL COMSER	RELNCO MSE
UNEM PLOY	1.0000	-.88540	.25949	-.017880	-.26106	-.30573	.58820
INCOME PC	-.88540	1.0000	-.55159	-.29649	.61251	.60845	-.61843
REL AGRI	.25949	-.55159	1.0000	.36066	-.65102	-.59741	.27318
REL INDUST	-.017880	-.29649	.36066	1.0000	-.60040	-.81406	-.36052
REL TRADE	-.26106	.61251	-.65102	-.60040	1.0000	.55465	-.32470
REL COMSER	-.30573	.60845	-.59741	-.81406	.55465	1.0000	-.073895
REL NCOMSE	.058820	-.61843	.27318	-.36052	-.32470	-.073895	1.0000

Source: Cambridge Econometrics Regional Database, own calculations.

Table 9: Co-movement of Regional Employment and Unemployment

1 Regional Correlation Coefficients 1983-1996 Employment Ratio (of Total Working Population) and Regional Unemployment Rate

2 Regional Correlation Coefficients 1983-1996 Employment Ratio (of Total Population) and Regional Unemployment Rate

3 Regional Correlation Coefficients 1983-1996 Female Employment Ratio (of Total Working Population) and Regional Unemployment Rate

4 Co-movement of Regional Female Employment Ratio (of Total Working Population) and relative Employment in Commercial Services

	1	2	3	4
R1 GERMANY	-0,9	-0,87	0,44	0,94
R11 Schleswig-Holstein	-0,68	-0,9	-0,62	0,29
R12 Hamburg	0,25	-0,38	0,07	0,67
R13 Niedersachsen	-0,54	-0,94	-0,24	0,95
R13A Braunschweig	-0,71	-0,71	0,44	0,34
R13B Hannover	-0,31	-0,7	-0,51	0,94
R13C Lüneburg	0,01	-0,04	-0,12	0,86
R13D Weser-Ems	-0,5	-0,96	-0,45	0,95
R14 Bremen	0,26	-0,74	-0,74	0,23
R15 Nordrhein-Westfalen	-0,18	-0,81	-0,42	0,97
R151 Düsseldorf	-0,31	-0,43	-0,06	0,89
R152 Köln	0,07	-0,73	-0,39	0,94
R153 Münster	0,46	-0,65	-0,71	0,89
R154 Detmold	-0,79	-0,93	-0,13	0,66
R155 Arnsberg	-0,55	-0,86	-0,46	0,67
R16 Hessen	-0,87	-0,92	-0,11	0,42
R16A Darmstadt	-0,73	-0,91	-0,2	0,39
R16B Gießen	-0,57	-0,83	-0,1	0,45
R16C Kassel	-0,7	-0,67	0,05	0,49
R17 Rheinland-Pfalz	0,17	-0,53	-0,31	0,97
R171 Koblenz	0,6	-0,18	-0,61	0,92
R172 Trier	0,73	0,4	-0,59	0,76
R173 Rheinhessen-Pfalz	-0,64	-0,93	0,1	0,9
R18 Baden-Württemberg	-0,75	-0,95	0,55	0,93
R181 Stuttgart	-0,76	-0,95	0,61	0,64
R182 Karlsruhe	-0,32	-0,58	0,19	0,88
R183 Freiburg	-0,84	-0,89	0,48	-0,02
R184 Tübingen	-0,49	-0,66	0,5	0,83
R19 Bayern	-0,68	-0,97	-0,51	0,86
R191 Oberbayern	-0,07	-0,68	-0,44	0,83
R192 Niederbayern	-0,27	-0,88	0,02	0,21
R193 Oberpfalz	-0,78	-0,92	-0,76	0,78
R194 Oberfranken	-0,41	-0,87	-0,59	0,44
R195 Mittelfranken	-0,78	-0,97	-0,56	-0,37
R196 Unterfranken	-0,55	-0,68	0,32	0,85

Table 9 (continued)

	1	2	3	4
R197 Schwaben	-0,72	-0,9	-0,26	0,85
R1A Saarland	0,42	-0,91	-0,48	0,91
R1B Berlin (West)	-0,55	-0,62	0,67	-0,03
R1C Brandenburg	0,11	-0,83		0,11
R1D Mecklenburg-Vorp.	-0,43	-0,77		-0,43
R1E Sachsen	-0,24	-0,84		-0,24
R1F Sachsen-Anhalt	-0,95	-0,99		-0,95
R1G Thüringen	-0,82	-0,87		-0,82

Source: Own calculations.

Figure 1: Unemployment in Major OECD Countries 1970-1998

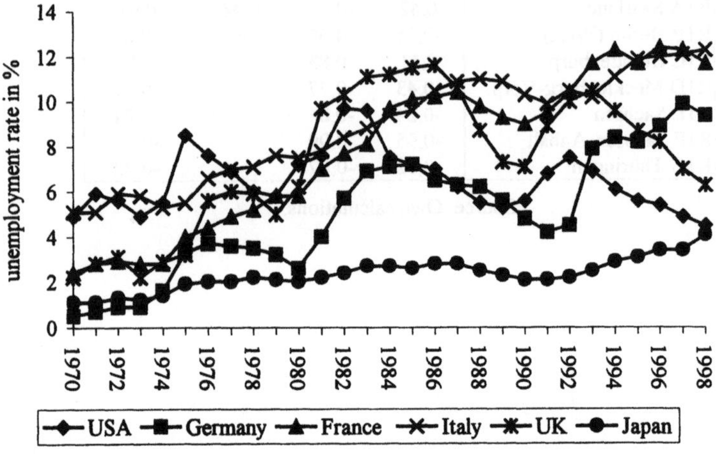

Source: OECD Economic Outlook (1996, 1999). Standardized unemployment rates in per cent of civilian labor force.

Figure 2: Regional Unemployment Rates in several EU Member States, in 1997 - minimum, average and maximum unemployment rate

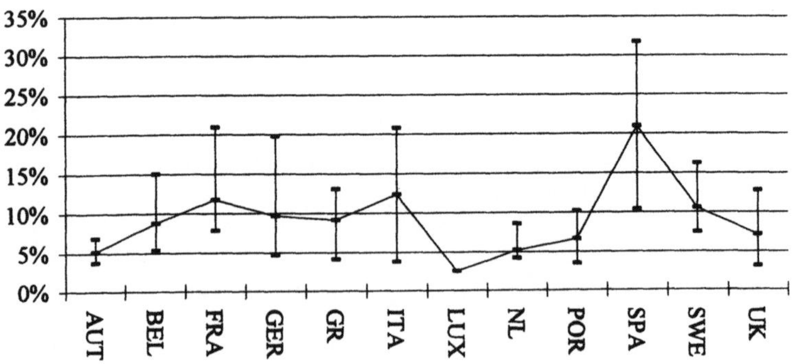

Note: NUTS 2 regions except for Luxemburg (national)

Source: Cambridge Econometrics Regional Database

Figure 3: NUTS 1 Unemployment Rates for Germany 1983-1996.

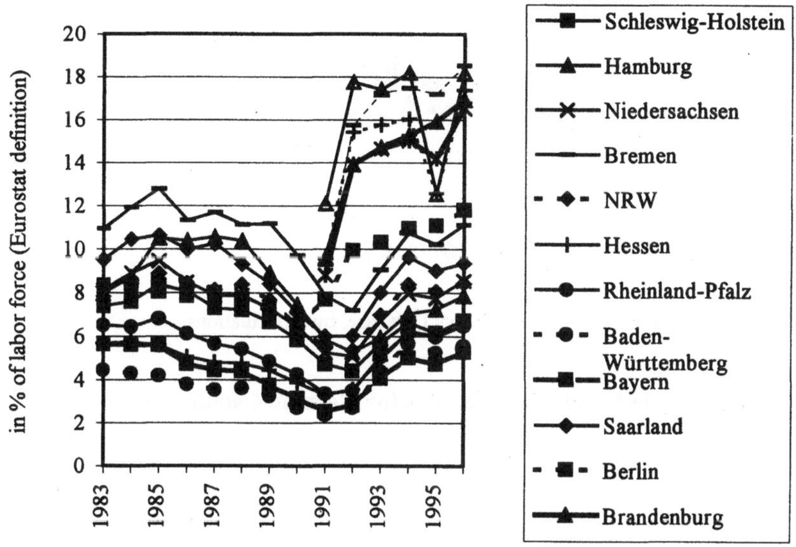

Source: Cambridge Econometrics Regional Database.

Figure 4: The four lowest and highest UR of NUTS 2 regions (West Germany)

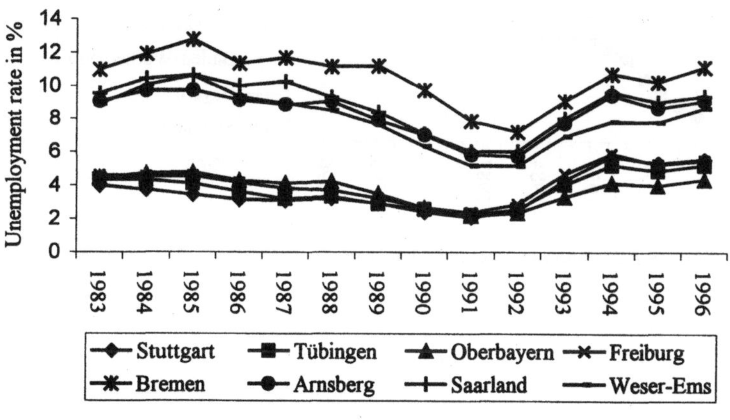

Source: Cambridge Econometrics Regional Database

Figure 5: Persistence of Regional Unemployment in Germany 1984-1994

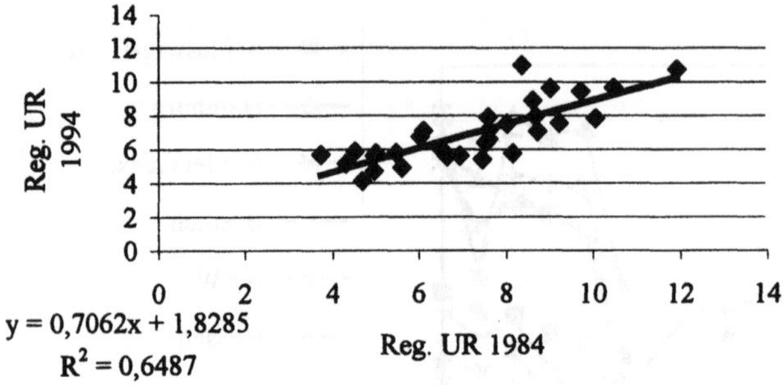

Source: Cambridge Econometrics Regional Database, own calculations.

Figure 6: Female Employment Ratios for German Laender, 1975-1996

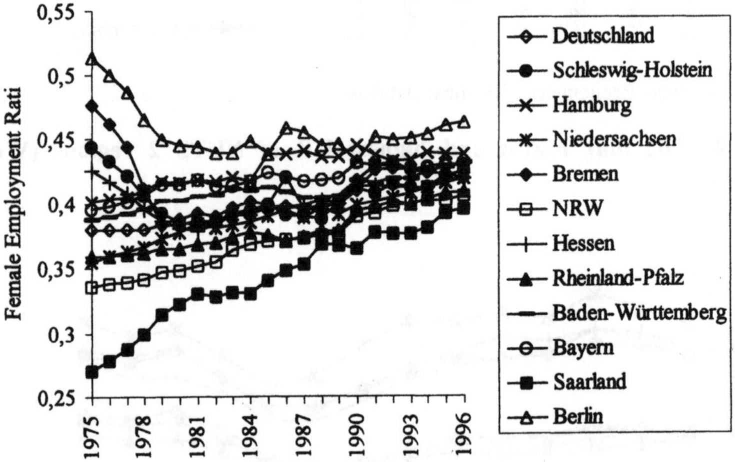

Source: Cambridge Econometrics Regional Database.

TEACHERS AND THEIR SALARIES IN ARGENTINA AND BRAZIL: DOES THE MARKET MATTER?

Mariana de Santis and Héctor R. Gertel[1]

1. Introduction

The remuneration of teachers in Argentina and Brazil is the object of this study. Salaries of teachers in these countries are ordinarily fixed through administrative decisions at the sub-national or local level, or collective bargaining, a political-economy mechanism which has apparently failed to explain why the relative welfare of workers employed as teachers has not improved in society. In this paper we seek to explain, through alternative approaches, why teachers salary have not improved in Argentina and Brazil relative to those of other workers. First, the role of the market in the determination of actual teacher salaries is studied with some detail and then, it is explored how these same forces will shape the future supply of teachers. In particular, after reviewing these issues, the paper will attempt to answer:

(1) How is the declining trend in teacher salaries explained under the political-economy approach?
(2) How do salaries adjust dynamically to market forces?
(3) How are the labor market characteristics of future teachers shaped by market forces ?

The paper is organized as follows: the next section reviews the issues in debate regarding teachers' salaries in industrialized and in less developed countries, with enphasis in Argentina and Brazil. Then, the political economy approach is reviewed. Next, the "dynamic shortage/surplus approach" is illustrated with data from Argentina. This is followed by a section on the "the graduate's decision approach" illustrated with Brazilian data to conclude with a more general discussion on whether market forces matter in setting the level of teachers compensation.

[1] Instituto de Economía y Finanzas, Universidad Nacional de Córdoba, e-Mail: hgertel@eco.uncor.edu

2. Teacher salaries: the issues at debate

The first issue has to do with the political economy of teachers salary decline. Earlier studies of teacher markets had shown that since the post war years the industrialized countries had gone through cycles of teacher over supply followed by years of shortages and that the evolution of teacher salaries responded positively to excess demand. In Argentina, a less industrial economy, teaching staff salaries deteriorated during the 1980's and did not recover during the 1990's. The performance of teacher salaries in Brazil, as in other NICs economies, was even poorer: salaries also declined during the nineties. In these countries, political-economy arguments have suggested that the absence of a political compromise and budget cuts due to structural-adjustment policies of the 1980s (Reimers, 1994, ILO, 1991) can explain why the average salaries of teachers performed so poor in spite of the fact that the employment of school teacher had grown fast and in a sustained way over time. Political economy arguments have also been used in the industrialized countries which characterized teachers markets as administered, or "political" markets where heavy state control was exerted over pay rise settlements. The political-economy explanations of teacher salaries decline ignored the influence of market forces. If the (nominal) wage level remains relatively fixed, the market will adjust the quantities demanded and supplied accordingly. In fact, the determination of teachers salaries has a complex nature because wages fluctuate over time, and these fluctuations are, at least in part, the result of changes in teachers' supply and qualifications on one hand, and school demands on the other, changes that take some time to materialize. The political economy approach failed to explain the mechanics of teacher markets; therefore, it was of little help for decision-makers. To explain why the average salaries of teachers performed so poor, we have to turn to the second issue.

The second issue is time. The trend in teachers salaries is dynamically affected by the trend in technology for two reasons: a) because the relative value of teacher skills to other professional skills in the market depends on the output-labor ratio and, b) because individual decisions in the labor market are responsive to changes in the regulatory framework (setting a ceiling on wages would generate under supply of teachers) (Johnes, 1993). Both aspects of technology and regulation are being strongly debated. For NIC's, such as Argentina and Brazil, technology trends in the 1980's and 1990's meant the accelerated adoption of new capital-intensive techniques of production that increased labor productivity and wages of professional workers holding credentials of similar level to those required to qualify as teachers (OECD,1996: 92-96). Similar to what has been observed for other countries, the education sector in Argentina and Brazil, did not received such a boost during that period, and teacher productivity improvements lagged behind those of workers with similar level of education employed in other sectors, probably because older technologies dominated the school system and output delivery was low (Hanushek, 1994: 33-34). The observed deterioration of relative teacher salaries is in part due to technological effects. The structure of the College market changed as a consequence of lower expected returs to teaching and of imperfect information, thus the best candidates began to drift off teaching and, as a result, in the long run, the predicted average skills and competency of the new teachers tended to decrease (Zabalza, 1979 a, Davini, et.al. 1997:56).

The third issue has to do with consistently poor performance of teacher salaries across countries despite the countries' individualities in teacher needs and overall primary school structure. We will concentrate in Argentina and Brazil whose primary school systems will be briefly described.

The total number of children attending primary school (K-7) in Argentina rose by 15 per cent over the period 1970-1980 and enrollments in teacher training institutes almost doubled. In 1980-94 primary school enrolments expanded by 20 per cent but the number of students in teacher training institutes did not change. An estimate of 320 000 employed teachers, 95 per cent of them females holding a College degree, and 5.1 million students attending primary school were reported in the Census of 1994. Almost every child had the opportunity to enter school at the age 6 although attrition was high (33.7 per cent in 1980 and 22.9 in 1990). Public expenditures in education over the period 1990-1997averaged 14 per cent of the consolidated Government budget in Argentina, representing about 4 per cent of GDP, below the 5-7 per cent share achieved by the OECD but higher than the ratio reported by most Latin American countries (Flood, et.al., 1998, OECD, 1997). The ratio of primary over total expenditures in education was 0.50, 0.41, 0.67 and 0.46 per cent in 1970, 1980, 1990 and 1996 respectively. Teacher salaries were on average eighty percent of total public expenditures in primary education (Morduchowicz and Iglesias, 1996). With a teacher-student ratio of 1:16 grossly representing the technology being used in public schools during the nineties (it was 1:20 during the previous decades), growing student population and a fluctuating fiscal environment, teacher compensation followed an erratic path: it was kept high in the seventies, then it plummeted in the eighties and might admittedly have stabilized (at low levels) in the nineties. Admittedly, political pressure to rise the salaries of teachers has always been high in the country. However, the economics would tell us that this can hardly be achieved given the conditions of the teacher market that prevailed in the country during the last quarter of the century.

The total number of children attending primary school (K-8) in Brazil has been estimated in 35.7 millions in 1999 (www.mec.gov.br). Brazilian education has advanced considerably over the past 10 years – and, quite remarkably for the past five years. The net schooling rate in fundamental education rose about 10 %

between 1991 and 1999, going from 86.1% to 95.4%. This means that Brazil, despite the pressure put by the 2 per cent annual population growth is about to guarantee universal access to fundamental education to all 7-14 year olds, a goal that Argentina achieved in the first half of the century. The participation rate in this age range, regardless of the level of education, has already reached 96.2%.. However, the average number of years of schooling for the Brazilian population is still too low, lagging well behind Argentine standards: in the period 1990 to 1996 the average number of school years went up from 5.1 to 5.7 for men, and for women, from 4.9 to 6, still almost half that of Argentina. With the advances in schooling rates, enrolment by the year 2000 is expected to be significantly higher than that of 1996 creating further pressures on teacher requirements. Another source for employment expansion comes from improved fundamental education transition rates in spite of the still high age/grade gap (46.6%). Promotion rate went up from 60% in 1990, to 73% in 1997 while, in the same period, repetition and dropout rates dropped from 34% to 23%, and from 6% to 4%, respectively. Thus, the rate of growth of teacher requirement that had expanded in the past faster than the population now had to focuss attention on new demands, the student-teacher ratio moved from 26 in 1980 to 24 in 1986 and again to 26 again during the nineties.

The 1994 Census estimated that 1.377.665 teaching posts existed in primary school in Brazil, less than half of the teachers employed had completed a College degree, ten percent have no secondary school diploma and regional disparities were high. In public primary schools, monthly salaries for teaching positions of 20 hours a week ranged from R$ 63 (teachers with secondary school diploma, starting position, in the state of Acre) to R$ 1259 (teachers with a Master's degree, at retiring age, in the Federal District of Brasilia) according to data collected in June 1996; these were low and unequal for the country and a significant number of teachers behave as temporary workers in search of higher rewards in other professions. The teaching force is considered quite young in Argentina and Brazil, 62% of the teachers are below 40 years old in Argentina (Argentina, MEC, 1994) and teachers in the public schools of Brazil are 32 years old on the average. However, while in Argentina almost all the teachers have completed 16 or 17 years of education and have an accredited degree, in Brazil the average education in the teaching labor force is about 12 years. The student-teacher ratio has remained at the 26:1 average level during the last 20 years in Brazil, but decreased from 21:1 to 16:1 between 1980 and 1994 in Argentina. Thus, in Brazil the under-supply of teachers is the most visible challenge to improve real access to equal educational opportunities for all children. In that country salaries of teachers exhibit substantial variation depending on the location, local wealth and the formal qualification of teachers (Brazil, MEC, 1996). *The National Fund for Primary Education Development and Enhancement of the Teaching Profession (FUNDEF)* was created in 1996 (by Constitutional Amendment n° 14) to attack the problems of a poor teacher supply. More specifically, the Fund aimed at reducing the extreme regional inequality in teachers' characteristics and salaries inherited from the failure of a highly descentralized finance tradition in Brazilian education, strong local control of schools and enormous local wealth imbalances. Today, FUNDEF effects the collection and redistribution of funds earmarked for basic education. This year, FUNDEF is expected to handle about R$ 15.200 million, according to National Treasury Secretariat (STN) projections to guarantee R$ 333.00 per student/year from 1st to 4th grade, and R$ 349.00 per student/year from 5th to 8th grade (which is less than the minimun standard allocation of R$425 claimed in previous Fund projections). Because an estimated 60 per cent of the fund should go to teacher compensation, by setting a lower standard, the contribution of the Federal Government to FUNDEF goals of improved salaries and equalizing opportunities are reduced (Farenzana, 1999). Notwithstanding, and despite continuous excess demand, as it is conventionally measured in the literature, salaries have remain low. Alternative explanations have either suggested that markts exert no influence at all on teacher salaries determination (a political-economy explanation) or, that markets matters but actual measures of excess demand are flawed and have, therefore, to be reexamined (for example, through dynamic market analysis and and career selection models).

3. The Political-Economy Literature on Teacher Earnings in Latin America

In Argentina and Brazil, as in many other countries, moving schools to more capital intensive techniques that would facilitate the rise in teachers productivity and wages confronts the problem of heavily regulated teachers labor markets (Psacharopoulos, Valenzuela and Arends, 1996); thus, the question of whether teachers are being under or over paid must also take into consideration distortions in employment associated with the use of non-competitive (bilateral-monopoly) policy practices. In fact, under the current educational policy practices, statements about salaries being below or above the trend line make little sense since schools are not allowed to recognize and reward differences in the quality of teachers. Under a centralized wage negotiation strategy, the Government "may end up paying too much for low-quality teachers and too little for high quality teachers" (Hanushek, 1994:81).

(i) The debate on "overpayment" and "underpayment"

The political economy literature on teacher salaries determination became popular during the eighties. It was shown that an association existed between the deterioration of teacher salaries and the fiscal crisis of the State, first manifested in the more industrialized countries of the North but that later affected the developing countries (Reimmers, 1994). Deterioration in teachers salaries was measured against the evolution of inflation as shown by the consumer price index. The conclussion was, generally speaking, that teachers were "underpaid". Then, a struggle to restore the prevaling purchasing power of teacher salaries was interpreted as a politically right movement that deserve the support of all progressive forces in society (ILO, 1991, ILO,1996, UNESCO, 1995). In counterbalancing this view, it also was shown that the teaching environment was transformed and had become increasingly bureaucratic with a larger portion of the payroll allocated now to "indirect" rather than "direct" teaching activities, and where extremely permissive rules meant the preservation of a bundle of historic rights, such as, extended leave of absence, early retirement, a shorter school year or lower student-teacher ratios which were almost impossible to match by the conditions of any other skilled worker in the market. These issues translated in rising average costs of schooling per teacher employed that were much higher that the average amount of salaries paid to teachers. Through the years, the preservation of these privileges produced an increased irritation among parents and other skilled workers in society. Thus, under this view, teacher salaries are today low because employment continuously over-expanded in the past, labor conditions improved but teachers' productivity levels fell down below any accepted standard. These, in turn, would explain the weaking political compromise with the teachers, now observed in many countries; hence, many are now arguing, that further discussions of increases in teachers pay, had to be linked to increasing the productivity of teachers (Hanushek, 1994:25-48). However, the political economy approach has not provided us with answers as to whether the depressed salaries of teachers would nevertheless represent a situation of market equilibrium or not.

This debate has traditionally emerged around issues of how to meassure changes in the real value of teacher salaries over time . As the price index has a tendency to rise over time, teachers observed, they were "underpaid" and they struggled to adjust their salaries accordingly so as to avoid losing purchasing power (ILO, 1996). But understanding how the market works and why teacher salaries stagnated or decresed in the eighties and nineties around the world would require a closer examination of productivity changes, as reflected, for example, in movements in the salaries of teachers relative to salaries of other skilled workers. In fact, decreasing (relative) teacher salaries has been associated with teachers showing less human capital as compared to those of other skilled workers over time. The corporation demanded, then, to increase teacher certification requirements, at least as these were measured by years of formal schooling. Teachers believed that after the length of their studies become equalized to that of other skilled workers, they would be automatically entitled to a pay rise that would improve their salaries relative to those of other skilled workers. However, this meant a message to Governments and teachers unions as well because, in practicing this principle, teacher markets should start moving towards a more open, transparent, descentralised and flexible system of salary and employment level negotiations than the one still existing today under politically regulated markets.

(ii) **What is an appropiate benchmark to compare?**

Any empirical determination of overpayment or underpayment would require comparison of teachers salary levels to an external benchmark. Overpayment was found in East Africa by an early study by Wolff (1984) after calculating the ratio of teachers salaries to the national income per capita. A recent comparative study from the OECD using data from European countries circa 1993 concluded that the richest the country, the lower the primary school teachers salary relative to the mean income in the population. In Argentina, teacher salaries have reached a ceiling due to budget cuts (Flood, 1998). Cox Edwards (1989) argued that the ratio of teachers salaries to other representative professional salaries is a better measure of market conditions. In his study, teacher salaries in the less developed countries were found to be below those of professionals requiring comparable training. In Africa, Asia and Latin America, on the average, these were half those of professionals in the non public sector with comparable training, reported Psacharopoulos, Valenzuela and Arends (1996: 402-403). Subsequent studies that applied this methodology have systematically found evidences of "underpayment".

(iii) **Salary evolution**

Is "underpayment" a temporary phenomenon?, or, rather, have teacher salaries declined over time? It is generally accepted in the industrialized countries that since the early 70's teaching staff salaries started losing their previous purchasing power or, teachers became "less affluent" each year with a manifest shortage of teachers. This trend has first been observed in the United Kingdom by Zabalza (1979b), Hanushek (1994) and Flyer and Rosen (1997) observed that the relative salary for teachers smoothly declined in the United States during the seventies but improved in the eighties, following a freezing in the public school demand for teachers. The recent comparative study from the OECD (1997) also revealed that primary school teachers salary growth between 1985/6 and 1993/4 was positively associated to improvements in efficiency as measured by higher student-teacher ratios that resulted from public education reforms introduced in those years (OECD, 1997). Psacharopoulos, Valenzuela y Arends (1996) use data of 12 Latin American countries to compare teacher salaries to workers in other occupations in 1979 and 1989. The data come from a series of Household Surveys and refer to characteristics and occupation of the individual. The study found that, in Argentina, Bolivia, Brazil, Peru and Uruguay, teachers earn, on the average, 21% less than a group of selected public and private employees excluding agricultural workers. In the remaining seven countries teachers earned on average 31% more than the comparison group. In the period 1979 – 1989, Argentina, Bolivia, Brazil, Uruguay and Venezuela teachers' earnings declined in relation to the comparison group, in Panama they remained almost unchanged, while in Colombia and Honduras they increased (see figure 1 in the annex).

Hence, the declining path in relative salaries of teachers was observed in Europe and the United States during the seventies and in Latin America a decade later, during the eighties (ILO/OIT, 1991), in the mid of severe inflationary processes, budget and balance of payment crisis and a wave of public sector structural adjustment policies designed to eliminate Government rampant deficits (Reimers, 1994). And an association between high inflation and salary deterioration suggested in the literature (Psacharopoulos, Valenzuela and Arends, 1996) may contribute to understanding differences between countries. Still, monetary wages and employment of teachers increased in Latin America during the 1980s because the student population expanded and, consequently, there were no significant changes in the teacher-pupil ratio. After the structural-adjustment years, however, it was salaries of workers in the less regulated sectors of the economy, included the salary of workers with comparable education, that slowed down or, eventually, plummetted in most of the less developed countries. Consequently, the ratio of teachers salaries to the average salary of other professional workers in recent years tended to stabilize or even improved. But under the political economy approach the question of how market forces interact in shaping the salary of teachers still remains unanswered.

4. The economics of teachers' supply in Argentina: An application of the "dynamic shortage/surplus approach"

In this section the "dynamic shortage-surplus approach" is explained with more detail and applied to study the economics of teacher salaries determination in Argentina. It will help to explore whether market forces exert a significant impact on what is generally assumed to be a highly political wage-setting mechanism. Interest in this type of models developed after Zabalza (1979b) observed, in England, an apparent inconsistency in the operation of the market for school teachers, that evolved from shortage in the sixties to surplus in the seventies despite the fact that salaries were declining. To challenge the prevailing view that this result is a consequence of the fact that the state of the market exerts no influence in the determination of teacher salaries, a dynamic model with lagged supply responses was proposed with data for 1963-1973.

The results lend support to the hypothesis that the inclusion of lagged variables in a simple supply and demand model helps to reconcile the observed decline in salaries with the (contemporary) elimination of the teacher shortage, notwithstanding the fact that teacher salaries in England are set in political markets. Dahlby (1981) interpreted the political market as a monopsony to explain the persistent shortage of teachers in England and Wales over the period 1948-73. In fact, he argued, "political markets" amount at saying that salary negotiations are heavily centralized, with the Government as the dominant buyer of teacher services and a, rather weak, national federation of teacher unions representing the teachers' interests. It concluded that England and Wales suffered in those years a persistent shortage of teachers because the local communities would like to employ more than the number of available teachers at the (below the competitive level) wage rate set by the monopsonist. Bee and Dolton (1995), examined the pattern of variation in the remuneration of school teachers in the U.K., over time and across individuals. The study demonstrates that market forces exert a significant impact on what is generally assumed to be a highly administered wage-setting mechanism

The economics of school teacher salaries in Argentina

In Argentina, the salaries of a primary school teacher relative to other salaries in the economy deteriorated between 1975 and 1988 (Petrei, Montero and Maraviglia,1989) and stabilized in the nineties (De Santis and Gertel, 1999). A plausible explanation comes from elastic teacher supply in the eighties and the trend in teaching productivity because the teacher-student ratio moved downward from near 1:30 in the sixties to 1:20 in the eighties to remain stable at this level during the nineties and employment adjusted accordingly through lagged supply responses.

Much of the political economy debate on teacher salary "deterioration" reviewed in the previous section revealed no distinction between absolute and relative deterioration. The political economy approach provided an explanation for the decresing trend in teacher salaries, however, it was rather simplistic because it did not take into account the role of time. Therefore, it is of practical interest to examine in more detail the dynamic suplus-shortages model to explain the economics of teacher salaries in Argentina.

The dynamic surplus-shortages model, which was developed by Arrow and Capron (1959), consists of a demand equation, a supply equation and a wage rate adjustment equation which relates the rate of change in the wage rate to the excess (defect) demand for labor.

A version of this model was applied in Gertel and De Santis (1999) to study teacher salaries determination in Argentina as follows:

$$\ln M^{D}_{t} = a1 - a2 \ln(s/p)_t + a3 \ln Z^{D}_{t}, \qquad a2>0 \tag{1}$$

$$\ln M^{O}_{t} = b1 + b2 \ln(sr_t) + b3 \ln Z^{O}_{t}, \qquad b2>0 \tag{2}$$

$$\ln (sr_t) - \ln(sr_{t-1}) = h(\ln M^{D}_{t-1} - M^{o}_{t-1}), \quad h>0 \tag{3}$$

The first equation is the demand equation, where M^{D}_{t} is the number of required teachers in year t; where t goes from 1981 to 1997; $(s/p)_t$ is the "real" salary and Z^{D}_{t} is a vector of variables exogenous to this model. The usual inverse relationship between quantity required and salary is expected, however, a small value for a2, the reaction coeficient, is predicted because in Argentina the market for teachers is a strictly regulated market. The second equation is a supply equation where quantity (M^{O}_{t}) reacts to relative salary (sr_t) and a number of exogenous variables (Z^{O}_{t}).

The third equation is a first order differential equation where relative salary movements from one year to the next depend on excess demand the year before. This, meaning that excess demand (supply) in one period would produce a salary rise (decline) during the next period. Equation (3) can be expressed as:

$$\ln (sr_t) = hG + (1 - h\, b2)\ln (sr_{t-1}) \tag{4},$$

where G is the summary computation for the demand and supply exogenous (unknown) effects:

$$G = a1 - b1 + a3 \ln Z^{D}_{t-1} - b3 \ln Z^{O}_{t-1} - a2 \ln(s/p)_{t-1}$$

If G can be assumed to be a constant, meaning that there have not been shifts in the supply and demand functions from one period to the next, then, the evolution of relative teachers salary would only depend on the value of (1-hb2) in equation (4), a standard result. If the absolute value of this expression is less than 1, the relative wage will converge to a stable market equilibrium level with excess demand equal to zero, in the sense that the market will reasonably clear all excess demand (supply). A value above 1would imply that any initial disequilibrium will accumulate from one period to the next and market clearence will only occur when exceptional and well behaved sector adjustment policies are introduced. Finally when the expression equals 1, there would be oscillation around the market equilibrium level.

Figure 2 (in the annex) shows the earnings of school teachers in Argentina for the period 1977 to 1997 using data from the province of Cordoba. The earnings of school teachers fluctuated around an upward trend from 1977 to 1980 and then declined from 1980 to 1991 to become stable until 1997 (althogh they then decreased sharply in 1981 and again in 1982, the years of the Falkland Island war and recovered part of the value between 1982 and 1985)

Consistent with the political economy explanation, there is a strong correlation with the fiscal, the balance of payments and the inflationary conditions in those same years.

Figure 3 (in the annex) shows the relative earnings of school teachers in Argentina using the ratio of the (initial) salary of teachers in the public school system of the province of Cordoba to the (initial) average earnings of clerical workers with a similar education level. The results, using relative instead of absolute earnings, show great differences. The relative earnings of teachers plummeted from 1978 to 1983, slightly increased from 1983 to 1987 and remained stable from 1987 to 1997. The dynamic surplus-shortages model would explain these movements in the relative earnings of teachers during a period of sustained demand increase if the growth rate of demand had been smaller than the growth rate of supply before 1983 and if the growth rate of supply had been smaller or equal to the growth rate of demand thereafter.

Equation (5) shows the estimation of a wage rate adjustment equation for the years 1977-1997. Data is for the Province of Cordoba urban primary school teaching staff. The excess demand variable is the difference between the number of teachers required to keep a 1:25 teacher-pupil ratio (the yardstick) and the number of teachers employed in direct teaching ($\ln M^D{}_t - M^O{}_t$).

Relevant information is provided in Table 1, Annex I. Salary differencials are obtained from time series of the initial salary of teachers in the province of Cordoba. Including seniority would only have the effect of a linear displacement of equilibrium, thus, conclusions are not altered although wage compensation calculations would become a little bit more tedious.

The estimated equation is:

$$\ln(sr_t) - \ln(sr_{t-1}) =$$

$$0.266(\ln M^D{}_{t-1} - M^o{}_{t-1}) - 0.70 \ln(sr_{t-2}) - 0.34 \ln(sr_{t-4}) - 0.06 \ln(sr_{t-6}) \quad \mathbf{R2} = 0{,}86 \qquad \mathbf{(5)}$$

(3,074) (-6.73) (-5.12) (-0.97)

Equation (5) confirms that market forces have influenced the rate of change of relative wages. The estimated coefficient of the difference between demand and supply of teachers, lagged one period, has the expected sign and it assumed the value of 0.26 < 1 then, the relative wage will converge to a stable market equilibrium level: clearence of a 10 percent "excess demand" (in the restricted definition of this paper) will require a modest 2.6 percent relative salary rise. There is an inverse correlation between the dependent variable and past movements in the level of wages meaning that a decrease of relative wages in t-2 or t-4 will stimulate a rise this year. Equation (5) can also be used to estimate by how much standards must move to restore equilibrium. If no relative salary rise can take place, elimination of excess demand can be achieved by rising student-teacher standards.

5. The economics of teachers' supply in Brazil: The "graduate's decision approach"

In reviewing the issues at debate, in section 2 above, the persistence in Brazil of a situation of excess teacher demand and depressed salaries over the period 1980-1996 has received the political economy interpretation that quality was adjusting downward. But how local wealth and the influence of local market conditions in wage determination has affected these results were not made apparent under this approach. In fact, more recently, teacher salaries were found to be higher than the salaries of other workers with similar education in the more developed states (Oliveira, 1997), a wealth effect, and teachers with higher educational attainments were found to earn more than teachers with lower credentials (Vegas, 1999), which is consistent with the human capital explanation of labor markets. The resulting policy was the implementation early in 1998 of a Fund aimed at equalizing per-pupil expenditures across states and municipalities while improving the quality of teaching through incentives to teachers to increase their education . Although it is still too early to evaluate the impact of this new Fund on the supply of teachers, understanding who are the teachers in Brazil and how this affects the choice of a carreer at the College level is critical for later assessing the impact that it may have on the supply of teacher and the quality of education.

The results reported in this section draw heavily on a recent research report by Vegas (1999) who studied the economics of teacher supply in Brazil. The paper revealed how teachers personal characteristics and wages compare to the earnings of workers with similar educational and other personal characteristics who are employed in other occupations using a combination of methods. First, the mean value for key variables representing personal characteristics of teachers and other workers are compared to assessed average differences. Second, a choice model helps to learn about the effects on the probability of being a teacher of marginal differences in individual characteristics. Third, an income equation of the Mincer type is run to assess how much teachers' hourly wages differ from those of workers in other occupations. Last, a similar income equation is run with the weakly wages as the dependent variable for a better understanding of variable effects on total annual earnings of teachers and other workers.

We are interested in the choice model here. Choice models have early been applied to learn about the decision to become a teacher by Zabalza (1979a) who calculated the probability to become a teacher for different types of individuals in the UK and Gales. The study concluded that expected earnings is the most influencial single variable in shaping decisions to enter or leave teaching. Murnane and Olsen (1989) revealed that decisions to enter the profession are heavily influenced by salary and unemployment levels in the market. The study carried on in Michigan found that individuals best qualified for teaching would prefer employment in other sectors where salaries for a similar profile were higher while individuals that found teaching economically rewarding are those who could not find employment in the best paid sectors. In England, similar findinds were reported in Dolton (1990). In Brazil, the choice model by Vegas (1999) found a strong effect of salaries on teachers' supply.

Suppose that job-related training (i.e. obtaining degree in a teacher training institute) is observed only where there are positive net benefits Zi, where i denotes the individual. In addition, there are unobservable individual attributes that may affect training participation, represented by e_i. Then, the probability that an individual i receives training is

$$\Pr[\text{Teacher}_i = 1] = \text{prob}(Z_i + e_i > 0); \qquad (1)$$

where the College student i selected teaching as the most beneficial choice. Then,

$$= \text{prob}(e_i > -Z_i), \text{ or}$$
$$= \text{prob}(e_i > XiA)$$
$$= 1 - F(-X_i A)$$
$$= F(X_i A)$$

where X_i is the vector of explanatory variables affecting Zi, A is the vector of a_i coefficients to be estimated and F is the logistic distribution function for e_i.

Thus, the probability to become a teacher is

$$\Pr[\text{Teacheri} = 1] = [1 + \exp(-XiA)]^{-1,} \qquad (2)$$

where the different Xi, in Vegas(1999), refer to gender_i, age_i, years of education_i, racial origin_i, marital status_i, rural/urban origin_i and household income of individuals in a 1997 nationally-representative annual Household Survey in Brazil.

Table 2, in Annex II, has been taken from Vegas (1999, page 26). It presents the estimated value of coefficients in the fitted logistic regression model of the (average) probability of being a full-time teacher in Brazil, defined as in equation (2), for three regions (Northeast, Center-north and South). The main results obtained in Vegas (1999) are summarized here: (i) The estimated probability of being a teacher, after controlling for other variables, is much higher for female than for males in all regions (up to 13 times higher, calculated as $e^{2.6}$); (ii) for married against single woman the probability of being a teacher, holding other characteristics constant doubled in the South and was 1.6 higher in the Center-north; (iii) The impact of age on the fitted probability of being a teacher varies by region but confirms that teachers in the economically depressed Northeast tend to be younger and less experienced than teachers in the other two more affluent regions; (iv) the impact of increased education on the estimated probability of being a teacher is high, strongest in the South, where each additional year of schooling increased the probability of being a teacher 1.7 times, other things equal and it is weaker in the Northeast.; (v)The education effect even compensate for the negative effect of being from a minority racial background. However, this may simply reflect "decreasing returns effects" because the average level of education for whites in higher than it is for individuals from racial minorities; (vi) Individuals living in rural areas, once the effects other variables are controled, have higher chances of being a teacher, a "lack of alternative opportunities" effect., and (vii) in all regions, keeping constant all other characteristics, teachers tend to come from households with lower incomes than do non-teachers, confirming that self-selection have heavily influenced career choice.

6. Concluding Remarks

The remuneration of teachers in Argentina and Brazil, as in most other countries, is considered by many to be too low as to generate the correct incentives for improving quality in teaching. Efforts to rise politically the relative salary of teachers in these countries have failed. Moreover, the political-economy approach have failed to explain why the salary of teachers have remain relatively depressed for long periods of time. These has been shown to be associated in various ways with a lack of interest in the examination of the forces of the market. This paper introduced two different kind of models that have paid attention to the market seeking to understand better why the salaries of teachers have not improved in Argentina and Brazil relative to those of other skilled workers. First,the dynamic model of wage determination applied to actual teacher salaries en Argentina led to the conclusion that continuos excess supply provide a strong statistical evidence that salaries followed the expected (downwards) direction. Then, using a choice model and data from Brazil, it was shown that, those that are most likely to end up working as teachers have less human capital and belong to families whose income is, on average below that of other skilled workers. Thus, in Brazil, career decisions of the young are strongly influenced by previous human capital accumulated and family income, and the fact that the demand for teachers (of a constant quality) will continue to expand seems to have created not enough incentives to the young to become a (qualified) teacher. The paper has shown that political economy solutions to fix salary levels in the past has provided wrong results. If quality of teaching is the ultimate goal, then, it is the long-run effect of depressed salaries on the future supply of teachers that should be analized more closely. And depressed teacher salaries are strongly affected by the temptation of governments to expand the supply of teachers with no true quality control on it.

References:

K.Arrow and W.Capron (1959), "Dynamic Shortages and price rises: the engineer-scientist case" *Quarterly Journal of Economics*, Vol LXXIII, 2, 292-308, may.

Brazil (1996), Ministry of Education and Culture, Document submitted to UNESCO/MINEDLAC 1996.

Brazil (2000), (indica4.shtm, and Brazilian National Reform)

M.Bee and P.Dolton (1995) "The Remuneration of School Teachers: Time Series and Cross Section Evidence" *The Manchester School*, Vol LVIII, 1, march.

Argentina, MCE (1997) El perfil de los docentes de nivel primario. Buenos Aires, Publicación del Censo de Docentes 1994, Serie C . No 4.

B.G.Dahlby (1981), "Monopsony and the shortage of school teachers in England and Wales, 1948-73" *Applied Economics*, Vol.13, 309-319.

María C. Davini (1997) "Asi ven su formación los estudiantes de magisterio" *Zona Educativa*, (Publicación mensual del MCE) marzo.

P.Dolton (1990) "The economics of UK Teachers supply: The graduate´s decision" *The Economic Journal*, 100, 400,91-104.

Estudio de coyuntura, Instituto de Economía, UADE, Nro. 147, enero de 1999.

Nalú Farenzana (1999) "Competencias Municipais e regime de colaboraçâo no financiamento do ensino fundamental: o contexto politico-normativo no Brasil e no Rio Grande do Sul". *IV Congreso latino-americano de administración de la educación* Buenos Aires, Universidad Nacional Gral San Martín, 20 al 22 Julio.

Cristina Flood, et.al. (1998) Caracterización y evolución del Gasto Público social 1980-1997. Argentina, M.de E. y S.P. Secretaría de Programación Económica y Regional.

D.S.Hammermesh (1993) *Labor Demand*, Princeton, Princeton University Press.

Eric A. Hanushek (1994), Making Schools Work, Washington, The Brooking Institution.

ILO/OIT (1991), Personal Docente: los retos del decenio de 1990. Ginebra. (Organización Internacional del Trabajo).

ILO/OIT (1996) Incidencia del ajuste estructural en el empleo y la formación del personal docente. Ginebra. (Organización Internacional del Trabajo).

Geraint Johnes (1993) The Economics of Education, London, The MacMillan Press

Henry M. Levin (1983) *Cost-Effectiveness: A Primer*. Beverlly Hills, Sage

A. Morduchowicz (1995) El financiamiento educativo argentino en un contexto de restricción de recursos, Progama Estudio de costos del sistema educativo, Secretaría de Programación y Evaluación Educativa, Ministerio de Cultura y Educación de la Nación (Argentina).

A. Morduchowicz y G. Iglesias (1996) El gasto público en educación y los mecanismos de asignación de recursos en el sector, Progama Estudio de costos del sistema educativo, Secretaría de Programación y Evaluación Educativa, Ministerio de Cultura y Educación de la Nación.

R.Murnane and R.Olsen (1989) "The effects of Salaries and Opportunity Costs on Duration in Teaching: evidence from Michigan" *The Review of Economics and Statistics,* Vol.71,2,347-352, may.

OECD (1997) Panorama Educativo 1996, Paris. OECD.

A. Petrei, M. Montero y A. Maraviglia (1989) "Estudio compartivo de las remuneraciones en el sector educación" en Humberto A. Petrei (Ed.) *Ensayos en economía de la educación,* Buenos Aires, edición propia.

George Psacharopoulos, J. Valenzuela and M.Arends (1996) Teacher Salaries in Latin America: A Review, *Economics of Education Review,* Vol.15, No 4, pp.401-406.

Fernando Reimers (1994) "Education and Structural Adjustment in Latin America and Sub-Saharan Africa" in *International Journal of Educational Development* , Vol. 14 (2), pp. 119-129.

UNESCO (1995), *Informe anual sobre el estado de la educación en el mundo en 1994*. Madrid, Santillana.

UNESCO (1996) Anuario Estadístico, Paris. Unesco.

Emiliana Vegas (1999) Teachers in Brazil: Who they are and how well they fare in the labor market? Draft version.

Lawrence Wolff (1984) Controlling the costs of education in Western Africa, Staff Working Paper 702, Washington, DC, The World Bank.

A. Zabalza (1979a) "The determinants of Teacher Supply", *The Review of Economic Studies,* Vol 46, No. 142, January.

A. Zabalza (1979b), "From shortages to surplus: The case of school teachers" *Applied Economics,* Vol.11, 1, 55-69.

ANNEX I

Table 1

Deficit of teachers in front of courses in the Province of Cordoba

Year	1980	1981	1982	1983	1984	1985	1986	1987	1988
T.F.C. required	7986	8267	8671	8921	9180	9218	9127	9322	9532
T.F.C. offered	7667	7751	8043	8121	8506	8537	8383	8624	8698
Def. / Surp. T.F.C.	319	516	628	800	674	681	744	698	834

Year	1989	1990	1991	1992	1993	1994	1995	1996	1997
T.F.C. required	9650	9603	9385	9246	9196	9201	9108	8845	9165
T.F.C. offered	9060	9133	9202	9226	9368	9308	9211	8501	9013
Def. / Surp. T.F.C.	590	470	183	20	-172	-107	-103	344	152

Source: Elaboration from official data

Note: T.F.C.: Teachers in front of courses.

Deficit/Surplus= (T.F.C. required/given a standard 25:1) - T.F.C. employed

Annex II

Table 2

Vegas (1999) Fitted logistic regression model of the probability of being a full-time teacher in 1997 on gender, age, years of education, marital status, racial background and household income

	South n=50,348	Northeast n=24,726	Center-North n=13,982
Intercept	-12.045***	-8.755***	-9.961***
	(0.231)	(0.297)	(0.335)
Female	2.644***	2.485***	2.461***
	(0.093)	(0.111)	(0.134)
Age	0.028***	-0.007~	0.018***
	(0.003)	(0.004)	(0.005)
Years of Education	0.521***	0.387***	0.492***
	(0.014)	(0.020)	(0.020)
Parda*	0.245**	-0.409	0.114
	(0.084)	(0.281)	(0.097)
Other	0.025	-1.173	0.179
	(0.164)	(0.748)	(0.330)
Married	0.750***	0.552***	0.494***
	(0.074)	(0.085)	(0.113)
Parda-Education**		0.057*	
		(0.024)	
Other Education		0.133*	
		(0.067)	
Rural	1.273***	1.385***	1.467***
	(0.123)	(0.107)	(0.189)
Household income	-0.0004***	-0.0006***	-0.0006***
	(0.000)	(0.000)	(0.000)
Pseudo R-squared statistic	0.364	0.344	0.365

~p-value<.1; *p-value<.05; **p-value<.01; ***p-value<.001; Standard errors in parentheses(1)

Source: Taken from Vegas (1999) Table 4.

* An F-test of the hypothesis that the main effects of race, Parda and Other, jointly affect the probability of becoming a teachers was conducted for the three models. It is statistically significant at the 5 percent level or better for all regions.

** An F-test of the hypothesis that the interaction terms, Parda-Education and Other Education, jointly affect the probability of becoming a teacher was conducted for the three models. It is statistically significant at the 5 percent level or better for the South and the Northeast.

Figure 1
Mean earnings ratio of teachers and comparison group (1989)

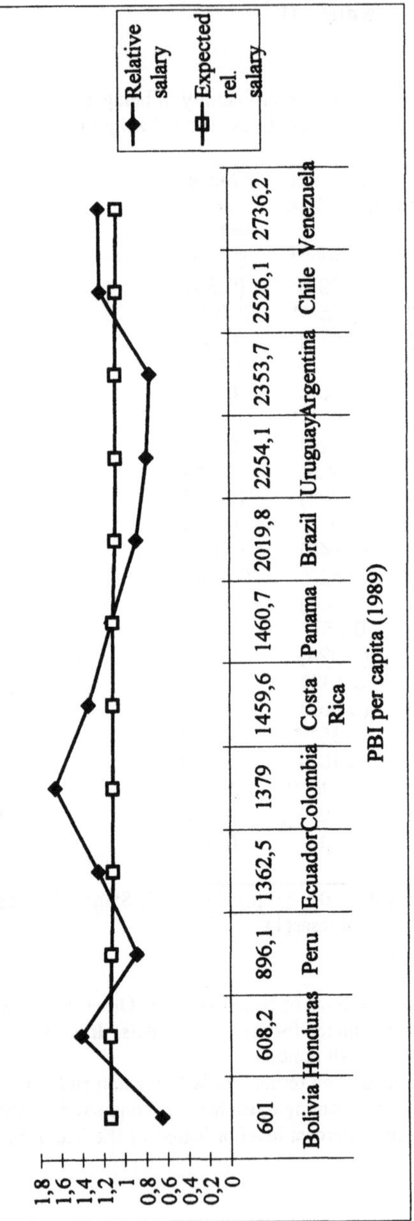

Figure 2
Initial salary of a teacher in Cordoba
(Index 1997=100)

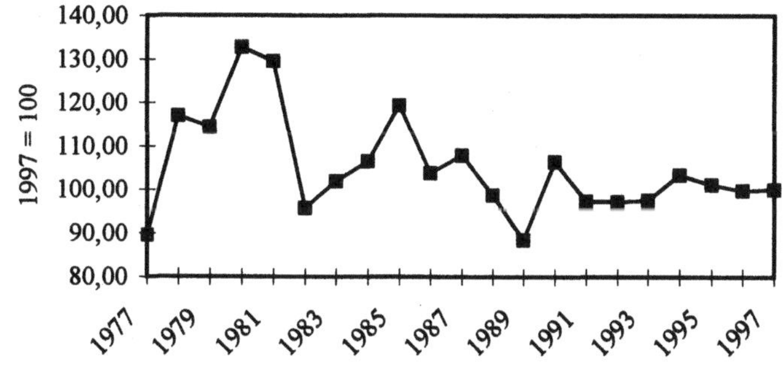

Teacher salaries are expressed in constant value
Source: Data available from the authors.

Figure 3
Ratio of teacher salaries relative to clerical workers in Commerce in Cordoba

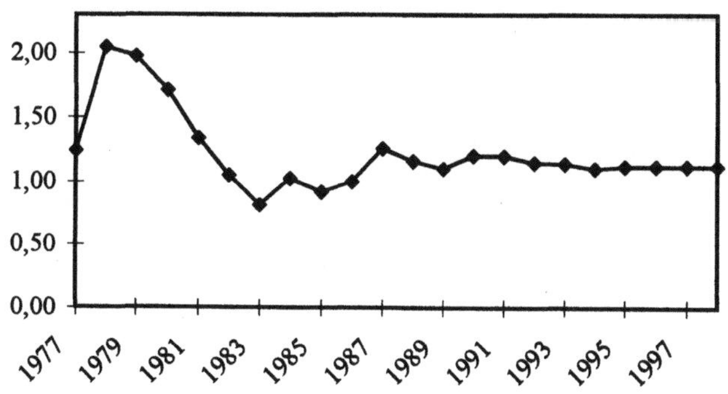

Source: Table 2 and data available from the authors.

LABOR REFORM AND ADJUSTMENT OF THE LABOR MARKET IN BRAZIL AND ARGENTINA[1]

Maria Cristina Cacciamali[2]

1. Introduction

Latin-American countries implemented labor reforms impelled by two contradictory elements, political and economic: the democratization of government regimes [3] at the end of the 80s; and the exhaustion of the import substitution model, in effect since the 30s. The first allows labor unions freedom of organization and collective bargaining without State intervention. This grants them political participation and influence in the definition of constitutional reforms following democratization of their countries, and therefore the expansion of social and labor rights. The second involves strong orientation changes in social policies, realignment of the productive structure, and the introduction of a new economic model of production and work organization. Unemployment affects union workers of the main professional categories and limits their bargaining power, leading many unions to intensify corporative practices in defense of their specific interests, in spite of the socioeconomic changes and the new social demands.

The labor reforms, among the different institutional changes carried out by the State during the 90s to face the new international order, are oriented to lower labor costs. To achieve this, the rules of labor contracts need to be made more flexible. These changes are implemented by national governments at different times, speeds, and with distinct political strategies. Chile was the precursor, at the end of the 70s, when the Pinochet Regime introduced profound changes in the labor legislation, allowing for different contract modalities. In the 90s, countries such as Argentina, Colombia, and Peru completely reformed their labor legislation following the same principles, while other countries such as Brazil,

---

[1] Paper presented at the IV Arnoldshain Seminar, Frankfurt/Arnoldshain, September, 2000.

[2]Doutora in Economics, Universidade de São Paulo, Brazil. At the moment Full Professor at the Department of Economics and President of the Graduate Program in Integration of Latin American of the Universidade de São Paulo. I thank Ana Maria Belavenuto de Freitas (PROLAM/USP) for her support in this research.

[3] Ecuador, 1978; Perú, 1980; Bolivia and Honduras, 1982, Argentina, 1983; Brazil and Uruguay, 1985; Guatemala, 1986; Paraguay, 1989; Nicaragua, 1989; Chile, 1990; Salvador and Panama, 1994 (BRONSTEIN, 1997:5).

Ecuador, and Panama, introduced important changes in the existing legislation in that same direction.

The main objective of this paper, discussed in the first section, is to identify the political strategies adopted in Brazil and Argentina to restructure the institutions of the labor market and their principal contents. The second section emphasizes the characteristics of the labor market adjustment in these two countries. One of the recurring arguments for implementing changes in the regulation of the Latin American labor market is the containment of illegally hired salaried workers, hence the second section emphasizes the development of that labor modality in the two countries. Finally, I present some final remarks and four hypotheses to be investigated on the increase of non-contract salaried workers in the labor market.

2. POLITICAL STRATEGIES AND LABOR REFORMS

The conception of labor reform is based on the presupposition that it is necessary to reduce labor costs in order to increase competitiveness and promote more employment. Labor laws formulated in most Latin-American countries in the thirties, and adopted, extended, and improved through the eighties, impose rigidity on the macroeconomic adjustment process of the countries and on the reorganization of firms, immersed in a mutable and intensely competitive world economic order, due to the greater liberalization and integration of the economies. In the Brazilian case, the entrepreneurial and government discourse favorable to reform is complemented by the urgency of transforming the labor union structure in order to create a negotiation atmosphere that engenders flexible rules in the employees' contracts, especially regarding hours and earnings. This would allow a rapid adaptation to the economic changes. Add to this – both in Brazil and Argentina – that the decrease of labor costs would restrain the growth of unregistered employees, that is, salaried workers without contracts in the labor market.

Labor reform, nonetheless, didn't constitute a priority of the Cardoso Administration in the period 1994-1998, or in the first two years of his second mandate (1999-2002). The strategy adopted was to avoid political confrontation with the unions, opposition, and public opinion and to apply discrete changes through exclusive measures of the Executive Power (Medidas Provisórias), which altered the 1941 Consolidation of Labor Laws (Consolidação das Leis do Trabalho). The practice of the new rules, over time, would constitute an accomplished fact. The sterilization of the inspection of Regional Labor Offices (Delegacias do Trabalho) would enforce this policy. Decree 865/95 prohibits charging fines in the case of incompatibility between the law and the collective agreements or conventions, the decision being left to the head officer of the

Regional Labor Office. Thus, over the last 6 years, 12 discrete but deep interventions were introduced in the Brazilian labor market rules, allowing or expanding new contract modalities, in contrast to the permanent contract[4], reducing labor costs, and making the allocation of salaried workers flexible. I highlight, among the most important, the following: Profit Sharing (Participação nos Lucros e Resultados) from Temporary Measure # 794/94, Professional Cooperatives (Cooperativas Professionais) - Law 8.949/94, Short-Term Contract (Contrato por Tempo Determinado) - Law 9.601/98, and Overtime Compensation System (Banco de Horas) - Law 9.601/98)[5].

The Profit Sharing Act was edited by the Itamar Franco Administration and republished periodically. It ensures the workers rights to participate in the profit and results of the company, unlinked to earnings. The negotiation between workers and companies on this matter may include a representative of the trade union, by option of the employer if circumstances call for it. This mechanism, in conjunction with wage disindexation, makes salaries flexible, because pay raises are offered in the collective bargain in the form of profit share and are not incorporated in the normal salary.

The Brazilian National Congress approved Law 8.949 in 1994, which allows the organization of labor cooperatives that provide services. The cooperative members don't belong to a trade union and their engagement does not follow the rules foreseen by the labor law in effect. The companies can, in this manner, hire permanent work under the cooperative form and thus avoid Social Security contribution (vacation, overtime, FGTS, Christmas bonus etc.) and indemnization of unwarranted dismissal.

Law 9.601 of January 21, 1998 and Decree # 2.490 of February 04, 1998 allow flexible daily working hours by creating a system of overtime compensation, which can be established through collective negotiation between employer and employees in any of the contract modalities. The weekly working hours may exceed the 44 hours defined by the 1988 Federal Constitution, and the compensation should be made within a year, according to Temporary Measure 1.709/98.

---

[4] The permanent labor contract or so-called classic or typical contract foresees full-time, only one employer, and dismissal can only occur without expenses in justified causes.

[5] Others are mentioned: wage disindexation for professional categories (MPs. # 1.053 and 1.079 of 1995); disindexation of minimum wage (MP of # 1906/97); Reproach from the ILO Convention 158 (11/95) on unjustified dismissals; limitation of the public service union organization and punishment of strikers (DEC. 2.066/96); expansion of temporary work (Decree 29/06/96); limitation of the time validity of agreements (MP 1620/98); part-time job (MP 1.709/98); suspension of the labor contract (MPs n°s. 1.726/98 and 1.779/99).

The Executive Power presented Law # 9.601 of January 21 1998 and Decree # 2.490 of February 4 1998 which allow companies to hire additional employees for a period of up to two years, through Short Term Contracts (Contrato por Tempo Determinado). In order to encourage contracting, the following is proposed: reductions of social burden[6] and overtime wage, and special access to BNDES credit. In addition, the hiring of short-term labor needs to be negotiated with the trade union and the law imposes limitations on the volume of short-term contracts[7].

Labor reform in Argentina was implemented by means of a distinct, more solid strategy, involving new contract modalities and the reduction of labor costs. The popular support and acceptance of the trade unions provided the conditions for the Menem Administration, at the beginning of the mandate, to present and get approval in the parliament for The National Employment Law (Lei Nacional del Empleo - LNE) # 24.013 of December 5, 1991, expanded, later, in 1995. This legislation, made up of 160 articles, deals with the labor market from several aspects[8], the most important of which are the short-term contract, unemployment insurance, and incentives for regularizing non-registered workers.

The Short-Term Contract (Contrato de Duración Determinada) foresees a minimum of 6 months and maximum of 18 months, allowing renewal for 6 more months. The employer has the benefit of total or partial exemption of his/her contribution to Social Security. These modalities are foreseen for companies that expand their staff above the average of the last 6 months, start activities, or have seasonal or occasional activities; and for the insertion of youths - people under 24 years of age. Furthermore, the LNE establishes unemployment insurance with varied payment duration, according to the time of contribution[9].

---

[6] That contract modality reduces by 50% the employers contribution to: SESI, SENAI, SENAC, SEBRAE, INCRA, educational contribution and work accident insurance; the contribution to FGTS decreases from 8 to 2% and the employer does not have to pay the fine of 40% regarding the FGTS individual total fund

[7] The limits are 50% (companies with up to 50 employees); 35% (companies between 50 and 199 employees); and 20% (companies with more than 200 employees).

[8] It deals, for example, with active policies to encourage and create employment, such as: facilitating productive investments in the private sector, mainly those with direct incidence on employment, elevating the levels of utilization of idle capacity within a perspective of economic growth; attenuating the unfavorable effects on employment of areas in decline and geographic zones in crisis, among others.
It foresees programs for special groups — youth and people over 50 - who have been unemployed for more than 8 months —, professional training, aid for geographical mobility, technical and financial support to create small business, mainly in the associative form etc.

[9] Contributions from 12 to 23 months—payment for 4 months; from 24 to 35 months—payment for 8 months; and above 35 months —payment for 12 months.

Two laws in 1995 mark the second reform. The first encourages the employment of women, people over 40, Malvinas war veterans, and the handicapped, through an exemption of 50% in the Social Security payment [10], without the right to prior notice or any compensation at the end of the contract. In addition, the trial period is extended from 3 months to 6 with reduction of costs. The second law produces a special contract for small companies[11]. It reduces the requirements and dismissal costs and permits the alteration, through collective bargaining, of other rules related to vacation, Christmas bonus, and internal mobility.

I should stress that LNE (5/12/91) addresses the regularization of non-registered and clandestine jobs, creating incentive and punishment, including pecuniary, to inhibit their maintenance and to stimulate regularization. The incentive for employers to register their employees is the exemption in the payment of social taxes and the punishment refers to compensation to be paid to the worker.

3. ECONOMIC AND LABOR MARKET PERFORMANCES

The diagnosis, shared by many authors, of the performance of the Latin American Labor Market is that the 90s – a period of implementation and institutionalization of structural adjustment programs - were characterized by insufficient creation of jobs and precariousness of said jobs, and stabilization of real wages and subsequent increases, without achieving the levels prior to the external debt crisis **(LÉON, 1999; TOKMAN, 1996; RENDÓN AND SALAS, 1996; CACCIAMALI, 2000a**). Add to this identification that the informality process[12], a phenomenon characteristic of the final decades of the 20th century, expresses itself in Latin American labor markets mainly by means of two facts:

[10] I agree with BRONSTEIN (1997:15) regarding women's inclusion with other mentioned groups: would being a woman constitute a negative attribute for those who elaborate the law? I add the hypotheses that legislators are motivating the expansion of women's work at low cost and low social protection, given that women's participation in the labor market constitutes the distinctive phenomenon of the last fifty years, especially in the last 20.

[11] A small company, defined by the law, is that which employs up to 40 workers and with annual revenue to be defined *ad hoc* by a commission.

[12] I define the process of informality as the redefinition of the production relationships, work processes, and labor insertions due to: I) the structural changes in the worldwide economy, and ii) structural adjustment processes, which have been implemented in different national economies. I define informal urban sector as productive units, small establishments, which present an undefined capital-work relationship, or a self-employment relationship, most of which workers do not contribute to the Social Security System and do not follow other social regulations (CACCIAMALI,1989, 2000b; OIT, 1995).

the expansion of non-contract salaried workers in the labor markets and the rise of employees in the urban informal sector, forms under which the largest part of the occupations were generated in the 90s. Brazilian and Argentinean labor markets are both inserted in this context.

The structural adjustment policies in Brazil and Argentina show two faces at first. One is the deepening, as in other countries, of integration to and dependence on the external sector: deficient trade balance, negative reserves, growing foreign debt, payment of high interests,[13] not to mention the financial dependence on short-run speculative capital accelerating the development of endogenous crises (Mexico, 1994; Brazil, 1999). The second is the recovery of investments, encouraged by the atmosphere of economic stability, privatizations, purchases of, and mergers with home companies. In Argentina, the investment share in GDP increases from 12%, at the beginning of the decade, to 22% in 1998. That variation for Brazil is from 19 to 22%. Economic growth, as a consequence, though presenting an unstable performance, accumulates, during the same period, an increase of 37% and 12% in the Argentinean and Brazilian per capita product, respectively (Table 1).

In Brazil, after the economic stabilization plan (1994), growth rates become lower and more unstable than in Argentina. This is due to the overvaluation of the exchange rate, which inhibits the level of domestic activity, and the fiscal crisis and inflation control which impose high internal interest rates and head in the same way. This recessive equation becomes exhausted in 1999, after the second Asian crisis, involves a depreciation of the exchange rate, and reduces Argentinean exports, disorganizing its economy and provoking a recession, while opposite effects are seen in Brazil. The political option of these two countries of not harmonizing their macroeconomic policies intensifies economic conflicts and slows the rhythm of the integration in MERCOSUR.

The substantial reduction and maintenance of inflation rates, especially in Argentina, close to zero and around 2% per year in Brazil, are the most remarkable gains of the stabilization policies. On the other hand, the increase of income concentration in Argentina and the maintenance of high inequality indexes in Brazil show the insufficiency of focusing the economic policies substantially on the stabilization program.

The labor market did not generate enough jobs to absorb the available workforce, and few were good quality. Economic activity, however, was capable of creating jobs and urban informal activities to accommodate the increase of occupational density - larger number of employed per family - mainly women. This rise occurs despite the increase of open unemployment, which reaches high

[13] The empirical evidence is located in CEPAL, 1999, chapters on those countries - Table 1 -. Argentina on pages 139-149; Brazil, 161-171; and Mexico, 253-263.

levels, especially in Argentina. Throughout the decade (1990-1997), the open unemployment rate in Greater Buenos Aires decreases from 25.4% for the Economically Active Population, to 14.3% and, in 1997, reaches a rate of 41% for the first decile of income distribution. This profile is from 3.7 to 8.1% and 13.3%, respectively for Brazil (CEPAL, 1999: 46, b).

Economic liberalization and exchange overvaluation alter the relative prices in favor of imported goods, reduce the profitability of the industrial sector and provoke a relative lowering of real salaries of the sector in relation to the salaries of tertiary activities, despite the productivity gains of the industrial sector, where the greater wage loss is in Argentina[14].

The industrial sector retracts its importance in the composition of employment, whereas services command the generation of new jobs based on a significant number of illegal contracts and informal activities. The first phenomenon is significant in both countries, whereas the second expresses itself in Brazil. In the region of Greater Buenos Aires, wage earners with clandestine contracts reach, in 1995, 32% of the total of salaried employment and encompass a greater proportion of lower level education workers, spouses, and young in contrast with more educated family heads (**GALIN, 1998**). In Brazil, the unregistered contracts reach 38% of the total salaried workers and present indexes over 40% in construction, services, and agriculture. They show greater relevance among women, youths, and small establishments (**CACCIAMALI, 1999; 1996**). In addition, the urban informal sector expands in Brazil, between 1990 and 1997, and the self-employment share in total employment grows from 22.8% in 1990 to 27.3% in 1998.

4. RESEARCH HYPOTHESES AND FINAL REMARKS

The introduction of new contract modalities achieves one of the goals of the labor reforms: to increase companies' competitiveness through the decrease of labor costs[16]. This result is obtained because they lessen companies' contributions to the Social Security System or because the short-term or temporary employees' earnings are lower, leading to a smaller total contribution. However, the new modalities did not prevent the growth of illegal contracts in the labor market, during the 90s. In a recent study, Argentina, Peru, Chile, and

---

[14] For this, I present the hypothesis of maintenance of the independent union organization - sectoral and central unions -, in Brazil.

[16] In a company, the maintenance of the productivity level at lower costs increases the competitiveness, and if the productivity increases, the competitiveness gains will be that much greater.

Colombia - countries that have accomplished labor reforms - present an increase in non-registered jobs. Only in Colombia has an increase been verified in the temporary employment contract **(TOKMAN and MARTINEZ,** 1999:23).

The maintenance of salaried workers without legal and registered contracts in the labor markets in Brazil and in Argentina has macrosocial and microeconomic explanations. I suggest four hypotheses that should be investigated. First of all, these kinds of contracts, among other modalities, present lower labor costs. The State does not enforce the law and the employer's risk of being fined is almost null. The entrepreneur does not compute the probability of that risk as a cost in the decision to hire employees. The second is related to the loss of political legitimacy of the Social Security System. The reduction of retirement pensions and social benefits and the financial crises shook society's confidence in the future of the System. People, especially youths, opt for individual or market solutions. The third hypothesis concerns the behavior of poorer employees. This group presents a high rate of discount related to future values, and would rather receive wages in the present with the addition of part of those contributions that are supposed to be paid to the government. Finally, the fourth hypothesis is related to the instability of the aggregate demand. This behavior generates pessimistic expectations and derives a restricted and unstable labor demand. Employers in this context avoid establishing permanent contracts or even legal contracts.

References

BOYER, R. *La flexibilidad del trabajo en Europa,* Madrid: Ministerio del Trabajo, 1988.

BRONSTEIN, A. S., "Reforma laboral en América Latina, entre garantismo ÿ flexibilidad", *Revista Internacional del Trabajo,* Vol. 116, n.1, 1997.

CACCIAMALI, M.C., "A informalidade na América Latina contemporânea. Argentina, Brasil e México". *IN: Anales del Congreso Latino Americano de Sociología del Trabajo*, Buenos Aires, Mayo de 2000 *(a).*

_____________, "Proceso de informalidad y sector informal: una discusión revisitada", *Revista de Ciencia Sociales*, Universidad Central de Venezuela, (no prelo), 2000 *(b).*

________________ "Assalariamento ilegal no mercado de trabalho urbano da Grande São Paulo: características e evolução, 1985-1992". **IN: FIGUEREDO, J.B.** *(compilador), Las instituciones laborales frente a los cambios en América Latina,* Genebra: Instituto Internacional de Estudios Laborales, 1996, pags. 219-233.

_____________, "Dégénérescence du droit du travail est ajustement sur le marché du travail au Brésil dans les annés 1990. ", *Cahiers des Amériques Latines*, n° 31, Paris: IHEAL Edition, pags. 105 – 126, 1999. ISSN 0008-0020; ISBN 2-907163-78-7

_____________"Expansão do mercado de trabalho não regulamentado e setor informal no Brasil". *Estudos Econômicos*, vol.19, número especial, 1989.

_____________"Setor informal e formas de participação: o caso do Município de São Paulo". *Estudos Econômicos*, n.3, vol.13, São Paulo, 1983, p. 607-627.

_____________*O setor informal e formas de participação na produção*, São Paulo: Editora IPE, 1983.

CACCIAMALI, M.C. & JOSÉ-SILVA, F., "Mais informalidade, menos cidadania. Considerações sobre esse círculo vicioso na América Latina". IN: *Brasil – 500 anos: Desafios do Próximo Milênio, São Paulo: Pontifícia Universidade Católica de São Paulo, 2000. (No Prelo).*

CEPAL, *Panorama social de América Latina*, Santiago do Chile: CEPAL, 1998, b.

______, *Estudios económicos de América Latina y Caribe,* Santiago do Chile: CEPAL 1998, a.

GALIN, P. E FELDMAN,S. "Sistema de información sobre el empleo no registrado en los países del MERCOSUR", *Oficina de la OIT*, n.52, Buenos Aires: OIT, 1997.

GALIN, P., "Empleo no registrado en el MERCOSUR y las políticas para reducirlo", *Oficina de la OIT*, n.61, Buenos Aires: OIT, 1998.

KREIN, J.D. E OLIVEIRA, M.A., "Mudanças institucionais e relações de trabalho: as iniciativas do governo FHC no período 1995-1998". *In: Anais da Associação Brasileira de Estudos do Trabalho*, *Belo Horizonte, outubro de 1999.*

LEE, E., "Mundialización y normas del trabajo – Puntos del debate", *Revista Internacional del Trabajo*, Vol. 116, n ° 2, 1997.

LEON, F., "Trabajo y trabajadores en los modelos económicos emergentes", apresentado no Seminário Internacional: *Brasil, 500 anos: desafios para o próximo milênio, Pontifícia Universidade Católica de São Paulo, 23 a 26 de agosto de 1999, São Paulo, Brasil.*

MARSHALL, A., "Empleo en la Argentina, 1991-1997? Nuevas pautas de comportamiento después de la liberalización económica?", *Boletín de la OIT nº 79*, Buenos Aires: OIT, 1999.

OIT, *15ª. Conferência de estatísticas do trabalho*, Genebra, janeiro de 1993.

_______, El *Empleo en el Mundo. Las Políticas Nacionales en la Era de la Mundialización*, Genebra, OIT, 1996.

_______ Panorama laboral '98, Peru: OIT, 1998.

TOLEDO, E. de la G., "La flexibilidad del trabajo en América Latina", *Revista Latino-americana de Estudios del Trabajo*, ano 3, n.5, 1997.

TOKMAN, V.E. "La especificidad y generalidad del problema del empleo en el contexto de América Latina". IN: Beccaria, L. E Lopez, N., *Sin trabajo. Las características del desempleo y sus efectos en la sociedad argentina, UNICEF, Buenos Aires, 1996.*

TOKMAN, V. E MARTINEZ, *D.*, *Flexibilización en el margen: la reforma del contrato de trabajo*, Organización Internacional del Trabajo, Lima: 1999.

Table 1
Macroeconomic Indicators
Argentina and Brazil
1990-1999

Years	GDP	GDP/ Capita	Unemploy-ment	Investment	Inflation
Argentina	(annual growth rate)		(annual rate)	(annual growth rate)	
	(%)	(%)	(%)	(%)	(%)
1990	-1,8	-3,2	7,4	-16,9	1344,0
1991	10,6	9,1	6,5	29,9	84,0
1992	9,6	8,1	7,0	32,6	17,6
1993	5,7	4,3	9,6	15,3	7,4
1994	8,0	6,6	11,5	20,7	3,9
1995	-4,0	-5,3	17,5	-16,0	1,6
1996	4,8	3,4	17,2	8,8	0,1
1997	8,6	7,2	14,9	26,5	0,3
1998	4,2	2,9	12,9	7,3	0,7
Brazil					
1990	....	....	4,3	....	1585,0
1991	1,0	-0,6	4,8	9,0	476,0
1992	-0,5	-2,1	5,8	-8,6	1149,0
1993	4,9	3,4	5,4	14,3	2489,0
1994	5,9	4,3	5,1	13,0	929,0
1995	4,2	2,7	4,6	8,1	22,0
1996	2,8	1,3	5,4	3,0	9,1
1997	3,7	2,3	5,7	9,0	4,3
1998	0,2	-1,2	7,6	8,5	2,5
Source: Elaborated by the author from CEPAL,1999 (a)					

Table 2
Unregistered salaried workers
Argentina and Brazil
1995-1996

	Argentina	Brazil
Primary Sector	n.a	72,6
Manufacturing	25,0	20,0
Construction	59,1	50,7
Commerce	42,6	32,8
Hotels&Restaurants	41,4	n.a
Transports&Communication	33,2	19,7
Financial Services	22,6	n.a
Personal Services	n.a	37,9
Education	7,7	n.a
Public Administration	6,3	38,4
Social Services&Health	18,0	30.4
Domestic Servants	87,4	76,4
Other Services	34,4	15,9
Total	32,0	38,0

Source: GALIN,1998 & CACCIAMALI, 1999.
Notes: n.a, not available

REGIONAL COORDINATORS

María L. Recalde de Bernardi
Instituto de Economía y Finanzas
Facultad de Ciencias Económicas
Universidad Nacional de Córdoba
Av. Valparaíso s/n
5000 Córdoba
Rep. Argentina
E-mail: lrecalde@eco.uncor.edu

Basília María Baptista Aguirre
Faculdade de Economía
Universidade de São Paulo
Av. Luciano Gualberto, 908
Cidade Universitária - São Paulo
SP 05508-900
Brazil
E-mail: basil@usp.br

Roland Eisen
Institut für Volkswirtschaftslehre
Fachbereich Wirtschaftswissenschaften
Johann Wolfgang Goethe-Universität
Mertonstr. 17-21
60054 Frankfurt
Federal Republic of Germany
E-mail: eisen@wiwi.uni-frankfurt.de

Peter Lang · Europäischer Verlag der Wissenschaften

Christian Lechner

The Competitiveness of Firm Networks

Frankfurt/M., Berlin, Bern, Bruxelles, New York, Oxford, Wien, 2001.
XXI, 418 pp., num. fig.
Regensburger Beiträge zur betriebswirtschaftlichen Forschung. Bd. 28
Herausgegeben vom Institut für Betriebswirtschaftslehre an der Universität Regensburg.
ISBN 3-631-37210-8 · pb. DM 118.–*
US-ISBN 0-8204-4832-X

Benetton, Sun Microsystems and IKEA, successful companies from different industries have common characteristics: These entrepreneurial firms are organized as firm networks and they have been successful despite their lack of resources. To understand their model, inter-organizational activities are the key. Christian Lechner analyzes how inter-firm networks can be a model for competitive advantage. „Competitiveness of Firm Networks" is about a theory of competitive advantage, a theory about the firm and a theory about networks. It explores relevant theories, formulates workable definitions, develops a framework for a strategic network management theory and refines this theory by own original research in the biotechnology and information technology industries.
This book – winner of the Lindner price for entrepreneurship research – is written for academics and managers interested in strategic management and entrepreneurship.

Contents: About Strategy and Networks · What is Strategy? · The Competitiveness of Firms · The Emergence of Networks · Relevant Theoretical Concepts for Networks · Networks and Entrepreneurship · Regional Networks · A Framework for a Strategic Network Management Theory · The Resource Based View of Networks · The Emergence of a Strategic Center · The Competitiveness of Firm Networks